Mistress

of the

VATICAN

Also by Eleanor Herman

Sex with the Queen

Sex with Kings

Mistress
of the
VATICAN

The True Story of Olimpia Maidalchini:
The Secret Female Pope

Eleanor Herman

WILLIAM MORROW
An Imprint of HarperCollins*Publishers*

FIRST EDITION

Designed by Ralph Fowler / rlf design

Library of Congress Cataloging-in-Publication Data

Herman, Eleanor, 1960–

  Mistress of the Vatican: the true story of Olimpia Maidalchini: the secret female pope /
  Eleanor Herman.—1st. ed.

      p.   cm.

  Includes bibliographical references and index.

  ISBN 978-0-06-124555-8

  1. Pamphili, Olimpia Maidalchini, 1594–1656.   2. Papal States—History—
  Innocent X, 1644–1655.   3. Women in the Catholic Church—Vatican City—
  History—17th century.   4. Papacy—History—1566–1799.   5. Nobility—
  Italy—Papal States—Biography.   I. Title.

DG797 .93 .P35H47 2008

945 .6' 3407   2007049233

08 09 10 11 12 WBC/RRD 10 9 8 7 6 5 4 3 2 1

This book is dedicated to

all women who refuse to

be locked up

Contents

Contents

Part Three

UNFORGIVENESS

Acknowledgments

One day in August 2004 I was speaking to Michele Giacalone of the Italian Cultural Institute in Washington, D.C., about setting up a lecture on Italian royal mistresses to promote my first book, *Sex with Kings*. Michele asked me, "Since you enjoy writing about controversial women, why don't you write a book on Olimpia Maidalchini Pamphili?"

And I said, "Olimpia *who?*"

Delving into the story of this forgotten woman, I was quickly fascinated and soon obsessed. My heartfelt thanks to Michele Giacalone, who heard Olimpia stories during his childhood in Rome. But for his timely suggestion, *I* would never have heard of her.

Nor would this book have been possible without the dauntless detective work of my assistant in Rome, Nancy Meiman, an American-born, Italian-spewing Sherlock Holmes of history, who tirelessly dug up places and sources related to Olimpia.

I am very thankful to Alessandra Mercantini and the staff of the Doria Pamphilj Archives in Rome for permitting me to peruse Olimpia's family letters. These letters allow Olimpia and her relatives to speak for themselves, and bring to life their daily vexations, hopes, and fears.

I would like to thank His Excellency Adhemar Gabriel Bahadian, Brazil's ambassador to Italy, who generously opened up his embassy and residence on the Piazza Navona, the palace Olimpia built. He gave Nancy and me a fascinating tour and permitted us to wander around for hours to puzzle out the location of ancient stables, kitchens, and servants' quarters. Many thanks to Fernando de Mello, the embassy's cultural attaché, who made this visit possible.

Francesco Colalucci of the Presidential Ceremonial Office was extremely generous with his time and knowledge by giving us a three-hour tour of the Quirinal, the papal palace, where Pope Innocent X spent the last six years of his life, and where he died.

I am especially grateful to Carlo Finazzi and Andrea Donatiello of the Council of Ministers for permitting me access to Bel Respiro, Olimpia's hilltop villa, despite the fact that renovations have resulted in the closing of the site to most visitors.

Don Gianni, rector of Saint Agnes Church, allowed us to enter the normally off-limits crypt, location of the ancient chapel built into an arch of the Domitian Stadium. And many thanks to the friendly custodian, Eraldo Sboro, who unlocked the doors for our voyage down a staircase that descended through time itself.

Vicenzo Ceniti, counsel of the Touring Club of Viterbo, took me to Il Barco, the hunting lodge of Olimpia's brother, and pointed out Olimpia's birthplace in Viterbo. My heartfelt thanks go to Alessandro Taddei and his wife, Elena Savini, for allowing me into their beautiful home to gaze at the gold eight-pointed Maidalchini stars still gracing their ceiling.

Mara Bastianelli gave me an in-depth tour of San Martino, including Olimpia's palace and church, and answered endless questions. Her husband, Colombo Bastianelli, has provided me with invaluable documents not found in any other sources, and gave generously of his in-depth knowledge of Olimpia's extraordinary life. It is Colombo Bastianelli who keeps Olimpia alive in her town of San Martino today.

My gratitude goes to Margherita Carletti Camilli-Mangani for allowing me to visit her beautiful seventeenth-century hunting lodge just outside the walls of Viterbo, which is associated with Olimpia's youth.

In touring the castles Olimpia bought in Umbria, I was welcomed and assisted by numerous individuals. Aleandro Tommasi and his wife, Irene Fabi, invited me to coffee in their home, the ancient hilltop fortress of Guardea owned by Olimpia. Nazario Sauro Santi, the mayor of Alviano, took me on a tour of Olimpia's jewel of a town. Roberta Proietti shared with me her thesis on Olimpia's feud of Attigliano.

Annalisa Marinetti and Paola Bonifazzi, who live in apartments in Olimpia's Viterban palaces, were kind enough to invite me in for coffee and permit me to poke around the gardens, former stables, and nooks and crannies of their beguiling buildings.

A surprising collection of Vatican letters and diplomatic dispatches from the pontificate of Innocent X has landed at the Folger Shakespeare Library in Washington, D.C. My heartfelt thanks go to the staff for their courtesy and assistance. Also stateside, Dr. Ken Gage of the Centers for Disease Control—known to his friends as "Dr. Plague"—kindly answered my questions about the bubonic plague that swept across Italy in 1656.

There are six biographies of Olimpia, all in Italian, and I am greatly indebted to their authors. Gregorio Leti wrote the first one in 1666. Ignazio Ciampi, relying heavily on Vatican archives, published his version in 1878. The twentieth century saw four more biographies, by Gustavo Brigante Colonna, Giuseppe Ciaffei, Donata Chiomenti Vassalli, and Alfio Cavoli. The research of these other biographers has been invaluable for this project.

Closer to home, I am grateful to Joseph John Jablonski, Jr., Esq., of Arlington, Virginia, for his help with certain Latin passages in Teodoro Amayden's 1655 *Elogia*, a description of Vatican personalities. And I am greatly indebted to Dr. Adi Shmueli, the renowned psychologist from Washington, D.C., for his insights, which helped bring to life a woman who has been dead for 350 years.

Finally, my thanks to my patient husband, Michael Dyment, and my encouraging sister, Christine Merrill, who have listened to my ceaseless Olimpia stories for three years.

Introduction

It is an age of exhausted whoredom, groping for its god.

—James Joyce, *Ulysses*

THE OLDEST ROYAL COURT IN Europe, the Vatican is a place of ancient secrets. The voluminous archives, though stuffed to the rafters with theological decrees, official correspondence, and accounting transactions, do not reveal much of the private lives of long-ago popes. Many records indicate only the most tantalizing fragments of murder, megalomania, and—heaven forbid—anything to do with women. Those stories that scandalized for a time were quickly suppressed or denied and soon forgotten. To paraphrase a modern saying, what happens in the Vatican stays in the Vatican.

One of the most interesting forgotten stories is that of Donna Olimpia Maidalchini ("My-dal-keeny") Pamphili—*donna* being the Italian title for "lady." The widowed sister-in-law of the indecisive Pope Innocent X (reigned 1644–1655), Olimpia was presumed to be the pope's mistress. Regardless of whether she was mistress of the pope, she certainly was mistress of the Vatican, appointing cardinals, negotiating with foreign powers, and raking in immense sums from the papal treasury. In a church that firmly excludes women from officiating as priests and even from marrying priests, Olimpia's story is clearly a discomfiting one for the Vatican.

The day that Cardinal Gianbattista Pamphili was elected pontiff, Cardinal Alessandro Bichi angrily declared, "We have just elected a female pope."[1] Mischievous Romans hung banners in churches calling her "Pope Olimpia I."

Olimpia's contemporary, Cardinal Sforza Pallavicino, bewailed the "monstrous power of a woman in the Vatican."[2] He fumed, "The court's predictions that if Cardinal Pamphili became pope, Olimpia would rule, came true. It was nauseating in a nation that excludes women from all participation, and it is much more abominable because she was not able to keep a lid on two female vices—those being ambition and greed. She fed her ambition by having her antechamber full of prelates and the principal ministers, who in their ceremony and etiquette recognized her almost as their boss, and it came to pass that even cardinals, in addition to their frequent visits, ran to ask for her intercession in their most serious business. One of these was not even ashamed to have her portrait hanging in his public rooms, as if she were a queen."[3]

Another contemporary chronicler huffed, "There has never before been heard of nor seen that the popes allowed themselves to be so absolutely governed by a woman. There was no more talk of the pope; all the discourse was of Donna Olimpia, many taking occasion to say, *That it were fit likewise to introduce the women to the administration of the Sacrament, since that Donna Olimpia was pope."*[4]

If someone broached a subject that the pope had not already discussed with his sister-in-law, he would ask, "What will Donna Olimpia say?"[5]

Savvy diplomats were prepared to flatter and bribe her to obtain the pope's favor. "If you cannot make a breach in the mind of the pope through our authority," said one powerful prince to his envoy, "try to gain it through the authority of Donna Olimpia with our money."[6]

Envied, admired, and despised, Olimpia was a baroque rock star, belting out her song loudly on a stage of epic exaggeration. Seventeenth-century Rome boasted the world's most glorious art and glittering pageants but also suffered terrors of apocalyptic proportions. Buildings spontaneously collapsed. Floods rolled through the streets, sweeping away horses and carriages. Swarms of locusts blocked out the sun and devoured the crops, bringing grinding starvation in their wake. Citizens burst out in black boils as plague culled its grisly harvest. Demons invaded the faithful, who writhed and hissed. Healed by saints' bones, the sick tossed away their crutches and danced in the churches.

Olimpia lived in an age of corruption and flagrant nepotism. Hers was a kleptocratic society, where everyone from the lowliest servant up to the pope's august relatives unblushingly stole as much as they possibly could. It was a time when dead pontiffs were left naked on the Vatican floor because their servants had pilfered the bed and swiped the clothes off the corpse. In this society theft was accepted, even admired, as long as the thieves were men.

Though Olimpia's tale was acted out larger than life on the international stage, there was an intimate, personal story behind it. Olimpia never recovered psychologically from her father's efforts to force her into a convent as a child. For the rest of her life she remained terrified of being locked up by men. An Italian Scarlett O'Hara, Olimpia vowed she would never be poor and powerless again. To avoid being crushed by men, she would have to acquire enough wealth and power to crush *them,* if need be. But how much was enough? In her efforts to find safety in a man's world, Olimpia made powerful enemies, which spurred her on to acquire even more to protect herself.

Unlike the story of the mythical ninth-century Pope Joan, patched together from rumor and fantasy centuries after she supposedly lived, that of Pope Olimpia has been attested to by numerous contemporary sources. Most touching are the personal letters of the Pamphili family kept in the Doria Pamphilj Archives in Rome, although there are, unfortunately, only a handful from Olimpia and the pope. Olimpia's legal papers—her wills and dowry documents—can be found in the Doria Pamphilj Archives as well as in the Archivio Storico di Roma.

Diplomatic dispatches reveal detailed information about Olimpia. A labyrinth of intrigue and corruption, Rome was the most difficult embassy posting, to which nations sent their ablest diplomats. Nothing was out of bounds in their weekly reports—even the pope's bowel movements were analyzed. As the pope's most influential advisor, Olimpia was carefully studied by the envoys of Catholic nations. Unfortunately, Protestant nations—England, Sweden, the Netherlands, Switzerland, and parts of Germany—had no ambassadors in Rome to titillate us with scandalous observations.

The most reliable source for Olimpia's story is Giacinto Gigli (1594–1671), who kept a diary from the age of fourteen until blindness in old age forced him to give it up. In recording the weather, politics, harvests, processions, murders, fires, and saintly miracles, he is a font of firsthand information for anyone wanting to understand life in seventeenth-century Rome. Gigli, who served on Rome's city council several times, and whose brother-in-law worked in the most important Vatican office, was well positioned to learn about the politics and scandal of the pope and his sister-in-law.

Another excellent source is Sforza Pallavicino (1607–1667), who became cardinal in 1658. A friend of Innocent's secretary of state, Cardinal Fabio Chigi, Pallavicino in 1665 wrote Chigi's biography, chock-full of Olimpia stories, which he either witnessed firsthand or heard about from Chigi, who had witnessed them.

The early seventeenth century saw the advent of the first newspapers. *Avvisi*—which meant "notices"—were handwritten news sheets of two to eight pages, consisting of small paragraphs in chronological order with no headlines. An *avvisi* writer sold subscriptions to foreign courts, banking houses, and wealthy individuals. From 1640 to 1650 the Vatican lawyer Teodoro Amayden (1586–1656) penned weekly *avvisi* to the court of Spain and Spanish embassies throughout Europe. A neighbor of Olimpia's who knew her and the pope well, Amayden included in his newsletters numerous stories about the pope's controversial sister-in-law.

Gregorio Leti (1630–1701), who wrote the first biography of Olimpia just a few years after her death, lived in Rome during her reign and enjoyed high-level Vatican connections. Normally, a contemporary biography like Leti's would be the best possible source, but unfortunately, Leti was biased against the Catholic Church in general and against Olimpia in particular. A convert to that rabidly anti-Catholic branch of Protestantism, Calvinism, Leti is accused by some Catholic scholars of making up his stories out of whole cloth. Yet most of his anecdotes are confirmed by the devout Catholic chroniclers of the time—Amayden, Gigli, Pallavicino, and the foreign ambassadors. In quoting Leti, however, we must bear in mind that he wrote for comic effect and exaggerated his stories to sell books.

Seventeenth-century Italians were extremely creative with their spelling of names, sometimes spelling the same name several different ways in the same letter. Pamphili is spelled Panfili, Panfilj, Pamphilj, and Pamphilio. Maidalchini is spelled Maldachino and Maidalchino. Cardinal Panciroli was also known as Cardinal Panzirolo. The reader is therefore warned of shifting Italian names in contemporary sources and is requested not to blame the copy editor or author.

Most sources disliked Olimpia's interference in Vatican affairs—she was far smarter than almost all the men in her environment, and it hurt. But some fair-minded ambassadors praised her for her intelligence, dignity, and financial acumen. The French ambassador Bali de Valençais admired Olimpia, informing Louis XIV that she was, without doubt, a "great lady."[7] Even Cardinal Pallavicino, who detested Olimpia, gave her grudging approval for her "intellect of great worth in economic government" and her "capacity for the highest affairs."[8]

While most men loathed her, and a few praised her, we don't have a single line from another woman discussing Olimpia. We do, however, have reports of Olimpia fan clubs—women who camped outside her palace for days just to get a glimpse of her, women who cheered for her. They were fascinated that a female from a modest background had, in the face of all social, legal, and church restrictions, acquired wealth and power and told the pope and cardinals what to do.

The exact nature of the relationship between Pope Innocent and his sister-in-law was the subject of intense speculation at home and abroad. Even while his brother, Olimpia's husband, was alive, the two were known to be unusually close. Most people believed that a physical relationship had stopped by the time Gianbattista Pamphili became pope, that the dignity of their situation and their advanced age—he was seventy when elected, and Olimpia fifty-three—would have precluded it.

Yet people couldn't help but notice that many days, as the sun slipped below the Seven Hills of Rome, Olimpia slipped into the papal palace. According to one source, "Donna Olimpia goes to the pope always through the garden, so that no one, not even the butler, knows when she comes and goes."[9] Sometimes she sat alone with the pope behind locked doors for as long as six hours. This nocturnal secrecy led to speculations of steamy senior sex in the Vatican.

But even if the rumors were true, it would not have been the sex that upset so many cardinals and diplomats, but the annoying fact that a woman wielded the power. Moreover, Olimpia was not running a secular monarchy like France or England; she was running the Papal States and the Catholic Church, making her position all the more shocking. The all-male bark of Saint Peter, guided so carefully through the shoals of fortune for countless centuries, now had a woman at the helm.

By the end of the seventeenth century, with new popes and new hopes, the scandal of Olimpia, which had gripped all Europe, faded and disappeared. Long forgotten now is her bittersweet tale of power, greed, and the glory of God.

Part One

THE GIRL FROM VITERBO

I

The Convent

O do not be born a woman, if you want your own way.

—Lucrezia de' Medici

O<small>N</small> M<small>AY</small> 26, 1591, as his wife's shrieks pierced the air, Sforza Maidalchini waited impatiently for the birth of his child. Everything depended on the child's gender. It absolutely must be a boy.

Born around 1560, Sforza was a man of humble birth and grandiose dreams. He grew up in the central Italian town of Acquapendente in the Papal States, a nation of some 1.5 million inhabitants covering roughly the central third of the Italian peninsula and ruled by the pope as earthly monarch. Looking around the world of late-sixteenth-century Italy, Sforza saw the yawning chasm between rich and poor, between those who feasted and those who starved. Wealth, position, prestige—these were the only things that mattered.

As a young man the ambitious Sforza was offered a job in the tax department of Viterbo, the capital of the province. His task was to assess the property and income of farmers and livestock owners in the fertile fields outside the town walls. Everyone who was anyone in town owned property outside of it, bringing in their own fresh vegetables and meat rather than buying them at market. Sforza's work put him in contact with the richest, most powerful and successful men in the region—Viterbo's wealthy landowners, politicians, and merchants.

While in many towns the tax collector was probably not the most popular man, Sforza had a special talent for winning the friendship of influential people, of making himself charming and indispensable. Working indefatigably, bit by bit Sforza moved up the ladder. He squirreled away money; he was promoted in his job. Over the years, his prestige increased in the community. In 1590 he was given the honorary title of castellan of Civita Castellana, an ancient fortress near Viterbo, and put in charge of the men-at-arms of the nearby towns of Sutri and Capranica.

His prestige was rising steadily, and the ambitious plan he had outlined for his life was unfolding perfectly. But what good was all this effort if he had no son to carry his legacy into the future? Only a son could make the mediocre name of Maidalchini resound through the centuries with greatness.

True, Sforza already had a son from his deceased first wife. Andrea, born in about 1581, was the focal point of his father's dynastic ambitions. But one son was not enough to guarantee the family line in a society where approximately 50 percent of children died young. Sforza knew he must produce an understudy for the role of heir to the future family greatness.

And to do so, the up-and-coming widower needed to find a replacement wife.

He did not need to look far. Sforza's boss, Giulio Gualtieri, was a nobleman of nearby Orvieto who had won the position of tax farmer of the province from the government of the Papal States in Rome. It is testimony to Sforza's hard work, thrifty habits, and valuable connections that Gualtieri gave him his daughter Vittoria in marriage with a generous dowry.

To his great joy, Sforza was now married to a nobleman's daughter with a comfortable pile of money in the bank. He moved into a home owned by Vittoria—perhaps part of her dowry—in the Piazza della Pace, the square outside the church of Saint Mary of Peace. It was not a grand nobleman's palace but a comfortable town house for a successful burgher. Built in the fourteenth century around a charming courtyard with a garden and well, it had been renovated in the early sixteenth century. In the main room Sforza had the ceiling beams adorned with gold, eight-pointed stars—the heraldic symbol of the Maidalchini family.

Poised to found a great dynasty, Sforza now needed only the insurance policy of a second son. Sons brought a family increased prosperity, prestige, and good luck. Sons cost very little to educate, given the huge pool of scholars willing to work as tutors. If the oldest son was heir to the family property, a second son could go into the church, a third son into the military. Sons were easy to dispose of, and each one that married brought money into the family in the form of his bride's dowry.

What Sforza greatly feared was a daughter. There was an Italian saying of the time—"to make a girl," which meant failure, disaster, plans gone awry. There was a reason for this. Girls sucked dry the family fortune with the dowries they required to marry honorably. A daughter would lessen the patrimony Sforza had saved for Andrea, dispersing it to another family. A girl would flatten the fortune and prestige of the rising Maidalchini name.

As the shrieks ceased and he heard the midwife's footsteps coming toward him, Sforza prayed fervently to all the saints. Was it a boy?

The saints, evidently, had not listened to his prayers. Sforza's child was a girl.

Children were baptized soon after birth, lest they die and their unbaptized souls be barred from entering heaven. And so, according to her recently discovered baptismal record, later that day Sforza's daughter was baptized by Carlo Montilio, the bishop of Viterbo, in the twelfth-century Cathedral of Saint Lorenzo. Sforza's standing in the community was shown by the fact that the child's godmother was Fiordalisa Nini, the sister of Nino Nini, the richest man in town.

The baby was christened Olimpia.

As Father Montilio sprinkled her with baptismal water, he spoke the sacred words that would mark the child's soul with an indelible stamp, signifying that as a Christian she belonged to God. "I baptize you in the name of the Father, and of the Son, and of the Holy Spirit," he said. Performing this baptism as he had hundreds of others, Father Montilio had no idea that kings and prime ministers would bow down to this unwanted girl, sending her lavish gifts and begging for her influence.

As he watched the ceremony, little did the dejected Sforza Maidalchini know that it would be his nuisance of a daughter, not his beloved son, who would make the Maidalchini family name great. No one had the vaguest idea that day, in the cool, gray church that smelled of age and mildew, that this mewling infant would become a pivotal personality in the history of the Catholic Church.

At the moment of her birth, Olimpia Maidalchini was encumbered by her father's disappointment in her gender and the question of the dowry that would loom ever larger as she grew up. But she was also burdened by a culture that blithely accepted women's inferiority to men. Pope Innocent III (reigned 1198–1216) confidently declared that menstrual blood was "so detestable and impure that, from contact therewith, fruits and grains are blighted, bushes dry up, grasses die, trees lose their fruits, and if dogs chance to eat of it, they go mad."[1]

Even the miracle of giving birth—the sole domain of women—was not considered an achievement of any particular value. The fourth-century B.C. Greek philosopher Aristotle and the Renaissance culture that quoted him believed that a uterus was a kind of soil—dirt, actually—in which the man planted his seed. A woman merely provided a nine-month lease for a warm rented room. In the *Oresteia*, the classical Greek trilogy by Aeschylus, the god Apollo argued that it was impossible for a man to kill his mother, since no one actually *had* a mother.

All pregnancies, it was thought, started off as male, nature attempting to replicate its own perfection. But at some point in about half of pregnancies, something went terribly wrong, an irremediable birth defect, and the fetus became female. A female's reproductive organs proved her defectiveness; they were small and misshapen, most of them tucked away in an evil-smelling cavity inside the body, unlike the robust, fully formed private parts of men, which enjoyed the fresh air and dangled proudly.

According to popular medieval literature, which was still widely read in sixteenth-century Italy, if a woman spread her legs very far, her female organs would fall out and she would become a man. If this were true, many ambitious women, including Olimpia, would have spread their legs wide, pushed their organs onto the floor, and luxuriated in the advantages of being a man in a man's world.

The church, too, looked on females as defective creatures. Jesus and his disciples had all been male. The church fathers, who in the second through fifth centuries grappled with Scripture to hammer out Catholic theology, were notorious misogynists. In the third century, Tertullian wrote a scathing commentary on women in the early church who preached, healed, and baptized. "The very women of these heretics, how wanton they are! For they are bold enough to teach, to dispute, to enact exorcism, to undertake cures—it may be even to baptize."[2]

In the thirteenth century, Saint Thomas Aquinas, arguably the most influential theologian in the history of the Catholic Church, declared women to be "misbegotten men," inferior by nature and therefore incapable of leadership. Defective women, it was believed, had no place in business, politics, or finance. They certainly had no place in Christ's church. The Latin word for woman—*femina*—was said to have come from *fe* for "faith" and *minus* for "less," since women were thought to be too weak to hold and preserve the faith. Moreover, it was believed that women's handling the holy Eucharist or stepping foot inside the Vatican would contaminate the holiness with their impurity.

The girl who would one day contaminate the holiness of the most holy Catholic Church was a born leader, a most unfortunate personality for a female. The only description of Olimpia as a child came from her first biographer, Gregorio Leti, who claimed to have spoken to people who knew her growing up.

"As soon as she attained the age of reason she was ambitious of commanding," he wrote. "Even at the most tender age, and as small as she was, she showed this inclination in childhood games. She always gave orders to the other children, and nothing was done without her commands. As a child she was reported to be dominating by nature. She decided which games to play and always wanted to win."[3]

Unfortunately, Olimpia had little education to back up her bossiness. She went to school in the medieval Convent of Saint Dominic in Viterbo, where her aunt was a nun. It was a rudimentary education at best. Times had changed since the early sixteenth century when women like the Roman poetess Vittoria Colonna (1490–1547) held salons, encouraged the arts, and spoke several languages.

Olimpia's world was shaped by the 1563 Council of Trent—the belated Vatican response to accusations of Church abuse lobbed by Martin Luther and his followers forty years earlier—and reforming bishops decided that wifely virtues were threatened by female education. An educated female would be less satisfied managing her household and raising her children; she would want to go gadding about town, meddling in government and business. Up north, the heretics would laugh at Catholics who couldn't even control their women. And so Olimpia would have learned to read and write Italian, do a bit of math, memorize the precepts of the Catholic religion, and sew.

Though she knew little or nothing of art, literature, philosophy, and foreign languages, Olimpia had two skills uncommon in girls. With regards to financial matters, her mind worked as if it were an abacus, adding, multiplying, subtracting, and calculating percentages. Within seconds of examining an economic issue, she could figure out the best financial advantage, a trait she must have inherited from Sforza. Moreover, Olimpia had a fantastic memory. She had only to read or hear something once to remember it forever.

Given her lifelong love of mathematical calculations and business, it is likely that Olimpia spent some time in her father's tax office. Perhaps she sat inconspicuously in the corner, watching Sforza chatting pleasantly with the landowners about their tax bills. As he added up the value of land, livestock, and crops, perhaps she did the figures in her head, coming up with the answers before he did. We can imagine Olimpia studying her father with her dark eyes, proud of him, wanting to grow up and be just like him.

While everyone acknowledged Olimpia's intelligence, there is some confusion as to her appearance during her girlhood. One source asserted that in her teens Olimpia was a "conspicuous beauty."[4] Another disagreed, calling her "not beautiful, but blond [light-skinned] and thin, pleasing, vivacious and always smiling."[5]

If she was not exactly beautiful, she was attractive and energetic, with an earthy sense of humor. From later likenesses we can extrapolate what Olimpia looked like as a girl. She was petite, with dark hair and chiseled features. She had a wide, high forehead, sparkling dark eyes under black, arched brows, and a beautiful, perfectly straight nose. Her cheekbones were wide, her lips thin, her jaw square, and her chin, though not overly large, prominent. It was a face of ambitious angles and resolute determination. It was a face that was intriguing on a slender blooming girl but that would become ferocious on a plump, hard-bitten older woman.

Olimpia grew up in a jewellike medieval town whose heyday had passed some three hundred years earlier. Viterbo sat snugly inside massive eleventh-century walls studded with turrets, towers, and gates. It was a town of thick strong stone the color of pearl gray and soft sand. Narrow streets wound between sturdy medieval houses and opened up onto charming piazzas with sparkling fountains. Adorning fountains, buildings, pillars, and palaces were stone lions—the heraldic symbol of Viterbo and the emblem of strength.

Rich volcanic soil and healing sulfuric baths had first drawn the Etruscans to the site, and then the Romans. In the eleventh century, Viterbo became a papal city, which the popes visited to escape Rome's malarial summers and perennial violence. The thirteenth century was a time of splendor, when new churches, towers, and palaces rose from the ancient citadel.

Viterbo's climactic moment in history came in 1268 after the death of Pope Clement IV in Viterbo's papal palace. Eighteen cardinals met to elect his successor but couldn't make up their minds. When the voting extended into 1269, and then 1270, Viterbans became frustrated at the lack of law and order in the popeless Papal States, and decided to make the electors' lives as uncomfortable as possible to hasten a result. Instead of allowing the dithering cardinals to return to their sumptuous palaces every night, they locked them in the building *cum clave,* the Latin for "with a key" and the origin of the term *conclave.*

When that didn't work, one cardinal jokingly remarked that the palace roof should be removed to give greater access to the Holy Spirit, who was believed to direct cardinals to elect the right man. Taking him at his word, the exasperated Viterban authorities removed the palace roof, exposing the cardinals to the wind, rain, and sun. They lowered down baskets of bread and water, all the food the sluggard cardinals could expect. The cardinals responded by threatening the entire city with excommunication, but this left the Viterbans unfazed. Finally, after two years and nine months, the longest election in church history, on September 1, 1271, the cardinals elected not one of themselves but a deacon named Teobaldo Visconti of Piacenza, who took the name Gregory X.

Some thirty years after the election, the popes became fed up with Rome, where noble families fought one another in daily street battles and sometimes held the pontiff himself hostage. The papal court moved to the peace and quiet of Avignon, in southern France, and the importance of Viterbo dwindled. When the popes returned to Rome for good in the fifteenth century, they had for the most part forgotten their once beloved haven, returning now and then only to soak in the salutary baths. By the time of Olimpia's birth, the town had no great political or church importance, though it was the seat of a bishopric.

Viterbo's bustling prosperity was due to its location; it was the last town of any size for visitors traveling to Rome from the north. Here countless pilgrims and diplomats ate, shopped for supplies, shod their horses, and rested before the last march to the holy city.

Pilgrims also prayed at the shrine of Saint Rosa. In 1250 fifteen-year-old Rosa led an uprising of Viterbans against their conqueror, the Holy Roman Emperor Frederick II, who had invaded Italy to seize territory from his enemy, the pope. Two years later Rosa died in a cell in her father's house, worn out by penance and bodily mortification, and, it was said, performed many miracles after her death. Each year on the eve of her feast day, September 4, her statue was carried through Viterbo in an elaborate procession that visited seven churches and ended at her tomb.

It was a festival that lasted for several days, involving the entire town and numerous visitors, and as a child Olimpia must have observed or participated in it. Perhaps Olimpia, realizing her own battle was looming, contemplated the audacious courage of a fifteen-year-old girl standing up to a warrior emperor.

When Olimpia was eight, Viterbo buzzed with scandalous news from Rome, fifty miles to the south. On September 11, 1599, the twenty-two-year-old noblewoman Beatrice Cenci was beheaded for playing a role in the murder of her violent father, who, it was whispered, had sexually abused her. Also executed were her mother and two brothers. A year earlier, the body of Francesco Cenci had been found at the foot of a castle cliff, his head smashed in. Aware of Francesco's brutal nature and the hatred his family bore him, authorities immediately suspected this was no accidental fall, but rather murder. And indeed, under torture the brothers admitted that the family had clobbered him and thrown him off the cliff.

It was the execution of Beatrice, young and beautiful, that captured popular imagination and became the stuff of legend. Such was the fate of a young woman who dared to rebel against her father, despite his violence and possible rape and incest. Though Beatrice Cenci's life and death were clearly tragic, the lesson learned was that daughters must obey, and that was that. Perhaps Olimpia thought long and hard about the courageous young woman who fought valiantly against the cruel fate imposed upon her by a heartless father.

As Olimpia grew up, the heartless Sforza Maidalchini was carefully considering the cruel fate he was going to impose upon her and her sisters, Ortensia and Vittoria. For his second marriage had resulted not in the longed-for son but in *three* daughters who threatened to siphon off the family wealth in the form of dowries. Many daughters of the time solved such family vexations by dying young. But Sforza's daughters did not oblige. They remained stubbornly healthy and grew unrelentingly toward marriageable age.

To marry honorably, that is, to marry a man of the same or higher social status, a girl would have to bring with her real estate, cash, furniture, jewels, or livestock. To marry a man of lower social status—a carpenter, blacksmith, or tavern keeper, say—would cost far less but would bring shame to a family such as Sforza's, perched on its upward climb.

In the fifteenth century the Papal States recognized the dangers of excessively high dowries: unwanted daughters with no religious vocation crammed into convents against their will, decreasing marriage and birth rates, and a resulting decline in economic productivity. The government legislated caps on dowry amounts, and any family going over the prescribed cap was forced to pay a substantial fine. But inflation and social pressure swelled the dowries, and the caps grudgingly followed suit. In 1586 the limit had risen to 5,000 scudi, and only twelve years later the average dowry had skyrocketed to 7,800 scudi. By the time Sforza married off his girls in the first decade of the seventeenth century, the combined dowries would have cost him some 24,000 scudi.

Since it is almost impossible to understand the value of a historical currency in modern terms, we must try to do so in contemporary terms. In 1600 a gold scudo could buy between twenty and twenty-five chickens or about a hundred pounds of flour, and represented almost a week's wages for a master builder. And 24,000 scudi would have bought some 600,000 chickens, or a large and profitable farm for Andrea. Yet how would Andrea make the family name great if so much of Sforza's money went to the girls' dowries, benefiting other families?

A father had very limited choices as to what to do with his daughters. And the reason was this: throughout history, women's lusts were considered insatiable, in contrast to the lethargic sexual desires of men. The daughters of Eve, if they were allowed to run free, would rape all the men and dishonor their families. After all, it was a woman who had gotten everyone thrown out of Paradise, and her daughters had to be locked up to keep society pure and wholesome. Oddly, no one ever came up with the idea that if a community truly wanted to become pure and wholesome—and less violent—it might consider locking up the men and handing the keys to the women.

A girl, kept under the stern eye of a father, would be handed over to a husband, who would fix an equally stern eye upon her. Or she would be walled up in a convent, where the abbess and bishop would make sure she got into no trouble and had no chance to escape. It was unthinkable for a woman to live alone, independent of men, unless she was a widow over forty, in which case she was thought to be so shriveled up that her private parts had turned to dust.

Looking at the gratifying patrimony squirreled away through years of hard work, Sforza decided there was no choice—all three girls would have to go into a convent so that his son would inherit an impressive estate. Although convents required dowries from the brides of Christ, Jesus in his infinite mercy was satisfied with one-tenth the amount demanded by flesh-and-blood sons of leading families.

It was the perfect solution for Sforza. His daughters would be honorably taken care of with very little dowry. Moreover, there was a spiritual benefit to having close relatives in monasteries or convents. Those who had been shut in would pray for those who had shut them in. And their prayers were guaranteed to be heard. The saints and the Virgin interceded first for the religious—the name commonly used for nuns and monks—before turning their ears to the selfish clamor of the worldly. The prayers of three daughters winging their way to heaven for decades to come would surely be heard by some saint, perhaps by the Mother of God herself, who would take action, ensuring success for Sforza and his son in this life, and easier access to heaven in the next.

Saint Peter, it was believed, would allow the religious to enter the pearly gates of heaven with barely more than a glance at their habits and a satisfied nod. It was the worldly he was on the lookout for, and these he would question rigorously. Turned away with only a tantalizing glimpse of Paradise, many would be forced to seek out that other place. For this reason, many of the most noble, wealthy, and worldly sinners insisted on being buried in the habits of nuns or monks, perhaps with the hope of fooling Saint Peter as they hurried by, the nun's veil or monk's cowl pulled over their faces, racing for the gates before the stern gatekeeper realized who they really were.

Though male and female religious were believed to have equal access to heaven, the life of a nun was far less interesting than that of a monk. Monks, though most lived in monasteries, were sometimes allowed to perform pious works in towns and cities, helping the poor and tending the sick in hospitals. Many monks were sent on missions to convert the natives of China, India, and the Americas. Male religious were also encouraged to make pilgrimages to holy sites, especially Rome and Jerusalem.

While the religious clergy were generally given to lives of contemplation, members of the secular clergy—priests—were extremely active in the community, baptizing, burying, and celebrating Mass. Priests could hope to become bishops, cardinals, even pope. But a nun could only remain a nun, with no place in the world. Lascivious creatures that they were, nuns were taken out of the community and guarded in what closely resembled a maximum-security prison.

Having studied at the Convent of Saint Dominic and boarded sometimes with her aunt, the abbess Giulia Gualtieri, Olimpia understood well what a nun's life was like. A nun slept alone in a narrow cell, on a hard bed, with an unlocked door through which the abbess could enter at any time to see what she was doing.

Fraternization was frowned upon as nuns, having devoted themselves to God, were not supposed to have any friends, even among their fellow nuns. Nuns who laughed and gossiped when cooking together or sewing in small groups could be subject to severe punishment. Forbidden to have pets, many nuns adopted the chickens they raised for eggs. Some nuns sent letters to their bishops complaining bitterly that the upstairs convent corridors were ankle deep in chicken turds because other nuns, looking for love where they could find it, kept so many pet chickens.

Nuns attended prayer service six times a day, and in between prayers they worked—tending the chickens in the henhouse, cooking the communal meals in the kitchen, doing the laundry, sewing, and cleaning. To become closer to God, they sometimes whipped themselves, starved, and spent their nights praying rather than sleeping.

They were not permitted to go into town. Servants bought supplies, knocked on the wooden window by the convent's front door, and, when it was opened, placed the items on a turntable that was spun inside. The nun receiving the goods had no contact with the servant, no friendly word, not the merest glance at a worldly person, and the entire transaction was handled exactly as if the convent were a leper colony.

Nuns were not supposed to have even a glimpse of the outside world and its temptations. All convent windows opened onto the inner courtyard, a place of contemplation, and never onto the rowdy street. Some convents even stopped up the ventilation shaft in the privies if it gave the nuns a view of the street below, or the street below, perhaps, a view of the nuns' behinds.

Nuns were allowed to meet relatives in the convent parlor, a gathering place where laypeople waited for a religious relative to come to the grille that separated the nuns' world from the real world. Male visitors were limited to a short list of fathers, brothers, and uncles, but female visitors could be more distant relatives, former neighbors, and friends. An older nun past the age of indiscretion—forty—was instructed to stand nearby and listen to the younger nuns' conversations in the parlors to make sure nothing inappropriate was said.

Usually the relatives would bring food and drink and make merry in the parlor, slipping wine and food through the grille to the nun while she, in return, slipped them the delectable convent cakes. Bishops routinely tried to clamp down on such excesses but just as routinely failed. It was, after all, the only fun a nun could have. And the rowdy relatives were not nearly as troubling as another problem in the parlor, which was becoming a favorite pastime of adventurous Italian youths. Boisterous young men—drunk, bored, or on a dare—pretended to be nuns' brothers, snuck in, and exposed themselves, waving their members and grinning at the shocked virgins behind the grille. The Neapolitans were the worst, some of them making the grand tour of Italy with the express purpose of flashing all the nuns.

Doctors' visits to nuns in their cells were viewed with suspicion. Physicians were encouraged to wait in the parlor and speak with patients through the grille without examining them. If the patient was too ill to rise from her bed, he spoke with another nun about her symptoms and prescribed remedies. The only men allowed in the convent with some sense of ease were priests, who were required to hear confessions and celebrate Mass. And sometimes even this resulted in pregnancy, thereby confirming popular beliefs about the incurable lechery of women.

Perhaps it is no wonder that so many nuns in Germany fled the confines of the convent as soon as the rising Lutheran religion allowed them to. Like rats on a sinking ship, they jumped out of their convents and paddled full force into the real world. In 1523 Katharina von Bora, the future wife of Martin Luther, escaped her convent hidden in a herring barrel and two years later ended up marrying the greatest heretic of them all.

Despite the hardships of a convent life, some young women wanted to be nuns with all their hearts. They saw it as a way of being closer to God and serving him every day. Others felt no strong vocation but chose to be nuns for other reasons. They would be spared the agonies of childbirth—many households had heard the cries of bone-shattering pain echo down the hallways and seen the suddenly silent almost-mothers carried out in boxes. Moreover, nuns were spared the brutality of men—drunken husbands who beat them or gave them syphilis picked up from whores.

But Olimpia Maidalchini was not one of those young women. Determined and domineering from her earliest childhood, at fifteen she knew she did not want a life sworn to poverty, obedience, and chastity. Olimpia most decidedly did not want to whip herself, adopt a chicken as her only friend, and sit in a stinking privy with its ventilation shaft blocked up. And she certainly did not want the only penis she saw in her life to be that of an impudent Neapolitan youth flashing her on the other side of the convent parlor grille.

It was Sforza's misfortune that his eldest daughter was in many ways just like him. Like her father, Olimpia yearned to be in and of the world—married, with children, social position, money, even power. Confronted with Sforza's decision to lock her up, she remained stubbornly defiant.

Olimpia's refusal to comply with her father's wishes was almost unheard-of in her society. In seventeenth-century Europe each member of the family was expected to sacrifice his or her dearest dreams to ensure the prosperity of the family as a whole. If their fathers desired it, swashbuckling soldiers became priests, and delicate scholars ran into the fray of battle wielding swords in their smooth white hands. Against their inclination, voluptuous bouncing girls swore themselves to lifelong virginity, and saintly maidens wed repulsive old merchants reeking with body odor. Family loyalty was fierce, and in pushing his daughters into convents Sforza was showing loyalty to the family. He expected nothing less from them in return.

Olimpia's younger sisters meekly submitted for the good of the family. Ortensia, who was thirteen or fourteen in 1606, and twelve-year-old Vittoria were safely tucked away in the Convent of Saint Dominic to the great honor and financial profit of the Maidalchini family. But there was still Olimpia to deal with, and though three dowries had shrunk to one, Sforza remained adamantly opposed to taking a penny away from Andrea's future greatness. Moreover, he must have been shocked by Olimpia's stubborn disloyalty to the family. By hook or by crook, he would get Olimpia into that convent.

It was not as easy as simply dragging her there. Sforza knew of the ruling of the Council of Trent—that no father could force his daughter into a convent against her will, and those found guilty of doing so would be excommunicated by the Catholic Church. This ruling was the response to the heretics' hooting and hollering that greedy fathers were jamming young girls into convents to drag out their days in virginal misery. According to the edict, each girl asking to join a convent would be interviewed privately by the local bishop, who would determine "whether she is being forced, whether she is being deceived, whether she knows what she is doing."[6]

Most girls, asked by the bishop in a private interview if they took the veil willingly, nodded their assent through tears, knowing their fathers were waiting outside the door with a big stick. But Sforza Maidalchini knew that the fearless Olimpia could not be badgered or beaten into submission. She had to be handled carefully.

It is likely that he started off in a friendly, persuasive tone, letting her know that their family's future depended on her. The brother whom she loved, who was by now married and a father, depended on her. Her sisters had obeyed, and Olimpia, too, must obey. Her family had loved her and cherished her, and now she must make a sacrifice for them. She would be well cared for in the convent. The family would visit her often.

Perhaps Olimpia found strength in the fact that four hundred years earlier another fifteen-year-old Viterban girl, Saint Rosa, had defied an emperor, and Sforza was no emperor. *Absolutely not,* Olimpia told her father. *No convent for me.*

Maybe cajolery would work. Sforza instructed Olimpia's aunt, the abbess of Saint Dominic, to persuade her. For a girl of Olimpia's strong personality and love of financial affairs, a convent offered the only path to a management position, Aunt Giulia explained. Olimpia could eventually become abbess herself, running the convent and its fields, farms, and orchards, administering justice and punishment to the nuns, dealing with the local bishop.

Using the small dowries the new nuns brought with them, the abbess made loans to trade guilds and private individuals, accruing annual interest, and bought rental properties, which she administered. The abbess invested in the *monti,* state-issued bonds with a guaranteed fixed income. A good head for business was required for the exalted position of abbess, and Olimpia, with her leadership skills, her abacus brain, and her financial genius, would, without doubt, make a magnificent one. She declined the offer.

When her aunt bemoaned the dishonor that would taint the Maidalchini family if Olimpia married beneath her, the girl replied firmly, "Lady Aunt, it is better that I should lose my family than my body should burn."[7] Olimpia was probably referring to Paul's letter to the Corinthians, in which he declared, "It is better to marry than to burn with passion."

By now Sforza had had enough. Olimpia's refusal was becoming a very public humiliation. Everyone in Viterbo knew he wanted her to join her sisters in Saint Dominic. Everyone also knew that his daughter was making him look like a fool.

We can imagine that one day Sforza has a servant call her into his sitting room. She finds him there with thunder on his brow, the grim paterfamilias, sitting in his large wooden chair, high-backed with thick arms. He begins yelling at her that she is only a girl, that she has no right to say anything about her own future. That this is a man's world, where men rule, and she will obey, not instruct. *That the only place for a girl like her is the convent.* He rises, towering over her, his angry words melting into a blur as the blood throbs in her ears.

And Olimpia, short and slender at fifteen, a mere slip of a girl, stands before him, tiny and defenseless. She gets smaller and smaller, shrinking beneath the verbal blows, the insults, and the threats. And as she shrinks, something inside her hardens. Her father, the one man who was supposed to love and protect her, is betraying her in the worst way possible. She will never forgive him. She will never forget. And she will find a way to wreak her revenge.

While Beatrice Cenci had murdered her tyrannical father, Olimpia Maidalchini would feel far greater pleasure in humiliating hers, in wounding him right where it would hurt the most, by shattering his reputation in Viterbo. There was the added advantage that a girl would not be beheaded for *humiliating* her father. Olimpia would bide her time and find a way to pay him back.

Undeterred by her latest refusal, Sforza came up with another idea. He put a young Augustinian confessor at Olimpia's side all her waking hours to convince her to submit to the paternal will. The man was highly regarded by the Viterban community for his patience and adherence to strict Catholic doctrine. Perhaps this likable priest, with his persuasive manner of speaking and his extensive knowledge of biblical precepts, could wear down the stubborn girl.

Olimpia listened silently to the priest's interminable harangues, one of which was most likely a sermon on "Honor thy father and mother." Through narrowed eyes, she must have seen the priest as her deadly enemy, in league with Sforza, the two of them trying to bury her alive. Well, she would pay them both back. One day Olimpia secretly took out her quill, her ink, and a piece of paper, and scratched a letter to the bishop of Viterbo, Gerolamo Matteucci.

It was Olimpia's good fortune that Bishop Matteucci was a strict churchman, described in the *Bishops and Dioceses of Viterbo* as "occupying himself in church business with perhaps too much severity."[8] He had sent several colleagues into exile for minor infractions, to the loud protests of the Viterban community. Such a stickler for the rules would not allow Sforza to disobey the Council of Trent with a wink and a shrug.

Sforza Maidalchini, she wrote, was trying to immure her in a convent without her consent, going willfully and knowingly against the rulings of the holy Council of Trent. And, for good measure, to further humiliate Sforza and punish the nagging priest, she added that the priest had tried to sexually molest her.

Perhaps Olimpia snuck out of the house and scurried across town to the bishop's palace, knocked loudly, and handed her letter to his butler. As she must have suspected, her accusation had the effect of a bomb exploding. Bishop Matteucci forwarded Olimpia's complaint to the tribunal of the Holy Inquisition in Rome. The priest was taken into custody, hauled up before the tribunal for crimes damaging to Christian morality, found guilty, and imprisoned for six months on bread and water, his career ruined. And the furious bishop forbade Olimpia's father to force her into a convent.

And so Olimpia had freed herself from the awful fate that loomed before her. But at what cost to herself and the Maidalchini family? As she passed in the street, people whispered, elbowed one another, and laughed. Many citizens of Viterbo felt she had made up the molestation story to get out of the convent, ruining the career of an innocent priest who had been quite popular with his parishioners. A rebellious, vicious girl, they said. Others felt she was telling the truth, that she was the innocent victim of a lecherous cleric, and everyone knew there were plenty of *them.*

But whether the Maidalchini girl was guilty or innocent, the scandal left an indelible stain on her reputation. On the surface at least, she didn't seem to care. She had accomplished many things with that letter, and indeed, she could be proud of herself. She had escaped the convent, humiliated her father, and punished the priest. She had carefully drawn her bow, aimed her arrow, and let it fly. It had hit its mark with deadly precision, punishing those who had hurt her.

Olimpia walked through town with her head held high, as she always would when under fire. As with many strong people, Olimpia never showed the cracks in her armor. She grieved secretly and put on a brave face to the world so no one would ever have the satisfaction of seeing her cry. Years later, when life's vicissitudes once more hit her brutally, publicly, when people threw stones at her in the street and spat on her, Olimpia was known to shrug and quote an old Italian saying. "I am like a beaten horse," she would say. "The beatings just make my coat glossier."[9]

Over time Olimpia's thirst for revenge and her stony face would cause the world to believe she was coldhearted. Indeed, it is a common mistake to think that those with strong leadership qualities never shed a tear in grinding sorrow, that they never feel the throbbing pain of a broken heart, that betrayal does not cut them as deeply as it does the easygoing. In fact, the opposite is usually true. Those who dominate, given their quick intelligence and high expectations, often feel the blow more keenly, suffer more cruelly, cry more bitterly.

And the fact that Olimpia's revenge was always so calculated, so deadly, was proof of how much she truly did care, of how much she had loved and hoped, of how deeply she felt betrayed. Those who had caused her bitter pain would suffer bitter pain themselves. It was, after all, only fair.

With the priest scandal, Olimpia had learned a valuable lesson that she would never forget. She had learned that she, a weak female, had the strength to break authority—the authority of the church, of the family, of society in general. And her tools in tearing down authority were lies, manipulation, and outright resistance. Only with these tools could she balance the handicap of being female. Given the cruelty men were always imposing on women, she must have viewed these weapons as permissible in her fight against injustice, in her right to protect herself.

Sforza, who had over the course of decades so carefully crafted his standing in the community, was devastated. The bishop was furious at him. The Holy Roman Inquisition frowned upon him. He had escaped excommunication by the skin of his teeth. His neighbors and business contacts either pitied him or ridiculed him behind his back. Sforza's well-intentioned efforts to protect his family had backfired disastrously. Given the magnitude of his disgrace, maybe Sforza was no longer up-and-coming. Maybe now he was down-and-going. And it was all Olimpia's fault.

There was another problem in addition to his damaged reputation, and this was a truly perplexing predicament. Olimpia had seen to it that a convent was out of the question. And it was unthinkable for a grown woman to live unmarried either with her parents or by herself. Yet whatever chance Sforza had had of finding a decent husband for her had surely vanished in the wake of the priest scandal. At this point, Sforza probably didn't *possess* enough money to persuade a man to take the scandalous Olimpia off his hands.

Who would want to marry her now? What on earth was he going to do with Olimpia?

But Olimpia knew she *would* find someone decent to marry her. She *would* have money, status, and power, and then no one would ever try to stuff her into a convent again. To prevent men from dominating her, she would dominate men. To prevent men from hurting other women, she would take the poor, the outcast, and the powerless of her own sex under her wing. And all those who were foolish enough to stand in her way would feel her wrath.

It was, after all, only fair.

2

The Wealthy Landowner's Wife

Wine maketh merry: but money answereth all things.

—Ecclesiastes 10:19

OVER THE NEXT YEAR or two after the priest scandal, when Sforza Maidalchini was at his wits' end over what to do with Olimpia, it became apparent that the richest young man in Viterbo had his eye on her. Twenty-year-old Paolo Nini was the nephew of Olimpia's godmother, Fiordalisa Nini. His father, Nino, had died, leaving him the sole heir to a large fortune that included two palaces in Viterbo, inns, vineyards, shops, farms, and rental property. In addition to wealth, the Ninis boasted several deceased relatives who had been high-level church officials.

Perhaps Paolo was attracted by the whiff of scandal that wafted about the bright-eyed girl like exotic perfume. Unlike the many dutiful, meek, obedient girls in Viterbo, any one of whom he could have married, Olimpia was exciting. Olimpia was rebellious. Olimpia was very, very smart. Olimpia would, perhaps, be a tigress in bed.

Nothing is recorded of Paolo Nini's character. But given what we know of Olimpia's, he must have been a good-natured young man whom she could easily dominate. Cheerful, jolly, easygoing—exactly the kind of man Olimpia would have been attracted to. She would never stand for a man likely to demean her for being a woman.

Maybe Sforza saw the young man's eyes follow his daughter's sprightly figure when she went to Mass. Or perhaps, at the annual procession of Saint Rosa, Paolo Nini's gaze lingered on her, and such a glance would not be lost on the eagle-eyed Sforza. Here was the perfect solution to all the family woes. If only Paolo could be enticed all the way to the altar despite the pitiful dowry, Olimpia would have the worldly life she longed for—a husband, household, children, and social position. The Maidalchini family prestige would rise dramatically. The terrible priest scandal would fade to a vague wisp of old gossip when compared with the reality of the prosperous landowner's wife.

In any event, it is likely that once Sforza was aware of the attraction, he did everything humanly possible to encourage it. We can assume that using his considerable charm, he invited Paolo to dinner, card parties, and hunting expeditions, events where Paolo and Olimpia could spend time getting to know each other. And we can assume that Olimpia, using the considerable Maidalchini family charm she had inherited from her father, did her level best to win the rich young bachelor.

Defenseless against the charms of both Sforza and Olimpia, Paolo Nini agreed to marry her for a dowry of only five thousand scudi, shockingly low given the wealth and social status of the groom. Paolo was clearly smitten, willing to sacrifice money and reputation to marry the scandalous Olimpia. The dowry documents were signed on May 18, 1608.

Some four months later, on September 29, seventeen-year-old Olimpia married Paolo Nini in the ninth-century Church of Saint Sixtus. The marriage of the richest man in town to the disgraced daughter of the town tax collector was an exciting event for Viterbo, and hundreds of guests must have crammed the church. Colorful tapestries would have hung from the drab, cold walls and the domed apse behind the altar, loaned by family and friends to add to the festive atmosphere.

The richly attired bride and groom would have walked down the aisle and up the fifteen steps to the main altar of Saint Sixtus for the holy sacrament of marriage—"What therefore God has put together, let not man put asunder." According to Catholic belief, this sacrament marked their souls with a holy seal indicating that they belonged together as long as they both lived.

After the wedding, the father of the bride was supposed to give a huge feast at his home. Sforza would have invited not only family but church officials, local dignitaries, business contacts, and their extended families. Perhaps Sforza winced at the cost but then remembered how fortunate he was to unload his embarrassing daughter on so prestigious a family for such a scant dowry.

After the reception, the guests would have escorted the newlyweds in a festive procession through the winding medieval streets to the groom's home. For more than seventy years the Nini family had owned two palaces facing each other across the narrow, curving Via Annio. Paolo's father had lived in one, and Paolo lived in the other.

Built in the early sixteenth century, the Nini palaces were what we would consider sprawling town houses. They were the most modern buildings on the street, with large, flat fronts and regularly spaced windows. Olimpia's new home was five windows across and three stories high. On the outside was an inscription in Latin stating that a Nini ancestor had enlarged and painted the house in 1543.

On either side of the building was a high arched carriage entrance, and underneath were stalls for the horses. The passages opened onto a courtyard. A courtyard was a most useful place for the day-to-day functioning of the household. Here the grooms brought the horses out of their stalls, brushed them, and hitched them up to carriages. Here was the tradesmen's entrance, where carts rolled up laden with firewood, barrels of wine, or animal carcasses to be dropped off at the kitchen door.

In the courtyard, if there was sufficient room, was an herb garden for the cook and a flower garden where the mistress of the house could sit in the shade of a tree and contemplate the blooms. Also in the courtyard, as far away from the house and garden as possible, were the outhouses, though many larger houses had inside privies which drained into a pit in the basement.

The courtyard usually contained the well, if there was one, and

Olimpia was fortunate enough to have one. Sometimes, though, servants ran to the nearest town fountain with buckets. Water from wells and fountains was used for washing dishes, clothes, and floors, for the periodic bath, and for washing the hands and face in the bedchamber and the hands at the table before each meal.

But water was not generally drunk. Given the stomach-wrenching bacteria that leached into the groundwater from the nearby outhouse and the ever-present animal waste, water was looked upon with great suspicion. Most Italians drank wine, often with just enough alcoholic content to kill the germs, generally about 2 percent. This low alcoholic content was fortunate, given the amount of wine the average Italian drank every day—two liters. Such wine often soured quickly, but even rancid wine had important uses—it was handy in washing down horses and mules and removing grease stains from wool and velvet clothing.

Entering her new home, Olimpia would have gone up the wide staircase to the *piano nobile,* or main floor, which was always above the noise and smell of the ground floor used by servants. And here she would have found a set of rooms that Paolo had newly furnished for her. The rooms were not sumptuous but high and airy.

Olimpia must have viewed her new home and impressive possessions with a sigh of relief and a tremendous sense of satisfaction. For lack of money, she had almost been imprisoned in a convent. By marrying Paolo Nini, she had taken the first step to making sure she would never be poor and powerless again. And the father who had betrayed her would have to acknowledge that she now had more money than he ever would, without his help. Plus, her house was several times the size of his, and she had another one just as big across the street.

The happy couple settled into their new life together. No doubt Olimpia had learned housekeeping skills from her mother, and the Maidalchini family would have employed several servants. Olimpia would now have her own *famiglia,* or domestic staff. Far more than mere servants, these individuals were, in a sense, family members, as their name implies. The master or mistress of a household was expected to bail a troublesome servant out of jail, pay for his medical and burial costs, and help his daughters with dowries. In return servants were fiercely—sometimes violently—loyal to their employers, ready to cut down anyone in the street who insulted them.

Olimpia's kitchen and staff dining room would have been located on the first floor of her palazzo, next to the stables and tradesmen's entrance. Seventeenth-century servants slept in the nooks and crannies of a house, in the basement next to the wine cellar, in the small rooms next to the kitchen or over the stables, and most commonly, in the attic.

The most important member of Olimpia's *famiglia* would have been her *maestro di casa,* an exalted butler, who supervised all her other servants. The *maestro di casa* arranged the delivery of meat, fish, fruit, vegetables, wine, and firewood from the Nini farms around Viterbo, and drew up contracts with local bakers, butchers, poulterers, fish mongers, and candle makers.

Olimpia and Paolo would have had two or three valets or footmen, who, wearing richly embroidered velvet livery and impressive hats with plumes, escorted them in their carriage whenever they went out, riding on the back of the carriage standing up. When the master or mistress was at home, these valets would welcome visitors and accompany them upstairs to the salon or, if the visitors were unwanted, prevent them from entering by a flurry of apologetic excuses. When not standing sentinel, the footmen took off their expensive liveries and did more menial work such as washing the floors, lighting fires, and replacing candlestick stubs with new candles.

One of the Ninis' servants would have played the role of master or mistress of the wardrobe, in charge of the purchase, laundering, storage, and repair of their clothing, sheets, tablecloths, and napkins. Only undergarments were washed. The outer garments of wool, silk, satin, and velvet, embroidered with gold and silver thread and edged with fur, would have been ruined by water. These were cleaned with wine, hung out in the courtyard overnight to air, and beaten with brooms to get the dust out.

As a rich landowner's wife, Olimpia was now in a position to buy gorgeous gowns. All the best velvets, satins, and dyes in Europe came from that portal to the East, Venice. But Olimpia did not much care for the gewgaws of contemporary females. Later in life she would laugh at other women for chattering an afternoon away over the merits of a ribbon or the cut of a sleeve. Though she would always love jewels, it was for their financial value. It is likely that as Paolo's wife she dressed simply but elegantly. She preferred to spend her time on business affairs, not women's foolishness.

Given Olimpia's thirst for business, and her husband's easygoing nature, it is probable that he allowed her to administer his estates. Farm tenants paid their rent in the form of crops, usually between 10 and 50 percent of the harvest of wine, olive oil, grain, livestock, fruit, and vegetables. Rents were due four times a year, regulated by the church calendar.

The first payment was expected on March 25, the Feast of the Annunciation, which celebrated the day when the angel told the Virgin Mary she would miraculously bear a son. Rent was again due on June 24, the Feast of Saint John the Baptist, Jesus' cousin, who baptized him in the river Jordan. The fall rents were paid on September 29, the Feast of the Archangels Michael, Gabriel, and Raphael, who had waged war in heaven against Lucifer. And the final payment was due on the Feast of the Nativity, that joyous day when Christ was born in Bethlehem. Olimpia would have made sure the rents were fully paid on time; she would have sold for maximum profit the produce her household didn't use, and carefully counted the coins.

At some point shortly after her marriage, Olimpia would have attended the profession ceremonies of her younger sisters at the Convent of Saint Dominic. After at least one year as a novice living the life of a nun, a girl was permitted to officially take nun's vows at the age of sixteen.

The profession ceremony was, in a way, much like a marriage ceremony, except a physical groom was absent. He was considered to be present, though unseen—the spirit of Jesus hovering above the altar ready to swoop down and claim the young nuns as his brides. As in a real marriage ceremony, the brides took new names. Ortensia became Sister Orsola, and Vittoria became Sister Margherita Vittoria.

In the profession ceremony, after the prayers and hymns, the bishop took each girl's right hand and put a ring on her third finger, proclaiming loudly, "I marry you to Jesus Christ, Son of the Father Almighty, your protector. Accept therefore this ring of faith as a sign from the Holy Spirit that you are called to be the wife of God." And in this moment it was believed that the girls' souls were marked with a spiritual tattoo proclaiming them to belong to God alone. Then the bishop added, "Forget your people, and your father's home."[1] But this injunction was almost never obeyed. Until the end of her life, Olimpia and her family would visit her sisters in the convent parlor, laden with food, wine, and gossip.

The girls stretched themselves out in front of the altar, their lips touching the cold stone floor. A black cloth was thrown over them, and lighted candles were placed at their heads and feet, the same ritual as in contemporary funeral customs. And indeed, to the world these young nuns *were* dead.

In ancient Greek legend, the warrior king Agamemnon sacrificed his adolescent daughter Iphigenia to the gods in return for favorable winds to take his fleet to Troy. Now, shrouded by the black death cloths, lay two baroque Iphigenias, sacrificial virgins to Sforza Maidalchini's dynastic ambitions.

Watching her sisters marry Jesus and die to the world, Olimpia must have shuddered and thought, *There but for the grace of God go I.*

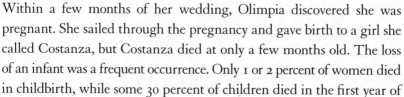

Within a few months of her wedding, Olimpia discovered she was pregnant. She sailed through the pregnancy and gave birth to a girl she called Costanza, but Costanza died at only a few months old. The loss of an infant was a frequent occurrence. Only 1 or 2 percent of women died in childbirth, while some 30 percent of children died in the first year of life.

Olimpia was pregnant soon again, and in early 1611 she gave birth to the long-awaited heir to the Nini fortune, Nino Nini, named after his grandfather. Perhaps Olimpia, carefully monitoring the health of her son, was surprised that it was her husband who became sick. Having survived the perils of childhood disease, most early-seventeenth-century men of Paolo's social status lived to be somewhere between fifty-six and sixty. But at twenty-three, Paolo Nini fell mortally ill. He died on June 6, 1611.

It is not known what caused Paolo's death. The plague, which ravaged Italian cities every generation or so, did not strike in 1611. Perhaps it was malaria, an errant mosquito that had flown to Viterbo from the swamps around Rome. Or maybe he caught a cold, which turned into bronchitis and then pneumonia. Paolo might have developed a walloping case of dysentery, which could quickly enervate a young, healthy person, dehydrating him into a parched husk within a week. In seventeenth-century Europe, the most robust individual could go from dancing to dead in a matter of days.

Twenty-year-old Olimpia was now a widow. We have no way of knowing how she felt about losing Paolo. Given the sentiment Olimpia hid beneath her hard crust, it is possible she grieved deeply. Though bereft of her husband, she still had her son, and little Nino was one very wealthy infant, having inherited all of his father's assets. Olimpia would administer the property for her son until he came of age.

But only nine months after Paolo's death, Olimpia was dealt another bitter blow. On March 9, 1612, one-year-old Nino also died. Olimpia had buried two children and a husband in less than three years. She had been abandoned once again.

She was abandoned, but very, very rich. For *she* was the heir of her son. All the Nini property bounced from the younger generation back to the older. Olimpia herself was now the proud and sole owner of the two Renaissance palazzos, inns, stables, taverns, farms, gardens, pasture lands, vineyards, municipal bonds, and mountains of cash.

Wealthy though she was, there was still the nagging question of her future. Society simply did not tolerate a young woman's living alone. Ironically, Olimpia faced the same two choices that had presented themselves five years earlier; she could bury her grief in a convent—not a likely choice, under the circumstances—or she could marry.

If she had been widowed nearer to that boundary of female decrepitude, the age of forty, she could have remained independent and respectable. But a young and attractive widow was thought to be more sexually insatiable than a virgin; she had known the pleasures of coitus and would likely do anything to enjoy them again. According to contemporary documents, even if a sex-starved widow found the strength to behave herself, she would most likely break out in pimples and lose her mind as the "naughty vapors" rose from her private parts up to her head. Suffering from the "unruly motions of tickling lust," she would require either a wall or a husband to keep her in line.[2]

The solution was clear. Olimpia needed to find another husband. And if she cringed at the thought of hearing the word *convent* suggested as a repository for her, she would have to dry her tears and marry fast.

3

The Roman Noblewoman

When in Rome, do as the Romans do.

—Saint Ambrose to Saint Augustine

O LIMPIA PUT THE WORD OUT that she was a rich young widow in search of a husband. Not any husband. At this point, armed with youth, good looks, and great wealth, Olimpia could afford to pick and choose.

What could she want from a husband that she didn't already have? Nobility, for one thing. As wealthy as Paolo Nini had been, and from a good old Viterban family chock-full of dead bishops, he had not been noble. Olimpia wanted to be the wife of a lord, a marquess, a count, or even a prince. "Princess Olimpia" had a lovely ring to it.

For another thing, she was tired of Viterbo. Though she would always love the region and often return to it, she longed to be in the beating heart of the Catholic world—the center of politics, finance, diplomacy, and church affairs. The land of glittering opportunities, Rome had always been so close but yet so far. Olimpia wanted to marry a Roman nobleman.

But even more than that, she wanted somehow to worm her way into political power. Given the irreparable handicap of her gender, Olimpia couldn't run for city council herself. But she could work on political matters through an obliging, politically connected husband who confided in her and asked her advice. And of course, the prospective groom couldn't be a domineering type whose abrasive personality would clash with hers. He must be a limp and languid person who would let her have her way.

As luck would have it, the perfect candidate presented himself as her son's body was still cooling in the grave. Olimpia's uncle Paolo Gualtieri had married Antonia Pamphili of Rome. The Pamphilis were a family of the minor nobility with a long tradition of church and government service. One of them had married the great-granddaughter of Pope Alexander VI, a Borgia, the one papal family no one liked to trumpet as ancestors. The family success was crowned in 1604 when Uncle Girolamo had been made a cardinal, reaping a harvest of wealth and prestige.

Girolamo lived with his widowed brother, Camillo, a papal historian who had fathered eight children. Two daughters had married honorably; two others had been honorably stuffed into convents. Two sons had died young, and two still lived in the Pamphili palazzo. Camillo and his sons enjoyed the financial benefits that were bestowed on Girolamo as a prince of the church.

But on August 11, 1610, Cardinal Girolamo Pamphili died at the age of sixty-six, the unfortunate result, according to Teodoro Amayden, of having slept in a room that had been recently whitewashed. Perhaps Camillo, too, inhaled the whitewash fumes, because he died two weeks after his brother. The income disappeared. Now, less than two years after the deaths, Camillo's sons were bereft of funds, living in a crumbling house, and in dire need of an heiress.

Born on May 6, 1574, thirty-eight-year-old Gianbattista Pamphili would have been closer in age to twenty-one-year-old Olimpia, but he was a priest trained as a canon lawyer—an expert in all matters of church law—and had the title of monsignor. However, his older brother, Pamphilio, the lay head of the family, was available, and it is unclear why he was unmarried. Perhaps he had been widowed early in life and had been reluctant to put his head in the noose again.

It is also possible that he had been a lifelong bachelor, though this would have been extremely rare among Italian nobles, as the oldest son was supposed to ensure the family's extension rather than its extinction. It seems, however, that the two brothers didn't particularly care about future generations of Pamphili greatness. In 1612 what they really cared about was paying the bills. This appears to have been the only incentive for bringing a woman into the house.

An inventory of 1611 revealed that Pamphilio possessed only two horses and his brother three, a pitiful stable for a noble family. Gianbattista paid for the hay and upkeep of all five horses, evidently from his salary as a canon lawyer, because his brother could not afford to. Although Pamphilio rented out shops on the street level of all three sides of his house, it seemed the rent didn't even cover basic living expenses.

Not only was Olimpia's suitor poor, but he was also balancing precariously on the precipice of what was considered old age for men—fifty. Yet contemporary reports noted that Pamphilio Pamphili was still strikingly handsome. He was known for his courtly manner and exquisite courtesy, traits he had acquired as a youth when he served as a page at the grand ducal court of Tuscany. Florence, the Italian capital of art and refinement, had given Pamphilio airs and graces that the riffraff Romans lacked. In his mid-twenties, Pamphilio returned home and was appointed to an office in the Campidoglio, the governmental center of the city of Rome.

It is not certain what position he held—perhaps taxation or administration—but whatever it was, it didn't pay much. This is odd, because Pamphilio boasted all the attributes necessary for financial success in Rome—blue blood, an excellent education, and high-level connections with the court of Tuscany, the Catholic Church, and the Roman civic government. Each year hundreds of men of humble birth marched on Rome armed only with ambition. Many of these got rich; a few even became pope. Adrian VI (reigned 1522–1523) was a carpenter's son. Pius V (reigned 1566–1572) had been a shepherd, and Sixtus V (reigned 1585–1590) had started his brilliant career feeding pigs.

But ambitious men had to wheel and deal, to bribe and cajole, to throw the right parties, to give the right gifts, and to plunge a figurative— or sometimes literal—dagger into the backs of their enemies at just the right time. It is possible that Pamphilio thought the most majestic course of action was to sit with noble dignity in his drawing room as the rain from his leaking roof dripped solemnly down on his head. Or perhaps he was simply too lazy to try very hard. One thing is clear: a Sforza Maidalchini he was not.

The one step he could take without terribly much effort was to marry money. And Pamphilio Pamphili was not alone in this predicament. Far older, more important families suffered along with him. The names that for a thousand years had made Rome ring to the clash of arms—the powerful Orsinis, Colonnas, Frangipanis, and Savellis—were dying out in mildewed palaces. Many decayed noblemen tried to boost the family fortunes by marrying into the *nouveau arrivé* papal families, trading their ancient lineage and impressive names for new Vatican money. The greatest prize of all was to marry a reigning pope's niece, who brought with her the staggering dowry of 100,000 scudi.

Pamphilio was not on the exalted level of a Colonna, of course, and had no hope of marrying into a papal family. But on a lesser level, he was ready to do the same thing. "Of course one must sometimes manure one's estates," sniffed one seventeenth-century noblewoman in reference to such marriages.[1] The manure for the Pamphili estate was to be Olimpia.

Their first meeting was likely arranged by Olimpia's uncle Paolo Gualtieri and his wife. Perhaps Pamphilio, in his slightly moth-eaten carriage, made the pleasant journey to Viterbo, not only to meet the young woman but to eye carefully her two palazzos on the Via Annio. Or maybe Olimpia, in a luxurious gilded and painted carriage with plump tasseled cushions and footmen standing on the back, made the exciting journey to Rome.

It is likely, under the circumstances, that Pamphilio would have readily married an obese elderly woman disfigured by smallpox to obtain her money, and that Olimpia would have wed a decrepit dribbling idiot to obtain his nobility and his house in Rome. Love was not a prerequisite for marriage, but it was always a bonus when the bride and groom did not disgust each other.

Such was the case of Pamphilio and Olimpia. Pamphilio must have been pleased with Olimpia's good looks and her Maidalchini charm. Olimpia was ingratiating. Olimpia was witty. Olimpia possessed a vigor that promised to rouse even a Pamphilio Pamphili from his noble torpor.

For her part, the shrewd Olimpia must have sized up the prospective groom at a glance. This handsome gentleman hid his insipid personality under a thick varnish of Florentine elegance, to the great admiration of all. She must have been relieved to see that here was no domineering temperament to compete with hers. Here was an easygoing man who would probably do as she asked just to keep harmony in the household. According to an anonymous document in the Vatican, Pamphilio "was a person who at the smallest hint would have made himself obey and respect his consort."[2]

Olimpia must have believed that such a man would be grateful for the clever advice of an energetic wife who could shoulder the burden of his governmental responsibilities. Pamphilio Pamphili could offer her everything she had been looking for in a husband, even political power. She jumped at the chance to marry him.

The dowry documents, signed on November 1, 1612, show a shocking inequality in the financial contributions to the marriage. Olimpia "promises to give him all her properties and inheritance which came to her through the death of Nino Nini, her son." In return for Olimpia's wealth, Pamphilio merely promised "to take her as his legitimate wife."[3]

Sforza Maidalchini must have watched with mixed emotions the meteoric rise of his perplexing daughter. He was proud of her, certainly, but also perhaps a bit afraid of her. He must have noticed her eyes narrow when she gazed at him, her lips almost imperceptibly tighten. Revenge is, after all, a dish best served cold. She had already served him one heaping helping of icy vengeance, and now that she had attained such an exalted position, she might be tempted to cram another one down his throat.

Though Olimpia's ample Nini inheritance served as her dowry, the nervous Sforza belatedly stepped up to the plate in an effort to redeem himself. He agreed to pay three thousand scudi the day of the wedding along with a valuable pearl necklace and matching earrings, other pieces of jewelry, and silver. He would pay an additional two thousand scudi in installments. Altogether, the dowry was worth about six thousand scudi.

"The marriage was celebrated in Rome with all the pomp possible," Gregorio Leti reported, "and with the entire satisfaction of both parties."[4] She was now Lady Olimpia—Donna Olimpia in Italian—which accounted for her entire satisfaction. She was a noblewoman, and no one would ever dare to try sticking *her* in a convent again.

Olimpia found herself the mistress of the old Pamphili family manse in the Piazza Navona, the heart of Rome. The site had a long and illustrious history. In A.D. 86, Emperor Domitian built a fifteen-thousand-seat stadium for athletic games called *agoni*. The lozenge-shaped arena was covered with travertine marble and adorned with statues of the gods and heroes. The emperor presided from his podium wearing his purple Greek toga, a crown of golden laurel leaves on his head.

When Emperor Constantine moved the capital of the Roman Empire to Constantinople in A.D. 330, the *agoni* stadium fell into disuse. Enterprising builders recognized it immediately as a free quarry, as most of imperial Rome had become. They arrived with horse-drawn carts, pried off the travertine blocks, and hauled them off to be used in houses and churches.

By the fifth century a tradition had arisen that a fourteen-year-old Christian virgin named Agnes had been martyred in the stadium in A.D. 303 during the persecution of Emperor Diocletian. When the executioner exposed Agnes nude to the hoots of the crowd, the angels made copious waves of hair sprout from her scalp to hide her nudity. But the angels didn't stay the headsman's axe. It is almost certain that the fictional Agnes developed from a corruption of the word *agoni*.

A little chapel was made to honor the saint under an arch in the decaying amphitheater, which in time became the tiny Church of Saint Agnes, located a few doors from Olimpia's new home. Those who still venerate Agnes's purported skull today must be aware that something is remarkably odd about it, since it is the skull of a seven-month fetus. But some legends are just too good to let facts interfere with them.

By the Middle Ages, silt deposited from recurring floods had raised the ground level of the old amphitheater by at least fifteen feet. Houses were built over the old stadium seats, many of which can still be seen in basements. The square began to be called the Piazza Agona and was further corrupted into Piazza Navona.

Around 1470, Antonio Pamphili came to Rome from the town of Gubbio, 130 miles to the north, and worked for Pope Sixtus IV as fiscal procurator of the Apostolic Camera—in other words, he was a Vatican tax collector. He bought a small town house first recorded in 1367 on the Via dell'Anima, the street that runs behind the Piazza Navona. Whenever a neighboring house came on the market, Antonio, as well as his son and grandson in later years, eagerly snatched it up, knocking out interior walls to incorporate the small houses into one larger house. By the time Olimpia moved in, the residence had its main entrance on the more impressive Piazza Navona and was the last house on the corner, with three sides overlooking streets.

Olimpia was probably not thrilled with her new home. The central location was excellent, but the building was a far cry from sumptuous, well laid out, or airy. A sketch from 1612 shows the house was narrow and four stories tall. It's façade had irregularly spaced windows of various sizes on different levels, and the *piano nobile* had three small windows fronting onto the Piazza Navona from two small rooms. Many of the rooms were not rectangular but trapezoidal, the result of cobbling together separate buildings in various stages of decrepitude.

The majority of rooms were on the side of the house, on the Via Pasquino, with another suite of apartments in the rear, on the Via dell'Anima. The rooms were grouped around a tiny courtyard and well, entered from a little alley on the Piazza Navona. The Casa Pamphili, called Casa—house—because it wasn't big enough to be a palazzo—was a huge step down from the Nini home in Viterbo, with its spacious entry hall, sweeping staircase, and elegant layout. But with her money, Olimpia could fix it up and decorate it, and keep her eye on neighboring houses that might come on the market.

It was difficult, however, to create a noble showplace on the very piazza where the Roman vegetable market took place every Wednesday.

Donkeys drank from three low fountains, one of them in front of Olimpia's main entrance. Farmers loudly hawked their produce, and at the end of the day the piazza was littered with manure, wilted lettuce, rotten tomatoes, and the enormous horseflies that buzzed around them. Olimpia detested the market.

Just as bad as the noise and crowds from the market out front were the noise and crowds around the statue of Pasquino located just behind her house. In 1501 when the Orsini family was expanding their palace, workmen unearthed a noseless, armless, horribly mutilated fragment of a third-century B.C. Greek sculpture of Hercules. It had almost certainly once been part of the statuary adorning the Domitian stadium. The statue was placed on a pedestal and began to be called Pasquino after a nearby papal tailor who, it was said, couldn't keep his mouth shut about Vatican gossip.

Almost immediately students began hanging virulently antigovernment poems and placards on the statue. These anonymous insults—on papal corruption, gluttony, sodomy, and incest—became known as pasquinades. Given the absence of a free press, by Olimpia's time writing a pasquinade was the only opportunity to express one's negative opinion of the government and have fellow citizens read it. And read it they did. They gathered around the statue at all times of the day and night to laugh, drink, socialize, and copy down the cruel poems so they could be read in taverns.

Pasquino had a friend. In the sixteenth century, a mostly intact colossal statue of a reclining river god was unearthed and placed at the foot of Capitoline Hill. He was called Marforio because he had been found in the forum (*foro*) of the temple of Mars. Marforio would "talk" to Pasquino, asking him his opinion of the pope, a cardinal, or a foreign ambassador. People would then run across town to see Pasquino's response. By the time they raced back to Marforio, his response to Pasquino's response would be posted. Other statues began talking to Pasquino.

Most popes usually let Pasquino and his friends have their say as a means of venting popular discontent against high taxes and injustice. But a few particularly annoying pasquinade writers had been incinerated at the stake. Even an execution didn't seem to dampen the ardor of would-be political columnists, and the crowds outside of Olimpia's back windows never seemed to go away.

Next to Pasquino was Rome's only post office. Here, before residents picked up their mail, or before their mail was sent abroad, inspectors opened letters and packages to search for heresy, libel, and treason. They compared book titles with the ever-growing list on the Vatican's Index of Prohibited Books. Though usually, for the price of a scudo an inspector would forget to look in a particular satchel.

Olimpia's Rome was a far cry from that shining marble metropolis of one million inhabitants under the Roman emperors. In the heady days of Emperor Trajan, who reigned from A.D. 98 to 117, eleven aqueducts pumped sparkling water to thirteen hundred fountains as well as countless public baths, swimming pools, and gardens. Eight sturdy stone bridges allowed pedestrians, horses, and carts laden with goods to cross the Tiber. But when Emperor Constantine left town, everybody who was anybody went with him, including almost all of the civil servants who had kept Rome running.

In the fifth and sixth centuries, Goths, Vandals, and Lombards surrounded the walls of Rome and cut the aqueducts, destroying most of the city's water supply. Swamps spread out over leaking pipes and became home to malarial mosquitoes, which caused massive epidemics. With no water, the famous Seven Hills were abandoned. For a thousand years, almost all Romans huddled around the Tiber River for water.

The empty imperial edifices on the Seven Hills were raided for materials to construct new buildings. Trees and vines covered what was left of them. Cows grazed in the formerly splendid Roman Forum, which became known as the Cow Field. The neglected Roman bridges collapsed of their own accord or were swept away in floods, until only two remained. By the twelfth century there were a mere thirty thousand inhabitants.

In 1309 the popes left Rome for Avignon and through a series of mishaps did not return for good until 1443. By this time wolves prowled the streets, digging up the dead and maiming the living. Those who entered the Eternal City in the returning pope's train were shocked at its utter ruin. The writer Aretino described Rome not by its impressive ancient title of *caput mundi*—the head of the world—but as *coda mundi*—the rear end of the world.

The narrow thoroughfares of Rome were often obstructed by mountainous heaps of ancient buildings collapsed by earthquakes or time. Streets were also choked by man-made obstructions: porticoes, or walkways over the street connecting houses, and balconies jutting out well into the street. Sometimes a road was completely blocked when a home owner, eager for a larger house, built an addition *across* the entire street.

Pope Sixtus IV (reigned 1471–1484) began an ambitious program to clean and widen the roads, a program that succeeding popes would continue. The *maestri di strada,* or street controllers, arranged for ancient rubble blocking the thoroughfares to be carted away. They tore down all the illegal home additions that had obstructed city roads. They forced citizens to clean up the manure, sewage, and refuse they had thrown into the street, and then imposed a hefty fine. The city hired dust carts to pick up the garbage and dump it where it was supposed to go—into the Tiber River, the main source of water for household consumption.

Fortunately, Sixtus and the popes who followed him repaired aqueducts, opening up new areas of the city for home building and commerce. Starting in the sixteenth century, cardinals built sumptuous palaces on the hills, enjoying fresh breezes and the cachet of living where Julius Caesar, Pompey, and Cato had lived fifteen hundred years earlier. Artists flocked to Rome from Florence and Venice, highly paid by popes to turn the heap of ruined monuments into a cultural center worthy of its glorious past. The population increased, art flourished, and business thrived.

But in 1527 Rome was invaded by a new horde of plundering barbarians, the troops of Emperor Charles V, who was angry at Pope Clement VII for siding with France in a political dispute. They murdered tens of thousands of citizens, stole their wealth, and destroyed some thirty thousand houses, or about half the buildings in the city. The German

Lutheran battalions vandalized papal tombs, using one pope's skull as a football, and massacred five hundred citizens who had gathered for protection around the altar of Saint Peter's. After the foreign soldiers left Rome, staggering under the weight of their plunder, the city was attacked by typhoid, famine, and flood. Anyone who could afford to leave the city—including the artists, architects, merchants, and bankers—fled, and Rome was once again moribund.

It took a decade for the city to get over the shock of the Sack and its aftermath. But Rome had, by now, some experience in cleaning up a moldering ruin. Rubble was carted away. The sounds of hammering and the sight of ropes and pulleys were everywhere as new buildings went up. The Roman pontiffs laid out wide roads to ease street congestion because the newfangled invention, the carriage, was choking narrow medieval roads. And every time a road was laid or a foundation dug, builders found the exquisite detritus of the previous civilization—marble columns, gorgeous statues, and mosaic floors. These were hoisted up and sold to the highest bidder—usually a cardinal—who integrated them into his own palazzo.

Despite the flurry of building, by the time Olimpia came to Rome in 1612, the city boasted only 100,000 inhabitants. The center of Christendom was only half the size of London and a fourth the size of Paris. Most neighborhoods were semirural in character. In the south and east of the city were orchards and farms. Monasteries and convents, set in large gardens, covered much of the western section.

Olimpia's house was in the most urban area of Rome. It was a short carriage ride from the Piazza Navona to the street of locksmiths, the street of booksellers, and streets reserved for rosary makers, glove makers, jewelers, carriage mechanics, and barbers who could shave a man's face, open a vein, and pull his rotten tooth with equal aplomb. Each establishment had a sign depicting the services offered within—a pipe for the tobacconist, a bleeding arm for the surgeon—so that illiterate Romans could find the shop they needed.

Rome made no products for export, such as cloth, ships, or guns. The economy was primarily focused on the church and its bureaucrats and the services that supported them. Architects, masons, carpenters, painters, and roofers built palaces for high-level Vatican officials. Cabinetmakers and drapers furnished them. Artists, sculptors, and gardeners adorned them. Tailors, seamstresses, hatmakers, cloak makers, and shoemakers dressed those who lived and worked in them. Grocers, butchers, bakers, and fishmongers fed them. A large chunk of the population worked as domestic servants for the rich—a cardinal usually employed a staff of two hundred individuals, many of whom took care of his one hundred horses and numerous carriages.

But Rome had countless poor citizens unable to find work in wealthy households. In Olimpia's time, the disparity between rich and poor was as great as it would ever be. The rich few lived in sumptuous palaces, gorged themselves to vomiting at banquets, rode in the finest carriages, and wore satins and silks embroidered with gold and pearls. The poor fretted over the number of ounces in the brown bread they bought on the street, a small loaf called the *pagnotta*. The price was fixed at one *bajocco,* which might translate into a penny, but the weight of the bread was determined by papal decree.

When Rome enjoyed peace and plentiful harvests, bread "rose" from its usual eight ounces to ten or twelve ounces. The poor survived well enough, working where they could and having just enough to buy bread, lettuce, and a little oil as salad dressing. But whenever Rome and its surrounding countryside suffered war, drought, flood, or epidemic— or when the pope withdrew Vatican bread subsidies to give the money to his greedy relatives—bread "fell" to six or even four ounces. Then the poor starved, dying on the street in a disheveled heap of ribs and rags.

The social safety net of the times was created not by the government, which did little to help the poor, but by confraternities—charitable organizations of laypeople attached to a particular neighborhood church. Each confraternity had its own special form of charity. Many attended the sick and dying. Some fed the hungry. Others provided dowries to poor girls or helped orphans and widows. One confraternity focused on reforming prostitutes, perhaps the most challenging job. Another one counseled death row prisoners in their cells, accompanied them in the tumbrel to the place of execution, and stood next to them as the execution took place.

But the generosity of confraternities was never enough to ease the boundless suffering in Rome.

Working-class Romans usually lived their lives outside. Markets were held in every square. Artisans worked in front of their shops. Women set up spinning wheels in front of their homes and yelled to their neighbors and passersby. The main occupation of Roman citizens, living on the street as they did, was gossip. They were quick to note who was going in and out of which house, how long they stayed, and what they looked like when they came out.

As comfortable as the Romans made themselves on the streets, they had to be ready to run at a moment's notice. In some ways, seventeenth-century Rome resembled a Hollywood version of the American Wild West. Street fights would erupt between the armed entourages of two feuding families or two dueling ambassadors. Shots would ring out, swords clash, and all those who had been lounging, working, or selling on the streets would vanish in an instant behind bolted doors and shuttered windows. Only once the violence had stopped would the Romans come out to gape at the dead bodies littering the pavement.

Worse dangers lurked in Rome than the spontaneous eruptions of baroque cowboys. Until 1875, when flood banks were built, the Tiber River was level with the streets and houses around it. Floods were an ever-present problem, and every decade or so a raging torrent killed hundreds of Romans in low-lying areas. In a few hours entire sections of the city could be flooded to a depth of ten or twelve feet. The Jews suffered most of all, as they had been crammed into the lowest-lying part of Rome right next to the river by papal decree.

Sometimes when the river surged suddenly, inmates incarcerated in Rome's Tor di Nona prison drowned in their cells as water poured in the barred windows and rose to the ceiling. During the two or three days the waters remained at their peak, Rome resembled Venice. Red-robed cardinals canoed through the streets offering blessings and—more important—bread to the starving, who lowered baskets from their second-floor windows.

When the waters receded, houses, roads, and public buildings were filled with sewage and mud. Sometimes typhoid broke out. And with each new deluge the ruins of the ancient forum disappeared a little more into the twenty feet or so of silt, deposited there by centuries of floods. The jagged tops of triumphal arches and colossal temples stuck out of the mud, tombstones commemorating the glories of a vanished race.

Fires, too, were an ever-present threat. Logs rolled out of fireplaces; untended candles shed sparks on straw-covered floors, and suddenly a whole city block was ablaze. As residents ran naked into the streets, dragging out chairs and tables, the volunteer fire brigade passed buckets of water from the nearest fountain, which was often quite a distance away. Since water thrown from a bucket had little effect on a raging inferno, most fires were simply allowed to burn themselves out, while "firemen" doused the roofs of buildings across the street to prevent sparks from igniting.

Even the ancient stones themselves posed a threat. In Olimpia's time most of the buildings were hundreds of years old and had been patched together from parts of imperial Roman baths and basilicas. The city had no salaried building inspectors, and every few months a house, a tower, or a wall would groan in pain and come crashing down with very little warning, killing everyone in its path. Even the most exalted Romans were not spared the dangers of falling masonry. In 1499 the ceiling of the Vatican audience chamber fell on Pope Alexander VI, knocking him unconscious and killing the servant standing next to him.

Casting a penetrating gaze around her new city, Olimpia must have realized it was dirtier, noisier, uglier, and far more lethal than Viterbo. But it was here, in Rome, where she would finally realize her lifelong dream of working in politics. Her new husband, Pamphilio, would surely want her advice.

4

The Brother-in-Law

I have a man's mind, but a woman's might.

—*Portia, William Shakespeare*, Julius Caesar

Ignor Pamfili her husband, like most Italian men, conducted his business affairs without asking his wife's opinion or
advice," reported Gregorio Leti.[1] In fact, the normally lethargic
Pamphilio was horrified when his vivacious new wife peppered him
with questions about his political business and cheerfully suggested she
become his advisor. If Pamphilio Pamphili had one firm opinion about
how the world should work, it was that women had no place in men's
business affairs. And here, for the first time in her life, Olimpia was
truly stymied. Pamphilio was adamant, and there was nothing she
could do to change his mind.

But even if she couldn't get involved in politics, there were many
tasks to keep Olimpia busy. There was, for example, charity work.
Though Olimpia could be tight as a tick with her money, she would
always be known for her generosity to nuns. She had great compassion for women who had not been clever enough to escape their lifelong imprisonment, as she had. In those convents with strict rules of
poverty, the nuns sometimes went hungry, the roofs leaked, and there
were no fires in winter. Olimpia visited convents often, chatting

cheerfully with nuns in the parlor. She brought bedding, linens, firewood, food, and cash for structural repairs. *There but for the grace of God go I.*

While most women spent an unconscionable amount of time gossiping with one another, Olimpia generally disliked the company of her own gender. "She spoke little when in the ordinary company of women," Leti noted. "But she spared no words when dealing with men."[2] Olimpia often said that chattering with women was a waste of time. Silly, empty-headed creatures, most of them, twittering about babies, balls, and bows. And yet, Olimpia must have made the requisite social calls on Rome's powerful noblewomen if only to ensure their assistance in the future, once she had figured out how she could use it.

But getting an entrée into society wouldn't be easy. Roman nobles inflated their importance based on their lineage. They pointed with pride to the popes and cardinals rotting in the family vault, to their ancestors' valiant feats of arms five hundred years earlier in the Crusades, to their mildewed palaces glimmering faintly with traces of bygone glories among the leaks and mold. The further these glories receded into the past, the less affably a noble family would welcome a wealthy nouveau riche newcomer. Many members of that closed and hostile society must have treated Olimpia with ice-cold hostility.

Olimpia would have known immediately the esteem in which her hostess held her by how far out of her audience chamber the noblewoman came to meet her. Roman etiquette was cruelly precise. The host or hostess showed the greatest respect by waiting outside for the guest's carriage to arrive, an honor usually reserved for royalty or the relatives of popes. A fairly well respected visitor was greeted at the bottom of the stairs. A visitor of so-so importance would find the hostess at the top of the stairs, mumbling apologies for not being able to come down.

Those who were genuinely disliked would be ushered all the way into the hostess's audience chamber by the butler to find the hostess sitting grimly in her chair. The same etiquette was used upon the visitor's departure. When the visitor rose to leave, and the hostess merely stood and didn't set foot outside the room, the visitor knew she was despised, or at least looked down upon as greatly inferior.

Olimpia would have found a few of her hostesses—those truly kind women eager to welcome a newcomer—at the top of the stairs. But later events would show that many had snubbed her badly when she first moved to Rome, and we can assume this snub took the form of calcified noblewomen glued to their chairs. A tax collector's daughter from Viterbo, these grand dames would have grumbled, who married an old man from the minor nobility for his title. Why should they get out of their chairs for *her*?

Back at her Piazza Navona palace, Olimpia must have suffered greatly from their unkindness. Though she seemed unflappable in public, she would never forget how these snooty women had treated her, and she would never forgive. One day she would wreak her revenge, she vowed, a vow that she would in time fulfill.

As a Roman nobleman's wife, Olimpia would have employed many more servants than she had as Paolo Nini's wife in Viterbo. A *scalco,* or meat carver, was a sign of great prestige. The *scalco*'s exuberant slicing of fish, beef, poultry, and game rivaled a theatrical performance. He was in charge of all the knives in a household and kept them sharp and sparkling. More important, he guarded the food from the time it was purchased until it reached his master's table, making quite sure no one had spiced it with a bit of arsenic. The 1668 butler's guide to a noble household, *Il perfetto maestro di casa,* declared that the *scalco* "has his master's life in his hands."[3]

The *coppiero,* or wine steward, was in charge of all wine and water for the table. He worked with local wine dealers and vintners outside Rome to purchase the finest vintages available for his master's entertaining. He obtained the cleanest water possible for the waiters to pour from silver ewers over the guests' hands at the start and end of meals, the water running off into silver bowls. He stocked the family carriage with a traveling bar of crystal goblets and fine wines should his master or mistress require refreshment on a journey. And he kept the wine under lock and key to make sure the other servants did not quaff it down and show up drunk for work, a common occurrence in noble households.

But according to *Il perfetto maestro di casa,* the *coppiero* had one duty of greater urgency than all others: he "must use great diligence especially in households where there are enemies, and hatred, keeping a watchful eye on the wine cellar and the lesser servants, because if wine, water, or their containers are switched, there can be disastrous consequences."[4]

The *credenziere* was in charge of all things related to setting the table and buffet—silverware, platters, pitchers, glasses, napkins, and tablecloths. To guard these valuables, which were made of silver, gold, and crystal, he slept in the pantry where they were kept. He had to wipe them clean before each meal to make sure no enemy had secretly entered the house and coated them with hemlock.

Olimpia's new household was required to follow the painstaking etiquette required for a Roman nobleman. For instance, whenever Pamphilio raised his glass to drink, all his servants standing stiffly in the dining room were required to remove their hats in veneration. And when the Ave Maria bells rang out from Rome's hundreds of churches at sunset, all the servants were required to fling themselves on their knees and pray while the nobles removed their hats and bowed their heads.

The dignity of a Roman nobleman was measured in the number of his retainers, most of whom rode noisily through the streets following his carriage no matter where he went—to church, to a friend's house, to his tailor, even to his mistress. When the *maestro di casa* rang a particular bell, within fifteen minutes all male members of the *famiglia* were required to be mounted on a horse, ready to fly through the streets of Rome behind their master. Those who were not ready would forfeit a week's meals. Even the cooks, gardeners, and servant boys would fling on the family livery and race madly through the streets, creating as much din and dust as possible.

The writer Aretino told the story of one Roman nobleman who couldn't afford to feed his servants. Before ringing the bell, he would hide their bridles, saddles, and stirrups so they weren't ready to ride in fifteen minutes. But Pamphilio Pamphili no longer had need for such ruses. Armed with Olimpia's money, he hired more servants and purchased expensive horses, which he had to board a block away as his tiny courtyard was not big enough for them.

After her arrival in Rome, Olimpia must have enjoyed the pageantry of religious and political celebrations in the Eternal City, the likes of which she had never seen in Viterbo. Some three months after her wedding Olimpia experienced her first Roman Carnival—that uproarious celebration right before Ash Wednesday. Carnival was permitted by papal edict for a specific number of days—usually ten—but permission was withheld if the Papal States were suffering from plague, war, or famine. A sorrowful face, liberally bedaubed with ashes, was more likely to win God's forgiveness than a jester's hat with jingling bells.

Carnival began with the tolling of a bell on a Saturday and a procession of city officials. Two days later naked Jews were forced to race along the Corso, the main thoroughfare of Rome and the heart of Carnival, to the cheering of thousands of spectators who pelted them with eggs, vegetables, and dead cats. But this was not meant as a special denigration to Jews. On other days there were naked races of old men, cripples, little boys, whores, buffaloes, jackasses, and riderless horses with tacks stuck in their backs to make them run faster, and everyone got pelted. Called *palios*, the races were considered great fun for all—except, perhaps, for the horses—and the prizes were valuable bolts of cloth. One race was reserved for naked hunchbacks, "very remarkable for the variety of their humps."[5]

A popular parade featured the King of the Defecators, hoisted aloft on a toilet chair and farting loudly. Horses, decked out with jingling silver bells and tall feathered headdresses, pulled extravagantly decorated floats through town. Carts rolled through the streets, some with musicians and others with costumed revelers. Jousts were held in large piazzas, including the Piazza Navona, along with mock naval battles as ships drawn on wheels shot firecrackers at one another. At night the entire city was illuminated with lanterns and torches, and fireworks were set off.

Day and night, costumed revelers thronged the Corso and surrounding streets and squares. Some paraded as doctors, lawyers, Jews, animals, and devils. Some men dressed as women, and some women dressed as men. All wore masks, and many were armed with syringes—the seventeenth-century version of a water pistol—which they squirted at one another. They also pelted passersby with oranges and painted eggs filled with scented powder, jam, perfume, or water. One popular prank was to pour honey out of an upper window onto the heads of pedestrians below.

On Ash Wednesday the boisterous extravagance of Carnival disappeared, replaced by the funereal atmosphere of Lent, which commemorated Jesus' forty days in the desert. During this time, Romans wore black, ate no meat, attended no festivities, and meditated on the sacrifice of Jesus on the cross. One Turkish ambassador visiting Rome was absolutely perplexed by the riotous Carnival followed by the sudden solemnity of Ash Wednesday. He wrote the sultan in Constantinople that Carnival was a ten-day mania that afflicted the Christians annually and was only cured by the application of ashes to the face.

Communion, which had been taken frequently in the early centuries of Christianity, had almost stopped completely by the sixteenth century. Catholic theologians argued loudly that the consecrated bread really *was* the body of Christ; this terrified people who thought it a desecration to have something so holy slide down their gullets, rumble into their stomachs, and come shooting out the other end.

Given the widespread fear of the Eucharist, the Council of Trent mandated that Catholics must confess and receive communion at least once a year. According to custom, most Catholics, having abstained from sex for three days, did this on the Thursday before Easter. The faithful received only bread as their communion, as the wine was reserved for priests. Laypeople with their clumsy hands could drop the chalice, thereby literally spilling the blood of Christ all over again.

In 1614 Olimpia would have noticed a novelty in her Easter confession, a grille between her and the priest. Pope Paul V had issued an edict mandating that all confessionals be outfitted with grilles because of the many complaints he had received from women who, when they confessed their sexual sins in graphic detail, suddenly found themselves pawed and groped by hormonally overwrought priests who could no longer contain themselves.

Olimpia would have seen many festivities taking place right in front of her house. The Piazza Navona was the heart of Rome's powerful

Spanish community. Here the Spanish ambassador lived, and right across from Olimpia's home was the Church of Saint James, the Spanish national church. Every June 28 the Spanish ambassador started out from his home with a cavalcade of some three hundred carriages headed for the Vatican. There he presented the pope with a beautiful white horse, the *chinea,* the nominal rent that Spain paid for the kingdom of Naples, which was, technically, the territory of the pope. It is likely that the ambassador's neighbors Pamphilio and Olimpia hitched up their carriage and joined in the procession.

Every August 7, Rome's Spaniards and their friends celebrated the Feast of Our Lady in the Piazza Navona by giving dowries to young women of Spanish descent who otherwise would not be able to marry. In 1613, twenty-seven women processed through the piazza and entered the Church of Saint James to receive dowries raised by the confraternity. Olimpia, if she watched from her drawing room window, must have been pleased.

Olimpia and Pamphilio were not the only Pamphili family members living in the Piazza Navona house. Pamphilio's younger brother Gianbattista also lived there. Gianbattista had been blindsided by his brother's sudden decision to marry. The writer of an anonymous document in the Pamphili family archives asked Gianbattista if he had been consulted about the marriage. The monsignor replied that he had been completely left out of the decision. But, he added, he had always known that if and when Pamphilio married, it would be a "most noble wife," that he approved of the bride wholeheartedly and wanted his brother to be happy.[6]

As head of the family, Pamphilio had a higher rank than Gianbattista. Pamphilio and Olimpia took the more important suite of rooms facing the Piazza Navona and wrapping around the side of the house. Gianbattista lived in the less honorable but more spacious suite of rooms in the rear.

It is amusing that the relationship of Olimpia and her brother-in-law, which would ultimately scandalize all Europe, got off on the wrong foot. When Olimpia first arrived at the Piazza Navona after her wedding, she swept through the rooms and joyfully exclaimed that all the lovely furniture was *hers*, including the room where Gianbattista had stacked his furniture to get it out of the bride's way. He had bought some fine pieces with his salary as a canon lawyer or had received them as gifts from Uncle Girolamo.

Evidently, in a moment of weakness Gianbattista, reluctant to anger his brother and frightened by his imperious new sister-in-law, told her she could have it. But he soon regretted it and put his position in writing. He had not given Olimpia the furnishings, he explained to Pamphilio, "but I placed them in the last room of the Piazza Navona house before Signora Olimpia came to Rome, along with my other things, to empty the rooms for the occasion, and if Signora Olimpia says that I gave them to her, I imagine that I only could have said so out of fear or persuasion of Signor Pamphilio. But I insist that it be returned to me at all costs."[7] It is not known exactly how the issue was resolved, but events proved it was patched up with no hard feelings.

Gianbattista had been the favorite of the late Cardinal Girolamo, who had recognized his diligence and intelligence while he was still a child. Girolamo encouraged him to study canon law at the finest school in Rome, the Jesuit Collegio Romano. At the age of twenty, Gianbattista received his doctorate in law. Though he took holy orders in 1597, he did not seem to have an inclination for the ecclesiastical life. Like most young noblemen of his time—lay or religious—he excelled in dueling, drinking, and womanizing, which earned him the nickname "Monsieur Pastime." The ambassador of Venice reported, "He had little capacity for such [scholarly] tasks and applied himself slowly to studies, passing his youth more in the pastimes of a cavalier than in learning the law. Despite his uncle's assiduous efforts, he could not make him forget his nocturnal pleasures."[8]

Uncle Girolamo was particularly concerned about Gianbattista's gaudy Spanish hairstyle—long frizzed ringlets—and his refusal to wear church robes. He implored his Vatican friends to persuade his nephew to adopt a more serious look, suitable for a priest and lawyer. Their persuasions had an effect; one summer when Girolamo was vacationing outside Rome his nephew appeared wearing the long dark robes of a canon lawyer, and had lost the curls and frizz. After that, his days and nights of debauchery were over, and a new, sober Gianbattista won the immediate approval of his uncle and his church colleagues.

The new look boosted his career immediately. In 1601 Pope Clement VIII, Uncle Girolamo's good friend, appointed Gianbattista a consistorial lawyer. Three years later, when Girolamo was named cardinal, the pope arranged for Gianbattista to take his uncle's position as an auditor of the Rota, the Vatican court that heard civil cases relating to matrimony, financial issues, and other matters.

When Olimpia first met Gianbattista, he was thirty-eight years old, tall and well built, but not handsome like his brother. He had a wide forehead, often puckered into a scowl, and small hazel eyes. Even in youth his beard, that benchmark of seventeenth-century male beauty, had never been thick and silky but rather was straggly and sparse.

Gianbattista was learned, courteous, and by now, sober. He was also indecisive to the point of paralysis, deeply suspicious of others, and subject to gloomy silent depressions. Over time, he had developed a highly effective defense to prevent others from seeing the doubts that lurked inside him—a wall of inscrutable dignity. Cloaked in ugly majesty, he never showed his weaknesses to other men, whom he regarded as backstabbing competitors.

Throughout his long life, Gianbattista was more prepared to trust women than men, as women could not compete with him in a man's world. But it is likely that he was also searching for a surrogate mother, having lost his own in 1580, when he was six. Gianbattista could confide in women, let down his guard, and openly discuss his fears. He was extremely close to an older sister, Agatha, a nun in Rome's Tor de' Specchi Convent, and visited her frequently for long talks in the convent parlor.

Suddenly, this new sister-in-law bolted into his life like a ray of sunshine. Olimpia was charming, amusing, and highly intelligent. We can imagine that one day over lunch, when Pamphilio was in his office in the Campidoglio, Gianbattista first spoke to Olimpia of the lawsuits before him. Most women would have been bored to tears by such a topic, but Olimpia's dark eyes would have sparkled with interest. Perhaps Gianbattista laid out the case, and the several possible decisions he could make, and the problems associated with each one. Perhaps he confided his horror of making the wrong choice. Olimpia's sharp mind would have cut through the cobwebs of Gianbattista's indecision, pointing out to him exactly the right choice to make.

Greatly relieved at the sudden clarity, Gianbattista would report to his office and do exactly as Olimpia had instructed him, and she was almost always right. He increasingly grew to rely on her and began spending several hours every day with her discussing his business. And it became clear to Olimpia how she would get political power. Not in Rome's civil government through Pamphilio, but in the Catholic Church, through Gianbattista. Moreover, the church was far more powerful than civil authorities because the church *ran* the civil authorities.

Olimpia was absolutely thrilled that *her* guidance was being employed in the Vatican courts. And Gianbattista was thrilled to have such an excellent counselor. Here, finally, was a person he could trust, a person who had only his best interests at heart. According to Gregorio Leti, Gianbattista "never undertook anything without consulting her beforehand as if she were the world's greatest oracle, and followed all her advice and her instructions."[9] In addition to helping Gianbattista's career, Olimpia was the only person who could pluck the taciturn monsignor out of his depression and, with her wit and cheerfulness, make him laugh.

Suddenly, Olimpia was no longer alone. There was another person who respected her, needed her, a man who valued her for her strength instead of hating her for it. Of all people in the world, she could trust Gianbattista Pamphili, who would never look down on her because she was a woman, who would never tell her to betake her unworthy self to a convent. She gave him absolute loyalty. Just as Olimpia would always find a way to revenge herself against those who hurt her, she was indefatigable in her efforts to help those who treated her kindly. And Gianbattista treated her more kindly than anyone else on the planet.

Olimpia and Gianbattista, both afraid of betrayal and terrified of losing dignity in the eyes of the world, had found in each other a soul mate. Each one offered the other increased power and prestige and a place of absolute safety with all defenses let down. It was like a marriage made in heaven, except, of course, Gianbattista was a priest and Olimpia was married to his brother.

Sometimes Gianbattista took her out in his carriage to see the monuments of Rome, tour the vineyards outside the walls, or take the air. The vegetable sellers in the Piazza Navona, the Pasquino gawkers behind the Pamphili house, and those coming to pick up their mail at the post office next door saw Olimpia and her normally somber brother-in-law laughing in their carriage brightly painted with the Pamphili coat of arms—a white dove holding an olive branch in its mouth.

Many Romans recalled the stories of Gianbattista only fifteen years earlier, when, as a young priest with frizzy ringlets, he had chased women, dueling over them in the street. Naturally, word got out that the two were conducting a very public affair right under the nose of Pamphilio Pamphili, the husband of one and brother of the other. And the affair would not only have been adulterous, but according to church law it would have also been incestuous. It was delicious gossip.

Leti sniffed, "This woman went more often in the carriage around town with her brother-in-law than with her husband. They were locked up for hours on end in his cabinet, longer than propriety could approve of, longer than her husband could tolerate. Sometimes he sought his brother and his wife without finding them, which is proof that he found it necessary to look for them together, and that she didn't take a step without being accompanied by her brother-in-law."[10]

Commenting harshly on Gianbattista's appearance, Leti continued, "One thing obliged many people to have a better sentiment of her conduct . . . which was, that they could not understand how a woman with an agreeable body and face could resolve to fall in love with the ugliest and most deformed man that was ever born, for such was her brother-in-law. . . . From this one can judge the grand ambitions that rule women. . . . And she, who wanted only to command, loved him all the more because he allowed her to govern."[11]

We have no record of Pamphilio's feelings about his brother's close relationship with his wife. It is possible the rumors did not unduly disturb him because he knew for a fact that the relationship was strictly platonic. On the other hand, if he was aware of an affair, perhaps he averted his eyes. Any children would, of course, still be Pamphilis.

Whatever was going on, Pamphilio was not in a position to protest too loudly. For Olimpia made it clear that she was willing to use all of her considerable skill and all of her vast piles of money to have Gianbattista made a cardinal. Why should the Pamphilis not have the best places in church on feast days, the most honorable seats at parties? All the power, prestige, and income had been lost in that tragic moment in 1610 when Cardinal Girolamo's heart stopped beating, his lungs clogged with whitewash fumes. Why shouldn't the Pamphili family boast another cardinal, Cardinal Gianbattista?

Most churchmen weren't made cardinals overnight, unless they were lucky enough to be closely related to a newly elected pope. The first step on the path to the cardinalate was to become a nuncio—papal ambassador—to a foreign court. The most prestigious posting was to Spain, the greatest supporter of the Vatican. Spain controlled large chunks of Italy—the duchy of Milan in the north, and the kingdom of Naples, which shared the southern border of the Papal States. The second most important posting was to France, Spain's inveterate enemy and historically a far less supportive ally of Rome. For centuries France had been angling for greater control of naming bishops, owning church properties, and keeping church revenues. France was often bristling with anger toward the Vatican, and its nuncio had to be a man of great diplomatic skill.

Gianbattista couldn't hope to be made nuncio to Spain or France on his first diplomatic posting, however. But there was Venice, the independent-minded republic in the northeast of Italy, and staunchly loyal Poland, that frontier outpost of Roman Catholicism in Europe. There were the German countries that had remained Catholic after the Reformation, and the Spanish Netherlands. But a more prestigious posting would be to the Holy Roman Emperor in Austria or to the kingdom of Naples.

Olimpia knew that Gianbattista had excellent qualifications for the position of nuncio. He had a stellar education and years of church legal experience. His wild youth firmly behind him, he possessed caution, discretion, patience, and a dignified manner. But his lack of sociability was a severe handicap. He was not one for wheeling and dealing, entertaining and glad-handing, for flattering the important and sending tasteful gifts to the powerful. On the contrary, for years he had stayed morosely in the background of the social scene, eyeing Rome's elite with thinly veiled suspicion.

But it was a handicap Olimpia could easily fix if she played the role of his hostess. She held the right parties and hosted the right people. Cardinals toddled in with their sisters-in-law and nieces, ambassadors with their wives and daughters. Olimpia was ingratiating, helpful, oozing with charm. Her keen memory allowed her to inquire after the illnesses of distant relatives and the harvests of distant vineyards, as if she truly cared. And, as Gregorio Leti remarked, "She went to great trouble to pretend to have the same sentiments as the person she was speaking to."[12]

At these events Olimpia could shine, discoursing on her favorite subjects—politics and finance—and drawing Gianbattista out of his hard-baked shell to show his fine grasp of Vatican affairs. Her guests admired her, and they began to see the excellent qualities of Monsignor Gianbattista. It is not known what they thought of Pamphilio, who was, perhaps, sitting glumly at the head of the table, drinking his 2 percent wine. No matter. Because of Olimpia, the Pamphilis were an up-and-coming family.

The dining table was the place where nuncios were chosen, cardinals created, rich pensions bestowed, and marriages negotiated. The quality of the wine and meat, the cut of the crystal, the skill of the servants, all contributed to a family's success. The table was always to present a cornucopia of abundance, a feast for the eyes, and never be bare for even a moment, which would indicate lack or poverty. Empty dishes were whipped off and full ones set down with military precision. With a grand flourish of knives, Olimpia's *scalco* sliced the finest meats. Her dapper *coppiero* poured liquid rubies into crystal goblets. Her *credenziere* proffered sparkling silver pitchers and platters, glinting in the candlelight. And all the servants did their level best to make sure there wasn't a drop of poison on anything.

Olimpia had, by now, totally immersed herself in the Vatican hierarchy. She knew all the cardinals resident in Rome, and also knew which ones were considered *papabile,* which translates awkwardly as "popeable"—that is, highly qualified to be elected pope. These qualifications included a ripening age, diplomatic experience as nuncio, knowledge of canon law, and a dearth of enemies among the rulers of Europe and in the Sacred College of Cardinals. These men—and their sisters, sisters-in-law, and nieces—she would turn into her best friends.

One of the most *papabile* cardinals was Alessandro Ludovisi. Born in 1554, Ludovisi was a canon lawyer who had worked amicably with Gianbattista for several years in the Rota. He had sterling qualifications in municipal, educational, and legal positions in the church. Pope Paul V made him archbishop in 1612, nuncio four years later, and cardinal in 1616. As Ludovisi slipped into his sixties, Romans whispered that there went the next pope. Olimpia must have courted him assiduously.

In the midst of this flurry of entertainment and plotting, the Pamphili family was blessed by a most surprising event. After seven years of marriage, Olimpia had a baby, a healthy girl she called Maria. Perhaps this one would live. Roman gossips scrutinized the baby closely not so much to determine her health but to ascertain whether she bore a greater resemblance to her father or her uncle. Meanwhile Gianbattista, feeling somewhat squeezed by the new addition to the family and servants hired to take care of her, rented the Teofili house next to the Pamphili residence.

On January 28, 1621, Pope Paul V finally died after a reign of sixteen years. The conclave that began on February 8 was shockingly short. The following day, the new pope was announced. Alessandro Ludovisi, Gianbattista's old friend, would take the name Gregory XV.

On March 26, 1621, Olimpia's nine years of hard work were crowned with success. Gianbattista Pamphili was named the new papal nuncio to the kingdom of Naples. And now *all* the ladies of Rome, no matter how snooty, would have to meet her at the top of the stairs.

5

The Papal Nuncio

Politics have no relation to morals.

—Niccolò Machiavelli

NATURALLY, OLIMPIA WOULD BE GOING with the new papal nuncio to Naples. Despite her eight years of tutelage, Gianbattista evidently did not feel confident enough to handle his first diplomatic posting without her by his side telling him exactly what to do. And she could hardly accompany the new papal nuncio without dragging her husband and her two-year-old daughter along to give the whole thing an air of respectability.

The Pamphilis would have been accompanied on the journey by their *famiglia,* those tried and trusted servants who would keep an eagle eye on their property in Naples to make sure it didn't wander off, and on their lives to make sure they weren't snuffed out. Romans believed that the Neapolitans were the most thieving, murderous wretches in the world.

It wasn't entirely the Neapolitans' fault that so many of them were thieving, murderous wretches. For some two thousand years Naples—and the other half of the kingdom, the island of Sicily—had been ruled by a succession of foreign invaders. The Greeks, Romans, Goths, Byzantines, Normans, Germans, French, and Spanish had governed the area, each conqueror squeezing the locals dry by brutal taxation and stomping them down with cruel repression. When the rich stole from and murdered the poor with impunity, this was called justice. When the poor, out of fury and desperation, stole from and murdered the rich, this was called stealing and murder. Over time, it would be called something else—the Mafia.

All male servants, walking or riding, would have been heavily armed with loaded pistols and knives. Bandits on the road between Rome and Naples were notorious, and the convoy of the new papal nuncio with his trunkloads of silver platters would have offered rich booty. As Olimpia and her family neared the city of Naples, they would have traveled under trees adorned with the bodies and body parts of bandits, hung there by the government as a warning to anybody so inclined as to rob travelers.

On April 3, 1621, the Pamphilis arrived in Naples unscathed and took up residence in the palazzo bought by Sixtus V in the 1580s to house the papal nuncio. But Gianbattista disliked the residence. "It is too small for the family of a prelate who will be situated in an indecent place," he wrote.[1] He wanted the pope to sell it and buy another palazzo, roomier, with better air. It is not known if the pope did so.

When Olimpia had settled into her new home, she would have had the chance to look around the city. Naples had three times as many inhabitants as Rome—some 300,000—most of them crowded in slum apartment buildings in a rabbit warren of narrow medieval streets climbing the volcanic hills. Laundry was strung across the street from every floor. Rubbish and night soil were flung out the windows onto the pedestrians below. Children, often without a stitch of clothing, scavenged among heaps of ordure, competing for food with dogs, cats, and rats.

Hygiene aside, the natural setting of Naples was infinitely more beautiful than that of Rome. At the city's feet spread out a sparkling carpet of sapphire blue, the Bay of Naples. Behind the city rose the peaks of Mount Vesuvius, trembling now and then and belching sulfuric fumes. In the harbor, connected to land by a narrow causeway, sat the square yellow Egg Castle, the Castel d'Ovo, named such, it was said, because the ancient Roman poet Virgil had hung an egg from the ceiling of a cave deep below the castle. When the egg broke, Naples would be destroyed. And whenever Vesuvius rumbled, many Neapolitans remembered the egg and crossed themselves.

When traveling in the city, even going to church, the Pamphilis would have been accompanied by an armed guard. Kidnappers could capture them and hold them for ransom or simply rob and murder them in broad daylight. Going out at night was a form of suicide. Once dusk fell, everyone but the criminals stayed inside and bolted their doors. A dinner party or ball naturally included an invitation to spend the night and return home in the morning.

Bristling with thousands of Spanish soldiers, its harbor stuffed with Spanish warships, Naples posed a constant low-level threat to the sovereignty of the Papal States to the north. The pope had only the tiniest standing army, relying on a sudden rush of volunteers or the hiring of mercenaries if invasion threatened. The papal navy consisted of a few ships manned by slaves and convicts. His Holiness relied on the goodwill of Spain, with its unlimited firepower, to protect him from invasion. However, if Spain decided to invade the Papal States, it could have easily rolled across the entire country with very little opposition.

But it was unlikely that Spain would do such a thing. For eight hundred years the Spaniards had waged a nonstop crusade against Muslims on Spanish soil, resulting in a militant Catholicism. Spaniards considered themselves to be more devoutly Catholic than any other nation in Europe, certainly more Catholic than the self-absorbed French or the rollicking Italians. In the late sixteenth century King Philip II said that religion was too important to be left in the hands of the pope.

His Excellency Gianbattista Pamphili and his staff would be working on a variety of issues with the Spanish viceroy, the personal representative of the king of Spain. Grain and other foodstuffs were shipped from Naples to the Papal States, and vice versa, depending on the harvests, and were taxed. The Vatican owned property in the kingdom of Naples— churches, monasteries, and farms—from which it received revenues. As a Catholic nation, Naples owed the Papal States a sum of money every year—which was negotiable, depending on war, famine, and plague.

Financial matters aside, there were numerous church issues that required attention. Requests for marriage annulments and dispensations would be presented to the Roman nuncio, who would look them over, write an opinion, and forward them to the Vatican. There was always the pesky problem of criminal clerics—a priest who robbed someone in Naples, for instance. Civil authorities were not permitted to pass judgment on ordained priests, who would be handed over to the nuncio's men and taken to Rome for trial.

Heresy was to be trampled, and literature on the Index of Forbidden Books was to be rooted out and publicly burned. Then there were issues related to greed and ambition. Neapolitans pushed for honors and pensions from the Holy See, and Roman nobles pushed for honors and pensions from the kingdom of Naples. Often, trades were made to keep everyone happy.

The papal courier service between Rome and Naples was efficient, the trip taking only three days on a fast horse. Gianbattista would have been required to write a weekly diplomatic dispatch that ran some fifteen or twenty pages. His reports would have been coded to prevent spies from understanding them. The easiest way to encode letters was to use numbers to represent the names of people and places, so that Gianbattista's Italian prose would have had numbers interspersed throughout. However, in highly sensitive cases every letter of every word was represented by a number. Back in Rome, the papal office of ciphers would decode them and deliver them to the pope. Similarly, the pope's instructions would arrive in Naples encoded, and Gianbattista's secretary would decode them.

As nuncio, Gianbattista would have been expected to set up his own espionage network, bribing servants in the viceroy's house or employees in his office. Information could always be bought for the right price, and the corruption of Naples made the corruption of Rome seem downright saintly in comparison.

In addition to the under-the-table bags of gold that stank of corruption, the papal nuncio was expected to give over-the-table gifts that smelled of ambergris—fragrant petrified whale vomit—and musk, the aromatic glandular secretion of the musk deer. The most popular gifts for government officials, local noblemen, and their female relatives were perfumed gloves. Seventeenth-century gloves were of supple leather, heavily embroidered with scarlet and gold thread, with huge tabbed cuffs extending halfway up the forearm, and adorned with tassels woven of real gold. Perfuming the gloves often cost twice as much as the gloves themselves, so rare were the fragrances. In fact, on May 29, 1621, less than two months after his arrival in Naples, Gianbattista wrote to Rome asking for a shipment of gloves.

The position of papal nuncio to Naples was a heavy financial burden and only awarded to the richest candidates willing to spend their own money. The salary was low and very few expenses were reimbursed by the pope. But it was a path to the riches of a cardinal's hat, and many churchmen were eager for the opportunity.

Without Olimpia's money, Gianbattista would never have been considered for the post. Olimpia paid for the servants, the food, the festivities, the secret bag-of-gold bribes, and all of those perfumed gloves. As careful as she was with money, all of her Naples expenses were well worth it. For one thing, she would do anything, give anything, to help Gianbattista, the one person who truly appreciated her, the one person she truly trusted. For another, her expenses were actually an investment. If he should be made cardinal, she would be paid back with interest. And most important of all, she exercised real power, which had always been her dearest dream.

We can assume that Olimpia was up to her elbows in intrigue and loving every moment of it—plotting, planning, bribing, manipulating, dictating coded letters, and decoding letters from the Vatican as soon as they arrived. Although they were not aware of it, the viceroy of Naples, the king of Spain, and the pope himself were all dealing with *her* political suggestions. It was worth all the money she spent to play such a major role in high-level international politics.

The Venetian ambassador to Rome, Alvise Contarini, reported that "to the same signora Donna Olimpia, [Gianbattista] declared himself to be very much obliged for the rich dowry carried into the Pamphili family and for having provided for his needs."[2]

Cardinal Sforza Pallavicino, who knew Olimpia well later in life, wrote that she "carried into the Pamphili family much patrimony that was used most instrumentally to honorably sustain the house, and from this came all the greatness which successively followed [Gianbattista]. Let me add that she possessed an intellect of great value in economic government, and she had always administered with care the possessions of the family, with great advantage to the purse, to relieve the cares of her brother-in-law."[3]

To Olimpia's joy, her brother, Andrea, moved just outside Naples and the two saw each other frequently. On September 23, 1621, Olimpia wrote her mother that Andrea was four days into his governorship of Aversa, a town five miles north of the city. Andrea was approximately forty years old and well on his way to siring the ten sons and numerous daughters he would have with two wives. Oddly, Olimpia never resented her brother for being Sforza's favorite or receiving all of the family wealth; she would remain very close to him until his death.

While close to her brother, Olimpia seems to have distanced herself from her husband. An anonymous document in the Vatican Archives does not beat about the bush when it comes to stating that Olimpia wore the breeches in the marriage. Olimpia, "married to Panfilio Panfilij in the second marriage, showed such a stubborn mind that many times . . . he was forced to tolerate her many importunities and many insolent rebukes."[4]

Despite the marital tensions or, as some said, *because* of them, a blessed event occurred. On February 21, 1622, some ten months after arriving in Naples, Olimpia gave birth to a healthy son she called Camillo. The Pamphili family, which had been grinding its way inexorably toward extinction for decades, now had an heir. The proud papa was nearly sixty and the mother thirty. With an uncle rising quickly in the church hierarchy and a rich ambitious mother like Olimpia, the boy, if he lived, was destined for a brilliant career. But many in Naples, aware of the strained state of Olimpia's marriage and her unusual closeness to her brother-in-law, wondered if the papal nuncio himself might be the father of the bouncing baby boy.

Shortly after the birth, Olimpia and Pamphilio returned to Viterbo for a few months to show her mother, Vittoria, her grandson and manage their business interests there. It is revealing that during her sojourn in Naples, Olimpia had placed her mother, not her father, in charge of her extensive Viterban properties. Family archives contain several letters to Vittoria from both Olimpia and Pamphilio regarding the rents, crops, and improvements. There are no extant letters from Olimpia or Pamphilio to Sforza, with whom relations were, apparently, strained.

In a letter to her mother dated October 11, 1622, Olimpia wrote, "I saw what Your Excellency said in your letter of September 27, and I did not fail to immediately write a letter to my father, which you will see here enclosed. If it seems appropriate to you then pass it on to him. I have tried to write lovingly so that he no longer has any doubts." At Christmastime, Olimpia sent warm seasonal greetings to her mother, adding, "and to signor father, too."[5]

Sforza died in the late spring of 1623 at about the age of sixty-three, suffering agonizing stomach pains. According to a letter Pamphilio wrote to Vittoria Gualtieri on July 22, 1623, Sforza had never finished paying the dowry he had promised Olimpia in 1612. Now Pamphilio wanted the money out of Sforza's estate. It is not known if he ever obtained it. Certainly, coming on top of the convent story, the dowry issue must have been an additional source of the father-daughter rupture.

It is uncertain when Olimpia's mother died. The last letter written to her in the family archives is dated 1629. But in their Viterban convent, Olimpia's sisters would live to old age in excellent health. From Naples, Olimpia often sent her sisters little comforts—macaroni, sweets, and linen undergarments. She frequently mentioned Ortensia and Vittoria in her letters to her mother, and probably wrote them letters that are now lost.

Pope Gregory XV was never entirely healthy during his pontificate and let his nephew, whom he promoted to cardinal, rule for him. "Just give me something to eat and you can take care of the rest," the pope said.[6] On July 8, 1623, Gregory died. "After the death of Gregory the treasury was empty and aggravated by huge debts, without anyone knowing how this occurred," the Roman diarist Giacinto Gigli wrote. The pope had given everything to his relatives, "who in twenty-nine months accumulated the greatest riches."[7]

The city of Rome tumbled into anarchy, which was usual when the

See was vacant. Gigli noted, "There was not a single day when there were not many fights, murders, betrayals, finding many men and women killed in various places, and many were found without a head. Many headless bodies were found that had been thrown in the Tiber. Many houses were broken into and robbed at night. Doors were smashed, women were raped, others killed, and many young girls disgraced, raped, and taken away."[8] For once it was actually safer to be in Naples than in Rome.

On July 19, fifty-five cardinals processed with great dignity into their tomblike accommodations in the Sistine Chapel to elect a new pontiff. It was a summer conclave, the dread of every cardinal. In the stifling heat, chamber pots grew rank and fetid. The smell of unwashed bodies oozed through red robes. And malaria struck, "the atmosphere being laden with putrid miasmas and sickening smells of decaying victuals that the potent perfumes of the young cardinals could not manage to disguise," one chronicler reported.[9] Then fleas invaded the premises, eating the cardinals alive.

The decision hastened by the spreading malaria, on August 6 the candidate favored by France, the Florentine cardinal Maffeo Barberini, was elected pope and took the name Urban VIII. Barberini had been papal nuncio to France from 1604 to 1607, and his continued good relations with the French government disgruntled Spain. At fifty-five he was younger than most newly elected popes and promised a long reign, which disgruntled the other cardinals, many of whom would never have another chance to become pope. But to get out of that stinking malarial hellhole of a conclave, the majority of cardinals would have elected the devil himself.

Urban had a square beard, hard, round eyes, and a snub nose that gave him the look of an alert schnauzer. The Venetian envoy Zeno was more flattering in his description. "His Holiness is tall, dark, with regular features and black hair turning grey. He is exceptionally elegant and refined in all details of his dress; has a graceful and aristocratic bearing and exquisite taste. He is an excellent speaker and debater, writes verses and patronizes poets and men of letters."[10]

The Barberini family coat of arms featured three gold honeybees on a blue shield, and indeed, it was whispered that two days before Urban's election a swarm of bees had hovered over his cell in conclave, forming themselves into the shape of a papal crown, surely an omen from the Holy Spirit. The family coat of arms had previously been three horseflies, but the rising family had had the good sense to change it. Bees, it was known, were attracted to honey, the nectar of the gods. Horseflies were attracted to manure, the nectar of horseflies.

At Naples, the Pamphilis waited for news of the conclave. Would the new pope recall Gianbattista from his nunciature, replacing him with a friend or relative as most popes did? The answer came quickly. Pope Urban VIII was pleased with his nuncio's work in Naples. Gianbattista— and Olimpia—should continue.

After four years as nuncio to the kingdom of Naples, Gianbattista was finally recalled to Rome in March 1625. Olimpia packed up her household and made the dangerous trip back, unloading at the old house in the Piazza Navona. It must have been a relief to be back in the relative safety of Rome. Even better, Gianbattista's recall involved not disgrace but honor. The pope had chosen him for a special mission.

Urban VIII had three beloved nephews. The eldest, Francesco, he made a cardinal in 1623 at the age of twenty-six, giving him the regal position of cardinal nephew, a kind of secretary of state who was accorded the honors of a sovereign. The second, Taddeo, would be the lay head of the family and marry. The third, Antonio, would be made a cardinal in 1627 at the age of twenty.

Cardinal Francesco Barberini was impatient to make his mark on politics and diplomacy. He prodded his uncle to send him on a difficult embassy to Paris. A dispute had arisen between France and Spain over a small area known as the Valtellina in northern Italy. France had ousted the neutral papal troops and replaced them with French troops, with Spain howling in protest. The pope wanted his diplomats to convince Louis XIII and his powerful prime minister, Cardinal Richelieu, to remove the French troops.

But the pope realized that his nephew was still inexperienced for such a delicate task. Though Francesco would technically head the mission and receive all the honor, Gianbattista, as special assistant to the cardinal nephew, would be the brains behind it. Olimpia would not be able to join her brother-in-law, as it was a temporary mission. And perhaps for the first time, Gianbattista felt confident enough to do without her.

Many at the French court, knowing the urgency of Gianbattista's mission, asked him for money, pensions, and honors from the Papal States in return for pushing his agenda forward. He routinely replied, "It can't be done," earning him the nickname "Monsignor It-Can't-Be-Done."[11] There was, unfortunately, a personality conflict between the suave silkiness of the French courtier and the prickly suspicion of Gianbattista Pamphili.

The mission to France failed utterly, but Urban realized this was due to French stubbornness rather than the ineptness of his envoys. After all, Cardinal Richelieu was known to dislike the pope's involvement in political matters, saying, "We must kiss his feet and bind his hands."[12] Urban immediately packed his diplomats off to the court of Madrid to convince Philip IV to force the French troops to leave Valtellina and allow the papal troops to return. But after the long voyage, when the two arrived in Madrid they learned that France and Spain had already made a secret peace. The Protestant enclave known as Grisons would control the Valtellina, quite a slap in the face of the Catholic Church.

Once again, Urban realized his envoys were not at fault. He recalled his nephew Francesco to Rome but instructed Gianbattista to remain in Madrid as the new papal nuncio to Spain. Gianbattista Pamphili, whose career had been stalled when Olimpia first met him, now held the single most important diplomatic position of the Papal States.

Olimpia was not inactive during her brother-in-law's absence. She continued to work on Gianbattista's behalf in Rome and was seen walking in and out of the French and Spanish embassies. Not slowed down a bit by the birth of her daughter Costanza in 1627, she invited the wives and daughters of ambassadors to dine with her, listen to music, attend card parties, and go hunting on the rolling hills around Viterbo. She had won over Urban's sister-in-law, Costanza Magalotti, the mother of the pope's three nephews. And, when Taddeo married Anna Colonna in 1627, Olimpia went to work on her, too.

An anonymous eighteenth-century pamphlet explained, "With great agility she insinuated herself into the graces of the Barberini brothers and particularly with Cardinal Antonio, through Signora Costanza Magalotti, sister-in-law of the pope and mother of the same Barberinis, and of Signora Anna Colonna, wife of Don Taddeo the prefect of Rome, procuring with her gentle manners the exaltation of the above-mentioned Monsignor Pamfilio to the nunciature."[13]

Despite the great honor of Gianbattista's new position, it was a difficult job, and Gianbattista didn't have Olimpia to advise him. Spain was bristling with rage at the pope, who was thought to be pro-French. But Gianbattista's caution came to his aid. In contrast to many diplomats of the time, puffed up with self-importance and surrounded by haughty servants brandishing weapons, Nuncio Pamphili was thoughtful, calm, and slow to take offense. He listened carefully to Spanish complaints and propositions and much later gave them a well-considered reply.

Perhaps this long delay had less to do with Gianbattista's careful deliberation than it did with the papal postal service, which took a full month to get a letter from Madrid to Rome and another month to bring back the reply. Gianbattista and Olimpia kept up an active correspondence during his time in Madrid, and it is certain that he asked her advice and she readily gave it.

Gregorio Leti claimed to have seen a letter written by Gianbattista to Olimpia during this time in which he asked her to respond to political questions outlined by his secretary. Leti recorded it as follows, "My dear Sister, my business does not succeed as well in Spain as it did in Rome because I am deprived of your advice. Far from you I am like a ship without a rudder, abandoned to the inconstancy of the sea with no hope of its own happiness. I feel obliged to let you know this because I would not know how better to show my affection. I ask you to have the goodness to respond at length to that which is attached by my secretary, and believe me always to be, Your Very Affectionate Servant and Brother-in-Law, Pamfili."

Leti harrumphed loudly about the letter: "It would have been almost impossible, if I had not read this letter, that a public official would have written in this way to a woman without considering his reputation, and without reflecting that letters easily go astray, as happened with this one. But although he had given himself over entirely to this woman, he didn't need to make it so public by confirming his love for her with his own signature. This letter was a great proof of the love between these two people and an entire confirmation of the rumors of the people, who amused themselves with speculations, that Donna Olimpia gave secret instructions to the Nuncio when he departed to go to the princes where he was destined."[14]

Considering that Gregorio Leti's works were the *National Enquirer* of his time—a mixture of exaggeration, innuendo, and God's honest truth—we must sift through his stories carefully. Yet later events, confirmed by cardinals and other reputable witnesses, confirm that the sentiments expressed in the letter, at least, were true.

Gianbattista Pamphili had good reason to write gushing letters to his sister-in-law in Rome. In late September he received the news that on August 30, 1627, Urban VIII had named him cardinal *in pectore. In pectore* meant literally "in the chest," and referred to the pope's holding this news secretly, in his heart, and not publicizing it. What it really meant was that Gianbattista would receive his red hat and officially become a cardinal when the next group of candidates was promoted sometime in the future.

Olimpia had triumphed. She had done it. Fifteen years of her hard work and brilliant intrigues had raised a mediocre prelate to papal nuncio and now cardinal. She had single-handedly lifted the fortunes of the Pamphili family as its men could never have done. She had rewarded Gianbattista for his love and loyalty. And every cardinal, of course, had the chance of becoming pope. Olimpia dreamed big.

Olimpia and her family, as relatives of a cardinal, would sit in the front row at festivities, and near the head of the table at banquets; they would ride in the front of church and diplomatic cavalcades. As the sister-in-law of a cardinal, she would be accorded great honors throughout Rome, as if she were a princess. But best of all, now the noblewomen of Rome would have to wait at the foot of the stairs when she deigned to visit them.

6

Cardinals

Whosoever will come after Me, let him deny himself,
and take up his cross, and follow Me.

—Mark 8:34

Gianbattista was finally reaping the financial profit of Olimpia's investment. Traditionally, the king of Spain gave the pope's envoy splendid gifts and annual revenues. Moreover, the pope expected his nuncio to Spain to sell honors and offices and pocket the money himself, thereby saving the Vatican great expense.

Gianbattista was doing so well financially that he not only paid all his extravagant expenses in Madrid but sent money back to Olimpia. There seems to be only one letter written by Olimpia to Gianbattista that has survived, and she penned it six weeks after hearing the news that Urban VIII had named him cardinal *in pectore*. She thanked Gianbattista for offering to send money to Pamphilio to pay for the gambling losses of Gualtieri, one of the sons of her uncle Paolo Gualtieri and Gianbattista's sister Antonia Pamphili. It seems that Gualtieri was troublesome, ungrateful, and ran off at the mouth.

Olimpia used numbers for names in case unfriendly eyes should read her letter. The entire tone is enigmatic, which we can assume was quite intentional.

Most Illustrious and Powerful Signor Brother-in-law;

I was resolved not to want to bother Your Illustrious Holiness with my letters, knowing how busy you are. But then I changed my mind, finding myself obliged to thank you for the offer that you made in a letter to Signor Pamphilio of money for gambling. But I do not want Your Holiness to be obliged with so much. It will not take a little to compensate for the whims of Gualtieri. And he will know well how to find the means so that Your Holiness will not be able to say no.

And what displeases me most is that he does it with the advice of 288 and 260 who have spoken a great deal with little regard of 110 112 and who will make him betray his own. And then it will be explained, here with me, that he never said these things. Instead, he has received from me all the courtesies that he could have desired and 288 thanked me for this, and I think I am the only one to do this.

In one mysterious sentence that evidently broached an extremely sensitive issue, Olimpia substituted numbers for letters of the alphabet. Gianbattista apparently wrote the letters above the numbers, though some vowels were assumed to have an *n* attached to them. He did not, however, decode the number 95.

Il ? c e a(n) c i a z i t o, m a
V.S. e prudente 15 41 nostro 95 18 40 14 18 15 14 12 15 54 55 46 14

n o(n) s i a m o f o r a d i s p e r a(n) za.
50 55 11 55 14 46 55 uu 55 12 14 di 11 19 40 12 14 14

Your Holiness is prudent. There is silent anxiety about our 95, but we are not without hope.

We can only imagine what "95" stood for. Intrigue? Plot? Love affair?

I will continue to serve your Holiness as much as I can. And I assure you I know of few actions that have not been for your benefit. I only regret that I do not have enough strength to do what I am obliged to do.

I hear that you have a beautiful place over there. However, I would not want you to forget your relatives in Rome. I will not bother you by writing any more. I will just remind you to stay cheerful and keep in good health, and I kiss your hand with great affection. Rome, October 11, 1627.

The Most Affectionate Sister-in-Law and servant of your Illustrious Holiness, Olimpia[1]

In 1627, the one hundredth anniversary of the Sack, Rome was undergoing a government-sponsored building program the likes of which it had not seen since the time of the Caesars. Though several popes since the Sack had widened roads, built fountains, and repaired churches, Urban VIII was the pope most responsible for creating the baroque city we see today.

As soon as he recovered from the malaria that almost killed him in conclave, Urban called together architects, engineers, artists, and sculptors to beautify the city. He affixed the Barberini bee emblem on every new building, fountain, and church, and even on old walls that had only been spackled. One visitor to Rome near the end of Urban's long reign actually went around counting concrete papal bees and found some ten thousand of them. Certain Romans, reflecting on the pope's numerous greedy relatives, commented that a swarm had invaded the Papal States and sucked the last drop of honey out of them.

For under the Barberini pope, nepotism flourished as never before. The word *nepotism* has its roots in *nipote*, the Italian word for "nephew." Though the word didn't come into use until the early seventeenth century, nepotism had started in the eighth century when Pepin the Short, king of the Franks, granted the papacy the central third of Italy as his realm. Suddenly the pope was also a king with lands, castles, and vast incomes to bestow on his relatives.

The fourteenth-century chronicler Lambert di Huy supported nepotism when writing of the then-current pope. It would "without doubt be inhumane if John XXII conferred on strangers, neglecting his own relatives of equal or superior virtue, those offices that the Church gives to lay people, and the associated stipends. . . . It is wise and praiseworthy that he continues to care for, as he has in the past, his relatives and friends. In fact, as the old proverb says, 'It is not good to bind strangers to your own navel.' "[2]

Papal nepotism was exacerbated by the fact that the throne was not hereditary, as in most secular monarchies. A cousin of Louis XIII would still be a cousin of Louis XIV, with the same position and income. But when a pope died, his relatives were immediately ousted from power and replaced by a new family. Because popes were usually elected when elderly and died after only a few years, their relatives had a limited amount of time to squeeze the Vatican treasury dry, conclude prestigious marriages, and obtain noble titles, castles, and lands. As soon as a cardinal was elected pope, his family descended on Rome in hordes, hoping to grab as much as possible before their elderly relative kicked the bucket.

While popes gave their lay nephews dukedoms, they made their religious nephews cardinals. There was a good reason for having a nephew in close proximity. In an environment rife with violence—and numerous popes into the Middle Ages were strangled, stabbed, or poisoned—a close relative was thought to be the best bodyguard possible.

In 1538 Pope Paul III instituted the official position of cardinal nephew. Living in the suite of apartments next to the pope's, the younger man would help his uncle in politics and diplomacy and truly look out for his best interests. The cardinal nephew would have every reason to keep the pontiff alive, unlike many other cardinals who might be tempted to slip something into his wine to hasten the next conclave.

The people of the Papal States were not, in principal, against cardinal nephews or the enriching of the pope's family. Sharing good fortune with relatives was, after all, a Christian virtue, and all levels of society did it. It was not the premise of papal nepotism but its execution that was disliked. Excessive sums were given to the pope's relatives, often from taxes imposed on the daily bread ration of the poor. Nepotism confined within the bounds of good taste would have been quite acceptable. But the seventeenth century was not exactly a time of restraint.

"Christ gave the keyes of his church to Saint Peter . . . and not to his nephews," Leti reminded his readers, but they wouldn't have known it by looking at the Barberini family.[3] Urban VIII would become the most nepotistic pope ever, routinely imposing new taxes on a beleaguered population suffering at different times from plague, flood, and famine. The pope taxed the staples of life—bread, flour, salt, and fruit—so heavily that in some years people starved on the street while his relatives received streams of gold from Vatican coffers.

Urban's deceased brother Carlo had sired three sons, and all were amply rewarded under their uncle's pontificate. Taddeo, who possessed very little when Urban ascended the throne in 1623, owned landed property worth four million scudi in 1632, a figure that did not include piles of cash and his art collection of Raphaels, Titians, Michelangelos, and Leonardo da Vincis. In 1630 he acquired the principality of Palestrina, becoming Prince Taddeo.

In 1627 Urban arranged Taddeo's marriage to the scion of one of Rome's most noble families. Anna Colonna had desperately wanted to become a nun and had successfully held out against marriage until the advanced age of twenty-six. But she suddenly found herself forced by the loss of her family's fortunes to marry the pope's *nouveau arrivé* nephew, whom she couldn't stand. Perhaps Anna Colonna was consoled by her husband's immeasurable wealth. The family jewels rivaled those of the royal dynasties of Europe. And no one ate from anything that was not of pure gold, silver, or rock crystal, studded with gems.

Anna Colonna must have enjoyed living in the most glorious palace in Rome. Prince Taddeo hired the greatest sculptor since Michelangelo, Gian Lorenzo Bernini, to design the Barberini family residence on the northwestern slope of Quirinal Hill. This monumental structure had an audience chamber with forty-foot ceilings painted with Greek gods. The niches all the way up the triumphal staircase held ancient Roman statues. Behind the palace were extensive gardens of rare flowers and lemon trees, adorned with ancient statues and fountains. The Barberini Palace was also known as the Palace of the Four Fountains.

Olimpia, the sister-in-law of an important nuncio and cardinal *in pectore,* would have called frequently on Anna Colonna, the first lady of Rome, to render her respects, attend social events, and loudly praise Gianbattista's work in Madrid. It is tempting to imagine Olimpia's feelings as she entered the lofty marble halls and strode through the fragrant gardens cooled by a wholesome breeze.

Olimpia's Casa Pamphili could never be as impressive as the Palazzo Barberini. Her home was hot, for one thing, in a low-lying, flood-prone area of the city where there were no cool breezes. There was no room for a garden in her tiny courtyard, and certainly not behind the house, hemmed in on all sides by busy streets, vegetable sellers, the post office, and drunken pasquinade writers. Though Olimpia oozed with charm at Anna Colonna's events, it is possible she was also lime green with envy. If Olimpia ever got Gianbattista elected pope, then *she* would be first lady of Rome and could own such a palace. Maybe even *this* palace.

Urban named Prince Taddeo the prefect of Rome, a title of great honor and income but only ceremonial duties. Yet with this empty title he created a diplomatic furor by claiming that he, as prefect, had precedence over all the ambassadors. *He* would march first in the parades; *he* would have the more honorable seat at dinner parties. The ambassadors of France and Spain, who were the personal representatives of their monarchs, were so insulted that they boycotted any function where the pope's obnoxious nephew would push them out of the way. They were finally recalled in protest by their kings, a huge snub to Urban.

The pope was more fortunate in Taddeo's brother Cardinal Francesco, who had accompanied Gianbattista to Paris and Madrid. The cardinal was a great scholar who translated ancient Greek, experimented in botany, and with his collection of rare books and manuscripts founded the Barberini Library, the most extensive library in Rome after that of the Vatican. With regards to his personality, however, he was not exactly a barrel of laughs. In 1630 the Venetian ambassador Alvise Contarini described Cardinal Francesco as "choleric, melancholy, greedy, and pretentious," though he was respected for his chaste way of life.[4]

Not so the third brother, Antonio, who became cardinal in 1627 at the tender age of twenty. "The great inclination he has had to women hath been no small blemish to his reputation," Leti wrote, and for once in his life Leti was being kind.[5] Cardinal Antonio was known for his astonishing agility in swinging both ways and caused scandal with both male and female lovers.

A sinister affair concerned Gualterio Gualtieri—Olimpia's cousin and Gianbattista's nephew—probably the same youth whose gambling debts she had mentioned in her letter to Gianbattista. Still in his teens, Gualterio entered the service of Cardinal Antonio as a page to learn cultured manners and the courtly way of life. Evidently, he learned other things as well. One day the cardinal called him away from the gaming table to attend him. "I have him in the ass all night," the young man cried, slapping down his cards. "He should at least leave me alone during the day!"[6]

The impudent remark flew around Rome like wildfire. Cardinal Antonio was so furious that he sent Gualterio to the battlefield in Germany to fight Protestants. No sooner had the boy arrived than he was killed on the field, many said shot in the back by an assassin paid by the cardinal. Whether he was murdered or not, his death had certainly resulted from his master sending him to war in a fit of rage. Gianbattista and Olimpia had been extremely fond of the boy and were devastated by his untimely death.

It was unfortunate that the prudish, studious Francesco was the handsomer of the brothers, while the swashbuckling, lecherous Antonio had eyes set ridiculously close to each other over an enormous nose. The two heartily disliked each other and jealously complained to their uncle if one received more money or honors than the other. The pope forced Francesco and Antonio to have breakfast with each other every morning, but usually the two ate in glum silence, never lifting their eyes from their plates. Once the two cardinal brothers got into a shrieking fight over the possession of a diamond-studded cross sent by Louis XIII; the pope yanked it from them and gave it to Taddeo.

Not all of Urban's relatives were lost to the deadly sins of greed, pride, and lust. The one member of the family—including the pope—who seemed truly called to a religious life was Urban's brother Antonio. Antonio had been a Capuchin monk for decades when his brother, newly elected pontiff, called him to Rome to be made a cardinal against his loud protests. He was a humble monk and wanted to remain so.

Leti found the new cardinal entirely unsuited to his glorious station. "Cardinal Onofrio, brother to Urban the Eighth, who was taken from a cloister of *Capucines*, and introduc'd into the Affairs of the Court, could never accustom himself to live in any other manner, but in that slovenly way of the *Capucines*," he wrote, "so that when he was to receive any Embassadours, he committed the most ridiculous pieces of clownishness imaginable." When the imperial ambassador asked him to convince the pope to assist Christian nations against the advancing Turks, the good cardinal began talking about "the excellence of Turneps, and the manner how the *Capucines* boil them in good fat broth; seeming to lick his fingers almost at every syllable and to swallow a Turnep at every word."[7]

On November 19, 1629, the papal nuncio to Madrid, Monsignor Gianbattista Pamphili, was proclaimed a cardinal by Pope Urban VIII, along with eight others. Gianbattista was not technically a cardinal until the pope placed a red cap on his head in a special ceremony, but he would now receive the remunerative revenues of a cardinal. These would enable him to pay the exorbitant expenses associated with the creation ceremonies when he returned to Rome.

The word *cardinal* was first used at the end of the fifth century and comes from the Latin *cardo*, which means "hinge." Scholars believe that the hinge referred to the flexibility cardinals were expected to show in leaving their local churches and swinging over to Rome to serve the pope. Early cardinals were a kind of super-priest, with greater dignity than regular priests, and over the centuries they steadily acquired more honors, income, and power. A cardinal was "created," and those cardinals created by a particular pope were known as his "creatures," a term that sounds extremely odd to us today.

Putting together a list of new cardinals was one of the most difficult tasks of a pope and sometimes took years of negotiations. It was not just a matter of selecting the most educated, diligent, and moral men of the church for the honor. The first consideration was political—France would be angling to have a French cardinal created, or at least an Italian cardinal who had served as nuncio to France and was known to be sympathetic to the national interests. Whenever France learned it would not be getting a cardinal, the French started mumbling darkly about Henry VIII. In 1533, when Pope Clement VII wouldn't grant Henry a divorce to marry his mistress, the king severed ties with Rome, declared himself the head of the Church of England, and never sent the Vatican another dime.

If France got a cardinal, Spain would screech shrilly if it did not get to choose one, too, and might, perhaps, rattle sabers loudly enough in Naples to make sure the request was heard in Rome. Venice and Florence, though smaller and less important than the "great powers" of France and Spain, would come flapping in pushing their own candidates, their dispatches laced with flattery, threats, and bribes. The Holy Roman Emperor in Austria, fighting to his west the heretics in what would become known as the Thirty Years' War and to his east the advancing Muslim Turks, would also insist on naming a cardinal. Every now and then a king of Poland would clamor for a cap for his brother, and it was hard to turn down the ruler of the last Catholic bastion next to Orthodox Russia.

Then there were the pope's family members—brothers and nephews, usually, though some popes into the sixteenth century nominated their own sons. In addition to these considerations, in the first list of cardinals publicized after his election, the pope was expected to name someone from the family of the pope who had created *him* cardinal decades earlier, as a way of expressing the Christian virtue of gratitude. And if a pope's niece married into a powerful Italian family, etiquette demanded that the pope name the groom's brother a cardinal as part of the marriage treaty.

And then, when all these positions had been filled, the pope could look around for a couple of truly brilliant, dedicated clerics from lesser-known families who had worked their way up in the church. It is not surprising that many popes were elected from among these cardinals of merit, rather than those who were created for reasons of politics and etiquette.

Urban VIII would have sent a special messenger to his nuncio in Madrid bearing not only the exciting news of his creation but also the robes of a cardinal. Gianbattista would wear a cardinal's mourning robes—in fuchsia, oddly enough—until he received his red hat from the pope's own hand in a special ceremony. Only after that could he wear the traditional red robes and hat. After receiving his fuchsia robes, Gianbattista did not leave Madrid immediately but spent another six months or so tying up loose ends.

In his diary entry of July 6, 1630, Giacinto Gigli noted that Cardinal Pamphili "made a pretty cavalcade" to officially enter Rome.[8] In the Piazza del Popolo, in front of Rome's ceremonial gate, hundreds of carriages bearing Rome's nobility, ambassadors, and cardinals lined up to welcome the new prince of the church and escort him to the Piazza Navona. We can assume that among them was an excited Olimpia.

According to etiquette, Gianbattista then called on the cardinal nephews Francesco and Antonio Barberini in the Vatican and generously distributed gold coins to their servants as a sign of gratitude to God for his good fortune. After dinner together, the Barberini brothers took Gianbattista to a private audience with the pope, where he knelt and kissed the pontifical foot. Urban took the red hat and put it on Gianbattista's head, proclaiming in Latin, *"Esto Cardinalis."* The celebrated red hat was called a *galero;* it was an enormous red velvet sombrero laden with ropes of red cords and huge drapery tassels. The hat was too big and too ridiculous to actually be worn other than in the creation ceremony, but it would be carried on a silver pole in parades and hung over the cardinal's tomb.

After the private creation ceremony, Gianbattista hopped into his carriage and made courtesy calls on all the pope's relatives, male and female. Then he returned to his house in the Piazza Navona, where he was expected to remain inside until his public Vatican ceremony five weeks later. Protocol dictated that he was not even to be seen at the doors or windows. Yet that first night he was seen with a look of supreme satisfaction on his face gazing out of the windows overlooking the Piazza Navona and, later, those in the rear of the house overlooking the Piazza Pasquino. He was glad to be home.

On the morning of August 12, 1630, Gianbattista burst forth from his cocoon blazing in red robes, leading a brilliant cavalcade to the Vatican. There, in a magnificent ceremony in the Sistine Chapel along with the other new cardinals, he officially received the red hat again from the pope. Olimpia attended the ceremony, beaming from her seat of honor.

Having been created cardinal, Gianbattista was required to give huge tips to all of his servants at the Piazza Navona house—from his private secretary to the little boy who shoveled horse manure in his stables. And countless employees of the Vatican were to receive tips—the dozens of secretaries, notaries, and office managers who had pushed his laborious paperwork through the system. The pope's personal servants also had their hands out, and Gianbattista would have handsomely tipped the papal master of ceremonies, clerks, singers, trumpet blowers, butlers, buglers, grooms, doormen, and gardeners at the proscribed rates. The protocol in *Il perfetto maestro di casa* declared that the papal servants alone received a total of 1,162 scudi. It was a huge amount, yet there was simply no way to get out of paying it without acquiring a terrible reputation for avarice as soon as the coveted red hat was plunked on one's head.

As cardinal, Gianbattista received a new honorific. On June 10, 1630, the pope decreed that effective immediately all cardinals were no longer to be called "Most Reverend" as they had been for centuries, but were to be addressed by the more honorable "Your Eminence," and were to take precedence immediately after kings. Feeling outranked by this title, European princes claimed for themselves the title of "Highness" instead of "Excellency." Furious at this title inflation, the pope instructed his cardinals to continue addressing the princes as "Excellency," with the result that such letters bounced back to them unopened. "My Master receives no Letters from him that knows not his Merit," wrote one prince's secretary.[9] Another stated, "the Cardinal has a drunken Secretary, and one that did not know what Titles Princes deserv'd."[10]

And so Their Eminences were forced to accept the new titles of Their Highnesses, and at the end of the day, the relative stature of cardinals and princes was the same as before but their titles had swollen significantly.

A new cardinal would be assigned to one or more "congregations" or church governing committees. Imbecile cardinals appointed for political or family reasons were assigned to congregations where they couldn't do much damage—the Congregation of Fountains, for instance, which met once a month to discuss the repair of water pipes, or that most popular committee, the Index of Forbidden Books, where for their homework the cardinals had to read the dirtiest books in Europe and write reports expressing their shock and outrage.

The French historian André du Chesne (1584–1640) wrote that Urban VIII respected Pamphili's "erudition," which he employed "in many of the most difficult negotiations and in the trickiest congregations."[11] Immediately after his creation, Cardinal Pamphili was assigned to one of the most important congregations of all—that of the Council of Trent—and in 1639 he would become its chairman. This group met twice a week, on Thursdays and Saturdays, to interpret the rulings of the 1563 council. Gianbattista's appointment to this prestigious congregation was a sign that he was widely acknowledged as an able churchman.

Cardinal Pamphili joined other important congregations, including the Congregation of Ecclesiastical Jurisdiction and Immunity, which protected clerics from civil prosecution of crimes and defined the often gray area between the legal domains of church and local governments. He accepted a position on the Congregation of Church Rites, which created saints after carefully examining the conduct of their lives and the miracles attributed to them after death. He was named to the Congregation of the Propagation of the Faith, which worked with missionaries spreading the Catholic faith in far-flung regions of the globe such as China and South America.

Cardinal Pamphili was also appointed to the Congregation of the Holy Office of the Inquisition, which included at least twelve reverend theologians who met with the pope every Thursday to look into accusations of heresy. The cardinal chairman of this congregation had a prison in the basement of his palace where he incarcerated unabashed heretics.

Heresy was no recent phenomenon but was almost as old as Christianity itself. Only twenty years after the crucifixion, Paul wrote the Galatians, "Some people are throwing you into confusion and are trying to pervert the gospel of Christ." From the earliest times, many converts had their own ideas about who Jesus was and what he meant. Those ideas that were not accepted by the mainstream bishops were labeled "heresy," which comes from the Greek *heresias,* "choice."

For the first three centuries of Christianity, heresy was punished by excommunication, not death. Early Christians looked disdainfully at Jews who stoned to death blasphemers; the followers of Jesus treated their disgraced brethren more mercifully. It was only when the religion became entwined with imperial power in the fourth century that disrespect of the church meant treason toward the emperor and the state and, therefore, merited death.

Ironically, heresy served as the impetus for the definition of orthodoxy. Reacting to heresy, theologians performed mental gymnastics to create new dogma. In doing so, they often went well beyond anything stated in the Bible. Over time, these writings of the early church fathers and the decrees of popes and church councils became accepted truth in the same way the Bible was.

The church rationalized this acceptance of later doctrine by concluding that divine revelation does not stop with Scripture. In John 16:12–13, Jesus said, "I have much more to say to you, more than you can now bear. But when he, the Spirit of truth, comes, he will guide you into all truth." In other words, God's word is continuously revealed by the Holy Spirit, inserted into the right time and place of the world's historical matrix. The Body of Tradition, as the church called it, added new layers of thought in between the meat of Scripture, creating a kind of theological lasagna.

The individual most responsible for slicing up the lasagna was a German monk named Martin Luther. A slight man with bruising cheekbones, a square face, and tiny blue eyes tucked beneath a Neolithic brow,

Luther studied his Bible and was perplexed to find the conspicuous absence of much of Catholic dogma. Where were monks? Where was the pope? Where was confession, pilgrimage, last rites? Not in the Bible. The writings of others had defined much of the Catholic Church as he knew it.

Beginning in 1517 Luther protested loudly against the Body of Tradition and soon had a rising German nationalistic movement behind him. For centuries the Germans had felt fleeced by Rome. Germany, consisting of some three hundred small states, could not present a strong unified front to the church, as France and Spain did, to protest taxes and political interference. Good hardworking Germans resented giving their gold into the smooth hands of slippery Italians doing God only knew what in their painted perfumed palaces with girls, or boys, or each other. "German money in violation of nature flies over the Alps," Luther wrote.[12] Given the financial advantages, numerous European princes suddenly found themselves convinced of Luther's theology.

As a belated response to the swelling Protestant movement, Paul III created the Roman Inquisition in 1542. Because the Vatican was the foremost legal organization of the modern world, the Inquisition imposed strict rules of law to prevent unjust executions. Witnesses could not accuse secretly but must come out and testify openly. All those who bore the defendant a grudge, including those who owed him money or were owed money by him, were banned from testifying. And for those cases involving witchcraft—stillbirths, bad crops, or sick farm animals—doctors and scientists were asked to testify about natural phenomenon that could have caused the complaints. With his rigorous sense of justice, his caution, and his fine legal mind, Cardinal Pamphili would have been a great asset to the Holy Office of the Inquisition and to those poor heretics and witches hauled before it.

In addition to their work in the congregations, cardinals had duties of a ceremonial nature. For instance, all cardinals were expected to ride with their train of gaily bedecked horses and servants to the Porta del Popolo to give a formal welcome to new ambassadors, foreign princes, and their relatives. Having greeted the exalted visitor, they would hop into their carriages and follow him to the Vatican in a colorful cavalcade.

But the most impressive cavalcade was that of the *obbedienza* ambassador, a special emissary sent by an old king to a new pope, or by a new king to the old pope, as a sign of obedience to the pontiff. An *obbedienza* procession was a kind of Ringling Bros. and Barnum & Bailey Circus, sometimes complete with camels and elephants. It had its roots in the imperial Roman past, when victorious legions marched in triumph through the streets of Rome carting booty and slaves captured in foreign countries. In the more civilized days of the Renaissance, foreign countries began sending their own booty, gifts designed to amaze the Romans and bring honor to their donors.

When the new king Ladislas of Poland sent Prince Jerzy Ossolinski as his *obbedienza* ambassador in 1632, he instructed him to carry out his mission to rival or even surpass the cavalcades of the king of France. "Where the French had silver he was to take gold; where they had gold he was to have precious stones; and where they had precious stones he was to use diamonds."

Ten camels carried the ambassador's luggage, and according to a contemporary report, "the astonishment of the Romans was specially roused by six Turkish horses which followed, whose trappings were studded with emeralds and rubies whilst harness, stirrups and even the shoes were of pure gold. The members of the embassy, too, were resplendent in cloaks set with diamonds. Ossolinski's *zupan* (Polish coat) of black cloth shot with gold, glittered with diamonds; his sword, set with precious stones, was valued at 20,000 scudi."[13]

If the Polish *obbedienza* amazed the Roman people, it is likely that some cardinals watched it while stifling yawns. A cardinal's lifestyle was just as regal. The glory of the church was reflected in the glory of her princes, in their gilded carriages, marble palaces, and sumptuous banquets. A cardinal needed to have a minimum of forty horses in his stables—though many had three times this amount—and rich velvet trappings for each animal to match the color of his robes.

The cardinal's apartments on the *piano nobile* of his palace consisted of a series of antechambers culminating in his bedroom in the corner of the building. The closer the visitor got to the bedroom, the more honored he was. In the audience chamber the cardinal's throne was placed on a raised platform under a canopy, or baldachino. When the cardinal was not in residence, the throne was turned to face the wall.

Cardinals drew income from owning benefices, or church lands. Though canon law decreed that each churchman could own only one benefice and must reside there to look after it, this decree was blithely ignored when it came to cardinals "to assist them to bear the burden of expense which their office imposed on them," according to a 1507 bull.[14] In 1503 the church declared that "having to perform higher duties so ought they to enjoy greater privileges than the other servants of Christ."[15]

In addition to these revenues, some cardinals were lucky enough to be named "cardinal protector" of a particular realm, a kind of in-house lobbyist paid to look out for the interests of a nation and send back secret reports of Vatican intrigues. The pope's nephews were given the plum assignments of aiding France and Spain, of course, but the king of Poland, aware of Cardinal Pamphili's intelligence, sobriety, and hard work, appointed him his cardinal protector. Poland couldn't pay as much as France and Spain, but it was a great honor.

A new cardinal required several sets of cardinal's robes and was, indeed, never again to be permitted any other wardrobe unless he was elevated to the papacy. Rustling in layers of dark red satin, with just a touch of lace, the cardinal presented a majestic and powerful figure. Cardinals had not always worn special robes but had dressed as regular priests until the reign of Pope Innocent IV (1243–1254), who invented the impressive red cap as a mark of distinction.

By the reign of Boniface IX (1389–1404), cardinals usually wore red robes as a sign of their willingness to be martyred for the church, though by the seventeenth century the color was mostly appreciated for its ability to conceal wine stains. On days of mourning—the forty days of Lent, All Saints' Day, and the ten days immediately following the death of a pope—cardinals wore fuchsia. On two feast days a year—the third Sunday in Advent right before Christmas and the fourth Sunday of Lent—they wore rose.

Cardinals first put on a *sottana,* a long, tight-fitting robe. Then they put on the rochet, a long-sleeved white shirt of finely woven linen adorned with lace, falling somewhere between the thighs and knees, and resembling a bridal negligee. In an era when most men wore ribbons, bows, high heels with pom-poms, ruffs, and puffs, the gorgeous rochet was the only concession to frivolity in a cardinal's costume. Over the rochet went the mozzetta, or elbow-length cape. The *sottana* and mozzetta were always of the same color—red, fuchsia, or rose.

The cardinal could choose between hats in the same color as his robes. Etiquette rigidly prescribed when it was appropriate to wear which one. For travel in the sun and rain there was a wide-brimmed felt hat tied under the chin with gold cords. The official cardinal's hat was the three-peaked biretta, used for formal wear, and for daily wear the small flat red *zucchetto*—what we would call a beanie—which was very similar to a yarmulke.

In fact, the similarities between the *zucchetto* and the yarmulke caused problems when, in 1636, the cardinal of Lyons, who was aged and shortsighted, was traveling through the streets of Rome in his carriage and saw a Jew wearing a red yarmulke. The cardinal, mistaking the Jew for a fellow member of the Sacred College, leaned out of the window and saluted him reverently in the name of Jesus Christ, the Son of God, as "Your Eminence." The horrified Jew scuttled away, but the ridiculous gaffe was witnessed by many. The story, being just too exquisite to keep quiet, leaped into the Vatican within the hour. The pope was so distraught about a Jew's being mistaken for a prince of the Holy Roman Church that he issued a new edict. Jews, he decreed, could no longer wear red yarmulkes. They would have to wear yellow.

Etiquette regarding the princes of the church was extremely exacting down to the most minor detail. Cardinals had to be seated in identical chairs. It would have been a gross insult to the church for one cardinal to have a lower seat than his colleague, or for one to have the honor of arms on his chair and the other to be dishonored by a chair with no arms. And it would have been unthinkable for one cardinal to sit disconsolately on a cushion with mere silver tassels while his counterpart exulted in a cushion tasseled in gold.

When the coaches of two cardinals met, there was also a rigorous protocol. According to Gregorio Leti's book on cardinals and their etiquette, "A Cardinal stops his Coach to another that is his Senior," and by this he meant not the older cardinal but the one who had been created first. "For it is to be taken notice of, that the most antient Cardinal is the last always that stops and the first that goes forward."[16] This rule was, of course, ignored when the cardinals were mad at each other, in which case they pretended not to see each other and galloped on by.

The position of the chairs in an audience chamber was also an important determiner of rank, since those facing the door were more prestigious. This custom had taken root in the Dark Ages when it was always possible that murderers could burst through the doors waving knives and those facing the door had a better chance of surviving.

Once, when the grand duke of Tuscany visited Cardinal Francesco Barberini, he found both chairs facing each other with their sides parallel to the door. The grand duke, a modest soul, moved his own chair a bit so as to place his back more toward the door, giving the cardinal the greater honor. The cardinal, equally polite, did the same. By the end of the conversation, both illustrious gentlemen had their backs to the door and were seated next to each other looking straight ahead, as if they were watching a movie. All that was lacking was the popcorn.

Diplomatic etiquette became so increasingly difficult over the course of the seventeenth century that in 1698 Peter the Great of Russia and the emperor Leopold of Austria had to meet at a "tavern" set up by their protocol officers, where Peter played the innkeeper and Leopold the peasant. They didn't need to worry about who sat on which chair and which direction the chairs faced, as one monarch cheerfully served beer and the other sat on a stool and drank it.

Stiff and suspicious, Cardinal Pamphili did not make friends easily and occasionally made inveterate enemies. His manner often came across as brusque, sometimes even downright insulting. In 1636 he criticized the artist Guido Reni for some decorations he had made for Saint Peter's Basilica. Reni was so offended that he decided to avenge himself in his next commission, a side chapel in the Church of Saint Mary of the Conception.

The artist painted the archangel Michael pushing the devil against a rock with the angel's foot planted firmly on his head. The devil looked exactly like Cardinal Pamphili, with his bald pate, furrowed brow, and straggly beard. When Gianbattista saw the painting, he knew immediately that it was his face on the devil and raced to confront the artist. But after hearing the cardinal's tirade, Reni merely shrugged. He explained that he had simply tried to paint the most horrible face imaginable on the devil. If Gianbattista Pamphili happened to look like that, it was not the fault of Guido Reni, it was the fault of the cardinal's face.

In his report to the Venetian senate, Ambassador Alvise Contarini had only a slightly more flattering opinion than Guido Reni. He wrote, "His stature is tall and dry, his eyes small, his feet big, his beard sparse, his complexion olive-green and sunburned, his head bald and, in short, a nice complex of bones and nerves."[17]

Looks aside, and despite his sometimes surly demeanor, Cardinal Gianbattista Pamphili had many excellent qualities that were true assets to the Sacred College. He was genuinely devout, and his tall, spare figure lent an air of great dignity to the ecclesiastical rites in which he participated. He was cautious in his congregations, but once he finally rendered a decision, he backed it up with solid canon law. He could be sulky and suspicious, but he also had a great deal of kindness. Even the humblest petitioners could easily obtain audiences with him, during which the cardinal listened patiently. And if he found that an injustice had been committed, he was quick to correct it.

Gianbattista was thoughtful and hardworking, and he did not gossip, except, of course, with Olimpia. He was respected for his diligence; though he was a late riser, he worked into the wee hours, burning the midnight oil. Unlike many cardinals, he was known for the moderation of his personal life, rarely spending money on himself. According to Ambassador Contarini, Cardinal Pamphili was sparing with food and wine and enjoyed robust health, which he attributed to keeping as far away from doctors as possible.

But for all his assets, the one black mark against Cardinal Pamphili was his ill-concealed passion for Olimpia. Gregorio Leti asserted, "The good cardinal was an excellent master in the art of dissimulating everything perfectly, except for the love he had for his sister-in-law. In the congregations he appeared gentle, in conversation he was very humble, and in church he was admirably devout. But with all of his skill, it was impossible for him to hide his affection for Donna Olimpia.

"He loved her," Leti continued, "he adored her, to tell the truth, in public and in private, and all the world was truly astonished that a Cardinal who had pretensions, although a long shot, to the Pontificate, worked so openly to win the good graces of a woman, and his sister-in-law at that."[18]

7

The Black Widow

Who in widow-weeds appears,
Laden with unhonoured years,
Noosing with care a bursting purse,
Baited with many a deadly curse?

—Robert Burns

WITH HER MASCULINE TASTES, Olimpia was interested in science and often discussed scientific advances with great animation at her dinner parties. The most salacious scientific news in decades was the 1633 trial of the astronomer Galileo Galilei by the Holy Office of the Inquisition. The highly respected sixty-nine-year-old Florentine had been hauled before the tribunal for heresy because his new book suggested that the earth moved around the sun. Scripture, which the church considered infallible in matters of science, clearly stated that the sun traveled around the earth. When Joshua, for instance, had prayed for enough daylight to finish smiting the Amorites, God had heard his plea and made the sun stay its course. Nothing was said about God making the *earth* stay its course.

Galileo had not come up with the theory himself but had picked it up from Copernicus (1473–1543), whose work, ironically, had been admired by the Catholics as a scientific advance and lambasted by Martin Luther as anti-biblical. But attitudes had changed by the early seventeenth century. The church felt threatened by the increasing power of

Protestant nations, by Rome's decreasing importance in international politics, and by a flurry of new scientific theories that contradicted Catholic dogma. In 1616 the Inquisition had warned Galileo not to publish any more books on a heliocentric planetary system. "The view that the sun stands motionless at the center of the Universe is foolish, philosophically false and utterly heretical," the Holy Office declared, "because contrary to Holy Scripture."[1]

But in 1632 Galileo published a book called *Dialogue Concerning the Two Chief World Systems,* a fictional discussion among three men on the structure of the solar system. The imbecile character Simplicio blindly defended the old cosmology with stupid arguments, which his more learned friends tore to shreds. Unfortunately, Simplicio greatly resembled Pope Urban VIII, who argued that God had the power to create whatever absurdities he wanted, and make it *look* like science. The blockheaded Simplicio explained that he clung to old science because its sheer antiquity made it more venerable than new discoveries.

"I must tell you I laughed my heart out when I came across Signor Simplicio," one of Galileo's friends wrote him.[2] But the pope didn't think it was very funny. Since he'd become supreme pontiff, Urban's ego had swollen. It was, most likely, not Galileo's science as much as his ridicule of the pope that landed him in boiling water.

The Inquisition found him "vehemently suspected of heresy" for supporting the Copernican hypothesis. He was required to make a solemn recantation in which he "abjured, cursed and detested [his] errors and heresies."[3] Due to his compliance, Galileo avoided being burned at the stake and was sentenced to life imprisonment. This sentence was commuted to house arrest due to Cardinal Francesco Barberini's impassioned intercession for leniency. In addition, the scientist was required to recite the Seven Penitential Psalms once a week for three years.

Many churchmen with scientific interests warned the pope that condemning Galileo would unleash a rabid anti-Catholic reaction across Europe. They were right. Up north the heretics, who had been so violently opposed to Copernicus a century earlier, switched sides and now accused the superstitious Catholics of being stuck firmly in the muck of the Dark Ages. How, they asked between chuckles, could an entire sixteen-hundred-year-old theology be threatened by a telescope and a book?

The prestige of the Catholic Church dropped precipitously in learned and scientific circles, even among devout Catholics. Those in the Vatican knew that the quickest way to send Pope Urban into a foaming-at-the-mouth rage was to whisper the name *Galileo*. Fortunately for his reputation, Cardinal Pamphili would not be appointed to the Holy Office of the Inquisition until later in the decade, or else his name would have joined the list of numskull cardinals who had signed Galileo's condemnation.

In 1634 Olimpia bought the two neighboring Teofili houses, one of which Gianbattista had been renting, and incorporated them into her own, thereby tripling the size of her residence and creating a true palazzo. As an important cardinal with papal aspirations, Gianbattista needed an impressive palace to hold audiences and entertain, and the narrow, jumbled Pamphili house had become an embarrassment. The architect Francesco Peperelli was hired to create a harmonious layout and an imposing façade.

For the better part of two years, from 1636 to 1638, the house bristled with scaffolding inside and out. Roofers crawled over the eaves, while carpenters, plasterers, and painters swarmed through the rooms, saws and paint buckets in hand. The sound of hammers rang throughout the corridors, and plaster dust coated the furniture. Olimpia kept a firm eye on the renovations, frequently meeting with artisans and inspecting their work.

Peperelli made a servant's entrance out of the narrow alleyway that had separated the two houses and extended the rooms above. In the new part of the palazzo, he created a large ceremonial entrance, which led to a wide courtyard, with room for horses and carriages, and a monumental staircase that swept up to the cardinal's waiting room.

The waiting room was where ambassadors, noblemen, and cardinals sat, chatting with the *maestro di casa,* eating snacks and drinking wine until Cardinal Pamphili could see them. This room was constructed from two floors of the old Teofili palace, each consisting of several rooms, to create one imposing chamber measuring some fifty by twenty-five feet, with twenty-five-foot ceilings. The new palace, though a great improvement over the old, was still not quite up to cardinalatial standards. The architect designed a false door at the end of the waiting room so visitors believed the house extended beyond it. It didn't. Beyond the door was the de Rossi house.

Nor could the new house hold all the horses and carriages required for a cardinal. Records show that from 1639 to 1644 Olimpia paid the monthly rent for nearby stalls and a carriage-storage area at the request of her brother-in-law. Though Gianbattista was now wealthier than he ever had been, he was not one of the richest cardinals. He was, in fact, on the pope's list of "poor cardinals," those beneath a certain income level who received an honorarium to help them maintain the requisite princely lifestyle. While some cardinals had a staff of two hundred servants, Gianbattista employed only twenty-five. Records show that Pamphilio and Olimpia had another fifteen servants between the two of them.

In the extended palace the Pamphilis continued to rent out shops on the ground floor. Architectural sketches show room for sixteen shops, though some tenants might have rented two adjoining rooms. Tenants included a fruit seller, a flax vendor, a leather-goods store, a restaurant, a lute maker, a grocer, a barber, and a tailor.

As a cardinal, Gianbattista now trumped his brother in position and was given the best suite of rooms, facing the Piazza Navona. Olimpia moved to the back corner of the house, overlooking Pasquino. Pamphilio's suite was at the rear of the house, overlooking the narrow Via dell'Anima. Olimpia's rooms had inner doors opening onto the suites of her husband on the one side and her brother-in-law on the other.

With her larger palace, Olimpia was now in a position to hold musical events for Rome's rich and powerful. If science was on the decline in the 1630s, theater and opera were on the upswing. The church limited theatrical performances to the anything-goes period of Carnival each February, but many nobles, including Olimpia, spent months preparing for their shows. They held amateur performances in their palaces, writing the plays and music, creating the sets and costumes, and even acting and singing in them. Tragedies were popular—suicidal lovers, sacrificial virgins, and breast-beating heroes dying on the battlefield. But comedies were even more popular, and Olimpia particularly enjoyed putting on humorous plays poking fun at contemporary figures.

Theater made use of "machines," contraptions of floats, pulleys, and levers that could lift actors and even horses into the air by means of almost invisible wires. Some machines held up to a hundred singing angels. Others were decorated as dragons, with flapping wings, swishing tails, and mouths that opened with a shriek to emit a fiery blast. Allegorical figures were extremely popular at the time; actors and actresses representing Divine Justice, Holy Religion, and Saintly Sacrifice would declaim onstage and then fly straight up to heaven.

Rome's foremost artists contributed to these events. In the sixteenth and seventeenth centuries, an artist did not keep strictly to one discipline but was expected to be the master of many. Painters sculpted, sculptors painted, and both were hired as architects for palaces and churches. They were called upon by the powerful to design carriages, furniture, clothing, and even spun-sugar desserts in the shape of statues and buildings. And the rich commissioned them to design machines, extensive sets, and costumes for their Carnival performances.

The darkly handsome Gian Lorenzo Bernini, though known primarily for his genius in sculpting marble, undertook his many theatrical commissions with gusto. He was a showman, a ringmaster who loved to surprise, startle, and frighten with his elaborate stage sets and special effects. Bernini was particularly admired for creating a gradual sunrise and sunset, and for darkening the stage at the approach of a sudden storm, followed by thunder, lightning, hail, and rain. This was an impressive feat, considering he had only torches, oil lamps, and mirrors to work with.

But his most impressive effect was his frightfully realistic simulation of the flooding Tiber for Carnival 1638. The river, which had been represented onstage in the form of wide tanks with actors canoeing on them, was suddenly diverted into the audience as the stage sets collapsed. Thinking this was an accident, the alarmed spectators stood up ready to rush off but soon realized there was a large basin in front of them to catch the roaring waves, and it had all been part of the show.

Opera became popular in Venice in 1637 and spread like wildfire to other Italian cities. While most nobles held performances on a temporary stage set up in their largest room—the reception hall or ballroom—in 1640 Cardinal Antonio Barberini built a theater seating three thousand attached to his palazzo. He and his brother Francesco tried to surpass each other in giving the best operas, each spending thousands of scudi on a single performance.

The brothers were often so immersed in their competing productions that they forgot to visit their uncle the pope, leaving him cooling his heels in the Vatican while they fidgeted with stage sets. Particularly troubling was when the pope went to hear Mass sung in the Sistine Chapel and the pontifical choir was missing; they were at the Palazzo Barberini theater, rehearsing for the next opera.

Olimpia attended the Barberini operas and must have had a good laugh at the 1642 première of Antonio's *The Enchanted Palace.* The performance, which had cost the cardinal eight thousand scudi, flopped due to malfunctioning machines. "His Eminence became fearfully enraged, threatening prison and similar things," wrote the musician Ottaviano Castelli to Cardinal Mazarin in France.[4]

We aren't told exactly how the machines malfunctioned, but it is tempting to imagine Divine Dignity toppling out of her flying chariot and landing on the stage below with a thud. Or perhaps a flying Christian Glory belting out an aria became stuck in the air, unable to descend, legs flailing helplessly until he was plucked to safety by a stagehand with a ladder. The audience, which was supposed to have been swept away by the glorious rapture of the moment, fell into paroxysms of laughter.

According to Castelli, the most irritating thing about it was that Antonio's own brother was seen laughing loudest of all. "It was believed that Cardinal [Francesco] Barberino laughed at seeing these disorders, as if from jealousy that Antonio had wished, with the display of a celebration superior to all the others, to obscure his own."[5]

Problems cropped up not only onstage but sometimes in the audience of noble guests as well. Competition for seats was fierce, and Cardinal Antonio kept order by marching up and down the aisles wielding a heavy stick, which he used to push unruly guests out of the way or to force people to sit more closely together. One evening before the performance started, the cardinal and several princely guests were seen giving one another the finger—yes, that particular gesture has been around for centuries—and calling one another sodomites.

Olimpia loved to attend her friends' operas as well as their tragic and comedic plays. But she preferred to give her own performances, in which she reconstructed the world as she saw it—a colorful place of ridiculous characters, with everything supervised and directed by herself.

Cardinal Pamphili's astonishing love for his sister-in-law had blossomed unimpeded by the constant presence of his brother Pamphilio in the Piazza Navona house. Not much is known about Pamphilio after the Naples sojourn, and he seems to have lived a secluded life in the 1630s, perhaps due to illness.

Certainly late in the decade, if not earlier, he suffered greatly from kidney stones. In the summer of 1639 one, in particular, tormented him, blocking up the flow of urine, causing violent shooting pains, high fever, chills, and abdominal swelling. The normal rhythm of the family ceased as attention was focused on the sick man. Olimpia would have stopped going out in her carriage—except, of course, to church—as friends and neighbors dropped by to check on Pamphilio's health. With the best of intentions, Pamphilio's doctors would have tortured their patient unmercifully, siphoning off his blood with leeches, causing violent diarrhea with enemas and uncontrollable vomiting with herbs known as pukes, all in an effort to dislodge the large kidney stone.

But nothing worked. On August 29, Pamphilio lay in the sweltering heat of a Roman summer, drenching his sheets in sweat and moaning in pain. The end seemed near, and a priest was called to administer last rites, the sacred words to ease the dying person along the path to God. Gianbattista, Olimpia, and her three children would have knelt in prayer with bowed heads.

It is hard for us to judge Olimpia's feelings as her husband lay dying. It was Pamphilio who had brought her from the backwater of Viterbo into the excitement of Rome. It was this marriage that had given her noble rank, social position, and power within the Vatican courts. Any sadness might have been assuaged by the freedoms of widowhood, however. A rich widow over forty could administer her own legal and financial affairs without any interference from a man, and certainly this would suit Olimpia better than having a husband as titular head of her household.

As Pamphilio lost consciousness and his breath grew labored, it is likely that Olimpia's eyes would have darted from her rosary beads to her servants. The author of a seventeenth-century book on household management related how servants of Italian noblemen, taking advantage of the uproar caused by their master's death, routinely stole from the family while the body was still warm in bed. The hall sweepers pilfered the brooms, and the meat carvers swiped the knives. The keeper of the wardrobe became the stealer of the wardrobe. The bedchamber servants purloined the sheets. The wine steward filched the last wine bottle. And the cooks ran off with all the food, pots, and pans. Most disturbing, the family chaplain stumbled out of the house groaning under the weight of the silver Holy Sacrament service. It is likely, however, that when Pamphilio Pamphili breathed his last, and Gianbattista and Olimpia's children dissolved into wretched sobs, Olimpia was making sure that not a single broom went missing.

Upon Pamphilio's death, Olimpia, who had never cared much about clothes, immediately threw on widow's weeds—a bone-chilling concoction of flowing black robes and a billowing black hood peaked over the forehead—which she would wear for the rest of her life. She wore velvet in winter, silk and satin in summer, over a plain white undergarment visible at the neck and wrists. These sober robes gave Olimpia the cachet of dignified virtue and offered the added advantage of saving her a great deal of money on clothing. In addition, she had put on weight in middle age, and black was always so slimming.

Olimpia paid for many Masses to be said for the benefit of her husband's soul, as each Mass was believed to cut the deceased's term in purgatory and speed him into heaven. Roman gossips, knowing she was much closer to her brother-in-law than she had ever been to her husband, said she put on these elaborate Masses and wore widow's weeds only for show, or perhaps to ease her guilt over having been unfaithful to him with his brother.

The most salacious rumor was that Olimpia had actually poisoned the old fellow who had been a stumbling block in her love affair with Gianbattista. After all, her first husband had died suddenly at the age of twenty-three, and she had inherited all his money. But it is unlikely that Olimpia had poisoned Pamphilio, if only for the fact that she had been married to him, and very close to Gianbattista, for twenty-seven years by the time her husband died. If she was up to poisoning Pamphilio so she could roll around in bed with her brother-in-law more freely, she would have dusted off her arsenic decades earlier. Moreover, an autopsy proved that a shockingly large kidney stone had done him in.

Whatever Olimpia's feelings about Pamphilio's death, Cardinal Pamphili was devastated. Two days later he wrote to a friend in Spain:

To the duke of Candia in Madrid.

I am obliged to your Excellency to inform you of the news of my family . . . , having lost the illustrious Pamphilio, my only brother, and head of this family at the age of 76, to my infinite grief, after a very painful illness of the stone, which turned out to have weighed six ounces, and was without remedy.

May it please the Lord God to keep him in glory, as I hope, for the resignation he always demonstrated to the divine will. I trust that Your Excellency will also be grieved, knowing what humanity has always accompanied your every sentiment. He has left an only son, my nephew Camillo, who will always recognize fully his obligations to serve Your Excellency. And so I kiss your hands, and pray for the prosperity of Your Excellency.

August 31, 1639 Rome."[6]

With the passing of a family member, Olimpia's *maestro di casa* would have hastened to the Jewish secondhand dealers to purchase a deluge of black bunting in which to drape the public rooms of the house, those that visitors saw. A house in mourning had all mirrors covered, as well as the chairs and tables, and black cloth was draped around all doorways and windows. Atop each door was hung the Pamphili family coat of arms, painted colorfully on large sheets of paper. The household used only black candles. The master of the stables covered the carriages in black and put black trappings on the horses. After the eight-month mourning period was over, the mountain of black cloth was usually sold back to the dealers.

While Olimpia was now legally entitled to administer her own Maidalchini-Nini money, Gianbattista insisted that she officially take charge of administering the Pamphili patrimony as well, which included payments for the comforts of his two sisters, Agatha and Prudenzia, in their convents. Being appointed administrator of a noble family's finances was a rare honor for a woman, but the ambassador of Mantua remarked that Olimpia deserved it for her "great intelligence and economy."[7] He added, however, that the real reason was Gianbattista's fear that if he did not show his sister-in-law sufficient respect, she would take all her money away from the Pamphilis by remarrying. Indeed, rumors abounded that Olimpia was going to marry Mario Frangipani, the scion of a line of princes stretching back much farther than the Colonnas, just to make Anna Colonna mad.

But Olimpia probably never considered a third marriage. First of all, now that she was forty-eight, there was no longer any talk of immuring her in a convent to protect her virtue. Tottering on the brink of the grave as she was, her advanced age alone would ensure her chastity. And surely she enjoyed being under no man's thumb—even a hypothetical thumb, since no matter whom Olimpia married, she would run the show. Moreover, Olimpia was now fulfilling the responsibilities of a cardinal, doing much of her brother-in-law's work. Anyone who wanted something from him was obliged to meet first with Olimpia, who would render a judgment and then tell Cardinal Pamphili what to say.

"It was said that if one wanted some favor from the Cardinal, he would have to ask the sister-in-law," Gregorio Leti explained. "But those who needed her for some affair were not permitted to address themselves to others. When they left the Cardinal little satisfied, he never grew angry but as they were leaving said, 'Perhaps he has not yet spoken to Donna Olimpia.'"[8]

In addition to her work as a cardinal, Olimpia had three children to think about and had, for some time, been plotting their futures. There was her only son, seventeen-year-old Camillo, now the official head of the family, although Olimpia would always hold the real power. And then there were two daughters. None of the three, she vowed, would enter the church. That would be a waste. Olimpia didn't mind paying a large dowry for her girls as long as they married into powerful families, creating a network of support and prestige for her.

Olimpia's daughters remain a cipher and seem to have lived in their mother's shadow. There are no known portraits of them. Neither are there any descriptions whatsoever of their beauty or lack thereof, which might indicate they were average-looking, neither waddlingly fat nor anorexically thin, neither radiantly beautiful nor clock-stoppingly ugly. Ambassadorial reports treat Maria and Costanza Pamphili as extras in the family saga, sweeping in and out of church ceremonies and family banquets with long silken skirts.

A few years later, one diplomat reported that of Olimpia's three children, the pious elder daughter, Maria, was Gianbattista's favorite. The youngest child, Costanza, "has no influence but is a good lady, and cannot be decried without doing her injustice, but neither can she be praised without exaggeration."[9] Given the universal lack of comment on their personalities, it is clear that they were in no way like their mother, whose forceful intelligence was much remarked upon.

In 1640 the twenty-one-year-old Maria married a promising young man of excellent family. The marquess Andrea Giustiniani was attractive and likeable, and even if he was not rich himself, he had very rich relatives. But Gianbattista thought the groom had uncouth manners and put up with him only for Maria's sake. The marriage soon proved fruitful. Within the year Maria had her first child, whom she named after her mother. But to distinguish the two Olimpias, the baby was called by the Italian diminutive, Olimpiuccia. She would prove much like her namesake in terms of her willfulness.

Olimpia fell in love with the infant at first sight. Here was someone she could truly give herself to, a noncompeting female, weak, needing to be nurtured and guided. Here was a safe place to pour out her love, to teach a girl the valuable lessons she had learned so painfully. Olimpia insisted she raise the child in her Piazza Navona palace. The parents gave her up willingly; after all, they were disappointed their child was not a boy. It would prove to be the deepest, longest-lasting love of Olimpia's life. In Olimpiuccia she would endeavor to create a new Olimpia in her own image.

Immediately after her granddaughter's birth, Olimpia called in her attorney to write a new will, arranging to leave the infant her own Maidalchini-Nini wealth, thereby disinheriting Camillo, who would receive only his father's wealth, which was, alas, not much. In an era when family assets were invariably hoarded for the son, Camillo must have greatly resented his mother's taking money away from him to give to a girl, and an infant at that. And Olimpia must have had a good laugh at her son's anger. Camillo was the cliché of a weak son dominated by a strong mother, and they bore each other a hearty dislike.

Camillo seemed the exact replica of his father. He had Pamphilio's sparkling dark eyes, wavy black hair, and strong, chiseled jaw. But as attractive as Camillo was, he was a bit of a dolt. There is no record of Camillo's having attended one of the excellent boys' schools in Rome, and Gregorio Leti reported that Olimpia hired tutors to teach him Latin, arithmetic, and deportment for as long as they could persuade him to sit still. With undisguised venom Leti added that Camillo was "so ignorant that he barely knew how to read at the age of twenty."[10] The French ambassador described the good luck the mediocre Camillo had in being born into the right family, sniffing, "Fortune supplied him with what nature had declined to give."[11]

As a result, Camillo grew up with the varnish of a seventeenth-century gentleman. He excelled at horsemanship and could cut a pretty figure on the dance floor. He crafted poetic verses with more enthusiasm than wit and spent hours at a time designing imaginary gardens on paper. He admired the great art collections of the cardinals and strolled imposingly around their galleries, tilting his head this way and that to examine statues and paintings. Camillo was charming. Camillo was polite. But Camillo was all varnish and no substance. He seemed to have no drive to excel in politics or finance, and he dragged himself through each day with a general air of lassitude.

If Olimpia looked at her son and heir with ill-concealed disappointment, she must have consoled herself with the knowledge that she had enough brains and ambition for the whole family. It was she, a poorly educated woman, who had raised the Maidalchini and Pamphili clans from nothing to the pinnacle of greatness. Looking at the inert, inept, insipid Camillo from her lofty position, she realized he was a hopeless ditherer.

But it was all right. Camillo could dither as much as he wanted as long as he performed the one duty his mother assigned him. He must marry the girl of her choice.

A widow was supposed to shun society, speak rarely, and fasten her eyes on the floor lest she be tempted by worldly vanities. She was to put away her jewels, pray daily for her husband's soul, never talk to unrelated men, and above all, never be seen laughing. A virtuous sense of shame was to imbue her every action. Interestingly, advice manuals of the time encouraged widows to shun the society of their brothers-in-law; while virgins didn't know what they were missing, widows were considered to be sexually insatiable and easily led astray by even the closest relatives.

Olimpia evidently did not read advice manuals for widows. She looked men straight in the eye, spent more time than ever with her brother-in-law, and, bedecked in diamonds, attended theatrical performances at which she guffawed most loudly of all. She also hunted regularly. Now and then the Viterbans were treated to the unusual sight of a grieving widow racing across the fields after a fox, her billowing black weeds flapping around her.

Nor did Olimpia give up speaking to unrelated men. According to the ambassador of Mantua, she was "haughty and entered into conversations more than was seemly for a widow, and spent many hours gambling."[12] Olimpia was passionate about card games and held late-night gambling parties in her palace. She loved beating her opponents, slapping down her cards with a cry of victory and raking in their cash. Gianbattista's cautious nature was adamantly opposed to gambling, but he enjoyed the parties nonetheless, talking with important guests and listening to the musicians.

Olimpia did not attend the balls or feasts of other noble families very often. Her contemporaries said this was due not to grief over her husband's death but to her avarice—she would then be required to reciprocate by giving expensive festivities of her own. Considering that she did give expensive festivities of her own from time to time—elaborate theatrical performances in her palazzo—it is more likely that she found the events of others boring. She far preferred small dinner parties at which she could talk to powerful men about politics and finance and win them over to support Cardinal Pamphili in the next conclave.

Olimpia had one sore spot in conversation. She became noticeably disturbed when those around her praised the generosity of other women. "Women," she would counter, "were to amass riches, not to dissipate them."[13] Most men would have disagreed with her.

In the late 1630s Olimpia found a clever way to avoid dissipating her riches when she wanted frescoes painted in her expanded palazzo. Hearing that the talented artist Andrea Camassei, who had worked for Urban VIII, had been thrown into debtors' prison, Olimpia generously offered to pull a few strings with her Vatican friends and spring him if he promised to paint her rooms for free. The artist was in no position to argue and worked the next year at the Piazza Navona house without being paid a single scudo.

In the 1630s and early 1640s, Olimpia had one goal—to line up sufficient cardinals to elect Gianbattista pope. He was, more than ever, *papabile,* having reached the age of sixty in 1634. His reputation as an able if stern churchman had been enhanced by increasing honors and positions of responsibility.

In 1637, Urban VIII suffered a serious illness from which it was thought he would not recover. He did recover, but his health was never the same, and ailments kept him in bed for weeks at a time. Papal power slipped into the hands of his cardinal nephews, and for several years a conclave was expected at a moment's notice.

One of the main stumbling blocks to Olimpia's papal aspirations was Cardinal Antonio Barberini, who had been responsible for the mysterious death of her young Gualtieri cousin in the early 1630s. Though Cardinal Pamphili was unfailingly polite, the mere glimpse of him seemed to Cardinal Antonio like a biting accusation. He simmered with resentment and often tried to provoke Gianbattista publicly by pricking and prodding him with cruel remarks. Here Gianbattista's lifelong habit of caution assisted him; at an insult flung at him by Cardinal Antonio, the older man would merely hold his tongue and politely bow.

It was unfortunate for Olimpia that the cardinal nephew of the recently deceased pope was invariably the leader of the conclave that followed. Antonio would do his best to prevent Gianbattista's election, if only to avoid the vengeance he so richly deserved for seducing and killing his nephew. Undeterred, Olimpia went to work on other cardinals. "She never spoke of her brother-in-law but with much modesty, trying however with every effort imaginable to discover the sentiments that the other Cardinals had for him," Leti wrote.[14]

Olimpia also had to win the favor of foreign ambassadors, particularly those of France and Spain, who had a say in papal elections. It was a delicate diplomatic balancing act. If she too openly courted one faction, the other would oppose Gianbattista in conclave. According to Leti, "When she had occasion to converse with someone from the Spanish faction, she assured him of her brother-in-law's inclination for this crown. On the other hand, when she spoke to someone from the French crown, she never forgot to persuade him of the secret affection he had for their interests, saying that he could better advance them in secret than in the open."[15]

Fueled by the bloody battlefields of the Thirty Years' War, the dramatic rivalry between France and Spain convulsed Vatican politics, as well as daily life in Rome. Partisans of Spain hung the Spanish royal coat of arms over their doors, and their enemies, the supporters of France, hung the French fleur-de-lis. Both nations sought to attract with lucrative pensions the prelates and cardinals of the Roman court, and some cardinals switched loyalties frequently, depending on which crown offered them the most money. The Roman people were amused to find that sometimes a cardinal's palace would bear one coat of arms as the sun went down and the rival coat of arms when it rose. As word spread, people would gather to point fingers at the new coat of arms over the cardinal's door and laugh.

Such was the case of Cardinal Virginio Orsini, who, according to Teodoro Amayden's newsletter of August 1647, "was a Spaniard and on his palace he had the arms of the Catholic King. When his son died he became a Frenchman and shortly afterwards a Spaniard once more; at present he is French again—for how long no one knows."[16]

One day Cardinal Mario Teodoli went to Teodoro Amayden lamenting that he had never received anything from Spain and had large debts to pay. France was offering him a generous subsidy if he would place himself in the French camp. The fiercely pro-Spanish Amayden met with the top Spanish cardinal, Gil Alvarez Carillo de Albornoz, to see if something could be done, but Spain, alas, could not afford it. Cardinal Teodoli said, "Since the Spaniards don't want to help me, I have gone into the camp of the French, though reluctantly."[17]

The rivalry of France and Spain had so infiltrated Roman society that even clothing reflected one's preference. Women showed their support for France or Spain by the side on which they wore their hair ribbons—on the right of the head for Spain, on the left for France. Men showed their allegiance by the color of their stockings—red for France, white for Spain. The position of the feathers in their hats was also indicative of political preference—right for Spain, left for France. Even the cut of one's beard had a huge political significance. Cardinal Teodoli first signaled his approaching shift into the French camp by wearing his beard in the clipped, pointed French style. Sure enough, a few days later his palace bore the French coat of arms.

Openly advertising one's allegiance in the form of stockings and beards often resulted in tumults in the street. Men wearing red stockings, for instance, might attack a group wearing white stockings, which sometimes resulted in murder and days of riots. Some men chose black stockings simply to avoid being assaulted the moment they went out their doors.

It was not known whether Olimpia was pro-French or pro-Spanish, and it seems likely enough that Olimpia was pro-Olimpia. She didn't wear hair ribbons of any color, and her political leanings seemed impenetrable under her long black widow's weeds. She instilled in Gianbattista the need to show strict impartiality so that no one faction would oppose his election in the next conclave. And his red stockings, if they could ever be glimpsed beneath his long robes, were simply part of a cardinal's uniform.

The enmity between France and Spain was further complicated in 1640 when Portugal, which had been a Spanish state since the last Portuguese king died in 1580, rebelled against its heavy-handed overlords. The Portuguese found a relative of the last king and proclaimed him King John IV. Spain was horrified by the rebellion; losing the huge harbor of Lisbon and the colony of Brazil would reduce it to a second-rate power. The Spanish king sputtered angrily about treason and sent soldiers to regain the rebellious region. The French were delighted at the revolt and supported Portugal with men, arms, and money.

But Portugal's status depended greatly on being recognized internationally. After France recognized the new nation, there was a deafening silence. Portugal pushed for recognition from the Papal States and sent as ambassador the bishop of Lamego in the summer of 1642. The Spanish ambassador, the marquis de los Vélez, was so furious at Portuguese effrontery that on the night of August 20 he attacked the bishop's carriage in the streets of Rome with a group of armed men. Seven retainers died in the brawl, after which the French and Spanish ambassadors, and the Portuguese bishop, galloped out of Rome in a huff.

While the dispute over Portugal only ruffled diplomatic feathers, the pope's disagreement with the duke of Parma led to a costly war. Odoardo Farnese, duke of Parma and Piacenza, despised Prince Taddeo's insistence on precedence and felt irreparably insulted by the pope's upstart nephew. On a visit to Rome in 1639, he refused to cede precedence to Prince Taddeo and snubbed Anna Colonna publicly. One morning he even barged into Urban's Vatican bedroom, yanked open the papal bed curtains, and complained bitterly to the startled pontiff under the bedspread about the arrogance of his nephews.

This behavior reminded the pope that Odoardo owed the Papal States loans amounting to 1.5 million scudi. The Barberini nephews thought this was an excellent opportunity to become dukes themselves, seizing Farnese's tiny duchy of Castro as forfeit for the loans. Urban sent ten thousand troops under the command of Prince Taddeo to take Castro. Cardinal Antonio strapped on armor over his red robes and rode into battle. But the French, Venetians, Mantuans, and Tuscans gave financial support and troops to the duke of Parma. The pope found himself politically isolated, and the cost of the war strained the papal coffers beyond their capacity.

With the Vatican treasury bankrupt, the futile campaign ended on March 31, 1644, when France mediated an embarrassing peace in which everything was returned to the way it had been before the conflict. But the scorched earth of Umbria, the Romagna, and Ferrara—historically the most fertile regions of the Papal States—could not so easily be returned to its former state. Neither could the empty coffers of the Vatican treasury fill themselves up again as if the war had never happened. The pope had spent some twelve million gold scudi on his army, though many thought that the Barberini nephews had pocketed a large portion of this sum.

In all probability the humiliation of the war of Castro hastened the pope's death. On July 2, 1644, the seventy-six-year-old Urban VIII became alarmingly weak. Cardinal Francesco informed his uncle that there were eight vacancies in the Sacred College at the moment and suggested he stuff the conclave with Barberini friends. But Urban, who knew that quite soon he would be standing before a tribunal even greater than that which Galileo had faced, would not hear of it. He died on Friday, July 29.

The camerlengo, or chamberlain, of the Holy Roman Church, Cardinal Antonio Barberini, performed the ancient and solemn ritual that took place immediately after a pope's death. He hit the dead pope on the forehead three times with a silver hammer, each time calling his name. If the pope did not answer, the camerlengo solemnly announced, "The pope is dead."

Surely the cardinals gathered around the bed would have been shocked if the pope had sat bolt upright and cried out, "I am still here. Stop hitting me on the head with that hammer." But like all popes before and since who were whacked with the hammer, Urban lay still. The camerlengo then broke the papal fisherman's ring—the pontifical symbol of office—and officially reigned himself until the election of a new pope.

During Urban's final illness, his servants had, according to tradition, descended on the papal apartments like ravenous locusts. They stripped his rooms of everything not nailed down, with the exception of the bed, which they generously spared for the dying man. According to Teodoro Amayden, Urban VIII "died like the other popes, unhappily, without a holy candle to light, and after much searching one was found in the church of Saint Mary of the Spirit, and taken to him."[18]

The papal funeral was held in Saint Peter's Basilica, the church richly festooned inside and out with black cloth and brightly colored canvases depicting the papal coat of arms. It was customary for the deceased pontiff to be laid out on a bier directly above Saint Peter's grave, dressed in pontifical vestments, surrounded by an iron grill through which only his feet protruded. This was to allow the faithful to kiss the holy feet but not steal the richly embroidered vestments. Sometimes, though, the shoes went missing.

Along with thousands of Romans, Giacinto Gigli went to pay his respects to the deceased pontiff. "On Sunday, July 31, the body of Urban VIII was exposed in Saint Peter's for three days to a huge crowd of people," he wrote, "and there was a great tumult, and two men were killed and there was a great stink coming from the cadaver, very bad on the first day, and on the others there were many homicides."[19]

It is doubtful that Olimpia wasted time joining the throngs to see the stinky corpse. The moment she had been working toward for more than thirty years had finally come. Now was the time to get Gianbattista— and herself, of course—elected pope.

8

Conclave

No one takes this honor upon himself; he must
be called by God.

—Hebrews 5:4

O N THE FOURTH DAY after his death, Urban VIII was laid in a
casket of cypress, which was placed in a lead coffin engraved
with his name, his coat of arms, and the years of his reign. According to custom, before the coffin was sealed, a scroll listing the dead
pope's pious deeds was placed at his feet. It is not known when or why
this tradition began. Perhaps it was for the dead pontiff to read to Saint
Peter to convince him to open the pearly gates.

Interestingly, a sack of gold was also placed beside the pope's corpse,
probably a vestige of the ancient Greco-Roman tradition of putting a
coin on the mouth of the deceased to pay the ferryman to take his soul
over the River Styx. Urban, however, as a Catholic, would have used it
to pay the heavenly gatekeeper if he had remained unconvinced by the
list of pious deeds. Armed with the scroll and the gold to help him on
his journey, Urban was laid to rest in Saint Peter's Basilica beneath a
magnificent marble effigy of himself in pontifical robes, with his right
arm outstretched in blessing, a black winged skeleton crouched at his

feet. Only half finished at the pope's death, it was being sculpted by the incomparable Gian Lorenzo Bernini.

While the funeral solemnities, rich with music and incense, took place inside the church, in the streets of Rome violence broke out against the dead pope and his greedy family. *Papa Gabella,* they called Urban; Pope Tax. He had placed sixty-three new taxes on the Roman populace to support his nephews, and despite the increased taxation, at his death the Vatican treasury was nineteen million scudi in the red. Angry mobs raced around Rome with hammers, disfiguring as many Barberini bees as they could reach on fountains, walls, and bridges. Crowds waving hammers tried to hack to pieces the statue of Urban in front of the civic government building of the Campidoglio, but soldiers with guns and cannon successfully defended it.

Ferocious pasquinades were placed all over the city. Giacinto Gigli noted sadly, "The people vented against the dead pope and the Barberinis with injurious words, their pens writing every evil, and there were an infinite number of compositions published, some in Latin, some in Italian, some in prose and some in verse, so that I believe there was never anything like it. . . . If Christians treat the head of their own church this way, what will the Turks and Heretics do? . . . Many other verses were against the Cardinals, making fun of the customs, vices, inclinations, and defects of each one, especially those who aspired to be pope."[1]

For centuries, the vacant See had been a time of anarchy in Rome. Those wanting to settle an old score would wait for years if necessary to carry out the deed after the pope died, when the police were hopelessly overwhelmed with crime. Every morning bodies, many headless, appeared on the streets or floating down the Tiber.

Vacant See violence was exacerbated by the fact that upon a pope's death, prisoners were let out of jail in imitation of Pontius Pilate's freeing Barabas at the time of Jesus' crucifixion. Sometimes debtors didn't want to be released, knowing that their creditors were waiting just outside the prison door ready to beat them. The jailers would try to smoke the reluctant debtors out, accidentally suffocating some of them.

On the day of the pope's death, Giacinto Gigli, serving a stint as one of Rome's fourteen *caporioni*—a kind of city councilman—went into one prison himself carrying a ring of large keys to unlock the cell doors. A huge crowd had gathered on the square in front of the prison to watch Gigli, followed by soldiers, drummers, and prisoners, march pompously outside.

After their release, many of the more violent prisoners immediately formed gangs, which roamed the streets, broke into houses, plundered, raped, and murdered. The princely households barricaded themselves inside and hired armed guards to stand watch with loaded pistols and drawn swords. Servants patrolled the roof, ready to throw rocks at any would-be attackers below.

Merchants hid their merchandise, schools ceased instruction, and courts were suspended. The entire city pulsated with suspense, hoping that a new pontiff, and the order he would bring with him, would come soon. The liveliest places in Rome were the gambling parlors where people wagered on which cardinal would become pope, the odds changing daily as news leaked out of the conclave.

According to tradition, a conclave was to be held in the Vatican commencing on the tenth day after the pope's death. But the low-lying Vatican was ghastly in August and September, roasting hot, shirt-soakingly humid, and without a breath of fresh air. Worse, it was subject to malaria, as the area had been a swamp for thousands of years. When the Roman emperor Vitellius stationed his army on Vatican Hill in A.D. 69, most of his men died of malaria. Sixteen centuries later, the mosquitoes seemed to retain an ancient memory, buzzing happily about their ancestral abode and diving down with bloodlust at the sight of red robes.

The threat of infection was compounded by the utter ignorance about malaria's cause, which was thought to be *mal aria*—bad air. In his *Book on Particular Matters,* the thirteenth-century scholar Michael Scot described malaria as "a corruption of the air that is not evident everywhere, but which moves about hidden from region to region, then settles down and maintains itself."[2] In Olimpia's time, Scot's definition was still believed; it was not until 1880 that the parasite *Plasmodium* was found to be transmitted by mosquitoes.

Given the heat and risk of illness, many cardinals petitioned to move the conclave to the other Roman papal palace, the Quirinal, situated on a breezy hill. The conclave doctor agreed that the Vatican was a lethal choice due to "the miasmas and the danger of infection."[3] But Cardinal Antonio, who as camerlengo had the final decision, held his ground for a Vatican conclave out of respect for papal traditions. Realizing the health risks, most cardinals made their wills before reporting for duty.

A papal conclave was thought to be guided by the Holy Spirit, who would inspire the cardinals to select the man chosen by God. But Olimpia was leaving nothing up to the Holy Spirit. She had, in fact, been preparing for this moment for more than thirty years. She had buttered up the Spanish, courted the French, venerated the Barberinis, discreetly bribed the cardinals and flattered all of their female relatives. Having positioned her kings, queens, and bishops on her chessboard, she now placed her pawns—spies in the conclave and in the houses of the French and Spanish ambassadors.

Leti wrote, "Due to the vacant See at the death of Urban, Donna Olimpia threw herself into keeping watch over all things carefully, and into making the most extreme effort to discover the intrigues, the plotting, and the intentions of the cardinals and ambassadors with regards to the election of a new pope. And even though she had a natural stinginess, she didn't fail to spend a great deal on spies to be well aware of all things. She staged a campaign to inform herself of the least intrigue from here or there and made every effort possible to learn what was happening."[4]

With an eye to a checkmate, right before the conclave Olimpia gave precise instructions to Gianbattista. Leti continued: "The evening they entered the conclave, Cardinal Pamfili spoke a long time with his sister-in-law, but I have never been able to discover exactly what passed between them."[5]

The conclave was preceded by the sound of hammering echoing from the Vatican halls as carpenters boarded up all windows in the cardinals' area. They left a couple of inches open at the top to let in a little humid air, swarms of mosquitoes, and a faint beam of light; candles would be used throughout the day. The boarding up of windows was supposed to prevent cardinals from making gestures or signs or giving messages of any kind to the outside world.

Though supposedly sealed off from communication with those out-side, the conclave leaked like a sieve and would continue to do so until Pope Pius X enforced absolute secrecy in 1904. Until then journalists and diplomats wrote daily newsletters with conclave updates, reporting with uncanny accuracy on who had voted for whom. Cardinal Antonio Barberini routinely corresponded with the French ambassador, the marquis de Saint-Chamond, who sent back replies. And Olimpia re-ceived frequent reports from Gianbattista, friendly cardinals, and their servants, and responded with new instructions.

Messages were often smuggled in and out of conclave in food plat-ters. Meals were brought in twice daily by the cardinal's household ser-vants, who marched in stately procession carrying large silver bowls swinging from wooden poles. Having arrived at the door assigned for food deliveries, they handed over the bowls to the guards, who were supposed to examine all platters and wine bottles for secret messages going in and out. But the guards often cast a careless glance at the vict-uals, even more careless than usual if a handsome tip was offered. In-structions to the cardinals were hidden among the roasted gizzards in a duck's body cavity, or tucked under the crust of a chicken pie. Cardinals replied by concealing messages in the secret compartment of a silver salad bowl returned for washing, or in a hollowed-out wine cork.

Cardinals lived in "cells," hastily constructed rooms ranging from about fifteen feet to twenty-two feet square. In the late fifteenth and early sixteenth centuries, when there were fewer than twenty-five con-clave cardinals, the cells had been built in the Sistine Chapel itself, where votes were cast in front of the main altar. But now that the Sa-cred College had been expanded to a maximum of seventy cardinals, the cells were built in the hall next door. Placed over each cell was a let-ter of the alphabet or two; after the letter Z came AA, AB, and so on. Before the conclave opened, cardinals had to draw letters out of a chal-ice to determine which cell would be theirs. This was to prevent squab-bling over the bigger cells.

As soon as Gianbattista learned the location of his cell, his servants would have hung all the walls with beautiful cloth—purple for cardi-nals who had been created by the just-deceased pope, as Gianbattista had been, and green for the others. The cells were built without roofs but were covered with a canopy, which could be opened for air circulation or closed for greater privacy. The servants would then have set up his bed, tables, chamber-pot chair, writing desk, stools, a chest with his clothing, books, washbasins, a little stove to reheat cold food, and eating utensils.

Each cardinal was allowed to have two servants, or *conclavistas,* who slept with him in his cell. Old, sick cardinals were permitted three. These servants were invaluable to their masters. They tidied their cells, served their food, cleaned their clothes, and emptied their chamber pots. But far more important than these mundane matters, *conclavistas* were their masters' eyes and ears. They performed tasks undignified for a prince of the church yet absolutely necessary all the same, such as peering through keyholes or placing an ear firmly against a thin wooden cell wall to listen to the conversation inside. Hidden in the shadows, they watched which cardinals visited one another. They often wore disguises at night—false beards, mustaches, or bulbous noses—and ghosted around from cell to cell negotiating with other cardinals on behalf of their masters.

Conclavistas spread false rumors, lied, flattered, and offered bribes to other servants for information. They smuggled letters in and out and sent news to the bookies to set odds on which cardinal would be elected pope. Armed with their inside knowledge, most *conclavistas* placed high wagers of their own, reaping a fortune when their favorite was elected. A cardinal chose his *conclavistas* from among his household servants, who eagerly sought the exciting, remunerative position. Among the emoluments was the right to sack the new pope's cell as soon as he was elected.

On the evening of August 8, 1644, singing hymns and saying prayers, fifty-five cardinals processed into the Vatican. Due to recent deaths, the Sacred College numbered only sixty-two, with seven cardinals living abroad; one of these, the nuncio to Madrid, was racing back to Rome and would join the conclave three days later. Other than the three Spaniards, two Frenchmen, and one German taking part in the conclave, the rest were Italians.

The very first evening, Urban VIII's brother, the cardinal of Saint Onofrio, was involved in a message-smuggling scandal. The good cardinal had evidently bribed a mason to make a hole in the outer wall of his cell through which he could pass messages too long and detailed to be hidden inside the tiny secret compartment of a food platter. While many cardinals smuggled messages, they all denied doing so and eagerly pointed fingers when their enemies were proven to be leaking news. And it was always the laborers, never the cardinals, who got arrested for the security breach. Giacinto Gigli reported, "There was discovered in his room a hole that gave onto the court of the Belvedere and therefore the cardinals of the opposing faction made a great noise about it and the hole was walled up, and they say that a mason was put in prison."[6]

Having settled into their cells, the cardinals met with various ambassadors for negotiations the next day. The French ambassador visited the cardinals individually or in small groups, advocating the favored candidates of Cardinal Jules Mazarin, prime minister of France. The impoverished Italian-born Giulio Mazzarino had worked his way up the church hierarchy in France by climbing into the widowed queen mother's bed. Since her husband's death in 1643, the dim-witted Anne of Austria supposedly ruled for her young son Louis XIV; but it was the luxurious Mazarin—mercurial, brilliant, and crafty—who held the power.

Five months before Pope Urban died, Mazarin heard of his steep decline and sent precise instructions to his ambassador regarding papal candidates. Mazarin's first choice was the sixty-five-year-old Cardinal Guido Bentivoglio, who for many years had been nuncio to France. His second choice was Cardinal Giulio Sacchetti, who at fifty-eight suffered the drawback of youth but was very friendly toward France. There was one other candidate Mazarin named. "As for Cardinal Pamphili," he thundered, "His Majesty cannot in any way consent that his ministers concur to his exaltation and orders them to oppose him by all means possible, first in secret, but overtly if necessary. He is a man who has given all his affections to Spain, and who has lost no occasion to give proofs that he has an aversion to France."[7]

Mazarin was incorrect in accusing Gianbattista Pamphili of blindly supporting Spain. Gianbattista was careful and just in all his proceedings and never rashly jumped to the side of Spain as did so many cardinals, even when he was nuncio to Madrid. Yet Mazarin could not forget that Gianbattista had been popular with the archenemies of France during his time in Spain. Additionally, those at the French court who remembered the cardinal during his 1625 mission to Paris recalled that his personality—awkward, severe, and cautious—greatly reminded them of their enemies the Spaniards.

Mazarin also sent instructions to Antonio Barberini, the cardinal protector of France. If Pamphili were to obtain a significant block of votes in conclave, Antonio was to announce that France had officially excluded him. An exclusion was not legally binding, and the cardinals could technically decide to ignore it. But if they did so, they would doubtless incur the anger of a major Catholic power against themselves personally—meaning the loss of the cardinals' revenues from that nation. Worse, the church herself might be penalized. The offended nation could withhold church revenues from Rome, or wage war, or, worst of all, pull a Henry VIII and cut ties with the Vatican altogether. Exclusions continued through the 1903 conclave, when Emperor Franz Josef of Austria derailed the election of the popular Cardinal Rampolla del Tindaro.

But then, as now, money spoke louder than threats. Mazarin sent sacks of gold to two friendly cardinals to distribute to fellow electors who seemed to be vacillating. Cardinal Alessandro Bichi reportedly received sixteen thousand scudi to hand out as bribes. The cardinal of Lyons received six thousand scudi and letters that he was to pass out in conclave, dictated by Mazarin but signed by the six-year-old king of France, discreetly offering more.

"My cousin," the letters read, "I have been so particularly informed of the affection that you hold for the advantage of this crown that I cannot prevent myself from showing my sentiments. If you have some good desires, you could explain them in all liberty and confidence to the marquis de Saint-Chamond."[8]

Not to be outdone by the French, the new Spanish ambassador, the count of Sirvela, arrived in Rome just as the conclave was about to begin. Teodoro Amayden accompanied Sirvela as he strode into the Sistine Chapel blazing in diamonds and fortified with rich Spanish bishoprics to bestow on cooperative cardinals, lovely princesses with huge dowries to give away to their nephews, and fine estates in the kingdom of Naples. And Spain's favorite candidate? Gianbattista Pamphili, who had left a good impression behind him after his embassy to Madrid fourteen years earlier. His stiff and sober dignity, which grated on Italians and Frenchmen alike, was most pleasing to Spaniards.

Swords were drawn along the usual French and Spanish lines before the conclave even began. Leti didn't mince words about the self-interested politics involved in choosing the Vicar of Christ. "Neither did the cardinals examine the virtues or vices of the competitors," he fumed. "Spain would exalt anyone, were he the wickedest man in the world or even the devil himself, as long as he was the enemy of France. The French would not worry about worshipping a demon, as long as he was the enemy of Spain. The nephews of the dead pope, guarding their own interests, would not bat an eye to advance a cardinal to the pontificate if he were the most detestable of all men, or even the Anti-Christ himself, as long as he was their friend."[9]

By midnight on August 9, the camerlengo, Antonio Barberini, cried, *"Omnes extra!"* at the top of his lungs, and all the wheeling, dealing ambassadors were forced to leave. The conclave had officially begun.

The first centuries of Christianity remain so shrouded in mystery that no one is certain how the earliest popes were elected. Saint Peter, later acknowledged as the first pope, had no throne, no incense-laden ceremonies, no great basilicas, and little Catholic dogma. Going house to house in a rough linen robe and sandals, Peter spread the word about his friend Jesus who had been crucified years before. Highly respected for his personal knowledge of Jesus, Peter was perhaps called an elder—a term that was later translated into *bishop*—or perhaps an apostle or a disciple. He was certainly not called pope, a term that was not used until some time in the second century when all bishops received the honorary title of *papa,* or father. Pope Siricius (reigned 384–399) was the first pontiff to claim that title for himself alone, though bishops in the Eastern Empire kept it until 1059.

According to tradition, Peter, knowing he would be martyred, appointed his successor, Linus, to tend his little flock of ragtag Christians in Rome. It is possible that dozens of popes after Peter also named their successors. When Christianity was legalized in the fourth century, the Roman senate, the clergy, and the people of Rome participated in the bishop's election, though we are at a loss to understand exactly how voting was done by such an unruly crowd.

In the first millennium of Christianity, any churchman, even a simple monk or priest, could be elected pope. But after Pope Nicholas II decreed in 1059 that only cardinals could elect the pontiff, they usually elected one of themselves, and since 1389 they have always done so.

Just as the papal election process changed over the centuries, so did the qualities required to be pontiff. In Christianity's first centuries the perfect pope was a man of deep faith who would willingly suffer martyrdom at the hands of pagan Roman emperors in their periodic persecutions. Given the likelihood of being thrown to the lions, there were fewer candidates for the position. Once Constantine legalized Christianity, the church became big business and more men vied for the job. Now the pope was a CEO; he must possess top administrative skills to spread the faith, appoint church leaders, build churches, manage money, and develop dogma.

When the last Roman emperor abdicated in A.D. 476, the remaining emperor was in far-off Constantinople. Sometimes he sent troops to help Rome, but more often he did nothing, having enough problems to deal with closer to home. As a result, the Roman people looked to the only authority figure in town—the pope—to perform the duties of a secular official. Instead of focusing on religion, the pope was now expected to feed the hungry, police the unruly, provide laws, and fend off invading barbarian hordes. Over the course of the next millennium, several popes strapped on armor and rode into battle against enemies.

By the Renaissance, the ideal pope was supposed to encourage the arts and letters. Nicholas V (reigned 1447–1455) founded the Vatican

Library, collecting moldering Greek manuscripts from across Europe and preserving a significant portion of the ancient literature we have today from being lost forever. The world's greatest artistic masterpieces—those by Raphael, Michelangelo, Bernini, and countless others—were commissioned by popes to glorify God and themselves. By the seventeenth century most pontiffs had legal training and diplomatic experience, abilities required to remain aloft in the shifting sands of baroque European politics.

The ideal candidate was rather advanced in years. Though John XI was eighteen or twenty when elected in 931, and Benedict IX was a teenager when chosen in 1032, by the Renaissance older cardinals were preferred for their wisdom and experience in church affairs. But the real reason for electing an elderly pope was the ambitions of the cardinals. If the new pope died sooner rather than later, the cardinals who elected him would have another chance to become pope themselves. It was a terrifying prospect for one man to hog the papal power for decades, depriving other worthy men of their chance, and the seventeenth century had already witnessed two such debacles. Paul V had had the bad taste to reign from 1605 to 1621, dashing the hopes of many meritorious sons of the church, and Urban VIII selfishly lived for twenty-one years after his election.

What was the perfect age for a new pope? By Olimpia's time, sixty was viewed as a venerable age, and cardinals under sixty were generally considered too young for the job. Younger cardinals, however, could be elected if their health was poor. In 1513 Cardinal Giovanni de' Medici became Pope Leo X at the age of thirty-seven, a teenager in terms of papal candidates. The young cardinal brought into the conclave his surgeon, who glumly informed the other cardinals that the candidate had few years to live, and he was immediately elected. In 1585 Cardinal Felice Peretti won the election by pretending to be weak and ill, coughing and hobbling around painfully with the aid of a cane, hoping to win the votes of the cardinals who wanted a short pontificate. Once he was elected, Sixtus V cast away the stick and rose before the astonished cardinals glowing with healthy vigor.

Even an elderly candidate would be considered unsuitable if he had several brothers itching for huge salaries and government positions, a dozen unmarried nephews hoping to be created cardinals and run the church, and a flock of sisters salivating over social status, palaces, and large dowries for their single daughters to marry into the highest echelon of Roman nobility. Such a pope would, within a few years, wrest most of the power, and all of the money, out of the hands of the cardinals and into the pockets of his own family. A cardinal with a throng of grasping relatives was highly unlikely to be elected pope, even if he possessed the most sterling qualifications to run the church.

At seventy, Cardinal Pamphili was considered healthy enough to live the requisite six or seven years and old enough to die shortly thereafter. He offered the great advantage of having three dead brothers and two sisters safely locked up in convents and sworn to poverty. He had only two nieces by Olimpia, one of whom was already married, and one nephew, who, though not terribly bright, was not known for greed, ambition, licentiousness, or free spending. And Gianbattista's dignity was a great point in his favor. Ambassador Contarini of Venice reported, "Many thought he was worthy of the pontificate because his words were few and weighty, which made people believe he was really wise."[10]

Despite these advantages, some cardinals heatedly expressed their dislike of both Gianbattista's appearance and personality. Cardinal Antonio Barberini described Gianbattista's character as "rigid and bitter." Another Venetian diplomat, Giustiniani, noted, "Some were offended by his dismal and saturnine aspect, the reflection of a contumacious and restless soul, and in him one could see customs poorly suited to the placidity that the person carrying the name of the universal father should have."[11]

Gregorio Leti was, as usual, crueler in his explanation. He asserted, "There were several reasons why Cardinal Pamfili was not desired by many people as I can well say. His poor expression, his somber sad air, and his ugly badly formed face made people take him for a bizarre and uncomfortable soul. Many took the occasion to say that it would not be good to make a universal father, a pope, who had a face so horrible and deformed that it scared the children."[12]

Gianbattista's looks aside, the specter of Olimpia hovered uneasily over the conclave. Ambassador Giustiniani had heard the gossip that the cardinal and his sister-in-law were sleeping together. He wrote, "Others were aware of the fact that the pontificate would be subject to female influence due to the boundless affection the cardinal showed his sister-in-law, absolute arbiter of all the most serious affairs that concerned the interests of his family, not without the opinion that his deeply rooted affection involved more than platonic sympathies, which was a very important point, considering the vehement spirits of that lady."[13]

Cardinal Antonio complained of the "cupidity and haughtiness of his sister-in-law."[14] He deplored the likelihood that despite Gianbattista's advanced age, his robust constitution would keep him alive for years, with Olimpia at the helm of the Vatican.

Francesco Mantovani, the ambassador of Modena, summed up Gianbattista's strong points: he was highly educated, hardworking, and just. But he added that Gianbattista would surely be handicapped in conclave by his "coarseness of spirit and the greed of the sister-in-law."[15]

What the diplomats and cardinals were complaining about was not so much Olimpia's character but that such a character should be encased in a female body. If Olimpia were Gianbattista's brother-in-law instead of his sister-in-law, her clever accumulation of power and wealth would have been lauded. As a man, Olimpia would have been a remarkable asset to any Holy Father. As a woman, she was his greatest vulnerability.

The casting of votes in conclave has a special name: a scrutiny. Twice a day, morning and afternoon, cardinals would anonymously write the name of a candidate on a folded piece of paper, disguising their handwriting, and toss it into a chalice in front of Michelangelo's daunting *Last Judgment,* which was splayed across the wall behind the altar of the Sistine Chapel. Visions of tortured souls being dragged to hell served as a constant reminder of what was in store for cardinals who voted selfishly and not according to the inspiration of the Holy Spirit.

Cardinal Antonio was confident of getting Mazarin's candidate, Cardinal Sacchetti, elected. But according to the old saying, "He who enters the conclave a pope, leaves it a cardinal."[16] And indeed, the only thing predictable about a conclave was its unpredictability.

From the moment voting began on the morning of August 10 to the end of the month, the Barberinis did everything possible to elect Cardinal Sacchetti pope. But repeatedly the Spanish cardinal, Albornoz, rose and cried that His Most Catholic Majesty, King Philip IV, knowing Sacchetti's ardent affinity for France, had excluded him. During the meetings held in between the scrutinies, and in late-night visits to cardinals' cells, the Barberinis used every method they knew to get the cardinals to ignore the exclusion—cajoling, bribing, and threatening—but to no avail.

The Barberinis asked the confessor of the conclave, the Jesuit theologian Vantino Magnoni, if such an exclusion were legal. With furrowed brow, the priest nodded, stating that while an exclusion was an interference, the will of so powerful a monarch as the king of Spain must be heeded or else evil could befall Christ's church.

Day after day of fruitless voting passed in the stifling heat. Hygiene deteriorated. Those locked inside the murky tomb were overwhelmed by the smells of body odor, urine, and excrement. Even worse, the mosquitoes began to bite. On August 27 two cardinals and five *conclavistas* declared themselves "incommoded," subject to projectile vomiting, migraines, diarrhea, and high fever.

Terrified of contagion spreading like wildfire in the enclosed space, the cardinals shifted uncomfortably. Given the stalemate over Sacchetti, they would need to elect another candidate if they were to leave the conclave alive. Some cardinals began to speak of Cardinal Pamphili. Stern, dignified, learned, with decades of church legal and diplomatic experience, surely he would make an acceptable pope?

The mosquitoes were on Olimpia's side. Receiving daily reports of the cardinals' discussions and moods from her conclave spies, Olimpia knew that opinion was moving toward Gianbattista. One day, waiting in her Piazza Navona palace for news from the Vatican, she received a sign from the Holy Spirit itself.

Olimpia's three-year-old granddaughter, Olimpiuccia, saw a white dove flying through the upstairs corridor. Delighted, the little girl chased it from room to room until it flew into the bedroom of Cardinal

Pamphili and perched on the canopy over his four-poster. Hearing the child's cries, Olimpia and some servants ran to find her. To their shock, they saw the white dove on Gianbattista's bed, flapping its wings, cooing, and blinking at them. All of them knew the story of how a swarm of bees—the bee was the symbol of the Barberini family—had entered the conclave of 1623 and hovered over Cardinal Barberini's cell just before he was elected. The dove, the symbol of the Pamphili family and of the Holy Spirit, which directs papal elections, had clearly been sent by God to indicate that Cardinal Gianbattista Pamphili would be the next pope.

Armed with such a sign from heaven, Olimpia played her hand. The only person still blocking Gianbattista's election was his old enemy Cardinal Antonio Barberini. She was well aware that Antonio was terrified that the family of an unfriendly new pope would prosecute the family of the old pope for stealing Vatican funds, a tradition that had existed for centuries. He also feared losing his political power, being pushed back to the ranks of unimportant cardinals.

In a message smuggled in to Antonio, Olimpia reassured him on both points. If he swung his block of votes to Cardinal Pamphili, Olimpia would have her twenty-two-year-old son, Camillo, marry Antonio's niece, the fourteen-year-old Lucrezia Barberini. This marriage would ensure the alliance and mutual support of the two papal families and offered the added advantage that the Barberinis could keep their powerful positions. By marrying Lucrezia, Camillo would give up any chance of being cardinal nephew and ousting the brothers.

Seeing the impossibility of electing his friend Sacchetti, Antonio was tempted by Olimpia's offer. He smuggled a message out to the French ambassador floating the idea. The marquis de Saint-Chamond replied with icy politeness, "I would like at the expense of my own blood to favor the exaltation of Pamphili, as much as for the esteem I have for his person and the particular affection I have had for him for twenty years, as for the respect of Your Excellency and to conform to your wishes which will always be law to me, *but it is impossible to go against the intentions of the King.*"[17] And so the stalemate continued.

On August 29, Cardinal Bentivoglio took to his bed with a raging fever, soaking his sheets in sweat. The other cardinals recalled that in the last conclave, that of 1623, eight cardinals had died of malaria along with forty *conclavistas*. On August 30, only twelve cardinals voted for Sacchetti, a far cry from the thirty-seven votes he needed for a two-thirds majority. In the afternoon scrutiny, Cardinal Francesco Cennini, an avowed enemy of the Barberinis and ardent supporter of Spain, got twenty-five votes from cardinals willing to elect a moron to escape the infected conclave with their lives. Antonio Barberini was stunned. Cennini would be far worse for the interests of France and the Barberini family than even Pamphili.

On September 2, Francesco Barberini became feverish but insisted on staying in conclave to vote. On September 4, Antonio wrote Saint-Chamond that Sacchetti's election was no longer possible. The other French candidate, Cardinal Bentivoglio, was dying of malaria. The only cardinal who stood a chance was Gianbattista Pamphili. If Pamphili promised to bestow significant favors on France—allowing Mazarin to name his candidates for cardinals, for instance, granting rich benefices to Mazarin's relatives, and other concessions, would Mazarin withdraw the exclusion?

Cardinal Alessandro Bichi, an avid friend of France, was furious at Antonio's capitulation, crying that he would die in conclave rather than vote for an enemy of France. He pointed out that no matter what Cardinal Pamphili promised France, once he was elected pope no one could force him to keep his promises. Over the centuries, countless cardinals had made generous promises to get elected, even swearing oaths on the Bible; but as pope they simply changed their minds, declaring such oaths invalid because they had been made under duress.

Faced with Cardinal Antonio's eager proposal and Bichi's warning, Saint-Chamond, the eternal diplomat, hedged. He asked Antonio to wait for twenty days before switching his votes to Pamphili, during which time he would send a courier posthaste to Mazarin asking if he wished to change his instructions. Antonio waited uneasily. Then, on September 7, Cardinal Bentivoglio died wretchedly in his cell. On the morning of September 10, Cardinal Gaspare Matthei was carried out of the conclave semiconscious, followed that evening by the vomiting Cardinal Giulio

Gabrielli. The electors were dropping like flies, and those cardinals who remained healthy were gripped by malaria hysteria.

While Olimpia was Gianbattista's most ardent supporter outside the conclave, his greatest champion inside was fifty-seven-year-old Giovanni Giacomo Panciroli. The son of a humble tailor, the intelligent Panciroli had worked his way up in the church and attached himself to Gianbattista's coattails. He had assisted him in the Roman Rota and in his missions to Naples and Spain. He had become a cardinal in 1643 in Urban's last creation and was named nuncio to Madrid. Hearing of the pope's fatal illness, he rushed back to Rome, arriving in conclave three days after it began. Pro-Spanish and pro-Pamphili, Panciroli would do everything possible to get his friend elected pope.

According to Teodoro Amayden, Cardinal Panciroli saw Cardinal Antonio's wavering. One day he approached him with flattering words. "See, Antonio, how fortune has carried you to high places," Panciroli said. "But this is nothing compared to what you can do today. . . . On you alone the Sacred College depends. You alone can create the pontiff."[18]

The idea appealed to Cardinal Antonio. For one moment, he would be more powerful than the pope himself; he would be the *pope maker,* the very instrument of God, crowning Saint Peter's successor. He suddenly decided that it would be better not to wait for Mazarin's decision. It was, after all, easier to apologize later than to ask permission and then act expressly against orders. If the decision was positive, all would be well. If it were negative, he had arranged to switch sides to Spain, and the Spanish ambassador promised to provide him with revenue equal to that which had been lost from France.

On the morning of September 14, Cardinal Antonio met with the cardinals of the Spanish faction and agreed to switch his block of votes to support their candidate, Gianbattista Pamphili. That evening, some fifty cardinals crammed into Gianbattista's cell to congratulate him, though many were forced to yell their good wishes from the corridor. As soon as they departed, their *conclavistas* squeezed inside to render their respects. "There was such a multitude of people in that cell," wrote an anonymous *conclavista,* "that they stole all his silverware."[19]

That night, Cardinal Antonio and the pro-Spanish cardinals set their spies to watch the cells of the pro-French cardinals to see if they were plotting a coup. Worried about a last-minute surprise, Cardinal Antonio called for the morning scrutiny to be held much earlier than usual, at dawn.

At 3 A.M. Gianbattista sent a messenger from the conclave to bang on the door of Olimpia's palazzo and give her the news of his imminent election. Standing in their nightclothes holding candles, she and Camillo received the message "with great pleasure," according to the 1650 autobiography of Cardinal Domenico Cecchini.[20] Gregorio Leti described "the transports of joy of Donna Olimpia. She was so beside herself with happiness that she seemed to be only 25 years old, although she was closer to 50."[21] (She was actually fifty-three.)

On September 15, as the sun rose over the Vatican, cardinals rubbing the sleep from their eyes stumbled into the Sistine Chapel. According to the diary of one *conclavista,* Gianbattista had not slept at all, "partly out of happiness and partly out of fear."[22] Now he bounced up and down nervously on his seat. "All your cardinals, are they there?" he asked the Spanish cardinal, Albornoz, who sat next to him. "Yes, they are there," was the reply. "Your Eminence must have good courage."[23]

One by one, the cardinals marched up to the altar and cast their votes into the chalice. When the votes were tallied, there was an overwhelming majority for Gianbattista. With one cardinal dead and two others sick at home, he had only needed thirty-six votes to win, but forty-eight of the fifty-three cardinals left in conclave had voted for him. Five cardinals, including the fulminating Cardinal Bichi, had voted against him.

Having counted the votes, the distinguished theologian Cardinal Juan de Lugo rose to his feet and said in a loud voice, "*Benedictus Dominus Noster, habemus cardinalem Pamphilium Pontifecum.*" Our Blessed Lord, we have Cardinal Pamphili as pope.[24]

Appalled at the choice of new pontiff, Cardinal Bichi raced back to his cell and fired off a letter to the court of France. "Gentlemen," he thundered, "we have just elected a female pope!"[25]

Part Two

THE FEMALE POPE

9

The Vicar of Christ

Here I am at the end of the road and the top of the heap.

—Pope John XXIII

U PON HEARING THAT Cardinal Gianbattista Pamphili was their new pope, all the other cardinals fell to their knees in adoration while their *conclavistas* rushed to his cubicle to sack it. Clothing, books, inkwells, quill pens, chamber pots and cook pots, sheets and pillows—everything was stripped bare in a matter of moments.

Cardinal Bernardino Spada asked Gianbattista which name he would like to take, and the new pontiff thoughtfully replied he would like to be called Pope Eugenio. But some of the cardinals reminded him that the last Pope Eugenio had been chased out of Rome in 1434 by angry citizens who threw rocks at his rowboat from the Tiber bridges. To avoid being stoned, the Vicar of Christ had to crawl under a shield in the bottom of the boat. Eugenio was, perhaps, an inauspicious name.

Gianbattista then proposed the name that his friend Cardinal Panciroli had suggested the night before—Innocent, Innocenzo in Italian. It was thought that he had selected this name because in the 1480s his ancestors had risen in prestige by serving Pope Innocent

VIII. But Roman wits would say he wanted to pretend he was innocent of sexual relations with his sister-in-law.

The canopies over the cardinals' stalls were lowered, and only that of
the new pope remained aloft. He was conducted behind the Sistine
Chapel altar to take off his cardinal's robes and put on the robes of a
pope. While cardinals usually wore a red robe, the *sottana,* since the
thirteenth century popes had worn a bright white one, the color of holiness and resurrection. Like cardinals, the pope wore a magnificent
white shirt of finest linen edged with lace, the rochet, over the *sottana.*
When Innocent went behind the altar, he found *sottanas* and rochets in
various sizes laid out for him to choose from.

The cardinals placed a red satin elbow-length capelet, the mozzetta,
over Innocent's white robe. In winter, the mozzetta would be red velvet,
lined with ermine. A red satin hat, the *camauro,* was placed on his head.
It was not like the three-peaked biretta of the cardinal but fit tightly at
the hairline and rose straight up for several inches.

Innocent emerged from behind the high altar in full pontifical dignity and sat on the papal throne. Members of the Sistine Chapel choir,
who had been waiting in the wings for precisely this moment, filed in
as their angelic voices filled the sacred space. One by one the cardinals
knelt before Pope Innocent X to kiss his feet and right hand. He bid
each one to rise and gave the ancient Christian kiss of peace on both
cheeks.

In Saint Peter's Square, a crowd had been waiting expectantly for
weeks, crammed into a piazza half its current width and ringed by a
jumble of barracks. There were two signs that a pope had been elected—
the bells of Saint Peter's would ring out in jubilation, and carpenters
would demolish the masonry that blocked the windows of the loggia
overlooking Saint Peter's Square. The tradition of sending smoke out of
the Sistine Chapel chimney after each scrutiny—black for an unsuc-
cessful vote, white for a successful one—was not instituted until 1903.

The bells began to ring, followed by the sounds of carpenters tearing out the boards. It was the task of the senior cardinal deacon to appear at the loggia of benediction to announce the great news to the
expectant crowd below. But Cardinal Carlo de' Medici was writhing in

such throbbing pain from a gouty toe that he was unable to perform the coveted duty. The second deacon, Cardinal Francesco Barberini, had recovered from his mild bout with malaria and would make the announcement.

But before he arrived, one of the workmen opening up the windows poked his head outside and grinned at the crowd.

"Who is it?" the people demanded.

"Innocenzo," he replied.

But the roar of the crowd and the ringing of bells muffled the carpenter's reply. Some people thought he had said "Crescenzio." Many of them raced to Cardinal Pier Paolo Crescenzi's palace and sacked it thoroughly, to the great delight of his family, who took this as proof that he had been made pope. Others, seeing boards pried free of Vatican entrances, raced into the palace to sack the cardinals' cells and brawled with the *conclavistas* guarding them.

At 1 P.M. Cardinal Francesco and Signor Domenico Belli, the papal master of ceremonies, singing "Ecclesiasticus Sacerdus Magnus," preceded the pope to the loggia of benediction. The bells ceased. The crowd waited breathlessly as silence pulsated. Cardinal Francesco appeared at the window and took a deep breath.

"Annuncio vobis gaudium magnum," he said, *"habemus Papam Eminentissimum et Reverendissimum, Don Iohannem Baptistum Pamphilium, qui sibi nomen imposuit Innocentium Decimum."*[1] We announce to you with great joy that we have a pope, the most eminent and most reverent Don Gianbattista Pamphili, who will take the name Innocent X.

The new pope appeared next to Cardinal Francesco and blessed the people gathered below. His gesture of benediction was greeted by a blare of trumpets and the cheers of the crowd. Across from Saint Peter's, looming over the Tiber, was the Castel Sant'Angelo, built as the tomb of Emperor Hadrian (reigned A.D. 117–138) but converted by the early popes into an impregnable fortress. Now cannon poking out from the crenellated bastion blasted loud salutes, a signal to every church bell in Rome to peal its joy once more.

The crowd was pleased that the new pontiff was a Roman, one of them. They hated foreign popes and had had bad luck with them. The horrifying Spaniard Rodrigo Borgia terrified Italy as Pope Alexander VI from 1492 to 1503, carving out an empire for his psychopathic son, the murderer and rapist Cesare, who rode boldly to battle wearing a black velvet mask to hide the fact that syphilis had eaten away his nose. The cheap and boring Dutchman Adrian Florensz, elected Pope Adrian VI in 1522, cut back on pageants and festivities and had the nerve to insist that Romans comport themselves with Christian morals and that women cover up their bosoms. When he died after a reign of only twenty months, someone hung a sign on his doctor's front door that read SAVIOR OF THE COUNTRY.

Italian popes were all right—those from Genoa or Siena, Venice or Milan. But only Romans truly understood Rome. It was far preferable to have a pope born and bred in Rome, and Gianbattista Pamphili was certainly one of their own, born in the old house on the Piazza Navona where his family had lived since 1470.

But Giacinto Gigli wrote in his diary that evening, "When they heard that it was Pope Pamphilio, the crowd did not celebrate so much, because he was held to be a severe man, and not very liberal."[2] Worse, he added, "It is believed that the widow called Olimpia, of the house of Maidalchini, will be the dominatrix of this pontificate."[3]

Olimpia was the true pope maker. She had made Gianbattista a nuncio, a cardinal, and now the Vicar of Christ. Without her he would probably still have been languishing in the Rota. Coming after thirty-two years of her hard work, his election must have been the sweetest victory of Olimpia's life. Now the Roman noblewomen would have to wait outside for her carriage. But even better than that, perhaps for the first time ever Olimpia felt safe. Now she had enough power, and enough wealth, so that no one would ever push her around again or suggest she enter a convent.

When the looters realized that the new pope was not Cardinal Crescenzi but Cardinal Pamphili, they stashed their ill-gotten goods and raced to Olimpia's house on the Piazza Navona. And it was Olimpia herself who threw the bolt and swung open the twenty-foot double doors into her courtyard, smiling graciously and bidding the mob welcome.

She could afford to be gracious because she had removed every stick of decent furniture, all the rich draperies and bed hangings, the priceless portraits and tapestries, and the silverware. It would have taken countless cartloads to transport her valuables to another location, perhaps to a neighbor's house, and she must have sent them off early in the conclave, just in case.

"Her avarice was so great that she removed and hid the most beautiful and best furnishings," Leti informs us.[4] The looters found only mediocre furniture, which Olimpia had possibly purchased at the weekly flea market, where Jews sold old rugs, wobbly chairs, and scratched tables. Carrying these disappointing items out into the Piazza Navona, the mob murmured, "The whore has cheated us."[5] Leti wrote, "Since that time the people—who didn't find anything good—began to conceive very bad sentiments for her and to esteem her extremely greedy."[6]

That evening, Olimpia and Camillo called on the pope. Protocol demanded that the first time a visitor was granted a papal audience, he or she kneel and kiss the pope's red velvet slippers embossed with gold crosses. Olimpia knelt but started to guffaw as she kissed her brother-in-law's feet. Innocent, for his part, was so overcome with emotion by what this woman had done for him that tears slid down his cheeks. He "received her with an extraordinary demonstration of love and affection."[7]

Olimpia then marched through the pope's rooms as if she were the mistress of the household. She issued orders to the servants to move the furniture around. She even plopped down on the pope's bed to "examine whether it was well made."[8]

A rush of visitors descended on the Palazzo Pamphili to congratulate Olimpia. She was now the first lady of Rome, and suddenly they called her Your Excellency and referred to her as *eccellentissima cognata,* "the most excellent sister-in-law."

"Donna Olimpia received so many visits that it is almost impossible to believe," Leti wrote. "One saw a crowd of ambassadors of the princes, cardinals, and grand noblemen approach her, and all the Roman ladies of quality. Initially, she gave the most obliging welcome possible to everyone, showing to each an agreeable face full of joy and giving everyone testimony of affection. But after only a few days she began to change her manner of dealing with people and to take on a proud and haughty air."⁹ After the initial tidal wave of joy had settled down, Olimpia realized there were old scores to settle.

The most shocking story Leti reported is that a few days after the election Olimpia swept into the Vatican and informed the pope and the cardinals meeting with him that she would take the apartments reserved for the cardinal nephew, which adjoined the pope's apartments. Such living arrangements would have been nothing new for Innocent and Olimpia, who had inhabited connecting rooms most of the time since 1612. Using an inner door, unseen by servants or other family members, Olimpia could pop into her brother-in-law's rooms to offer advice, and he could duck into hers to ask for it.

Leti confidently declared that Innocent, who was not planning on having a cardinal nephew, initially seemed willing to give Olimpia the official suite of rooms. But Cardinal Panciroli was almost apoplectic at the idea. He "had a hard time diverting the pope and Donna Olimpia from this resolution, representing this design as scandalous, not only for the city of Rome but for all the earth and which would confirm all the rumors that ran throughout the world."¹⁰

The pope finally concurred with Cardinal Panciroli that Olimpia should continue to reside in the Piazza Navona palace. Olimpia acquiesced, but she would hold an eternal grudge against Cardinal Panciroli. The pope, however, gave her carte blanche to visit him at any time, day or night. Her visits usually lasted from sunset to midnight, as Innocent was a night owl and did his best work after dinner.

Innocent and Olimpia made preparations for his coronation as the 243rd pope going back in unbroken succession to Peter. Indeed, the power of the Catholic Church rests on Jesus' statement in Matthew 16:18–19, in which he called his friend Simon bar Jonah by a new name. "And I tell you that you are Peter, and on this rock I will build my church, and the gates of Hades will not overcome it. I will give you the keys of the kingdom of heaven; whatever you bind on earth will be bound in heaven, and whatever you loose on earth will be loosed in heaven." Papal coronations were held in Saint Peter's Basilica, where, it was thought, the power of the saint himself would be transferred directly to his new earthly representative.

The grand basilica of Innocent's time had risen from the humblest beginnings. In 500 B.C., Etruscan professional soothsayers called *vaticinia* lived in the swamps there at the foot of a modest hill. For a price, they would slaughter an animal and read fortunes in the shape and color of the liver. Vatican clay was used in pots, bricks, and roof tiles.

Around A.D. 40, Emperor Caligula built a stadium, called a circus, for chariot races on the site. Inside he placed an immense twelve-hundred-year-old red-granite obelisk he had swiped from Egypt. Since no one wanted to live in a mosquito-ridden sinkhole outside the walls of Rome, a pagan graveyard sprouted outside the sports arena. Emperor Nero even buried his favorite chariot horses there.

In A.D. 64 when the great fire of Rome was blamed on Nero, the emperor, in turn, blamed that strange new sect, the Christians. Since the Colosseum would not be built for another fifteen years, Nero held his executions in the Vatican Circus. Christians were made to don animal skins and run from ravenous dogs, who tore them to pieces. Others, smeared with tar, were nailed to crosses and set alight, human torches for nighttime entertainment. Two particularly troublesome Christians, Paul and Peter, were dispatched. According to Catholic tradition, as a Roman citizen Paul was beheaded and his body buried outside Rome. But the poor fisherman from Judea was crucified. Peter reportedly refused the honor of dying in exactly the same way Jesus did. Crucify me upside down, he said, and they did. It is possible the last sight Peter saw on earth was the great Egyptian obelisk, which now stands in front of Saint Peter's Basilica.

Executed criminals were often denied burial, their bodies tossed into the Cloaca Maxima, Rome's great sewer. It is likely that Peter's friends came that night to the circus to cut down his body and, unable pull out the nails in his feet, cut off the feet at the ankles. They placed his body in a hole dug on the side of Vatican Hill—about 150 feet up from the road—and covered it with roof tiles, the poorest kind of Roman burial.

The guards who entered the circus for cleanup the following morning would have found only the old man's feet, still nailed to the cross.

The location of Peter's illegal grave must have been a closely guarded secret among the early Christian community. But the growing flock wanted a place to pray close to the body of Jesus' best friend. Within eighty years or so of Peter's death, when rich pagan Romans were building elaborate garage-sized mausoleums nearby, the Christians erected a pagan-looking altar above Peter's humble grave. They could visit the shrine, pray, eat, and drink in commemoration of the departed, just as they would have at a pagan grave. No one would have known it was a forbidden Christian tomb.

During the persecution of the 250s, Emperor Valerian dug up the body of a Christian saint and threw it into the Tiber. Evidence indicates that leaders of Rome's Christian community, fearing he would do the same to Peter's bones if he discovered their location, scooped them up from beneath the altar, wrapped them in a purple shroud, and placed them in a cavity of the altar wall; other bones were scattered in the tomb to fool any desecrators.

In the 320s when Constantine decided to erect a huge new church to honor the saint, Pope Sylvester I told him the secret location of Peter's grave but not that the bones were hidden in a wall of the old altar. This secret, it seems, had died out, or perhaps the pope feared Constantine might jump back to paganism and dig up the holy bones.

The emperor designed the church so that the high altar would be located directly over the saint's grave. Unfortunately for Constantine, Peter's tomb was not on the flat area near the circus but on the side of Vatican Hill, and it would have been a desecration to move the bones from their initial resting place. Using slave labor, imperial engineers had to remove a million cubic feet of earth from the top of the hill and dump it at the bottom to create a flat surface. Around the saint's tomb they constructed enormous brick foundation walls seven feet thick and up to thirty-five feet high.

The church was built in the form of the Roman court of justice, the basilica, a rectangular building separated into three sections by two rows of large columns. Indeed, much of early church architecture and customs was based on the Roman imperial judicial system. This was because Constantine, realizing that Catholic bishops were among his most educated subjects, granted them judicial responsibilities to settle a variety of legal disputes. A bishop assumed the robes, rings, and special insignia of a judge of the Roman Empire. Bishops were also accorded the ceremonial rites of Roman judges—in their basilicas they sat on thrones, took center stage in processions accompanied by incense and torches, and expected those speaking to them to kneel. The altar of Minerva, goddess of wisdom, present in all pagan basilicas, became the altar of God in a Christian one.

As Christianity spread throughout the empire, Rome loudly claimed primacy over all other bishoprics because the holy bodies of Saints Peter and Paul were buried there. Constantinople, the glistening new capital of the empire, had such a dearth of apostolic bodies that starting in A.D. 356 Saints Timothy, Andrew, and Luke were imported. And Jerusalem, the location of Christ's crucifixion, could hardly claim to have his body. Gradually, other bishoprics accepted Rome's primacy and looked to Rome for direction, acknowledging the pope as universal father and Vicar of Christ, appointed by God himself to nurture his bride, the church.

Although barbarians periodically poured into Rome and pillaged, the Goths, Lombards, and Huns were semi-Christian and spared Saint Peter's Basilica out of respect or, perhaps, superstition. But when the Muslim Saracens marched on Rome in 846, church officials knew the undefended basilica—outside the city walls—would make a tempting target for plunder. Pious officials opened Peter's tomb below the altar and took the skull they found to safety, not knowing, of course, that the real bones were hidden in the tomb wall. Retreating behind the stout walls of Rome with the skull, church officials placed it in the Church of Saint John Lateran, where for centuries it was the object of intense veneration, though it might have been the skull of a pagan or even a woman.

While the power of the church waxed over the centuries, the structure of its holiest basilica was sliding into dereliction. By the time the popes returned to Rome for good in 1443, the eleven-hundred-year-old building was leaning dangerously off-kilter—one wall was six feet out of plumb and slowly pulling the perpendicular walls with it. Given the shifting sand beneath the basilica, it was a testament to the skill of Constantine's engineers that the structure had lasted as long as it did.

Late-fifteenth-century popes pondered what to do with the tottering basilica, hesitating to destroy something so sacred. But the irascible warrior pope Julius II (reigned 1503–1513) had no such scruples. The ancient basilica was torn down, its ancient papal tombs relocated and some of the art incorporated into the new church. Throughout the sixteenth century the new basilica was raised by fits and starts. Italy's greatest architects—Bramante, Raphael, Sangallo, and Michelangelo—argued over the design, particularly over the trailblazing dome they wished to build as a beacon to all Christendom.

Shoddy construction required the tearing down of years of work. Some popes, facing war, plague, famine, the Sack of Rome, or a bankrupt treasury, ignored the project entirely. There are several contemporary etchings of the partially built basilica with large trees growing out of the piers. But late-sixteenth-century popes raced to finish construction, and the new basilica was dedicated in 1615.

Saint Peter's is not the orderly work of one architectural genius who labored to create a harmonious design. It is a collage of centuries of conflicting personalities and historical upheavals, organized haphazardly in an immense space. In Olimpia's time the basilica was not much different from the Saint Peter's of today, only lacking certain later embellishments. Then as now, the visitor is immediately overwhelmed by the sheer size of the structure. The eye tries to find a focal point but cannot, distracted by the multicolored marbles, gilding, bronzes, statues, tombs, reliefs, lamps, pilasters, columns, and ornate vaulted ceilings. In 1638 a visiting John Milton found Saint Peter's so dizzying that years later, when he wrote *Paradise Lost,* he located Pandemonium there.

The chief purpose of Saint Peter's Basilica was public relations, perhaps best summed up in the 1455 deathbed speech of Pope Nicholas V. "To create solid and stable convictions in the minds of the uncultured masses," he said, "there must be something which appeals to the eye; a popular faith, sustained only on doctrines, will never be anything but feeble and vacillating. But if the authority of the Holy See were visibly displayed in majestic buildings, imperishable memorials and witnesses seemingly planted by the hand of God himself, belief would grow and strengthen. . . . Noble edifices combining taste and beauty with imposing proportions would immensely conduce to the exaltation of the chair of Saint Peter."[11]

The new basilica was, and still is, the largest church in the world. It is 693 feet long, 404 feet high under the dome, and 232 feet wide, holding some 20,000 people. It is much larger than the footprint of the old church, which was 395 feet long and 212 feet wide. The altar is in the center of the church, visible on all sides, and not flush against the far wall as it had been in the old basilica.

In 1626, Urban VIII commissioned the twenty-seven-year-old Gian Lorenzo Bernini to construct the baldachino, the 100-foot tall, 186,000-pound bronze canopy supported by twisted columns, directly over the high altar and Saint Peter's tomb. When digging the four ten-foot-square foundations to support the columns, workmen realized that below the basilica there were mausoleums and streets, an entire underground city of the dead. The laborers who cautiously walked through the brightly colored rooms, holding their torches high, were surprised to find that the cemetery was both pagan and Christian.

Upon opening the coffins, they found some bodies wrapped in ancient Christian clerical garb. Other tombs bore frescoes of dancing naked goddesses. Urban considered the inscription on the tomb of a certain Flavius Agricola so revolting that he had the sarcophagus thrown into the Tiber.

If the pope was afraid of desecrating the holy grave that he hoped was down there, he was absolutely terrified that the grave wasn't there at all—many Protestants insisted that Peter had never even set foot in Rome and the Catholics had made up the story to solidify Roman power. Urban instructed Bernini to disrupt as little as possible beneath the altar.

Unbeknownst to Innocent and Olimpia, beneath the baldachino, beneath Michelangelo's giant dome, slumbered the bones of Saint Peter, tucked away in the cavity of the second-century altar wall. They would be discovered in the 1940s and identified in 1968 as the remains of a robust man, some sixty to seventy years old at death. The bones were dyed purple—a rare and expensive dye reserved for royalty—from an ancient, disintegrated cloth. Pieces of every bone in the body (including the skull) were found except the feet, which had evidently been severed. The lack of foot bones almost certainly confirms the identification as Saint Peter, who, according to the most ancient tradition had been crucified upside down, unworthy to die like his Lord.

10

Celebrations

God has given us the papacy! Let us enjoy it!

—Pope Leo X

O N THE MORNING OF OCTOBER 4, 1644, Pope Innocent X was dressed for his coronation in ceremonial vestments—an *alba,* a floor-length white linen robe; a cincture, or linen belt; and a *stola,* the long band of silk worn around the neck and crossed on the breast. Around his shoulders hung the cope, a heavy, stiff cape with glorious gold and silver embroidery of biblical scenes, studded with pearls and precious gems. A dazzling bejeweled miter was placed on his head.

After Mass in the Sistine Chapel, Innocent climbed onto his pontifical chair to be carried into Saint Peter's Basilica. The chair was a golden throne affixed to a platform with gilded wooden rods on each end. Servants picked up the rods and carried the chair on their shoulders so that the people could see their pontiff lifted high above the crowds. If the pope needed to travel through Rome, the chair could be affixed to an elaborate wagon and pulled by horses. Then, when the wagon reached its destination, the servants would lift the chair and carry the pope up the stairs and into the building. Above the chair was a baldachino, a covering on four gilded columns to protect the pope from the wind, rain, and sun. The sides of the chair were adorned with enormous ostrich-feather fans.

During the coronation ceremony, Camillo, as the pope's nephew, sat next to him on a lower chair. As part of the ancient coronation rites, the pope ritually washed his hands several times, a gesture oddly reminiscent of Pontius Pilate. First Rome's city magistrates—the conservators—poured the water over the pope's hands. Then Camillo did the honors, followed by the French ambassador and the envoy of the Holy Roman Emperor. As the Sistine Chapel choir sang, Innocent was given the fisherman's ring, which the Vatican jeweler had crafted for him, and took his place on the throne. Two by two, the cardinals came forward to kneel in adoration, followed by the ambassadors, prelates, and nobility.

Then Signor Domenico Belli, the papal master of ceremonies, stood before the new pontiff with a bunch of flax on the head of a cane and set it on fire. It burst into flame and turned to ash immediately as Signor Belli solemnly intoned, "*Pater sancte, sic transit gloria mundi.*"[1] Holy Father, thus passes the glory of the world. It was the reminder that the pope, no matter how exalted at that moment, was mortal, and his power transient. He, too, would return to ashes and dust.

Throughout the ceremony, there were two centers of attention. Most spectators, as if watching a tennis match, glanced from the pope to Olimpia and back. According to the author of the *Relatione della Corte di Roma,* who witnessed the coronation, "The Most Excellent Signora Donna Olimpia Maidalchini" sat in the place of honor near the main altar on a platform adorned with rich crimson damask and embroidered heavily with gold. "Next to her sat the Marquesa Giustiniani, her daughter, niece of His Holiness; Donna Anna Colonna . . . and a great number of titled ladies."[2]

Olimpia was beaming with joy because for the first time ever her chair was more honorably positioned than that of Anna Colonna, who sat next to her. Anna Colonna had insisted on equal honors for her chair, given that she was of blue blood by birth, a niece of the recently deceased pontiff, and wife of the prefect of Rome. But Olimpia would have none of it, and it must have felt good to tell the haughty Anna

Colonna that Urban VIII was *dead,* thank you very much. Her chair would be several inches behind Olimpia's.

The ambassadors and princes who attended the coronation were impressed by Olimpia's appearance. The new power behind the papal throne was a stately widow renowned for her intelligence and financial acumen. Diplomatic dispatches posted that day described the "prudence and valor" of Donna Olimpia. She would certainly be a tremendous asset to the pope, playing his hostess as first lady of Rome.[3]

After the ceremony, the pope was carried to the loggia of benediction to be crowned in front of the crowd in Saint Peter's Square, most of whom had camped out overnight to get a good spot. Cardinal Francesco Barberini removed Innocent's jeweled miter, and Cardinal Carlo de' Medici, whose gouty toe was healing, placed the shining triple crown on the pope's head.

The papal tiara was unique among the crowns of European monarchs. Until the late eleventh century the pope wore a simple white cap. But as the papacy increased in power and majesty, so did popes' hats, which rose like overyeasted loaves. Originally the high hat had two bejeweled circles—the tiaras of the temporal and spiritual realms. But by 1300 the power-hungry Boniface VIII had enlarged his crown to resemble an enormous pointed dunce cap with *three* jeweled tiaras—the triple crown. It was said that the three crowns stood for the Father, Son, and Holy Spirit, though no one really knew. By Innocent's time the triple tiara was lower, and wider, shaped something like a potato.

At his coronation each pope was expected to choose a motto for his reign. Innocent selected an invocation to God: "Give to your servant a docile heart to judge your people."[4] Many snickered that the pope's heart was already docile enough, at least where his sister-in-law was concerned.

As the sun set, Innocent prepared a new delight for the people of Rome. Vatican servants with mountain-climbing experience tied ropes around their waists and knotted them on iron hooks along the observation point at the top of Saint Peter's dome. Easing down the dome, they affixed torches in the iron spikes projecting out every few feet, all the way down the dome, and then down the façade itself. When darkness descended, the entire basilica glowed and shimmered and seemed to be aflame.

According to one eyewitness, Girolamo Lunadoro, "There was not a street that was not full of lights, not a palace without illumination. . . . It is sufficient to say that for many, many years Rome has not been as jubilant as it is now for the happy exaltation of its prince, to whom Divine Majesty concede the years of Nestor and the strength to execute his holy thoughts."[5]

In seventeenth-century Rome, any individual who found himself suddenly possessed of a fortune was expected to share it with his family. After all, that was what a good Christian of any social standing was supposed to do. Sitting on the zenith of the social pyramid, the pope was no exception.

Moreover, as monarch of the Papal States, the pope was a sovereign and his family members were, therefore, temporary royalty, holding their vaunted positions until their elderly uncle breathed his last. But unlike the Bourbons of France and Habsburgs of Spain, many of the popes had worked their way up from the humblest backgrounds, and the citizens of the Papal States did not want their monarch's relatives mending nets in fishing hovels or feeding pigs on pork farms. Most of the pope's subjects wanted to point to their ruling family with pride— the princes and princesses setting out from their sumptuous palaces in elegant coaches and six, just as the royal families of France or Spain did. Over the period of twenty-one years the rapacity of the Barberini family had, of course, exceeded the bounds of good taste. It was hoped that the Pamphili pope would practice a more dignified nepotism.

On September 24, nine days after his election, Innocent made a new will in which he left all his worldly goods to Olimpia, whom he designated as his heir, expressly stating that she could do whatever she wanted with his money. It was highly unusual for a pontiff—or any Italian nobleman, for that matter—to choose a woman as his heir, especially when he had a healthy young nephew. But Camillo, Innocent knew, was a thoughtless ditherer. Olimpia was the only one capable of managing the increasing family wealth. And Innocent's decision must have made Camillo hate his mother even more.

But Innocent did not reward Olimpia to the exclusion of her three children. Her eldest daughter, Maria, now twenty-five, had married the marquess Andrea Giustiniani in 1640. During the conclave Giustiniani's uncle had had the good grace to die and leave him his immense wealth. The pope gave Giustiniani the title of prince of Bassano, and Maria became a princess. Innocent also made him the castellan of Castel Sant'Angelo, an honorific post that brought a good income.

At seventeen, Olimpia's younger daughter, Costanza, was unmarried. Two promising candidates immediately made offers for her hand. The handsome prince of Caserta, twenty-three, seemed a perfect match, but the thirty-one-year-old Niccolò Ludovisi, who had placed two wives in the grave and was casting about for a third, was the most titled man in Italy. He was the prince of Piombino and Venosa, the duke of Sora and Arce, the marquess of Populonia and Vignola, the count of Conza, the signor of Elba and Montecristo, and a grandee of Spain. Some of his titles descended from his great-uncle Pope Gregory XV and others from his dead wives.

Though he dragged such impressive titles in his wake, Prince Ludovisi offered the decided disadvantage of being obscenely fat, so fat that Roman gossip speculated as to whether he was in any position to have children. Looking at his slender, handsome bachelor opponent in the race to marry the pope's niece, Ludovisi was "debased and humiliated and oppressed," said one diplomat.[6] But in the end, titles won out over looks as they usually did.

The dowry documents were signed in October. The pope gave Camillo 20,000 scudi to give Costanza as her dowry, a pitiful sum for a pope's niece, who usually fetched 100,000 scudi. But Prince Ludoviso accepted eagerly; the position of pope's nephew, even a nephew by marriage, almost always guaranteed immense political power. On December 21, Costanza married the fat prince in a grand ceremony in the Sistine Chapel presided over by the pope himself.

The choice of the ardently pro-Spanish, anti-French groom had dangerous international implications. The Venetian ambassador to Rome,

Contarini, reported to his senate, "Prince Ludovisi is bursting with private hatreds and is too inclined towards the Spanish faction."[7] Spain rejoiced and France was outraged, demanding that the papal nuncio explain if this was a sign that the new pope despised their kingdom. Innocent sent a calming missive to Paris, explaining that most eligible bachelors in Rome were of the Spanish persuasion, and he was merely trying to find his niece a suitable husband.

With the girls' futures arranged, that left Camillo. By the end of the conclave, Olimpia had already made plans for him to marry Lucrezia Barberini, sealing the deal she had made to win the Barberini cardinals' crucial votes for her brother-in-law. But Camillo proved unexpectedly intransigent. It was his life's greatest misfortune that he had been born not to a woman but to a force of nature. Camillo was fed up with his mother's domination. Here he was, the pope's nephew, the number two man in the country, being treated as if he were a mindless child.

Camillo told his friends that he would not marry Lucrezia Barberini because that was precisely what his mother wanted him to do. Moreover, as an art connoisseur he could not have been pleased that the potential bride's eyebrows were blacker, thicker, and bristlier than most men's mustaches, or that her nose took up an inordinate amount of her face. Camillo would not marry her. He would become cardinal nephew and wield more official power than his bossy mother ever could.

Camillo's stubborn refusal to wed Lucrezia put Olimpia in a terrible bind, and he must have relished it. The furious Barberini cardinals would suffer a double loss—Francesco and Antonio would not keep their powerful positions, which would be taken over by Camillo, nor would they be immune from prosecution for corruption as members of the new pope's extended family.

Olimpia, for her part, wanted to bring the powerful Barberinis into the family for her own protection. Innocent had reached the age of seventy in a century when most men died in their fifties. Whenever Innocent died, the Barberinis would bounce back from ignominy and, using all their wealth and connections, be in a position to harm Olimpia. In Roman politics, one hand always washed the other, and because of Camillo's stubbornness both of Olimpia's hands remained hopelessly filthy.

Many Romans expressed surprise that the only son born to the Pamphili family in seventy years would join the church, ensuring the extinction of the line. There was a way around this, however. If the male heirs died out, as happened frequently in the best families, many noble Italians gave the family name to a daughter's second son to extend it into the future.

In his *avvisi* of October 15, 1644, Teodoro Amayden informed his readers, "The news of the antechamber is that Signor Camillo will be made a cardinal. . . . And in the meantime there could be born sons to the Marquesa Giustiniani which would be enough for both families, as a son has already been born and she is pregnant again."[8]

Knowing his nephew's difficulty in applying himself, Innocent did not give Camillo the impressive title of "cardinal *padrone,*" which Urban VIII's nephew had held, but called him the "cardinal superintendent of important affairs."[9] On October 24 the pope appointed his good friend Cardinal Panciroli secretary of state. In addition to doing most of the work, Panciroli was to instruct Camillo in foreign affairs.

On November 14, 1644, Innocent created Camillo cardinal. When Camillo approached the throne, his uncle was overcome with emotion. Innocent "seemed not able to speak, and ended his speech with some words concerning the affection of blood relatives."[10]

As cardinal nephew, Camillo enjoyed huge wealth. He received the income of the governor of the Papal States, along with the revenues from Avignon, the county of Venassino, and the priory of Capua, together with numerous benefices and posts he received from foreign nations eager for his support. Spain gave him the archdiocese of the metropolitan church of Toledo. The republic of Venice inscribed him among its own nobility.

Though furious at Camillo's insistence on becoming cardinal nephew, Olimpia decided to make the best out of a bad deal. Knowing her son's indolence, she initially believed that she could run the Vatican through him. She insisted—and the pope agreed—that Camillo continue to live with her in the Piazza Navona palace instead of taking up the cardinal nephew's apartments in the Vatican, the very ones she had wanted for herself. Cardinal Panciroli moved into these. Nor would

Camillo be allowed one of the chief privileges of his position—bestowing honors and incomes on his friends. Innocent made him first obtain his mother's approval.

But as usual, Olimpia was doomed to be disappointed in her son. Each evening, when his gilded carriage returning from the Vatican clomped into her courtyard, she pumped her son for information on his daily activities and made suggestions on how to handle business. But Camillo, sweeping past in his crimson robes, rebuffed her.

Wednesday, November 23, was the date of the pope's *possesso,* the ceremony in which Innocent officially took possession of the pope's titular church, Saint John Lateran. This was the greatest of all the celebrations for the new pontiff, and the colorful procession, winding its way across Rome, lasted for hours. The day had started off windy and cold with a driving rain, but by the time the parade left the Vatican at noon the clouds had parted and the sun warmed the tens of thousands waiting to watch the show. The government had spent the eye-popping sum of twelve thousand scudi on the costumes and decorations, and no one wanted to miss it.

Mounted on horses, the *sbirri*—the municipal police force—pushed the spectators back toward the buildings to keep a clear path for the procession. Faces crowded each window; bodies filled every doorway and balcony and crammed onto every roof. The buildings were alive with the devout, the sneering, and the curious.

All the streets along the procession route had been thoroughly cleaned of dirt—animal droppings, vegetable peels, and night soil—no mean feat. Holes had been filled in, loose stones replaced, and the pavement swept and scrubbed. Flags bearing noble family crests were placed on the roofs and façades of palaces and snapped joyfully in the breeze. Saints' relics and sacred images were placed in the windows of houses and displayed in front of churches. The season's last flowers were strewn on the streets.

Precious tapestries, removed from drawing room walls, were hung from windows and balconies. Those who could not afford the outrageously expensive hand-embroidered tapestries hung bolts of cloth, even bedspreads or drapes. The important thing was to have a brightly colored something hanging out of the window. Those items within reach of the crowds below were firmly secured as thieves were known to grab the precious objects, run off with them in the throng, and sell them later to the used-furniture dealers in the flea markets.

John Evelyn, a young Protestant gentleman traveling in Europe to avoid the English civil war, was in Italy when he heard that Innocent's *possesso* would soon take place. He raced to Rome and got himself a good observation point at the top of the high steps of the Church of Saint Mary of the Altar of Heaven. Armed with paper and pencil, he wrote down a detailed description of the parade: "Then came the Pope himselfe, carried in a litter or rather open chaire of crimson velvet richly embrodred, and borne by two stately mules; as he went he held up two fingers, blessing the multitude who were on their knees or looking out of their windows and houses, with loud *viva's* and acclamations of felicity to their new Prince."[11]

The parade climbed up to the Campidoglio, the civic heart of Roman government on the top of Capitoline Hill. Between two huge papier-mâché female statues—Rome the Peacemaker and Rome Triumphant—the cortège filed in. Other statues represented Wisdom, Vigilance, and Discipline. The procession marched under an enormous plaster arch with life-sized horses on top.

At the crest of the hill, three palaces framed a large square, in the middle of which stood the colossal bronze equestrian statue of a Roman emperor thought to be Constantine. Here the militia awaited Innocent. The senator of Rome, Orazio Albani, wearing a brocade robe embroidered with gold, got off his horse and marched up to the pope. Kneeling, he ceremonially placed the ivory scepter of state at the pope's feet, which he kissed. Rising, he offered Innocent the keys of the Capitoline rock as trumpets blared and artillery crackled.

Olimpia, who had not taken part in the procession, watched Innocent receive the scepter and keys from the balcony of one of the three palaces overlooking the square. She had invited twenty-five of Rome's most influential ladies to join her for the celebrations in the Palace of the Conservators, in a huge hall frescoed with scenes of ancient Roman legend. As the papal procession moved on, the ladies turned from the windows. It was time for Olimpia's banquet to begin. And now, thirty-two years after she had come to Rome and been snubbed by the noblewomen, it was time for a buffet of revenge, served very cold, which was all that some of her guests would eat that day.

According to Giacinto Gigli, "When it was time to eat, she called eight of them, and led them with her to eat, and the others remained mortified at the windows without being invited."[12] Evidently, the eight that Olimpia invited had been kind to her from the beginning. The other seventeen had offended her. It was payback time. And she must have been absolutely delighted.

The pope's procession descended Capitoline Hill and marched past the ancient heart of Rome, the Forum, where cows grazed among the tops of arches and columns that stuck out like blackened bones from the dirt of a millennium. Along the route wooden posts had been erected and ropes strung between them. From these ropes hung posters specially painted for the ceremony by noble families, expatriate communities, and various charitable organizations.

As the cortège veered around the Colosseum, the pope saw that the Jewish community of Rome had hung sixty huge posters featuring beautiful paintings of Old Testament scenes inscribed with Bible quotes in Hebrew and Latin. At the end of the posters Innocent halted, and the chief rabbi handed him a magnificent jeweled Torah, imploring the new pontiff to be merciful to the Jews of Rome.

It was a straight shot from the eastern side of the Colosseum to the fourth-century Lateran basilica. Inside the church, the choir sang, candles burned, and incense filled the air with heady perfume. Innocent was seated on a magnificent red porphyry chair with lion legs, one of a matching pair. Dug out of ruined imperial baths in the eighth century, the chairs had been instantly recognized for their beauty and value. As the finest chairs in Rome, they had been drafted for papal coronations in Saint Peter's Basilica.

The chairs had an unusual feature—a keyhole-shaped opening in the seat. Though many thought the pope's throne had once been used as a toilet chair, the reclining back makes this doubtful. Given that the chairs had been found in the imperial baths, it is probable that they had been used in the sauna. The sitter could lie back and relax as the sweat ran off his body and out the hole in the bottom of the seat. But the strange hole in the pope's chair gave rise to the story that during his coronation each pope had his testicles felt by a cardinal to make sure that he was in fact a pope and not a popess. According to the tale, the cleric assigned the task knelt before the pope and, lifting the papal robes, put his hand under the seat. When he felt the pontifical balls, he cried, "He has testicles!" and the people replied with a heartfelt "God be praised!"[13]

It was commonly believed that the testicle-feeling ceremony was instituted after an androgynous-looking woman had become pope in 855, Pope Joan. Her terrible secret was revealed three years later during a papal procession when she fell off her horse, gave birth in the street, and died. The problem with the Pope Joan story is that it was first reported almost four hundred years later by a Dominican monk. Another problem is that a pope named Benedict III reigned during those years. The story was most likely inspired by a real-life woman named Marozia, who ruled the Vatican behind the scenes in the tenth century and was the lover, mother, grandmother, great-grandmother, and great-great-grandmother of popes. But the legend of a female pope was just too delicious for truth to get in the way.

The tale of Pope Joan and the testicle-feeling chair had become so widespread by 1513 that Leo X had the chairs moved from Saint Peter's Basilica to the Lateran, where they were used for the *possesso* ceremonies. But the story stubbornly lingered. In describing Saint John Lateran, a 1543 book reported, "Nearby are two porphyry chairs where they check to see if the new pope has testicles, as they say."[14]

One Protestant Swedish gentleman, Lawrence Banck, actually stated in his 1644 book on his travels that he had seen Innocent X getting his testicles felt up. Perhaps this story was anti-Catholic propaganda, or perhaps the author, watching the cardinals crowd around the papal throne, couldn't tell *what* they were doing.

A more reliable witness, John Evelyn, pencil in hand, had followed the procession all the way to the church but was, alas, unable to enter and report on testicle feeling or lack thereof. "What they did at St. John di Laterano I could not see by reason of the prodigious crowd," he wrote in his diary, "so I spent most of the day in viewing the two triumphal arches which had been purposely erected a few days before."[15]

That evening all of Rome was illuminated by colored lanterns, torches, white wax candles, and fireworks. The magnificent dome of Saint Peter's was once more glowing with a thousand torches. But the most impressive display was in the Piazza Navona, and we can assume that Olimpia had returned home from her chilly banquet in the Campidoglio to watch the festivities from her drawing room window. A huge Noah's ark had been built on top of an artificial mountain. Noah and his family were portrayed on deck in plaster of Paris, as elegantly sculpted elephants and giraffes poked their heads out of windows.

In the book of Genesis, God sent a white dove with an olive sprig in its beak to the ark as a sign that dry land was close at hand. And now, a large papier-mâché dove with a burning torch in its mouth was sent careening down a wire from the roof of Olimpia's palace. When the dove reached the ark, it lit off a barrage of fireworks and firecrackers. Animals went flying out of the ark in a streak of sparks, and comets blasted from the hull into the night sky. The ark and its inhabitants sizzled and crackled and finally went up in a thunderous explosion of red smoke and orange flames. By the time the smoke had cleared, only the dove, still hanging by the wire, remained unscathed. Everything else was ashes. This was seen as an extremely good omen for the success of the new pope.

11

Women in the Vatican

Well-behaved women rarely make history.

—Laurel Thatcher Ulrich

THOUGH OLIMPIA WAS PREVENTED FROM moving into the Vatican, she set about transforming her Piazza Navona palace into a papal showplace. Her first act was to finally have the pope ban the Wednesday-morning vegetable market. Grumbling, the vendors took their produce, flies, creaking wagons, and donkey droppings to another locale. Olimpia must have been overjoyed that after thirty-two years of the weekly din and mess, it was gone.

Her next step was to buy the two houses next door to the Palazzo Pamphili, the small de Rossi house and the large Palazzo Cibo, and incorporate them into her own. Back in 1634 Olimpia had tripled the size of the old Casa Pamphili to create a cardinal's palace. With her 1644 purchases she doubled the house again, making it a palace worthy of a papal dynasty. With unlimited funds at her disposal, she could choose from among Rome's top artists, sculptors, architects, engineers, and craftsmen to redesign her palazzo.

She hired a team of famous architects, the father and son Girolamo and Carlo Rainaldi, to do the designs, and Francesco Borromini to oversee the project. Olimpia met frequently with her architects, studying their drawings, three-dimensional models, and watercolor sketches of paintings suggested for the ceilings. The palace would not be finished until July 1648, and in the meantime Olimpia would have to live once more with hammering, scaffolding, and the ever-present sneeze-inducing film of plaster dust.

The final façade was five stories high and eighteen windows across, with four doorways and a balcony over each. A painting of her finished palazzo in 1651 shows it painted pale gray with white woodwork. Olimpia's carriage entrance remained the same, though the high double doors were now in the center of the palazzo instead of on the far right side. To the left of the courtyard was the same covered triumphal staircase of the cardinal's palace. But on the right of the courtyard she had the old de Rossi house demolished and built four stories on top of magnificent arches through which horses and carriages could travel to a second courtyard, where the stables were kept.

Her private apartments—some seven rooms across the front of the palazzo facing the Piazza Navona—were, in seventeenth-century terms, in restrained good taste. The carved doorways were of red marble, splashed with white. The floors were parquet. The sixteen-foot coffered gilded ceilings depicted mythological scenes. Beneath them for about a yard, matching frescoes adorned the walls.

The baroque era was a time of decline politically and economically. The peach was a bit overripe, still beautiful and fragrant, but mold was beginning to form. After the perfection of the Renaissance, there was no place for art to evolve other than into wild excess. Painting comprised the heroic, the theatrical, and the colossal. It attempted not to re-create reality but to idealize it. Amidst sea monsters, dragons, saints, and angels, human bodies twisted and writhed, muscular, fleshy contrasts of light and shadow. Waves crashed. Ships floundered. Among the larger-than-life figures, mouths hung open in shock and eyes blazed with fury. Arms were raised to bestow a heavenly blessing or a fatal blow. And above it all, plump laughing cherubs tossed rose petals.

An extravagant manifestation of the glories of militant Catholicism, Roman baroque art was a counterweight to the decline of papal power. In fact, the word *baroque* was first used derisively by those classicists who disliked its melodrama. The word was derived from a Portuguese term that meant "deformed pearl."

Uneasy about leaving any surface unadorned, baroque artists paid particular attention to the ceiling, that most neglected part of a modern room. When those of the twenty-first century enter a neighbor's house, we never automatically throw back our heads to gape at the ceiling. If we did, we would no doubt be rewarded by the sight of white paint and a lightbulb. But in the seventeenth century, the observer would look up immediately to see clouds parting, revealing Paradise, and must have felt as if he could climb a ladder and just keep going right into heaven itself.

The most awe-inspiring ceiling of Olimpia's expanded palace was at the end of her seven chambers facing the Piazza Navona. The reception room, designed by Borromini, stretched from the piazza all the way back to the Via dell'Anima. This chamber, measuring one hundred feet long and twenty-four feet wide, was used for balls and large receptions. It is called the *galleria* of Pietro da Cortona because the famous artist painted the story of Aeneas on the thirty-foot-high curved ceiling. Oddly enough, the pope was depicted as the god Neptune, bare-breasted and holding a trident, his right arm extended to quell the wind and waves. Around him naked youths blow conch shells, as laughing nude girls swim by. In the sky, worried cherubs hold the reins of white horses rearing out of the water.

In addition to her *galleria,* Olimpia created an enormous music room in the central section overlooking both courtyards. Here she staged her operas and comedies. The acoustics were almost perfect, a great advantage in an era without microphones.

But Olimpia had another building project in addition to the Piazza Navona palace. On October 7, 1645, Innocent named her the princess of San Martino, a church-owned territory three miles outside of Viterbo. The site included a medieval church and abbey and a few hunting lodges of the rich, including one owned by her brother, Andrea Maidalchini.

Olimpia hired Francesco Borromini to design a suite of princely apartments on top of the fourteenth-century abbey and reinforce the load-bearing walls to sustain the extra weight. Suffering from arthritis in her knees, she could no longer walk up stairs. Borromini created a double snail staircase, a spiral within a spiral. The inside spiral comprised low, gentle stairs, and the larger outside spiral was a wider ramp of terra-cotta for her sedan chair or possibly her carriage.

She hired Gian Lorenzo Bernini to decorate the seven-room suite. The large room at the end of the palace was made into a papal audience chamber with a throne for Innocent when he came to visit. For this room Bernini designed a unique movable ceiling. Made of incredibly light wood, sculpted and painted with Innocent's papal coat of arms, gilded garlands, and riotous flowers, the ceiling was attached to a series of ropes and levers. In cold weather it could be lowered by servants working from the crawlspace above. In warm weather, it could be raised.

Olimpia's rooms are elegant, with intricately carved and gilded sixteen-foot ceilings and doorways of red marble spattered with white. The windows look out over the church and piazza, toward hills blue-gray in the mists. Oddly, Olimpia's bedroom is very plain. It is the only room with a hidden spiral staircase in the wall going down to the first floor. The stairs were probably too steep for Olimpia's aching knees, but perhaps they were used by messengers bringing her secret dispatches from Rome. As in the Piazza Navona palace, Olimpia's bedroom was connected by a small inner door to the bedroom she designed for the pope. Unseen by servants or visitors, the pope and his sister-in-law could visit each other at night.

The new princess of San Martino set about creating a model town of some 250 houses around the church and palace; these she gave as dowries to dowerless girls who would otherwise have been forced to enter convents. Though documentation is lacking, it was said that she also invited fifty recently released convicts and fifty reformed prostitutes to San Martino with incentives to settle down.

Since time immemorial, European towns had always grown helter-skelter around a castle or river. San Martino, which Olimpia built in a slightly off-kilter form of the Piazza Navona, was one of Europe's first planned towns and became a model for later urban design.

While Olimpia rolled up her black silk sleeves to begin her construction projects, the new pope settled into his princely suites in the Vatican Palace, a rabbit's warren of buildings, corridors, gardens, libraries, offices, and staircases connected to Saint Peter's Basilica. Innocent lived surrounded by the greatest works of art of any palace in Europe.

From the 300s to the 1300s, the main Roman papal residence had been the Lateran Palace on the other side of town, connected to the Church of Saint John Lateran. Nicholas V (reigned 1447–1455) improved the Vatican Palace, creating the clifflike pink building that still stands today, rising to the right of the basilica as the observer stands in the piazza. The papal apartments consisted of a series of antechambers, one leading into the other, culminating in an audience chamber, with the bedchamber behind that.

In the 1490s Pope Alexander VI had commissioned the famous artist Pinturicchio to paint the Borgia family in three large, dark rooms in the papal suite, which are today called the Borgia Apartments. But when his successor, the ill-tempered Julius II, moved into the rooms, he couldn't bear to wake up each morning and look at his worst enemy, the fat-jowled Borgia pope, on his knees in prayer, sinking under the weight of his gold jewel-studded cope. Nor did Julius wish to see the pope's daughter, the wiltingly beautiful Lucrezia, and her barbarous brother, Cesare, a sadistic gleam in his eye. In 1508 Julius moved into the suite of rooms a floor higher and commissioned Raphael to paint them. Here, when the pope woke up, he saw edifying works of ancient philosophers, saints, and popes disputing theology, and not a Borgia in sight.

It was across one of these glorious frescoes that during the Sack of 1527 a German soldier used his sword to scrawl, in three-foot-high letters, "Martin Luther." As soon as the pope returned to the Vatican after the Sack, the graffiti was painted over, of course. But at certain times of day, when the light hit it just so, the name of the arch heretic could be seen as big as life in the pope's apartments, and it can still be seen by tourists. Sixtus V (reigned 1585–1590) built a new wing of the Apostolic Palace with far more light and fresh air than the old residence. It was this wing that Innocent inhabited in 1644, and where popes have re-sided ever since, though they moved to the top floor in 1903.

Innocent's Vatican household included countless secretaries, transla-tors, notaries, accountants, scribes, and decoders. His kitchen served hundreds of meals a day to visitors and servants and employed squad-rons of cooks, waiters, and wine stewards. A team of men looked after his clothes, working with launderers, tailors, and embroiderers. Others cared for his jewels, keeping them polished and in good repair.

Innocent had four masters of ceremonies, who planned all ceremo-nial events down to the last detail and dealt with the irksome issue of which individuals would have the seats of greatest honor. He had his own Sistine Chapel choir, consisting of men, boys, and castrati, who sang for him during his meals. It was said that the unnatural sweetness of the eunuchs' voices caused the listeners' hearts to break.

Though the new pontiff was pampered in every way by his efficient palace servants, Olimpia was not about to give up the homely services she had always performed for her brother-in-law. She personally looked after laundering his undergarments, which were delivered to her at the Piazza Navona. There she made certain that his shirts, stockings, and underpants were washed, bleached, starched, and pressed just the way the pope liked it. For this service Olimpia received a monthly salary of eighteen scudi from the papal treasury.

Olimpia's shirt laundering for the pope would not have disturbed the Vatican power structure. This was a womanly task, the kind that many papal sisters- and nieces-in-law had performed over the years to the ap-probation of onlookers. That was, after all, what women were supposed to do, stay in the laundry to look after the needs of men. But naturally Olimpia did not limit her ambitions to a tub of hot soapy water.

One of Olimpia's first acts after her brother-in-law's election was to search for the priest of Viterbo whom she had accused of trying to sexu-ally molest her nearly forty years earlier. The priest was found. His ca-reer had never gone anywhere due to the scandal of 1606. Olimpia called him into her audience chamber at the Piazza Navona and asked him where she would be at that moment if she had followed his advice and become a nun.

The priest said with a sigh, "Most Excellent Signora, my goal was not to advise you to do evil."

Olimpia replied, "No, but if I had done it, I would not have done well because I would not have become what I now am."[1]

Then, to show him her absolute power, and to assuage the guilt that must have rankled subtly over the years, she had Innocent make him a bishop. Having made amends with the priest—sort of—Olimpia turned to helping oppressed women. She continued giving generously to nuns and was now in a position to assist another group of women forced into a life they would not have chosen under different circumstances—prostitutes.

Rome, a city with a large population of single men—priests and monks—and men who had left their wives back home—pilgrims and laborers from the countryside—had always boasted a thriving sex trade. The 1650 census reported 73,978 male residents of all ages and 52,214 females. These figures, however, did not include visitors, which would have inflated the preponderance of men even more. The census also listed 1,148 "courtesans" and 32 "concubines." We are not sure what the difference was, but possibly a concubine was rented by one wealthy client for months at a time. And these were only the women who kissed and told. We can assume there were many more who kissed and clammed up.

In the Renaissance the *cortigiana onesta,* or honest courtesan, played the role of a geisha girl, reciting poetry, strumming the lute, and singing at Rome's best gentlemen's parties. Many of these women owned their own palaces and rode through the streets in luxurious carriages attended by several servants on horseback. Then there were the lowly *cortigiane alla candela*—candle tarts—who lit a little candle when their customers arrived and stopped working the moment the candle burned out.

The infamous Borgia pope, Alexander VI, invited prostitutes to the Vatican for orgies as a form of court entertainment, awarding prizes to those of his servants who made love to them the greatest number of times. In the wake of Martin Luther, most popes were stricter with prostitutes. Pius V (reigned 1566–1572) tried to banish them entirely, but the Roman senate begged him to reconsider. If amorous priests could not visit prostitutes, it was argued, they would seduce the wives and daughters of virtuous citizens. Other popes encouraged confraternities to reform the whores of Rome and give them dowries for marriage, which culled a few off the streets. Sumptuary laws were passed limiting the luxury of the clothing they wore in public and forbidding them to keep carriages.

Morals aside, the Roman civic government was concerned about prostitutes because of the illnesses they spread. The Hospital of Saint James, with beds for up to three hundred patients, specialized in treating syphilis. Every day the patients would be bled and administered a concoction that contained mercury. Although mercury diminished the symptoms of syphilis, it made the hair fall out, and eventually the teeth, and sometimes the mind would follow the hair and teeth as they rattled into oblivion.

Olimpia decided to take the prostitutes of Rome under her wing, evidently in return for a substantial donation. This transaction was not unusual as various groups in Rome paid an influential person to act on their behalf as a kind of lobbyist. Having won Olimpia's official protection, prostitutes affixed her coat of arms over their doors, a warning sign to the police and church officials that they were under the personal protection of the pope's most excellent sister-in-law. They were permitted to ride in carriages if they painted her coat of arms on the carriage door.

Teodoro Amayden was scandalized. He wrote in his *avvisi* of August 30, 1645, "The prostitutes parade in their carriages in the most solemn religious festivals, because Donna Olimpia, after having been given presents by the same, was content to take them under her protection, and permitted them to tack the arms of Her Excellency above their door and allowed them to go in carriages without any regard, as if they were honorable people."[2]

But there was more scandal to come. It was, indeed, an unusual sight for a woman reputed to be the pope's mistress to go in a great cavalcade of carriages to the Vatican for political consultations. Olimpia alighted from her coach clutching stacks of petitions and requests for the pope, along with the replies she had already written for the pope to sign. She then stepped into a sedan chair, which was carried up to the pope's private apartments. In meetings with Innocent and various cardinals, she told them exactly what she wanted them to do, as the pope nodded in agreement.

The Venetian ambassador wrote, "And she from time to time with masterly haughtiness is carried into the palace with a file of petitions, most of them her own decrees, and spends hours with His Holiness to discuss the matters. . . . The jokes that went about the court were hidden from the pope."[3]

The Mantuan ambassador stated that Olimpia clattered around Rome with such a staff of pages and retainers that her "magnificence rendered the sisters-in-law of the three prior popes almost modest."[4] On February 11, 1645, the Florentine envoy reported, "Olimpia's influence grows daily; she visits the Pope every other day and the whole world turns to her."[5]

Cardinal Pallavicino concluded, "So adding up the pope's feelings toward her, the close affinity, obligation, esteem, the conformity of interests, and his popularity right after his election, there began to be verified the predictions of the court, that if Cardinal Pamfili would be pope, Olimpia would be the ruler."[6]

As pope, Innocent became more suspicious of men than ever, and the only churchman he completely trusted was his secretary of state, Cardinal Panciroli. But Olimpia trumped Panciroli, and the cardinal knew it. Though later events would show that he was irritated by her influence, to keep the pope's friendship he paid court to her. Gregorio Leti wrote that Panciroli "was fain to go in person very often to wait upon her, and give her an account of all the secret negotiations of the court, and everything that passed through his hands, after which she would from time to time go to the Vatican, followed by a numerous company of coaches."[7]

In addition to Panciroli, many other cardinals had the good sense to fawn on Olimpia, flattering her, sending her presents, and asking her advice. They even hung her official portrait in their audience chambers, right next to the pope, as if she were a sovereign herself, or perhaps co-pope.

Olimpia's house became a second Vatican court. The Piazza Navona was crowded with the carriages of powerful churchmen and ambassadors who came to call on her. Cardinal Pallavicino wrote, "She fed her ambition by having her antechamber full of prelates and principal ministers, who in their ceremony and etiquette recognized her almost as their boss, and it came to pass that even cardinals, in addition to their frequent visits, ran to ask for her intercession in their most serious business."[8]

In a document from 1651, Abbot Gianbattista Rinalducci wrote that Olimpia "had all the vices of a woman, and none of the virtues. She was avaricious, insatiable, haughty, scornful, implacable, arrogant, impetuous, sensual, and drunk with the financial prosperity of the papacy, which she alone absorbed."[9]

The French ambassador, Bali de Valençais, had a better opinion of Olimpia. In his instructions to his successor in Rome, he compared Olimpia to the mythical Pope Joan. "One cannot deny that Donna Olimpia is a great lady," he wrote. "Great, because she knows how to advance herself, to absent and present herself in the favor of the pope with such prudence that the court of Rome, which is used to marvels, is amazed. Being a woman, she appears to want to accumulate with too much industry, enjoys vendettas and, finally, makes a great show of her predominance. But I must repeat that she is a great lady, and if one pretends that a woman attained the papacy in former times, she would have had to have been as wise, shrewd and prudent as she. . . . Your Eminence must procure her affection, and this should not be so difficult seeing how she is the genius most adapted to want good for France rather than to please Spain."[10]

The Venetian ambassador, Nicolò Sagredo, wrote that Olimpia's "judgment is truly of a marvelous quality. She knows how to satisfy all her desires with the authority of a minister."[11]

Even Leti, who heartily hated Olimpia, gave her grudging kudos. "Truly this woman deserved all sorts of praise for her mind and judgment, even if some criticized her and called her avaricious and impious," he declared. "It is certain that no one but Donna Olimpia could have governed even six months in those bad circumstances let alone six years."[12]

In addition to her political work, Olimpia had the more traditional responsibilities as the pope's official hostess and first lady of Rome. The liturgical calendar was crammed with saints' feast days and processions, and every few months another foreign prince would send an *obbedienza* cavalcade. At these events Olimpia sat proudly in the seat of honor. Additionally, when the wives of new ambassadors or traveling princes arrived in Rome, they first called on Olimpia to pay their respects. She was then expected to accompany them to papal audiences for the supreme honor of kissing the pope's holy feet. Visiting men, however, usually called on the pope first, and then on Olimpia.

As the sun set, Olimpia often returned to the Vatican for secret work sessions. She sat alone with the pope behind locked doors, sometimes for as long as six hours at a time. One anonymous source noted, "Donna Olimpia goes to the pope always through the garden, so that no one, not even the butler, knows when she comes and goes."[13] People began to wonder why Olimpia sneaked into the Vatican at night, why she stayed so long, and what she and the pope were *doing* in there.

But Olimpia was, most likely, doing something infinitely more pleasurable than having sex with her brother-in-law—setting the Vatican finances in order, just as she had done with the Pamphili family finances. Gregorio Leti grumbled, "This woman made the pope retrench all expenses she deemed superfluous, obliging him to reduce wages and the appointments of officers . . . and finally putting him in the mood to see so great an economy even at his own table."[14]

"In everything one sees an exquisite slenderness," Giacinto Gigli wrote in his diary.[15] So slender, in fact, that during the first anniversary celebrations of Innocent's coronation, the bells of Rome's churches remained stonily silent because Olimpia had fired the bell ringers.

Olimpia's official monthly stipend as first lady of Rome was only 250 scudi, plus the 18 scudi a month for laundering the pope's underwear. But she would make far more money by taking bribes for influence peddling.

The Mantuan ambassador wrote, "Having great authority with the pope, all recognize her to get honors, offices, and favors, purchasing her efficacious intercessions in the form of extravagant gifts, so that giving them becomes obligatory."[16]

According to the Venetian ambassador, "Donna Olimpia Maidalchini, sister-in-law of His Holiness, the only recipient of the favors of the pope, is a lady of intelligence and masculine spirit and only makes herself known as a woman through her haughtiness and avarice, from where it is necessary that the favor-seekers at court give her incessant obsequiousness and continual gifts."[17]

The ambassador of the republic of Lucca explained, "The signora Donna Olimpia, sister-in-law of His Holiness, governs absolutely the business of the house of Cardinal Pamphili her son. And at the age of 48 or thereabouts [she was 53], of singular valor and greatly esteemed by the pope, it is the universal opinion of the court and of all Rome that she is the most powerful and efficacious means to obtain graces and rewards from His Beatitude. She goes frequently to private audiences with His Holiness once or twice a week where she is always needed, and in this favorable environment she obtains commodious honors and great gifts."[18]

The culture of the time didn't look at gift giving as corruption; bestowing handsome presents in the hopes of influencing the powerful was, after all, only common sense. Olimpia had done it for decades to position her brother-in-law to become nuncio, cardinal, and pope. Now, sitting at the pinnacle, she would reap her reward as other ambitious people gave gifts to her. It was only fair.

Bribery was endemic not only in the Papal States but throughout Europe. When Peter the Great began executing corrupt state officials, one of them summed up the international situation when he quipped, "In the end you will have no subjects for we are all thieves."[19]

Pasquino had a field day with the cartloads of gifts trundling into Olimpia's Piazza Navona courtyard. In ringing Italian rhyme he said,

He who wishes a favor from the sovereign,
Bitter and long the road to the Vatican.
But the shrewd person
Runs to Donna Olimpia with full hands,
And there who wants it attains it,
And the street is wider and shorter.[20]

Olimpia, always short, had indeed been getting wider lately.

As a close relative of the reigning pope, Olimpia was doing nothing new in accepting bribes in return for her influence. Her zeal for power and wealth would have been lauded in a man; after all, almost every cardinal and Roman nobleman had the same aspirations. But there was one problem with Olimpia: she was a woman, operating at the apex of the oldest continuously existing misogynistic institution in the world.

⁓

To understand Olimpia's position in the Vatican, and public reaction to it, we must first take a look at the historical relationship of the Catholic Church and women. It had started off well enough; Jesus and Paul had been close to women, traveling with them to spread the word of God. Jesus' female followers stood loyally at the cross when his male disciples ran away to hide. After the crucifixion, many apostles traveled with their wives to spread the gospel. In 1 Corinthians 9:5, Paul wrote, "Don't we have the right to take believing wives along with us, as do the other apostles and the Lord's brothers and Peter?"

For three centuries after Jesus, Christianity was not an official Roman imperial religion and as such had no public churches for worship. Church services were held in homes, the accepted domain of women. And here women played a major role—teaching, disciplining, and managing material resources. According to tombstones found in France, Turkey, Greece, Italy, and Yugoslavia, some of these women were priests.

Women lost ground when Constantine legalized Christianity and built grand basilicas—the public sphere of men—for the church. A new generation of male leaders marched in, casting the women aside. The flexible hierarchy of the house churches yielded to a more rigid structure of parishes and dioceses, all run by men.

To excise traces of women's role in the early church, the apostle Junia, whom Paul hailed in Romans 16:7 as "foremost among the apostles," was transformed into Junias, a male name that incorrectly persists in Bibles today. In the ancient Roman Church of Saint Prassede, the mosaic of Bishop Theodora has had the feminine ending of her name scratched off, leaving Bishop Theodo wearing a woman's headdress.

Yet in southern Italy the tradition of women priests was not easily uprooted. Pope Gelasius I (reigned 492–496) expressed his outrage to Christian communities there. "We have heard," he thundered, "that divine affairs have come to such a low state that women are encouraged to officiate at sacred altars and all matters reserved for the male sex."[21]

Not only were women prevented from becoming priests, there was a growing movement afoot to prevent them from marrying priests. Pope Siricius (reigned 384–399) issued the first decretal denying marriage to the clergy. Yet the Bible makes clear that Saint Peter was married, and for 350 years after him the church had no policy against clerical marriage. Paul wrote in 1 Timothy, "A bishop must then be blameless, the husband of one wife, vigilant, sober, of good behavior, given to hospitality, apt to teach . . . one that ruleth well his own house, having his children in subjection in all gravity. For if a man know not how to rule his own house, how shall he care for the church of God?"

Later popes realized that a bachelor priest would not have family issues distracting him from his work and could devote himself fully to the prosperity of the church. But there was a more pressing problem. For more than a thousand years after Constantine, married priests bequeathed their churches, the lands around them, the silver sacrament chalices, and their priestly incomes to their sons. If a priest had no sons, he would give the church buildings to his daughters as dowries. Church property became something owned not by the Vatican but by individual families, passed from generation to generation. Priests' wives, with a position to maintain, paraded about town decked out in finery paid for by alms intended for the poor.

Some forty popes up until the seventh century were the sons of priests. Several popes were the sons of popes. The major attack on priestly marriage did not occur until the late eleventh century, and even then, most priests ignored it. Some married priests of the time were much like Catholics today who practice birth control—otherwise good Catholics ignoring a papal decree that proves so inconvenient to their personal lives.

Married priests were unfazed by threats of fines or loss of income. They might have to send their wives and children away if a visiting bishop came to town, but they would bring them back the moment he left. Many town leaders refused to accept bachelor priests, fearing they would seduce their wives and daughters. Churchmen sent from Rome with decrees outlawing priestly marriage were often beaten up and kicked out of town, as townsfolk threw the papal documents into a bonfire.

The church had more control over what occurred in Rome. In 1051 Pope Leo IX enslaved priestly wives, making them cook food for the bishops and scrub the church floors. After that, few Roman women wanted to marry priests. But overall, the path to priestly celibacy was long, drawn-out, and hard-fought.

The church believed sexual continence was good for the soul. Finding no decree of abstinence in the Bible, Martin Luther believed it to be a pitiful waste. Sex within marriage, he reasoned, was good. Virginity was displeasing to God, who gave people reproductive organs with the express purpose of bringing children into the world. Priestly celibacy was the real sin. God said in the book of Genesis, "Be ye fruitful and multiply." By wrongfully insisting on celibate priests, the Catholic Church had prevented the fruitful multiplication of millions of people.

Luther believed there was another problem with prohibiting priestly marriage. Sex, he reasoned, was a valid bodily need just like urination. God created the body to get certain things out of the system. To deny the body sex—or, for that matter, urination—was sure to generate a terrible explosion sooner or later. And scandalous sexual explosions occurred across the board, from the lowliest parish priest up to the popes themselves.

According to accusations made after his death, Boniface VIII (reigned 1294–1303) often said, "To lie with women or with boys is no more sin than to rub one hand against the other."[22] Many popes in the fifteenth and sixteenth centuries had children. Innocent VIII (reigned 1484–1492) was credited with sixteen, though this was probably an exaggeration. The Borgia pope had at least eight that we know about, by three of his mistresses. Julius II (reigned 1503–1513) had at least one daughter, whom he handsomely maintained, and possibly two more. Paul III (reigned 1534–1549) sired four children, whom he amply rewarded when he became pope, making his grandsons cardinals. Pius IV (reigned 1559–1565) had three bastards, and Gregory XIII (reigned 1572–1585) had one.

As the droves of papal children proved, it wasn't sex that bothered the church; it was marriage, with its rights of inheritance of ecclesiastical property. Mistresses, male lovers, and bastards posed no threat to the prosperity of the church, as they had no inheritance rights. And so the word *celibacy* came to denote lack of marriage, rather than lack of sex. Morality became a bit twisted when sex without marriage was deemed a lesser sin than sex within the bonds of holy matrimony, as the Lutherans were quick to point out.

While most papal mistresses stayed quietly in the background, there were a few exceptions. The charming Cecile, countess of Turenne, believed to be the mistress of Pope Clement VI (reigned 1342–1352), evidently did the same things that Olimpia would do three hundred years later and received the same criticism. The scintillating countess sold offices, received bribes for her influence, and paraded around with great haughtiness.

Clement's contemporary, the Florentine merchant Giovanni Villani, wrote of the pope, "When he was an archbishop he did not keep away from women but lived in the manner of young nobles, nor did he as pope try to control himself. Noble ladies had the same access to his chambers as did prelates and, among others, the Countess of Turenne was so intimate with him that, in large part, he distributed his favors through her."[23] When the pope's confessor warned him that he must give up women for the good of his eternal soul, Clement reportedly shrugged and said he had gotten used to women during his youth and only continued sexual relations now on the advice of his doctors.

Some 150 years after the countess of Turenne, Cardinal Rodrigo Borgia, who became Pope Alexander VI in 1492, took as his mistress the voluptuous brunette Giulia Farnese. When the affair began in 1489, Giulia was a bride of fifteen and Borgia was a fat cardinal of fifty-eight. Giulia wanted no power or riches for herself but accepted Borgia into her bed as the price she had to pay for getting her brother Alessandro made a cardinal.

Unambitious though she was, Giulia was a target for Vatican favor seekers. Anyone who wanted something from the pope stopped off at Giulia's house to give her presents and heavily larded compliments. "The majority of those who want to receive favors from the pope pass through that door," said one writer, referring to the large doorway of her palazzo.[24]

Her brother Alessandro, an able and diligent churchman, would forever feel uneasy about the manner in which he had obtained his red hat. Pasquino called him "the Petticoat Cardinal," an infuriating name that caught on with the Roman people. Giulia, who had advanced his career, was now a stumbling block to it long after Alexander VI's reign. She showed her brother great consideration by dying in 1524, a full decade before the Petticoat Cardinal become Pope Paul III.

The other Vatican woman of Borgia's reign was his daughter Lucrezia, who in 1501 at the age of twenty-one was given official power to run the church and the Papal States when her father toured lands conquered by her brother. Reports spread by Borgia enemies had Lucrezia sleeping with both her father and her brother, and slipping poison from her ring into the wine of enemies, none of which is likely.

Lucrezia was a pawn moved about on the bloodstained chessboard of her male relatives to advance their own selfish objectives. Highly intelligent, she survived in a brutal, male-dominated world by playing the fragile female. Twittering apologies for her headaches and fatigue, Lucrezia was permitted to remain in her rooms for days at a time, temporarily removing herself from the sinister machinations of her male family members.

Washing her ankle-length blond hair was an all-day affair, as it took hours for her ladies to comb and dry it, in front of the fire in cold weather, out on the balcony in warm. Periodically the simpering Lucrezia begged for a retreat to a convent, to get closer to God, she said, though it was more likely she wanted to escape from Vatican men. Lucrezia presented herself as weak, meek, and not terribly bright. Yet she was smart enough to get her way. Not even the most savage warlord, looking at Lucrezia's golden tresses and trembling smile, would refuse her a hair wash.

Men were less impressed by a woman like Olimpia, stomping into the Vatican with no headaches, no blond curls, and no apologies for being a weak, stupid female. She knew she was smarter than the men and didn't bother to hide it. And their resentment grew.

12

Vengeance on the Barberinis

*Even on the highest throne in the world,
we are still sitting on our ass.*

—Michel de Montaigne

OLIMPIA AND INNOCENT STARTED OFF their papacy with an extremely dangerous enemy—Cardinal Mazarin, prime minister of France. Due to Olimpia's conclave machinations, the good cardinal found himself in the unfortunate position of having to congratulate a pope who had been the only candidate he had expressly excluded from the papacy.

In a fury, Mazarin fired Ambassador Saint-Chamond, believing incorrectly that he had taken a bribe to allow Pamphili's election. He then punished Cardinal Antonio Barberini's betrayal by taking away his lucrative French protectorship and stripping him of all French honors, incomes, and titles.

Gazing from afar at the new pope and his family, Mazarin realized that he could not bare his fangs openly and covered them with an oily professional smile. In November 1644, Mazarin instructed the French ambassador to Venice, Nicolas de Gremonville, to travel to Rome to present Innocent X with the homage of six-year-old King Louis XIV. Mistakenly believing that the cardinal nephew would hold the greatest influence over the new pontiff, Mazarin instructed Gremonville to bestow on Camillo the abbey of Corbie, the second richest in France, with an annual income of twelve thousand scudi.

To win over Olimpia—whom Mazarin reckoned would always have some influence over Innocent—Gremonville was instructed to lose money at her card parties. The ambassador of Lucca observed that on certain evenings the Pamphili palazzo on the Piazza Navona became a gambling den, "where run princes, high prelates and other sorts of nobility, each believing himself greatly fortunate to have rotten luck in this gaming, as losing could acquire the protection of this signora in their interests and cause her to affectionately and efficaciously advance their causes to His Holiness."[1]

Losing money to Olimpia was, of course, a form of bribery, but more fun for her than simply receiving a bag of money or a diamond necklace. At the card table she could truly *win*. It is amusing to picture the grandees of Rome and ambassadors of foreign powers racing to Olimpia's house intent upon losing vast sums to her at the seventeenth-century equivalent of poker. Given the whims of Lady Luck, there must have been a few courtiers who won, despite their best efforts to lose, and walked away humiliated by the gold coins stuffing their pockets, knowing that now they would never get anywhere with the pope.

The courtly Gremonville managed to lose such great sums that Olimpia demonstrated "with words and a great expression of affection the desire to earn his approval, declaring herself his special servant, exaggerating that there would never be an occasion where she would not do her best to serve him."[2]

Having cleverly lost a fortune to Olimpia at cards, the ambassador then informed the pope of Cardinal Mazarin's dearest wish, the one tiny favor that would cement the friendship of France and the Papal States forever—a cardinal's cap for Mazarin's brother, the Dominican priest Father Michel. This request was not out of Mazarin's love for Michel, whom he considered an idiot, but out of his dynastic ambitions.

By making some of his relatives high-level churchmen and marrying others into powerful European families, Mazarin could strengthen his tenuous hold on power. He was prime minister neither by election, nor by parliamentary approval, nor by the king's personal appointment because the king was still a small child. Jules Mazarin held power because he was the queen mother's lover.

While the French might have shrugged and winked when it came to taking the queen to bed, what they could not forgive was that the prime minister of France wasn't even French. Though he dripped in opulent French lace and clipped his silky beard in the sharply pointed French fashion, beneath his overpowering French cologne there remained the annoying whiff of spaghetti sauce. The powerful nobles grumbled, and Mazarin lived uneasily, knowing that he could be toppled at any moment.

Unfortunately for the prime minister's dearest wish, Innocent knew Michel Mazarin and despised him. In fact, many people wondered if Michel was all right in the head. He seemed to be a child, giggling one moment, stomping his foot in rage the next, apologizing after that. In addition to his impetuosity, Michel was known for his "indiscretions," which we can presume to be sexual in nature.

Innocent had too great a respect for the church to make such a man a cardinal. When the pope's list of cardinals was announced on March 6, 1645, it included Orazio Giustiniani, the brother of Andrea Giustiniani, who had married Olimpia's older daughter, Maria. It also listed Niccolò Albergati, a cousin of Niccolò Ludovisi, who had married Olimpia's younger daughter, Costanza. These creations were all well and good as etiquette demanded that the pope select a cardinal from each of the families that had married into his own. But of the five other cardinals, not one of them was named Michel Mazarin. Worse, all seven were known to be pro-Spanish.

Ambassador Gremonville marched into the Vatican protesting loudly, and Innocent declared that he would *never* consider Michel Mazarin worthy of the honor of being a cardinal. When Jules Mazarin heard the news, he was so insulted that he loudly threatened to follow the ways of Henry VIII, creating an autonomous church of France and never paying another penny to Rome. He ordered his ambassador to leave Rome immediately. Nursing his wounded pride, Mazarin considered the best way to humiliate the stubborn pope.

Meanwhile, Cardinal Antonio Barberini found himself in a terrible situation. Having lost his French income, he called on his old enemies the Spaniards, who, in order to obtain his support in conclave for Cardinal Pamphili, had promised they would restore any loss of French funds. Now Spain apologetically backtracked, saying they could not offend their ally, the duke of Tuscany, who hated Antonio Barberini. Besides, they really couldn't afford it. And so he was left with no money and no honors. In the streets of Rome, people hissed and hooted and threw dung at his carriage. Many cardinals avoided him, and Cardinal de' Medici pretended not to see him at all, looking straight through him so he would not have to render his respects according to protocol.

Worse was to come. While Innocent was initially kind to the Barberinis, letting them know how much he appreciated their votes in conclave, he found himself increasingly besieged on all sides to investigate them for corruption. The Vatican treasury was nineteen million scudi in the red, and the useless Castro war alone had cost twelve million. There were, all in all, tens of millions of scudi missing. And much of it could be found in Barberini palaces and art collections.

Olimpia, too, was pressuring the pope to punish the Barberinis, who were furious at her. She had betrayed them, they complained, promising to marry her son to their niece, when all along she must have known Camillo was planning on becoming cardinal nephew. Fantastically rich, still powerful in their connections, the Barberinis could wreak the most excruciating revenge on Olimpia as soon as Innocent breathed his last. Better to have them poor, powerless, and exiled. The warm feeling of safety that Olimpia had enjoyed when Innocent was elected hadn't lasted very long. The highest position in the land was not so much a sanctuary as a target. Now Olimpia had more enemies, who could do her more harm, than ever before.

Innocent was tortured by indecision. He was keenly aware that without the Barberini votes he would never have been elected pope, and he was always ready to show gratitude to those—like Olimpia—who had helped him. On the other hand, with his strict sense of justice and strong streak of parsimony, Innocent knew the Barberinis had had their hands in the till. Pressured by Olimpia, numerous cardinals, advisors, Pasquino, and the people of Rome, the pope named a commission to investigate the Barberini family for corruption. He wanted a detailed accounting of all monies the family had received from the Vatican and how they had been spent.

But the Barberinis had kept lousy account books and in many cases hadn't kept any records at all. For the twenty-one years their uncle was pope, they had used the Vatican treasury as a personal bank account for building palaces, buying art, and helping the poor. Awash in money, they had seen no reason to keep a record of it. Waving away the Barberini excuses, the commission insisted loudly on getting the accounting records, and the family grew desperate.

Mazarin realized that he could become a thorn in the side of the pope by taking the Barberini family back under his protection as the persecuted victims of a cruel pontiff. Forgetting his fury and vengeance against them only months earlier, he secretly extended his welcome and promise of financial assistance if things got too hot in Rome.

As usual, Pasquino, with his psychic abilities, made an accurate prediction, crowing: "From what people are saying, I think that we will see Innocent chasing away from Rome the family of the bee."[3]

Cardinal Antonio immediately took Mazarin up on his offer. Though all Barberinis had been guilty of corruption above and beyond the accepted level, Cardinal Antonio had possibly been guilty of murder as well. There had been that little matter in the early 1630s when he sent Olimpia's young nephew to war and he died soon after, shot in the back, it was said, by a henchman of the good cardinal. Now Antonio felt he was in grave danger. In September, without obtaining the mandatory papal permission to travel, he fled Rome for France. Upon hearing the news, Innocent was shocked.

In December Prince Taddeo and Cardinal Francesco Barberini unearthed some records for the war of Castro, which they delivered to the commission. But the commissioners found the records highly irregular; the war had cost some twelve million scudi, but the entries had gaping holes, with large sums unaccounted for. As a result, all Barberini bank accounts were frozen and all Barberini family members were put under surveillance. Servants were taken away for questioning—a polite word for torture. Word on the street was that the Barberinis would be put in prison, perhaps a dank, dark cell in the dungeons of Castel Sant'Angelo, a place from which few people ever emerged.

Dressed as huntsmen, Cardinal Francesco, Prince Taddeo, and his children sailed away from Rome in January 1646, leaving the imperious Anna Colonna to defend what was left of the family property. Just when Olimpia thought she could take over the Palazzo Barberini, Anna Colonna defiantly raised the French flag over the entrance, declaring that she had given the house to Louis XIV, and brought in French soldiers to defend the property. It was a clever move, because now if Olimpia made any attempt to take it, France would have cause to wage war on the pope.

Though Anna Colonna kept her palace, it was cold and empty. All the exquisite furnishings had been hidden from the pope. The princess, who had used only utensils of pure gold and silver, was seen waving a rusty tin fork in the air as lamentable proof of how far the family fortunes had fallen due to the vengeance of the Pamphilis. Many who knew her, however, said she still had the gold and silver utensils safely hidden in a palace wall and used the rusty tin forks to make herself look pitiful.

Mazarin welcomed the fugitive Barberinis in triumph, greeting them outside Paris with a cavalcade of more than a hundred carriages. He held lavish banquets for them and restored their French incomes. The French government decried the unjust persecution of the poor innocent cardinals.

Documents indicated that when Innocent heard of Mazarin's exuberant welcome of the Barberinis to Paris, he threw a temper tantrum, screaming and jumping up and down in his white robes. "The heretics are laughing," he said, "and the Catholics are scandalized to see a pope so scorned as I am."[4]

While the pope was fretting about his loss of dignity, Olimpia was not above having a good laugh at the situation. For the Carnival of 1646 she gave a play in her palazzo, attended by Rome's elite, in which a staggering drunk (Francesco Barberini) was held up by a man dressed half-French, half-Italian (Mazarin), who picked him off the ground each time he fell. Those with more delicate sensibilities thought the play in very poor taste given the dangerous international situation. But Olimpia's cackles rang out loudly at this earthy scene. Word of the Carnival comedy winged its way swiftly to Paris, where her humor didn't translate very well into French.

Mazarin considered his next step. Though he couldn't very well attack the Vicar of Christ, he could wage war on the pope's ally, Spain, in territories uncomfortably close to the Papal States. In the spring of 1646, a French fleet left port in Provence, captured the Spanish isle of Elba, and raided principalities along the Italian coast. To show the pope that the war was, indeed, a personal vendetta, France captured the Spanish territory of Piombino, owned by Olimpia's son-in-law Prince Ludovisi.

But French successes were short-lived. Plagued by military setbacks, Mazarin suddenly looked ridiculous, waging a stupid war against Spain just because his idiot brother was not given a cardinal's cap. Some called it a tyrannical abuse of power.

In addition to his reverses in the war, Mazarin soon discovered that he did not like the Barberini brothers, who had become a thorn in his side. They seemed ungrateful for the income he had given them, whining that it was not nearly as much as they had enjoyed in Rome. They were reduced to such a disgraceful state, they lamented, that they couldn't even throw decent dinner parties. They wanted to go home. They wanted their Roman titles, honors, commissions, positions, and properties restored. Surely the all-powerful Mazarin could make this happen.

Given the lost battles, huge costs, political unrest, and the Barberini complaints, the beleaguered prime minister couldn't stand it anymore. What had seemed like a political stroke of genius was quickly turning into a disaster. Mazarin sent a new ambassador to Rome, the abbot Saint-Nicolas, to negotiate the Barberinis' return in a manner that would allow both France and the Holy See to keep face. On June 20, Saint-Nicolas was received by the pope, who insisted that the Barberinis write him a letter of apology and pay a hefty fine of 600,000 scudi. When Saint-Nicolas spoke of reducing the amount, the pope inveighed against "the consummate dissimulation" of the family that cried poverty "while from the dust of their palace you could get a fortune, and that Donna Anna used the same lies when eating on earthen plates."[5]

As negotiations proceeded, Olimpia was also having second thoughts about the Barberini exile. If she brought them back, they would be extremely grateful to her. Perhaps it was not too late to arrange a marriage between the families, and all would be forgotten. She told Innocent it was time to let bygones be bygones and sweep the whole untidy affair under the rug. On September 12, Innocent acquitted the Barberinis of criminal intent and did not impose his threatened fine, but he stubbornly insisted on receiving letters of apology before he permitted their return. And the matter of their confiscated property would have to be attended to later.

On December 16, Cardinal Antonio wrote three letters asking pardon, one to Innocent, one to Olimpia, and one to Camillo. On the same day, not by coincidence, Saint-Nicolas called on Olimpia, who welcomed him with a great show of friendship. Saint-Nicolas, knowing exactly what to say to win her over, thanked her obsequiously for using her immense influence with the pope on behalf of the Barberinis. When Olimpia demurred, saying she hadn't really done anything, he assured her of her great power. Later that day the ambassador wrote to Mazarin, "She would have been plenty mad if we believed she didn't have any."[6]

Mazarin, having finally put away his warships, felt increasingly well disposed toward the pope. First of all, he was going to get the troublesome Barberinis off his hands. Second, Mazarin felt that Innocent was not in a position to refuse a cardinal's hat to his idiot brother, Michel. And now he truly understood who had the power to obtain it for him—Olimpia. Saint-Nicolas had informed Mazarin that all efforts should be concentrated on Olimpia, and that it was perfectly useless to speak with the cardinal nephew. "It is better not to go there at all," he advised, "because he only responds with compliments."[7]

~⁀⁀⁀

"'Tis a tedious thing to Princes' Ministers who are old Stagers in Councils and Affairs, to have to do with raw unexperienced Persons," wrote

Gregorio Leti about the cardinal nephew.[8] And indeed, Camillo's favorite part of his vaunted position was the honor, precedence, and income he received, along with those dazzling red robes. We can picture him trying them on in front of a full-length mirror, tilting his biretta rakishly and admiring the result. The only thing he hated about his job was the work.

Camillo was horrified that his uncle expected him to sit in an office all day and meet with ambassadors and other cardinals who talked about the most *boring* subjects—politics, finance, defense, and trade agreements. His visitors, for their part, were insulted that as they spoke about matters of international urgency, the cardinal nephew was doodling on a piece of paper—sketching gardens and designs for his new villa.

As soon as his uncle became pope in 1644, Camillo decided to build a villa on a large property his father had bought in 1630. Located on the top of Janiculum Hill, with a magnificent view of Saint Peter's dome, the land was just begging for a pleasure house with extensive gardens. As cardinal nephew, Camillo now had unlimited funds to build his dream villa, which he called Bel Respiro for its fresh, bracing air. He hired the sculptor Alessandro Algardi to work with him, and soon the villa began to rise.

While digging the foundations, Algardi realized he was actually building on an extensive ancient Roman cemetery that included the tomb of Nero's bodyguard. This was a happy turn of events because the excavators unearthed quantities of statuary that Camillo wanted to use on the façade. Unfortunately, many torsos were lacking heads, and the heads they found were missing torsos; and arms and legs had disappeared during destruction by Goths, Vandals, and Saracens. Camillo solved this problem by having Algardi glue available heads on available bodies and sculpt the parts that were missing, then strew the finished product all across the façade.

At first glimpse the villa is an impressive confection, pale blue, covered with white statues and friezes that look like elaborate frosting on an ornate wedding cake. But upon closer inspection, the heads and bodies clearly don't match—the heads are too big, or too small—and there

seems to be no rhyme or reason for these statue parts and their place-
ment. The overall impression is that the villa, while lovely, is also inex-
plicably strange. But Camillo thought it was wonderful, and during his
meetings with high-level officials his mind wandered off from war with
France to marble body parts for his villa.

Complaints about Camillo's uselessness began to percolate up to the
pope, who lectured him sternly. He must stop sketching and do something useful. When Camillo told Innocent that he had always been interested in the military—probably because he looked so dashing on a
horse—his uncle gave him the commission of building ships for the
papal navy. In his *avvisi* of August 5, 1645, Teodoro Amayden reported
that Camillo's first vessel was launched in a great ceremony attended by
his mother and the pope. But the boat had been built so badly that it
immediately listed to one side and was in danger of sinking. It was sent
back to the boatyard, where it was probably scuttled.

Innocent, who had always worked diligently for the church, was furious over his nephew's indolence. Leti explained, "The Pope, having
created his Cardinal Nephew, had no other design than to instruct him
bit by bit to render him capable of administering political affairs, already being aware of the little wit he had. But the Nephew, instead of
advancing, seemed rather to reverse. So much so that, not profiting at
all from the good instruction of his Uncle, he was incapable of managing the smallest negotiation, so that every day he was poorly treated by
the pope who made always a thousand reproaches for his ignorance."[9]

Some days the Vatican corridors echoed with the pope's shouting at
Camillo, tearing into him for being a lazy bum, leaving all the hard
work to his poor elderly uncle. In response, the cardinal nephew locked
himself in his rooms on the Piazza Navona and took to his bed for days
on end, claiming illness.

Olimpia graciously offered to read those petitions that Camillo found
too boring to bother with, and to write his answers. But Camillo certainly didn't want his *mother* telling him what to do. One day after a
particularly bitter argument with her, he raced in his carriage to the
Vatican and begged the pope to lock Olimpia up in a convent, the
proper place for meddling women.

There it was again, the sound of the bolt grinding shut behind her. She would never forgive Camillo for that. She would make him pay for that.

Seeing Camillo's uselessness, Olimpia's son-in-law Niccolò Ludovisi hoped to be assigned high-level political offices. After all, it was the only reason he had married Costanza at such a bargain-basement dowry. Gregorio Leti asserted, "This Prince had enclin'd to this match, out of an opinion of making great advantages by it, as seeing at the time that Cardinal Camillo was made Cardinal, and altogether unfit for business, so that he flattered himself with an opinion of being the only Nephew and governing the Pope and Church."[10]

But Olimpia wanted all the power herself and was certainly not going to let the fat prince acquire any at her expense. Luckily for her, the pope didn't like him anyway. Innocent "had no great tenderness for him," the French ambassador reported.[11] Sometimes Prince Ludovisi had to fight even to obtain an audience with the pope. When he did see the pontiff, Innocent "had no other conversation than topics of drollery and never entered into anything of importance. And if he initiated some discourse, the pope always interrupted him with gossip and foolishness which seemed to the poor prince that the pope wanted him to serve as a court jester rather than as a nephew."[12]

When he complained to his mother-in-law about the lack of honors and offices that were his due as pope's nephew, "Donna Olimpia answered him in a haughty manner, that it was honor enough for him that he had been preferred to marry her Daughter over so many competitors of as great a quality as himself. Whereupon the Prince, being unwilling to come to a rupture with one who had so great an influence upon the Pope, would hold his tongue and be quiet."[13]

The prince vented his rage by telling anyone who would listen that he would never have debased himself by marrying the daughter of a cheapskate nobody like Olimpia if he had known he wouldn't be getting any Vatican power in return. Word got around Rome, and we can only imagine how Costanza felt.

On May 4, 1645, at Olimpia's suggestion, the pope appointed Prince Ludovisi commander-in-chief of the fleet sent to aid Venice in defending

Crete against invading Turks. That would get him out of her hair for a while and stop him spreading such nastiness around Rome. Maybe, if she was lucky, he wouldn't return. But when the fleet finally arrived in the Aegean after many delays, they found that all but one of the Christian forts had fallen, and the Turks were in control. After a few inconclusive skirmishes at sea, the prince bounced back to Rome, a war hero, gloriously wounded in the finger.

As if Innocent didn't have enough on his hands, it appeared that the new façade of Saint Peter's Basilica was in danger of falling down. The church was the grandest building in all the world, a marvel of engineering, and proof in stone of Catholic supremacy. Even a partial collapse would signal greater fits of laughter from the heretics, and louder sobs from the Catholics, than had yet been heard.

Clement VIII (reigned 1592–1605) had established a committee specifically for the building and maintenance of the basilica, the Congregation of the Fabric of Saint Peter's. Working with this group, Innocent should have found it a simple task to have experts examine the cracks and propose solutions. But the pope was caught in a power struggle between the two most talented artists of his time, who, unfortunately, both happened to be living in Rome, competing for the same work, and nursing deadly hatred for each other.

Gian Lorenzo Bernini, born in 1598, had achieved unheard-of success at an early age. Discovered by Cardinal Nephew Scipione Borghese as a child, Bernini sculpted some of the most phenomenal works of art ever created. Known as the new Michelangelo, Bernini had been the darling of Pope Urban VIII. The day Urban was elected in 1623 he called the young artist to the Vatican. "Great fortune is yours, Cavalier," he proclaimed, "to see Cardinal Maffeo Barberini become pope. But even greater is our fortune, that Cavalier Bernini lives during our pontificate."[14]

Bernini had entrée into Pope Urban's apartments twenty-four hours a day and swashbuckled around the Vatican as if he owned the place. He was a handsome man with noble features, flashing black eyes, and high cheekbones. Sensual full lips poked out beneath his silky black mustache. His jaw was square, and an adorable cleft marked his chin.

He had quite a reputation as a womanizer and apparently sculpted the likeness of his rowdy mistress as Divine Love on the pope's tomb. When Bernini turned forty, Urban announced that it was time for the loyal son of the church to marry and settle down. The pope had, in fact, already found him a wife, the most beautiful girl in Rome, Caterina Tezio, whom Bernini dutifully married and with whom he had eleven children.

Bernini's extraordinary success at an early age, flamboyant personality, and dashing good looks irritated his fellow artists, who were less successful, less flamboyant, and less good-looking. But the most irritated of all was the sullen Francesco Borromini, born in 1599, the absolute antithesis of Bernini in appearance, demeanor, and personality. Borromini was not an attractive man, with his small, hard eyes, hooked nose, and thin lips. He had a disheveled appearance, and those who saw him must have restrained themselves from whipping out a comb and trying to tame his hair. There were no woman stories wafting about Borromini like cheap perfume, nor were there any boy stories, either. He lived a solitary existence, pouring his passions into his work and his vengeance.

Borromini felt that he would be Rome's top architect if only that windbag Gian Lorenzo Bernini had not come into the picture. In terms of solid engineering skill and architectural originality, Borromini had the advantage over his rival. While keeping colors and costs to a minimum, he created designs that were unique, unexpected, employing inverted geometrical forms in ways that had never been done before.

For all his startling genius as a sculptor, Bernini's architecture employed conventional forms overlaid with lavish colorful materials. Engineering was his weakest point. He had gone through a baptism of fire—literally—when casting the bronze baldachino in Saint Peter's. Toward the end he realized the structure could not bear the weight of the risen Christ he had designed for the top. The four colossal statues Bernini had placed on the piers surrounding the baldachino had been designed to react to the figure of Jesus in the center. But they ended up gasping and gesturing in response to something that didn't exist, which they still do to this very day.

Rome's art commissions, like marriages and political appointments, were decided at the dinner table. Bernini's wit sparkled like the crystal goblets he drank from. Draped in his eternal, old-fashioned black clothes, Borromini was more like Death eating an onion, his face scowling and puckered, lacking only a sickle to complete the picture. As it was unpleasant to have Doom as a dinner guest, he usually wasn't invited back. When clients did give him work, he was often so temperamental that they fired him, or he stormed off the job in a blistering rage.

Borromini felt that Urban VIII should have given him the two great commissions of the 1620s—the construction of the Palazzo Barberini and the design and casting of Saint Peter's baldachino. The pope gave both jobs to Bernini, and Borromini worked under his archrival for one tenth the pay. As Borromini saw it, he had crafted the guts of the projects while Bernini was toasted at all the best parties and took all the credit, never sharing a shred with his team of talented workmen. "I do not mind that he has the money," Borromini would say, "but I do mind that he enjoys the honor of my labors."[15]

Frowning in the shadows, Borromini waited for his chance to pounce on his despised competitor. And it came. The façade of Saint Peter's was always meant to have bell towers, or campanili. In 1618 the great architect Carlo Maderno had begun to build foundations for low, modest towers at each end of the façade, but work stopped when Paul V died in 1621. In 1638 Urban VIII commanded Bernini to build magnificent three-story bell towers, some two hundred feet high, loaded with pilasters, arches, colored marble inlay, and marble columns.

When he heard of Bernini's latest papal commission, Borromini grumbled that the foundations had not been built to support the heavier weight and the façade would crack. But those who heard him were mindful of his sour grapes, and his warnings were ignored. Borromini kept a careful eye on his enemy's construction and was delighted to find that as the south tower rose, alarming cracks appeared in the church façade. The added weight was indeed pushing the south part of the building into the shifting, sandy soil below.

In 1642 work on the towers ceased. Pope Urban needed all available funds for the Castro war. Before his death in 1644, no decision was made as to how to proceed with the bell towers—whether to shore them up or tear them down. But the new pope was faced with the urgent decision his predecessor had put off. One of Innocent's first decrees after his election was to form a committee of architects, engineers, and the eight cardinals of the Congregation of the Fabric to look into the problem. A shaft was dug to examine the foundations of the south tower, into which members of the committee descended on rope swings.

The first meeting was held on March 27, 1645. The most outspoken critic of the bell towers was none other than Francesco Borromini, who claimed the heavy towers would pull the façade with them as they settled, and the entire front of the church would collapse. Borromini presented mathematical calculations to show that the tower was three times higher and six times heavier than it should have been. "The prudent architect does not first erect a building and then make a sounding to see if he finds cracks in the foundation," he declared, making it clear to all that Bernini was a most imprudent architect.[16]

Innocent attended the next meeting, on June 8, as did both Borromini and Bernini. Borromini presented new drawings to show that the whole thing was poised to topple with a thunderous crash. "He declared publicly against Bernini in the pope's presence with all his heart and all his strength," Domenico Bernini wrote in his biography of his father.[17]

Borromini and other jealous architects, wounded by years of papal neglect, beat their breasts. "These were the ruinous results visited on Rome," they cried, "by those popes who were pleased to give all the work to one man alone, although there was an abundance of meritorious men in the city."[18]

In the face of such vehement opposition to his bell towers, Bernini offered to work with other architects to study the foundations and perform tests over a period of time. Everyone on the commission except Borromini agreed that there was no imminent danger of collapse. The cautious pope found Bernini's suggestion a wise one, and so the matter was left.

But Bernini's flamboyance got the better of his common sense. In

February 1646, at the behest of Olimpia, he wrote and produced a Carnival play at her palazzo for a crowd of cardinals and nobility. Bernini made the sets and costumes and joined the young noblemen of Rome in acting. Unfortunately, the play made fun of the pope and the cardinal nephew. The ambassador of Modena, Francesco Mantovani, explained, "There was depicted in the play a youth who had good will but who never did anything and an old man who never could make up his mind."[19]

Though the script has, tragically, been lost, we can still hear Olimpia's loud guffaws as she poked fun at her inept son and her indecisive brother-in-law. She must have seen no harm in it because other Bernini plays given at her palazzo poked fun at Olimpia herself, making her out to be a greedy, power-hungry vixen; she chuckled hardest at these.

When he heard about the play, the old man who could never make up his mind couldn't make up his mind about it. Draped in his brittle dignity, Innocent had never been one to laugh at himself. He asked Cardinal Panciroli his opinion about Bernini's play. The cardinal reassured him that it was just another silly piece of Carnival revelry that would soon be forgotten.

But the young man who never did anything was furious. Camillo complained bitterly to the pope that the play had his mother's "tacit approval and reinforced the caricature of the cardinal nephew circulating at court." He told his uncle the play was "foul."[20] Everyone in Rome was talking about it and making fun of him.

Camillo vowed to wreak his revenge. Though Olimpia seemed untouchable at the moment, Bernini was in a very delicate situation due to the bell towers. He was also fragile politically; the spoiled darling of the reviled Barberini family, he stood on a precipice, ready to tumble after them into the fissures of disgrace.

While the enemies of the Barberinis circled their prey, and the jealous architects of Rome pounced, it was the cardinal nephew who bit into the jugular. According to Bernini's contemporary biographer, Filippo Baldinucci, when Innocent retired to an estate outside Rome for a few days, "enemies of Bernini and the Barberini family, especially a certain person semi-skilled in art whom the pope greatly trusted," persuaded the pope "by intensive arguments" to have the bell towers torn down immediately.[21] The certain person semi-skilled in art was Camillo.

It was reported that the pope also decided to fine Bernini the cost of dismantling and reconstructing the bell towers, a whopping 160,000 scudi. "It is a miracle that the *Cavaliere* has not been condemned to prison," Mantovani marveled. But, the ambassador continued, Bernini tactfully gave Olimpia a thousand gold coins and presented Camillo with a valuable diamond ring given to him by Queen Henrietta Maria of England. The threat of a fine was dropped, but the beautiful half-built bell towers came down. Now Saint Peter's would forever be too wide for its height.

For the first time in twenty-five years, Bernini was no longer the chief papal architect. Now Borromini, who had smoldered with ill-suppressed rage for decades, swaggered about the Vatican, dizzy with victory. It is not surprising that the stiff, uneasy pope was perhaps the only person in Rome who actually liked the stiff, uneasy Borromini. Bernini's razzle-dazzle enthusiasm had frayed Innocent's nerves.

Though disgraced, Bernini was allowed to complete the elaborate sepulcher of Urban VIII in Saint Peter's that he had been sculpting on and off since 1628. It is just to the right of the far altar as the spectator looks at it, balanced by the equally magnificent monument of Paul III just to the left. The figure of Christ on the cross in the center caused some wits to call the statues of the nepotistic popes on either side the "two thieves."

Bernini's very public downfall and the triumph of his inveterate enemy made him ill for a while, and it seems that he sank into a deep depression. When he recovered, he found he had countless high-priced commissions from noblemen and cardinals for paintings and sculptures. But Bernini first made a statue for himself, a giant female image of Truth, which he kept in his home. This prompted Pasquino to quip that the only truth to be found in Rome was in Bernini's palazzo.

13

~ ⌾

The Despised
Daughter-in-Law

Between daughter-in-law and mother-in-law,
the devil is at work.

—Italian proverb

THOUGH CAMILLO WAS BORED by his work, he had never been bored by beautiful women. And indeed, the dashing cardinal nephew, with his flashing black eyes, glistening black curls, and swirling red robes, was the object of fascination of numerous noble Roman ladies. But Camillo, who flirted with many, was particularly fascinated by one of them, Olimpia Aldobrandini, the princess of Rossano, who was, unfortunately, the wife of Prince Paolo Borghese.

A slender woman who took up a great deal of space in a room, the princess of Rossano was the spectacular amalgamation of sparkling wit, exquisite breeding, a peerless papal bloodline, and radiant beauty. She had a gloriously rich mane of chestnut curls, strong black brows, and sparkling dark eyes. Her complexion was peaches and cream, her nose straight, her lips full and wavy. Her figure was perfect, and her taste in clothing exquisite. When the princess of Rossano entered a gathering, jaws dropped—even those of the oldest, most chaste cardinals.

In addition to being beautiful, she was spirited, bold, and confident, one of the few women in Rome considered well worth listening to.

Swishing into a room with her long silken train, smiling and nodding to the men assembled there, she opened her mouth and they were spellbound. "Highly gifted by nature and by fortune,"[1] Cardinal Pallavicino wrote of the princess, who was "furnished with intelligence, grace, and excellent power of speech."[2]

Clothing styles had changed since Olimpia's youth. Gone were the clunky wheel-shaped farthingales sticking out from the waist. Gone were the enormous platter-sized ruffs, the heavily embroidered and stiffly bejeweled velvets. By the 1640s women's fashions had a flowing ease to them that had not been seen in well over a century. Women gleamed in shining silk that threatened to slip entirely off the shoulders. Their décolletage was so low it barely covered the nipples. A puffy undershirt poked through full elbow-length sleeves sliced open in front and held loosely together by jeweled pins, as if they had been placed there as an afterthought.

Hair, too, had completely changed. In Olimpia's day it had been severely scraped back from the face, secured over horsehair pads or metal frames, and loaded with gems. Now it was cut shoulder-length and curled, swinging and bobbing gently as a lady nodded, with tiny pin curls framing the face. Large teardrop-shaped pearls were worn in the hair and ears.

When the princess of Rossano—all bouncing curls, gleaming silks, and lustrous pearls—swept into Olimpia's palazzo the day after Innocent's election to render her congratulations, the usually loquacious Camillo appeared to be struck dumb, his mouth agape. Many visitors chuckled at his mute ecstasy, but little account was taken of it; it was known, that particular month, that Camillo was in love with a ballerina.

Olimpia Aldobrandini had a most interesting and romantic story. She was related to Pope Paul III (Alessandro Farnese, reigned 1534–1549) and was a cousin of the Farnese duke of Parma. She was also the great-grandniece of Pope Clement VIII (Ippolito Aldobrandini), who had died in 1605, leaving enormous wealth to his cardinal nephew's nephew, Ippolito Aldobrandini. By the time Cardinal Ippolito died in 1638, his only surviving relative was his niece, Olimpia, a girl of fifteen.

Father Ridolfi, general of the Dominicans and a friend of her deceased uncle, placed her immediately in the Monastery of Saint Sixtus outside Rome to prevent her being kidnapped and forced to marry a man who could then claim her wealth.

The Barberinis had their eye on her, and while they were figuring out which young family member she would marry, they instructed the abbots that she was not to receive any visitors whatsoever. However, Father Ridolfi, looking out for the girl's best interests, arranged a marriage with the heir to the Borghese fortune. The handsome Prince Paolo, sixteen, also belonged to a papal family. His grand-uncle Paul V (reigned 1605–1621) had siphoned off untold riches from the Vatican coffers, most of which had descended to the young man. In addition to owning the principality of Sulmona and several palaces, Paolo reportedly had four million gold pieces stashed in his house. One day Father Ridolfi secretly took the princess bride from the monastery to marry the young prince.

A few days later, Donna Costanza Magalotti, the mother of the Barberini cardinals and Prince Taddeo, arrived at the monastery to claim the girl. To her grinding chagrin, she found that the heiress had gone, and worse, that she was already married. A luscious fortune had slipped from the Barberini hands while they dillydallied. There was nothing they could do other than fire Father Ridolfi from his post as Dominican general.

The young couple moved into the Villa Borghese, surrounded by extensive gardens, orchards, fountains, aviaries, and a zoo, on a hill just outside the main gate of Rome. It was also known as the Villa del Sale— the salt villa—because Paul V had put a tax on salt to pay for it. The villa was not a home so much as a museum, built by Cardinal Nephew Scipione Borghese to showcase the sculptures and paintings that he had begged, borrowed, bought, and stolen. From his uncle's election in 1605 to Scipione's death in 1633, whenever men digging holes came across a gorgeous statue or elegant mosaic, messengers raced to him with the news. Scipione, in turn, raced to buy the new discovery.

In addition to his ancient works of art, he had bought paintings by the best Renaissance artists—Michelangelo, Raphael, Caravaggio—and owned some of the largest, most inspired sculptures by the young Gian Lorenzo Bernini. Scipione was even known to steal paintings off church walls, causing howls of protests, which his uncle the pope had to smooth over. His palazzo was a gorgeous home for the bride, though she had to be careful when moving about her airy, frescoed chambers not to knock over a statue.

In quick succession, the princess had three children, two boys and a girl. One boy died young, which presented a problem. While the first son was to take the Borghese name to continue his father's line, a second son was required to take the Aldobrandini name, as that line had died out. Her uncle Cardinal Aldobrandini had left a will stating that his entire fortune would go to Olimpia's second son if he took the Aldobrandini name.

On June 24, 1646, at the age of twenty-four, Prince Paolo Borghese died. To avoid the ten-thousand-scudi fee for bringing a dead body into Rome, the family smuggled him into the city hidden in a hay cart and secretly interred him in the family crypt. Olimpia Aldobrandini, the princess of Rossano, was now a widow—a very beautiful, very rich young widow who urgently needed to remarry and bear a son to reap her uncle's fortune.

As soon as Prince Borghese's death was known, speculation began about who would marry the princess. She must endure eight months of mourning before remarrying, during which time a prince of Naples offered his hand and the ruler of Modena sent flattering letters. But it was the French government, as usual, who knew what was really going on. Their spies were the best, working as indispensable servants in all the most powerful households. Wise in the ways of human nature, these spies were always looking for the woman stories, which is why the term *"cherchez la femme"* exists in French and no other language.

On June 25, 1646, while Prince Paolo's body was being stuffed into the hay cart, the French ambassador, Saint-Nicolas, sent word to Cardinal Mazarin in Paris, "Here is a rich widow who people already say will marry Cardinal Pamphili."[3]

What the French already knew, Rome soon found out. Perhaps they saw Camillo's carriage with the pope's coat of arms making its way up to the Villa Borghese more frequently than was suitable for a man of the church. Perhaps people noticed the meaningful glances the two exchanged at Roman society parties or Vatican events. It seemed that the rich widow, dismissing her princely suitors, was going to marry the cardinal nephew.

The marriage of a prince of the church was not necessarily forbidden. Until 1917 cardinals were not required to be ordained as priests. The pope had wisely conferred on Camillo only minor orders and not priestly ordination, a sacrament that was thought to tattoo the human soul with an invisible but ineradicable seal that prevented marriage. The cardinalate, on the other hand, was a dignity. And a dignity was like a coat; it could be put on and taken off at will. Remaining unsealed, Camillo could legally take off his coat and marry.

Though it was rare for a cardinal to renounce his position, a few did. Usually these were the brothers of rulers who died without heirs, cardinals who suddenly found themselves kings and were required to marry, have children, and rule a nation.

We might wonder why the princess, who could have married anyone, would want to marry a cardinal. Perhaps the cachet of scandal appealed to her—the forbidden romance, the man who had everything giving it up for *her*. She was a seventeenth-century version of Wallis Warfield Simpson, the American socialite for whom King Edward VIII of Great Britain gave up his throne in 1936. The princess was thrilled to be the woman for whom a king—or in this case a cardinal nephew—renounced his throne.

The frisson of scandal aside, we might also wonder what the princess saw in Camillo himself. Gregorio Leti recounted the general surprise among noble Romans "to see a princess so universally sought after and desired by so many princes and great noblemen give her affection to a man who was already known to everyone as a very simple person."[4]

True, Camillo was handsome, with his fine features and dark, silky beard, but so were dozens of other Roman noblemen. This was, after all, Italy, which boasted the best-looking people in Europe. Camillo could write a pretty verse and discuss the latest theories of gardening, but so could any Roman schoolboy. He had plenty of money from his two years as cardinal nephew, but the princess of Rossano's fortune was so immense that money was not an issue. It is likely that her interest was heightened by Camillo's close relationship to the reigning pontiff. As papal niece, *she* would be first lady of Rome, shoving aside the papal sister-in-law. The princess wanted not only to take first place at ceremonial events, she was itching to take over Olimpia's political power and run the Vatican.

The bride's rival would not relinquish her position cheerfully, of course. And by far the worst burden that came with Camillo Pamphili was his vampire of a mother, who would sink her teeth into anyone— especially a beautiful young woman—threatening her control over the pope. The image of this harpy as a mother-in-law would have struck fear into the hearts of many a young noblewoman who otherwise might have been interested in Cardinal Camillo. But the princess of Rossano was not like other women.

Perhaps the frightening mother-in-law was actually an attraction for her. Here, at last, was a worthy opponent with whom she could thrust and parry. Here was a duel in which she could use all her bounteous talents to draw some blood. The princess of Rossano accepted the cardinal's offer of marriage and sharpened her sword to do battle with his mother.

When Camillo told his mother that he wanted to marry and his choice had fallen on the princess of Rossano, Olimpia was horror-stricken. She had encouraged him to have an affair with the princess as a means of keeping him far from the Vatican so that she could do his work. According to the Venetian ambassador, "His mother consciously fomented a love affair to distract him from the applications of business, sending him often to various gatherings and conversations" with the princess.[5] Now her plot had backfired horribly. She had never envisioned that he would want to *marry* the woman.

She was not appalled at the idea of Camillo's marrying; she of all people had known he was hopelessly ill suited for the job of cardinal nephew. But Olimpia realized that allowing the princess of Rossano into the family would be like opening the gates of Rome to the Goths, or perhaps inviting the Lutherans back in for another sack. This was not a woman to meekly accept orders from her mother-in-law. Here was a woman as smart, grasping, ambitious, and manipulative as Olimpia herself.

It is likely that Olimpia was not averse to fighting her battles with a daughter-in-law—she had, over the course of her life, taken on much worse and come out victorious. But what frightened her most was the thought of the pope's reaction to this charming new niece. There would be frequent interaction between Innocent and the princess, of course— lunches, dinners, banquets, religious events, and the more official papal audiences in which the lovely bride would request honors and benefits for her family and friends and would try to influence papal policy. Olimpia knew that the princess of Rossano, with her words as smooth, sweet, and golden as honey, would be able to convince the pope to do whatever she asked. And those honors and benefits could very well be the exact ones Olimpia had her eye on, and those papal policies might directly contradict what she was conniving at.

Olimpia knew that even if by some saintly miracle she could suddenly once more become twenty-three, the charms of the princess would have beaten hers hands down; and now she was fifty-five. The princess's figure was slender, shapely, achingly perfect. Olimpia's was, well, that of a fifty-five-year-old who enjoyed her dinners. Her jowls were sagging, and then there was that pesky double chin.

Olimpia was of mediocre birth, the unwanted daughter of a rural assistant tax collector. The princess boasted close connections to three papal bloodlines and was a cousin of the reigning duke of Parma. Olimpia had received the most rudimentary education; her conversation was a slab of brown beef thrown on the table. The princess's conversation was, in comparison, sparkling peach champagne, bubbling with erudite witticisms uttered in several languages ancient and modern.

Even though there had not been the slightest rumor of the pope's having sex with a woman—other than Olimpia, of course—Innocent was undoubtedly drawn to attractive women and listened to their advice. Hadn't Olimpia herself managed to wrap him around her little finger when she was at the height of her beauty? He was still tightly wrapped, of course, but that might not last long with the princess of Rossano prancing before him, flashing him brilliant smiles, batting her long black lashes, and playing the sexy dancing Salome to Innocent's entranced Herod.

Europe's elite were kept well informed of the romantic stalemate in Rome, which provoked much laughter, speculation, and wagering. On December 20, 1646, Cardinal Mazarin wrote a friend that Olimpia "feared that the princess would take ascendancy over the spirit of His Holiness."[6] Gregorio Leti explained that Olimpia "feared that the pope would have greater pleasure in talking with a young niece than with an old sister-in-law."[7]

Olimpia resolved to put a stop to it. No, she would never tolerate the union. If Camillo insisted on marrying, Olimpia would find him a girl of excellent connections to be sure, but a lumpish girl—awkward, painfully shy, and humbly obedient. Pimples would be a great advantage, as well as pigeon toes, bad teeth, a flat chest, and eyes that were ever so slightly crossed.

And she had just such a girl in mind. Lucrezia Barberini was now an unattractive seventeen-year-old, her eyebrows bushier than ever, living in French exile with her uncle, Cardinal Antonio. By marrying Camillo to Lucrezia, the Barberinis could come back immediately and remain forever grateful to Olimpia, especially in the next conclave. And the timid Lucrezia would never have the nerve to interfere in papal policy.

But Camillo remained firm. He would never marry Lucrezia Barberini. Never. He was in love with the princess of Rossano. According to French reports, the unhappy cardinal made desperate threats—perhaps suicidal in nature—and Olimpia was close to bursting with rage. The French envoy Saint-Nicolas reported to Mazarin in January 1647 that the pope was, as usual, torn by indecision. Certainly he was delighted at the idea of getting rid of his useless cardinal nephew. He also sympathized with the young man, in love, wanting to do the honorable thing and continue the Pamphili family line. And clearly Camillo could not have picked a more magnificent bride.

But there was Olimpia's fury to deal with. The pope couldn't go against that. And there was another problem. Innocent told Saint-Nicolas that he was afraid of looking stupid, what with Camillo's putting on and taking off the red hat in such a ridiculous manner. Camillo was ready to peevishly throw away the incomparable honor of being a prince of the Catholic Church, and this would reflect poorly on his uncle, who set high value on the dignity of the Holy See. Camillo, the pope continued, had been importuning him for the marriage since August. Afraid of tarnishing his reputation, the pope inclined against it.

Cardinal Panciroli weighed in on Camillo's side for two reasons. First, he was delighted to lose such a millstone around the neck as Camillo had been while pretending to work in the Vatican. Second, he enjoyed upsetting Olimpia, who had so interfered with his political affairs. Hearing of Panciroli's support for the marriage, Olimpia marched into the Vatican several times, venting her fury, crying "that this marriage was an obscenity and that if her son planned to marry she would approve of no other than Donna Lucrezia Barberini because in this manner it would firmly stabilize the friendship and union of the two families."[8] In response, Panciroli shrugged and smiled.

Though Camillo had Cardinal Panciroli's support, he knew that the pope usually followed Olimpia's advice. With Olimpia against him, Camillo needed to bring out the big guns in his defense. His trump card was Sister Agatha, the pope's beloved older sister in the Tor de' Specchi Convent.

A convent, like a harem, keeps its secrets to itself, secrets that die with the nuns. We know of Sister Agatha only from a few scrawled letters in the family archives and numerous reports of her tireless efforts to make peace among her warring relatives. Forgiving, compassionate, and kind, Sister Agatha was required frequently to intervene among the fractious Pamphilis. Given her advanced age and the fact that she was the pope's sister, she was one of the only nuns to have carte blanche in coming and going from her convent.

When her desperate nephew begged her to intervene on his behalf, obediently the little nun went to the Vatican to implore the pope to agree to the marriage. The pontiff now found himself hounded by Olimpia, Cardinal Panciroli, Sister Agatha, Princes Giustiniani and Ludovisi, and a myriad of cardinals, ambassadors, and advisors who weighed in on one side or the other. Paralyzed by indecision, the pope became ill and took to his bed.

The first week of January 1647, Innocent crawled out of bed and went to the Piazza Navona to have lunch with Olimpia and a long talk about what to do with Camillo. By this point, the cardinal nephew's very public agitation to get married had created a huge international scandal. Over lunch, the two must have decided to put the matter to bed, literally—allow Camillo to marry but privately, not in a big wedding in the Sistine Chapel. Let the world see that the pope was concerned for the dignity of the church and quickly get Camillo out of the limelight where he could make trouble. Let the new couple live in quiet exile outside Rome.

Given the spirited natures of the two women, clearly the city was only big enough for one Olimpia at a time. But perhaps there was an added reason for the exile; a year or two earlier Camillo had tried to convince the pope to lock up his mother in a convent, an unforgivable suggestion that still rankled deeply. Now she would lock up Camillo in the country and see how he liked that.

On January 7, news flew around Rome that the cardinal nephew would renounce his hat in the next consistory, an important meeting to which the pope called all his cardinals. The *avvisi* of January 26 reported, "Finally in the consistory of this past Monday [January 21], Cardinal Pamphilio renounced his hat. . . . His Holiness cried with tenderness and showed far greater emotion on this occasion than when he made him cardinal."[9] But perhaps the pope was crying less out of avuncular tenderness than because of the mess he was in.

As the marriage negotiations inched forward, Olimpia was horrified to learn that the pope had received a list of conditions from the princess of Rossano. In his diary entry of February 3, Giacinto Gigli detailed them. "Everyone is waiting to hear news of the marriage of Don Camillo with the princess of Rossano," he wrote, "and for many days we heard nothing more of it. Then it was said that there were many difficulties, and the princess who had had a husband and had tasted what it was like to have a mother-in-law . . . did not want to subject herself again, and therefore sent a letter to the pope with many requests. One of them was that she be married by the pope himself in the [Sistine] chapel as the wife of the pope's nephew. Also that she wanted to be the mistress of her own wardrobe without being subject to anyone." The "anyone," we can presume, was her future mother-in-law.

Gigli continued, "That she did not want to live with Donna Olimpia, her mother-in-law, but in her own palaces. That Donna Olimpia her mother-in-law promise Don Camillo that at her death she would leave him all her possessions. That the pope would let her pick a future cardinal whoever it might be."[10] These requests were not likely to meet with Olimpia's favor. She had already made a will leaving all her money to her little granddaughter, Olimpiuccia, and *she* controlled the list of cardinals.

Gigli wrote, "This lady, becoming the wife of the pope's nephew, showed spirit and desire to dominate, which would not seem at all to be pleasing to the pope's sister-in-law Donna Olimpia, who truly in this pontificate is the only dominatrix. I could easily believe that this induced Camillo to renounce his hat and take a wife, because even if he was a cardinal and the pope's nephew . . . , he was not allowed to do a favor for anyone. Whoever asked him for one, he had to excuse himself, and could not do it without his signora mother."[11]

Surprisingly, although the pope did not agree to meet a single one of the princess's conditions, she married Camillo anyway. According to a letter written by a wedding guest, on the morning of February 10, the bride left the Borghese Palace in Prince Ludovisi's carriage, accompanied by Olimpia's daughters and their husbands. When the princess arrived at her country estate, the Castello di Torrenova, Camillo was standing in the courtyard. Watching her descend, he "was overcome by excesses of ardor, and stupefied, but finally, animated by these princes [his brothers-in-law], he embraced the loved one, offered her as a pledge a kiss, which from fear he did not let pass the confines of the neck. . . . Monsignor Vice Regent celebrated the Mass and married them in the name of His Holiness, and afterward they went to table sumptuously laid out."[12]

While the bride and groom had assembled a group of illustrious guests, the two most important relatives were conspicuous for their absence. Olimpia, however, did have the good taste to send the bride a nice pair of earrings. An *avvisi* records that on that same day, a Sunday, the pope went to visit the Basilica of Saint Paul Outside the Walls, as if making a public gesture that his health was good enough for a short journey, and he could have attended the wedding had he so chosen.

Teodoro Amayden expressed his shock that the couple did not return to Rome to kiss the pope's feet. "I know that His Holiness tenderly loves his nephew, but seeing that Signora Donna Olimpia did not have satisfaction with this marriage, and believing that between the mother-in-law and daughter-in-law there would be great disgust, he prudently wanted to prevent the gossip of the common people. . . . The pope is upset with his nephew who wanted more than anything in the world to become a cardinal and then, to the pope's disgust, tossed aside the hat."[13]

The princess of Rossano and Camillo honeymooned in the sumptuous Villa Aldobrandini at Frascati, thirteen miles outside Rome. Once the wedding festivities had ended and the scandal and romance had died down, the bride was suddenly struck by the fact that she could not return to her beloved Rome, the center of power and politics. Because of her nasty mother-in-law, the magnificent princess of Rossano was stuck in the country mud.

Prodded by his wife's nonstop needling to get the exile lifted, Camillo secretly went to Rome in a plain carriage to ask his cardinal friends to intervene on his behalf with the pope. But when Cardinals Panciroli, Federico Sforza, and many others broached the delicate subject, according to Amayden, the pope abruptly interrupted and said "that they should not speak to him about it and should mind their own business."[14]

Back in the country, while the princess of Rossano connived and manipulated at getting the exile lifted, Camillo made plans for his Bel Respiro villa. The exterior had been completed in the fall of 1646, and now he was eager to decorate the interior with stucco reliefs and frescoes of mythological heroes and ancient Roman emperors. Though the pope wouldn't let him visit the villa to work with his architect, Alessandro Algardi, Camillo and the artist traded letters with plans and sketches.

He was also interested in improving his wife's Roman palaces, adding to her magnificent art collection, and designing new gardens. To think, people had made fun of him for sketching flower beds and statues. Now Camillo would use those skills as a wealthy art connoisseur—that is, if only his mother would let him come back to Rome.

14

∿

The Imbecile Cardinals

*The ship of Peter is shaken by the waves, the fisherman's net
is broke, the serenity of peace turns to clouds.*

—Sacred College to Pope Clement V

O N AVERAGE, MOST ITALIAN NOBLEWOMEN who survived
childbirth lived to their late fifties or early sixties. Of the many
fatal illnesses that struck women, ovarian cancer was the worst;
it announced itself with a slight pang in the abdomen that gradually
became bone-shattering pain as it slowly ate out the surrounding organs. Breast cancer was almost as bad. Sometimes doctors sliced breast
tumors off with a knife without benefit of painkiller, but this never
slowed the disease, as the medical profession knew nothing of lymph
nodes spreading invisible cancer cells throughout the body.

As bad as suffering got, suicide was never an option, as it was considered a direct route to eternal damnation. Far more enviable than any
lingering malady was a fatal bout of dysentery or fever. But best of all
was a massive stroke or heart attack, provided the individual had freshly
confessed her sins.

At the age of fifty-six, taking a frank look at what was probably her
near future, Olimpia decided to build her tomb. It was not an unusual
or macabre plan, this preparation of a grave while one was still healthy.

Most wealthy people did it, working with their favorite artist to design sculptures and picking out the colored marbles and Bible phrases with the eagerness of a modern housewife designing a new kitchen. It was, after all, the only way people could make sure they had the tomb they wanted, especially when they couldn't count on their cheap nasty relatives.

Olimpia would not build her tomb in Rome where it would be lost among the throng of marble monuments competing for attention. She would be laid to rest in the Church of San Martino, in the principality where she had done so much for dowerless girls. Unfortunately, the four-hundred-year-old church was in a sad state of decay. Olimpia commissioned Francesco Borromini to shore up the sagging structure, refurbish the interior, and replace the crumbling bell towers with majestic new ones in the medieval style. As the finishing touch, he would design her tomb. They would bury her at the high altar, beneath a simple yet elegant pavement of gold and red marble, with a black border around it and the white Pamphili dove holding the green olive sprig in its mouth. In the upper corners were ghastly huge yellow skulls with red eyes and ragged hair that could only have been designed by the mournful Borromini. The slab was about twenty feet square, and each of the four corners was adorned with the gold eight-pointed Maidalchini star.

The text reads:

Olimpia Maidalchini Pamphili
Princess of San Martino
Aware of human mortality
Anticipating the last day
With the thought of spiritual immortality
Here chose to erect her sepulcher
As religious piety suggested to her
To feel she was protected in life as in death
By the eternal aid of the Holy Spirit
And to ask at the same time
Abundant prayers and intercession with the Lord
From the inhabitants of her feud

Who are asked to remember her by this monument
And among whom she lived
To the increasing and greater dignity of the town
With the loving care of
Universally bestowed charity
She wishes to establish
A lasting testimony of affection
1647

The date of death would be filled in later. It is interesting that Olimpia used the term "to feel she was protected in life." Clearly, she felt *unprotected,* unsafe, as though something awful was waiting for her just around the corner.

Because it was not an elaborate tomb with numerous marble and bronze statues such as many Roman nobles commissioned, it was completed quickly. Now Olimpia could die at any time and have a fitting resting place ready to receive her.

Ice was melting off the relationship between France and the Papal States. Mazarin had stopped playing war games and was sending friendly letters to the pope. As the thaw set in, he hoped that soon his dearest wish would become a reality—a cardinal's hat for his idiot brother. And now he knew exactly who could get it for him.

At the end of May 1647, the new French ambassador, the marquis de Fontenay, arrived in Rome with a most brilliant suite—twenty-four pages, forty valets, and three hundred men, the entire retinue and their horses dazzlingly attired to outshine the rather tarnished glory of Spain. The marquis called first on Innocent in the Vatican. Next, his train of carriages made their way to a more important meeting at the Piazza Navona. To receive the ambassador, Olimpia had created a kind of court with herself as queen and numerous ladies-in-waiting hovering attentively nearby. The marquis respectfully saluted her, noting that she "was accompanied by ten principal ladies of Rome, richly dressed."[1]

Fontenay was dumbfounded by the dignity of a woman whom he

had heard to be a yokel from Viterbo. In a letter to Mazarin he gushed, "The Queen [Anne of Austria, queen mother of France] has not demonstrated more gravity and majesty than this lady on that occasion."[2]

Mazarin wrote back, "We must do favors for the signora Donna Olimpia, and it must go beyond everything His Holiness could desire for her."[3] The prime minister now considered Olimpia his best friend. Indeed, the two were remarkably similar; born to nothing, they had both scrambled up to the pinnacle of wealth and power because of their street smarts. Gazing at each other from either side of the Alps, each saw the other as a useful pawn on the chessboard of power; it is also likely that they greatly admired each other.

With French panache and Gallic charm, the new ambassador set to work on Olimpia regarding the little matter of the red hat for Michel Mazarin. We can presume that he, like his predecessors, eagerly lost money to her at card games. Certainly Olimpia knew a large reward would be forthcoming from France if she could only prevail upon the pope to make Michel a cardinal. Surely, she must have told Innocent, it would be a small gesture to establish goodwill between nations, and heaven knew there were centuries of precedents for popes creating feebleminded cardinals for the sake of peace among Christians. But Innocent, hating the thought of creating a feebleminded cardinal himself, procrastinated.

However, Innocent knew that with Camillo married and gone, he would have to create a new cardinal nephew. It was unthinkable *not* to have one. Unfortunately, Camillo was the pope's only nephew. In such cases a pope could look a bit farther afield in his family, giving the job to a niece's husband's single brother. And both the pope's nieces had married into well-connected families with numerous single males.

Olimpia would have loved to have the job herself. After all, no one in the family was as clever, hardworking, and manipulative as she was. No one looked out for the family interests the way she did. But a female cardinal nephew was, alas, impossible, even if that female were Olimpia. The uproar both in the church and among the heretics would be too great, and this would be one request the pope would never consent to.

A 1653 French print. The text reads:

Donna Olimpia Maidalchini, Princess of San Martino, widow of Don Pamphilio Pamphili, brother of Pope Innocent X, and mother of Don Camillo Pamphili, Prince of Rossano, formerly cardinal, and of the princesses of Bassano and Piombino. Having come to these honors by the good will of the pope.

(From the author's private collection.)

ABOVE: Pope Innocent X by Diego Velasquez, 1650.
(Seat/ALINARI Archives, Florence.)
OPPOSITE: Olimpia Maidalchini by Alessandro Algardi, circa 1650.
(© ADP/ALINARI Archives, Florence.)

RIGHT: The unimpressive Casa Pamphili in 1612 when Olimpia moved there. Her building is the one on the left, separated from the neighbors by an alley. *(Archivio di Stato di Roma. Granted by the Culture Ministry of Italy, ASR28/2007. No reprints permitted without specific permission.)*

BELOW: Palazzo Pamphili as it looked when Olimpia completed it in 1648. The church of Saint Agnes is on the right. Olimpia's palazzo is a statement in stone of her accomplishments. *(Marcello Leotta—Artphoto, Embassy of Brazil, Rome.)*

Pope Urban VIII, who made Giovan Battista Pamphili a cardinal in 1630, setting him on the road to the papal throne. Portrait by Gian Lorenzo Bernini, circa 1625. *(Archivio Fotografico Soprintendenza Speciale per il Polo Museale Romano.)*

RIGHT: Camillo Pamphili, a terracotta bust by Alessandro Algardi, 1647. Olimpia's handsome but feckless son became a cardinal, left the Sacred College to marry, and then wanted to become a cardinal again. *(The State Hermitage Museum, St. Petersburg.)*
BELOW: Olimpia Aldobrandini, the Princess of Rossano, the scintillating daughter-in-law Olimpia despised. *(© Arti Doria Pamphilj srl.)*

ABOVE: Pope Alexander VII by Giovanni-Battista Gaulli, known as Il Baciccio. The successor of Innocent X charged Olimpia with stealing from Vatican coffers. *(© Civici Musei, Castello, Udine.)*
RIGHT: The dashing but useless Cardinal Camillo Astalli-Pamphili, Innocent X's "fake" nephew. *(Courtesy of The Hispanic Society of America, New York.)*

San Martino, the town Olimpia built for dowerless girls
as she had once been. Her palace is on the left, next to the church
where she is buried. *(© Maurizio Vecchi.)*

Unable to take the position herself, Olimpia already had a replacement picked out. She needed someone who was young enough and obedient enough to permit her to run the Vatican by serving as a front for her and doing every little thing she said. She found the perfect candidate in Francesco Maidalchini, the seventeen-year-old son of her half-brother, Andrea. Olimpia had originally planned for him to marry her granddaughter, Olimpiuccia, thereby keeping all the money in the family, but now she saw a better opportunity. Soon after Camillo's resignation, she had Francesco named abbot of her church at San Martino and a canon of Saint Peter's. She told the pope that this boy would be his next cardinal nephew.

The minimum age requirement for a cardinal was twenty-two. But the pope could grant a dispensation to make a newborn a cardinal, if he wanted. For political reasons Paul V gave the red hat to a ten-year-old Spanish prince in 1619, knowing that youth was the one handicap guaranteed to pass away with time. And manhood came earlier in past centuries. Seventeen-year-olds married, fathered children, slashed their way across battlefields, and toiled in their professions.

But Francesco Maidalchini had very little in the way of intelligence and an unattractive appearance to boot. Gregorio Leti described him as having "a stupid expression, neither the air nor the appearance of a man, with no experience of the world, ignorant of letters and even incapable of learning them, brutal and disagreeable in his actions and his words, badly made in body and mind, and carried away entirely with exercises and diversions low and unworthy to people of quality."[4]

The pope was fond not only of attractive women but of handsome men as well. He could barely stand to look at ugly people—it seemed to truly pain him—and he believed a person's appearance reflected the virtues and intelligence radiating from within. It is not known what Innocent thought when looking in the mirror, but he was clearly displeased when looking at little snub-nosed Francesco Maidalchini.

Seeing the pope's hesitation, Olimpia offered to put the boy under the instruction of top cardinals to bring him up to speed quickly. "But this was no more than to sow Corn upon a Rock," Leti wrote. "Maidalchini had no capacity to receive any thing at all, having brought an incredible stupidity along with him, even from his Mothers belly."[5] And alas, Francesco's ignorance would prove invincible.

Whether he was stupid or not, Olimpia insisted on the boy's appointment, and the pope finally relented. Leti reported that "the rest of their Eminences were all astonish'd at the Election of such a person, and I know above forty of them were displeas'd, and would willingly have gone out of Rome to have avoided the sight of him, but in spight of their indignation, they were forc'd to be content to visit him as the rest, and to swallow that bitter Pill in the Cup of Patience, without speaking one word to the Pope against it."[6]

Making Francesco Maidalchini a cardinal trailed another problem in its wake. For three years Innocent had refused to give the nitwit Michel Mazarin a cap, explaining that a man of such low intelligence was not worthy of the honor. By caving in to Olimpia's pleas to give her nephew a hat, the pope found he could no longer use this excuse.

It was no coincidence that on October 7, 1647, Francesco Maidalchini was created a cardinal along with Michel Mazarin. When the former ambassador Saint-Nicolas asked the pope what had changed his mind, Innocent was very frank, explaining that if he gave a cap to one imbecile, he might as well give a cap to the other imbecile, too. "Here is the entire secret of this affair," Saint-Nicolas informed his prime minister.[7] But Mazarin didn't care what the pope thought of his brother. Michel had received the red hat, thereby increasing the prime minister's power and dignity, and that was all that mattered.

The creations were done to the deep regret of a pope who wanted to make only the brightest men cardinals and, political and family considerations aside, usually managed to do so. Innocent must have been consoled by the fact that he had, at least, made peace with France and kept Olimpia happy. Immediately after the consistory where the pope announced Maidalchini's creation, Innocent had himself carried to the Piazza Navona, where he gave Olimpia the good news. On the same day, he instructed Cardinal Panciroli to start teaching the youth politics and diplomacy.

In rendering his courtesy visits to all the other members of the Sacred College and the foreign diplomats in Rome, Cardinal Maidalchini tried hard to remember the polite compliments Aunt Olimpia had taught him to say. He ended up stiffly repeating the same words again and again, "like a song that he had learned by heart. Moreover, he was not capable of producing anything more than abrupt changes of subject and ridiculous discourse."[8]

The Giustinianis and Ludovisis were furious that the selection had not fallen on a worthier candidate from one of their families. They stormed into the Vatican and let the pope know what a ridiculous choice he had made.

Unfortunately, the uproar over the boy's promotion was not limited to the pope's family. The people of Rome, who eagerly fell in love with a good-looking face and an impressive figure, could not pardon Cardinal Maidalchini's unpalatable appearance. The new cardinal nephew, it was said, bore an uncanny resemblance to Pasquino, that battered statue with no nose. The day of Cardinal Maidalchini's creation ceremony, someone hung a sign on Pasquino's friend Marforio that read,

DON'T CRY PASQUINO,
AS A COMPANION YOU WILL HAVE MALDACHINO.[9]

Leti grumbled, "And in fact this cardinal will forever be the laughing-stock of the Sacred College, the scandal of the church, and the disgrace of all the Roman court. The instructions given him by his aunt, who did everything to persuade him to always keep beside him learned men, didn't help much as he didn't have the mind to reap any advantage."[10]

Olimpia knew she could not let this boy loose in the Vatican. Camillo, while forced to live with his mother, had still worked in the Vatican offices. But Cardinal Maidalchini would not only live with Olimpia, he would also hold court there. In his impressive office in the front rooms of the Piazza Navona palace, Cardinal Maidalchini held his meetings with Olimpia sitting next to him, elbowing him to blurt out the answers she had taught him.

Giacinto Gigli wrote, "She didn't want him to stay in the palace next to the pope, but to live in her house so she would not lose dominion. And she did not want the prelates and the rest of the court, who without doubt would have gone to the antechamber of the cardinal, to abandon her own antechamber."[11] Finally, the beating heart of the Vatican had been transferred to Olimpia's own house.

But it did not last long. Cardinal Camillo, at least, had been a good-looking man with refined manners, dignified in his crimson robes. When he had managed to climb out of bed, he had politely discussed art, poetry, and gardening, though politics had seemed to escape him. But poor little Cardinal Maidalchini was hopeless. Confronted with experienced diplomats of the most powerful sovereigns in Europe, he sat numb with terror as they spoke of treaties, trade agreements, war, and taxation. His memory was awful, and he had a hard time sputtering out the statements Olimpia had taught him the night before.

Olimpia persuaded her nephew to espouse the cause of Spain. "But finding by degrees the little esteem the Spaniards had for him," Leti explained, "by their several times neglecting to call him to their Assemblies, in which the intrigues of that Court were transacted, and all because they knew he had not judgement enough to give them any Councel, he turned to the French, who receiv'd him very readily, if for no other reason to secure his voice in the Conclave."[12] One good thing did result from his hobnobbing with the French. Over time, Cardinal Maidalchini picked up a veneer of French elegance, and his conversation began to improve.

The Spaniards weren't the only diplomats who found they were wasting their time talking to a pimple-faced boy in a cardinal's costume. Other than the French, they all began sidestepping him and went right to Cardinal Panciroli in the Vatican.

As a reward for Olimpia's invaluable aid in obtaining the red hat for Michel Mazarin, the queen of France suggested sending her a splendid tapestry and a silver dinner service. But Mazarin, in a rare and egregious miscalculation, instead sent Olimpia a large trunk of the queen's old clothes. The gowns, of the finest materials edged with the richest lace, were valued at four thousand scudi, a significant sum. Perhaps the prime minister thought Olimpia would be honored to have the clothes of a queen who, a widow like her, always wore black. But he was dead wrong, and Olimpia was highly insulted to be given hand-me-downs from a queen or anyone else.

When Ambassador Fontenay next called on Olimpia, she threw a royal conniption fit about the gift. The horrified diplomat wrote Mazarin immediately, letting him know he had made an awful mistake. On November 17 the prime minister replied, "I believe that it is most important for the service of the king to correctly cultivate her friendship, and to omit nothing possible to conquer her entirely, knowing full well that her credit will prevail always with the pope over all his other relatives for the duration of this pontificate. . . . I ask you to discover what would please her most in terms of silver plate, precious stones or beautiful tapestries, and if she desires that these gifts come from the queen or from myself, if she prefers that the gifts go to her nephew [Maidalchini] or to her, if the thing should be publicly known or extremely secret, in fine, to conform exactly to the above punctually and in a manner that would be the most agreeable to her."[13] It is probable that the gifts were sent by the queen instead of the cardinal, to Olimpia instead of her nephew, and quite publicly.

While Mazarin was sending splendid gifts to Olimpia, back home the people of France took note. In addition to the old dresses and whatever other presents Olimpia received, she would also have pocketed a cash commission. Speculation ran high as to exactly how much it had been. The president of the French Parlement declared that Michel Mazarin's red hat had cost France twelve million gold pieces, which Olimpia Maidalchini had stashed in her bottomless pockets. The Venetian ambassador Nani wrote back to his senate that the price had actually been a mere one hundred thousand. Other French politicians said they knew for a fact she had received only thirty thousand, which is probably closer to the mark.

Having placated France by giving Michel Mazarin the red hat, the pope still had the prickly problem of Portugal to resolve. France, now the pope's best friend, pushed him to recognize Portugal as a sovereign nation. Spain, on the other hand, insisted that he proclaim Portugal a rebel state, excommunicate the whole country, and have nothing to do with its government until it rejoined Spain. And Portugal, which had been hovering uneasily since 1640 as a kind of disembodied ghost nation, threatened to keep for itself the significant sum in church taxes sent annually to Rome if the pope did not recognize its sovereignty.

King John IV found himself in a bit of a bind. Technically, he could not send an ambassador to Rome to negotiate the pope's recognition of Portugal until the pope had recognized Portugal. But if he sent a bishop with the ostensible purpose of discussing church business, the pope had to receive him. Unfortunately, when the Portuguese bishop arrived in Rome in 1647 for his official audience, he kissed the pope's foot and blurted out that he was actually there on behalf of "the king, my señor."[14] The Spanish ambassador howled in protest and threatened to gallop back to Madrid in a fury. The pope had to cut short the discussions since it was clear the bishop had been sent not as a bishop but as an ambassador.

The Portuguese, having seen the French success in winning over Olimpia, had not come to Rome empty-handed. Portuguese agents called on Olimpia and presented her with a portrait of the pope in all his pontifical majesty, with King John IV at his feet in abject veneration. More important, the portrait was set in a massive frame studded with huge pearls and sparkling diamonds. And suddenly Olimpia, who hadn't received a dime from the Spanish, was convinced of Portugal's right to self-determination.

But for once Innocent refused to take her advice. He stubbornly protested that recognizing Portugal would create uproar in Spain. Shaking his head, he waved his sister-in-law away. Such strange behavior put Olimpia in an uncomfortable situation. The Portuguese ambassador was furious and told everyone that he had bribed Olimpia without getting a thing in return. Even worse, Olimpia must have been mystified about why the pope had refused to take her advice.

For years Spain had been squeezing the kingdom of Naples dry through increasing taxation. There were taxes on meat, bread, salt, wine, candles, and firewood—the very necessities of life for rich and poor alike. The tax on flour cost nearly as much as the flour itself. On July 7, 1647, the Spanish viceroy, the duke of Arcos, imposed high fees on the sale of fruit and vegetables—the only untaxed foodstuffs and the staples of the poor.

Tommaso Aniello—called Masaniello—was an illiterate Neapolitan fish seller who had had enough. He called out to the poor of Naples to rebel against the heavy-handed overlords. Suddenly the city was alive with revolution. Rebels set fire to the customs office, plundered the royal palace, and broke into the jails, freeing the prisoners. Soon Masaniello himself became a victim of the mob. On July 16 some of them grabbed him and cut off his head.

The mob proclaimed a republic. Never again, they vowed, would they be ruled by Spain. Some of them wanted the pope, as feudal lord of the realm, to march south with his armies and claim the territory that was his by right. But Innocent knew that if he merged the kingdom of Naples into the Papal States, he would be at war with Spain, which owned most of northern Italy, was closely allied to Tuscany in central Italy, and still had plenty of forts in the south bristling with soldiers. The pope had a few ships but hardly a fleet. Though the Papal States had Swiss Guards to protect the pope, and Corsican Guards to keep order in Rome, it had only a token standing army of about three thousand men in garrisons outside Rome, always relying on the firepower of Spain to protect it.

When the people of Naples did not get an immediate response from the pope, they offered the kingdom to France. Mazarin didn't hesitate for an instant. He established relations with the rebels and sent them money, weapons, and food. He equipped a fleet to bombard the Spanish coastal fortresses. But in October 1647 a Spanish fleet appeared before the coast of Naples, commanded by the courageous Don John of Austria, bastard son of King Philip IV. Don John's ships bombarded the city with cannon fire, bombing rebels and loyal citizens alike, and several times hit the papal nuncio's palace.

Watching the ancient enemies have at it, the pope heaved a sigh and decided to remain neutral, calling himself "the common father of the sons of discord."[15] Without saying so, he hoped that Spain, that loyal mainstay of papal power, would win the war. He hated the idea of the narcissistic French—ruled by none other than the detestably oily Mazarin—taking such a huge chunk of Italy bordering on the Papal States.

Throughout the rebellion Olimpia, as usual, didn't support one power against the other. Though doing so would have won her some friends, it also would have created inveterate enemies, and Olimpia was always thinking ahead to her life post-Innocent. Ever the efficient businesswoman, she realized that there was a killing to be made in cornering the Roman grain market. The winter floods of 1646 had resulted in less grain than usual, but she bought up what she could and sold it at high prices to Spanish garrisons.

Many Romans, either to profit financially as Olimpia did, or to support their French or Spanish friends fighting in the south, sent grain from their estates outside Rome down to Naples. Suddenly, there was very little grain left in Rome. The weight of the *pagnotta*, the little loaf of bread the poor bought for one *bajocco*, decreased from its usual eight ounces to six, and then to four. With little or no grain to be had, bakers made foul-smelling bread of beans, peas, stalks, and wood chips.

Hopes for a good harvest were dashed in December when a flood of biblical proportions rolled into Rome. Giacinto Gigli observed, "It began to rain copiously without stopping so that on the 6th the Tiber left its bed and flooded all the low parts of Rome. . . . In the Tor di Nona Prison four prisoners were drowned, and many people drowned in their own houses for not being able to flee in time, while others drowned while trying to save their possessions, and many canoed up and down the streets distributing bread to those who couldn't get out. . . . There drowned carriages full of people, pulled by six horses, and men on horseback, and others escaped as if by a miracle, like a woman who was pulled from the water alive, being grabbed by her dress with a hook while the torrent was carrying her off. . . . Masses were held continuously to restore tranquility to the weather."[16]

Eager for a scapegoat, the Romans blamed Olimpia for their hunger. Knowing of her grain speculation with the Spanish, they ignored war, revolution, floods, and the hundreds of other nobles who had shipped grain south, and blamed her and her alone. Whenever the huge double doors of her palazzo swung open, mobs descended on her carriage crying, "Bread! Bread!" To disperse them, Olimpia was forced to throw coins to the crowd, who scrambled for them, thereby allowing her carriage to pass.

Even more troubling to Olimpia was the sudden illness of the pope. He suffered intense pain from a kidney stone—the same ailment that had killed his brother—and for twenty-four hours was unable to urinate. Olimpia was worried that if he died, the mob would break into her palazzo and tear her limb from limb. Teodoro Amayden wrote, "These past few days due to the indisposition of the pope and the lack of bread, the house of Signora Donna Olimpia has been guarded by sentinels and a company of Corsicans."[17]

Teodoro Amayden's November 30, 1647, *avvisi* reported that the princess of Rossano wrote to Sister Agatha that she was pregnant, and her mountain palace of Caprarola was extremely cold. She complained that she was being punished for having committed no crime. Sister Agatha went immediately to see the pope about the matter, but the exile was not lifted.

In December Camillo came secretly to Rome and met with his uncle while his wife stayed quietly with Sister Agatha in the convent. Camillo complained that he had left in the Piazza Navona house numerous valuable pieces of furniture—items he had either received as gifts or bought himself during his tenure as cardinal nephew. Yet when he had asked his mother to send them to him, she had refused and was keeping them for herself. Camillo's complaint was an interesting echo of the pope's own protest thirty-five years earlier when Olimpia first moved into the Pamphili house and claimed *his* expensive furniture.

Innocent summoned Olimpia to the Vatican and ordered her to give Camillo the items he wanted so that the Vicar of Christ didn't have to be bothered with such nonsense. According to Giacinto Gigli, "Donna Olimpia replied that she did not want to, and the pope said to her that she should not appear before him anymore, and she returned home sick and it was said she was very bad off."[18] Having taken possession of his furniture, Camillo trundled back to exile with his wife. Olimpia must have been doubly dissatisfied. She had lost the furniture, and once again the pope had refused to do as she said.

On December 14 a courier raced into Rome with news from Paris.

That night Gigli noted in his diary, "Don Taddeo Barberini has died, 44 years old, his death no doubt due to the sufferings he felt in the persecution of his house."[19] Two days later an *avvisi* recounted that Olimpia received the not-so-grieving widow, Anna Colonna, "with particular demonstrations of affection." At this meeting Olimpia expressed her great displeasure that her son had not married Anna's daughter Lucrezia and had unwisely chosen that other one. "To which Anna Colonna replied in general terms," the report continued.[20]

Certainly it could not have been pleasing to the princess to think of her daughter's alliance with an upstart family such as the Pamphilis. She was most likely delighted that the match had fallen through. Her blue blood must have pulsed with irritation at the necessity of getting into her carriage and visiting the vulgar Olimpia that day. But if she were to bring back her family from Paris, obtain the restitution of their property, and take her silver forks out of hiding, visit the vulgar Olimpia she must.

Anna Colonna's titanic sacrifice was successful. Olimpia negotiated the return of the Barberini family to Rome. All charges against them were dropped, and much of their property would be restored, along with honors, incomes, and titles. On February 27, 1648, Cardinal Francesco returned to Rome after two years of exile in France. His brother Antonio had not accepted the pope's offer of clemency and restitution. Mistrustful of Innocent and Olimpia, Antonio remained in Paris along with the children of Taddeo and Anna Colonna.

Despite Antonio's recalcitrance, Olimpia was pleased. Now if the pope were to die from a stubborn kidney stone, she would be protected by the grateful Barberinis.

15

Birth, Famine, and Bitter Peace

*Like all the best families, we have our share of eccentricities,
of impetuous and wayward youngsters and of
family disagreements.*

—Queen Elizabeth II

In March 1648 the six-months pregnant princess of Rossano, ignoring the decree of exile, once more clattered into Rome with her husband. This time she was here to stay, and a convent wouldn't do. She moved into the magnificent Palazzo Farnese. Built in the mid–sixteenth century by the family of Pope Paul III, with some decorations designed by none other than Michelangelo, the imposing palace belonged to her cousin the duke of Parma. It was a wise choice of residence; should the pope's guards try to throw her out, she could claim diplomatic immunity.

The princess had a very specific reason for flouting Innocent's mandate to remain in the countryside. Teodoro Amayden wrote, "The princess is said to have come to Rome so that there is no opposition made to the truth of the birth."[1] Giving birth in exile was dangerous. The princess knew that her mother-in-law could cast doubt upon the child's parentage. Olimpia might say that it was the illegitimate child of a farm laborer and maidservant that the disgraced couple was trying to pawn off on the Pamphili family to elicit sympathy.

The princess of Rossano also knew that even giving birth in Rome in the presence of a midwife or doctor was not enough. Olimpia could still claim the baby was not hers but had been smuggled into the room in a warming pan or laundry basket, and the doctor and midwife had been bribed to lie. To prevent a rumor that would haunt her child forever, the princess arranged a public birth as if she were a queen. Putting aside any shred of modesty—and we can assume she didn't have many such shreds—she invited numerous noble ladies of Rome and several ambassadors to witness it when the time came. No one could accuse this throng of accepting bribes.

Rome was abuzz with the exciting news of the princess's flagrant disobedience. Saint-Nicolas wrote Mazarin that Olimpia had a huge fight with the pope because he did not want to throw the pregnant princess out of Rome. Once again, she must have returned to her Piazza Navona palace mystified at Innocent's stubbornness.

The unexpected arrival of the princess and Camillo caused a vexing problem for the cardinals and members of Rome's diplomatic community who twittered with unease about whether or not to call on the couple. Would the pope punish them if they did? But if they didn't visit, and the pope reconciled with his nephew and made him powerful, would Camillo wreak vengeance upon those who had not called on him? They wrung their hands in frustration.

Only Cardinal Girolamo Grimaldi, who enjoyed insulting Olimpia publicly, immediately called at the Palazzo Farnese in great state. Mulling his options, Cardinal Panciroli went a bit later to pay his respects, but the princess of Rossano gave him a very rude reception. When Cardinal Panciroli next called on Olimpia, he informed her of the obnoxious behavior of her daughter-in-law. Olimpia replied dryly that she forgave him.

Olimpia did not forgive the princess, however, when she held dinner parties with poetry contests, awarding prizes to those who could make up the most scathing poems about her mother-in-law. In one poem she described Olimpia as a jackass clothed in pontifical vestments and made insinuations that "touched, not lightly, upon her honor."[2]

In April 1648 Don John reestablished Spanish control over Naples. The rebellion was put down, but throughout the Papal States the famine continued. It is likely that Olimpia and Rome's municipal officials kept the severity of the bread shortage from the pope. Without benefit of live CNN coverage or anything like a free press, the elderly pontiff, sitting in the rarified atmosphere of the Vatican nursing his kidney stones, believed what his advisors told him.

Giacinto Gigli reported that bakers were ordered to bake fine white loaves and pretend to be selling them on the street whenever the pope passed by so he wouldn't realize how dire the situation was. When the ragged, hungry souls eagerly gathered to buy the delicious bread, the bakers refused to sell it. It was, they said, just for show to keep the pope happy.

The princess of Rossano went into labor on June 24, 1648, the Feast of Saint John the Baptist, the pope's own saint's day. It was a good omen. At the first pang, her servants donned their best livery and raced around Rome knocking on the doors of the ambassadors and nobles, inviting them to come immediately to witness the historic event. They congregated in her bedroom, eating, drinking, and gossiping, the women doing needlework, the men playing cards. It must have been a great shock to all when Olimpia strode in to see for herself what was going on. She could not have failed to notice that between her gut-wrenching contractions, the princess had a gleam of triumph in her eye.

At 7 P.M., through narrowed eyes Olimpia saw the baby's head push out between the thighs of her detested daughter-in-law. When the doctor plucked the baby out and proclaimed it a healthy boy, the princess cried out that he would be called Gianbattista after the pope. The guests cheered but Olimpia did not. She stood up and, without saying a word, left.

When the vice-regent of Rome, Signor Rivaldi, raced to the pope breathless with the news of a healthy boy, Innocent could not contain his joy. "God be praised!" he cried, his face aglow with happiness.[3]

Olimpia knew the birth of little Gianbattista Pamphili would bind the tenderhearted Innocent to Camillo and his wife more than all the princess's youth and beauty. This birth would cause him to lift the exile for good, to invite the presumptuous princess to the Vatican, to listen to her political suggestions. This birth would push the old Olimpia out of the Vatican limelight, supplanted by the new, younger, more beautiful Olimpia.

The old Olimpia marched into the Vatican and had a long talk with her brother-in-law. When he emerged, the pope was once more his usual sober self. He refused to accept congratulations from the ambassadors, cardinals, and noblemen who waited in his antechamber. Thinking this was the most propitious time to request an audience with his uncle, Camillo arrived at the papal palace hat in hand. But the pope sent his steward out to tell him to go home and not come back.

Despite the pope's insistence that the birth of Gianbattista Pamphili not be celebrated, the international community of Rome reacted as if a royal prince had been born. Ambassadors dispatched couriers to France, Spain, Austria, Tuscany, Germany, Poland, and the Netherlands with the glorious news. The noble palaces of Rome were illuminated with white torches and colorful lanterns. Fireworks were set off in the piazzas. Cannons blasted, drums rattled, and trumpets blared. The pope issued instructions to cease the celebrations at once, but no one listened.

A few days after the birth, the princess told some friends that she intended to order a magnificent gown to wear the first time she went out in public. Hearing this, Olimpia sent her daughter-in-law a note, instructing her to make sure it was a gown suitable for the countryside, as she would be going back very soon.

But Camillo cashed in more chips with sympathetic cardinals and ambassadors who once again knelt before the pope and implored him for mercy. This time, mercy was granted. Innocent was incredibly touched by the arrival of his namesake, who, though his grandnephew, was actually his grandchild in papal terms. Little Gianbattista Pamphili was the continuation of the family line, which for so long had seemed to be tottering on the brink of extinction.

Powerless in her efforts to exile the family, Olimpia was at least able to impose conditions on Camillo and his wife if they wanted to stay in

Rome. They were to leave the Palazzo Farnese, owned by the inveterate enemy of the papacy, the duke of Parma, and move to the princess's Palazzo Aldobrandini on the Corso. They were not to involve themselves in any important matters. Camillo, who had earlier tried to have Olimpia locked up in a convent, still found himself locked up by *her*, this time in Rome. The revenge was exquisite.

On June 28, four days after the princess's delivery, the annual procession of the *chinea* took place, a magnificent pageant in which the king of Spain, through his representative, gave the pope a gorgeous white horse as symbolic payment for the realm of Naples. The horse had been trained to kneel upon command and would do so at the pope's feet as a sign of Spanish submission. Since there was at the moment no Spanish ambassador to the Holy See, the king of Spain had selected Olimpia's son-in-law, the staunchly pro-Spanish Prince Ludovisi, for the astonishing honor of leading the horse.

Olimpia had never been overly fond of the fat prince, always trying to push himself into papal government and trudging around town crying that he never should have married Costanza for such a cheap dowry. And now, still licking her wounds over the birth of little Gianbattista, she was forced to watch her unappetizing son-in-law, swollen with pride on this, the greatest day of his life. Huffing and puffing, the prince marched solemnly forward holding the diamond-studded reins of the white horse. The sweat dripped off his red face onto his rich black velvet suit, dimming somewhat the blazing glory of his sewn-on diamonds.

After the ceremony, Cardinal Giovan Battista Pallotta, a man of strict morals, took Innocent aside and informed him of the dire bread shortage in Rome. Perhaps while riding in the procession that morning the cardinal had seen wretched, ragged people begging for bread, or worse, too weak to care anymore. Whatever the reason, Cardinal Pallotta flatly informed Innocent that the people of Rome were literally starving to death, and that he was furious the pontiff had done so little to help them. With a parting swipe at Olimpia, whom he must have blamed for the fiasco, he added that he would rather be in a monastery obedient to a monk than in Rome under the domination of a woman.

After Pallotta left, Innocent was uncertain what to do and, as usual, called in Olimpia to ask her opinion. She was livid to hear that the cardinal had spoken to the pope in such a manner, and she yelled at her brother-in-law for putting up with it.

As Olimpia dejectedly rode home, her carriage had the misfortune to cross that of Cardinal Pallotta, whose driver stopped to salute the pope's sister-in-law out of respect. Olimpia and the cardinal glared at each other from open windows only a couple feet apart. Then Olimpia started shrieking that Pallotta and his family were spies and yanked down her carriage window shade "in his face," according to Giacinto Gigli. But worse was to come. Yelling at the pulled-down window shade, "the Cardinal replied that he was no spy, but that it was certainly a shame that the government of Rome was in the hands of a whore, and other such similar injurious words, and they departed. It was publicly known that Donna Olimpia had slept with her brother-in-law before he became pope, and people were always talking about this."[4]

It was a very public display of bad temper, a tantrum thrown in front of dozens of people on the street who must have enjoyed seeing the pope's sister-in-law insulting a cardinal who then called her a whore to her face. Word leaped into the Vatican, and Innocent mulled over his waning dignity.

There would be more street battles to aggravate the pope. Unfortunately, the palazzo of the princess of Rossano was only a few blocks from her mother-in-law's, and the adversaries were bound to run into each other. One day Olimpia's carriage met Camillo's carriage on the street. Inside were little Gianbattista and his nurse. Camillo's coachman stopped to salute Olimpia, as courtesy demanded, and Olimpia's coachman stopped to return the salute. But Olimpia poked her head out of the window and screamed at her coachman to keep going. Numerous bystanders witnessed the altercation, and word of Olimpia's latest public display of bad temper flew back to the pope.

Innocent called her to the Vatican and chastised her severely. Yes, the princess had behaved disrespectfully to her mother-in-law, but she had the excuse of youth on her side. Olimpia had long ago lost *that* excuse and as a wise and venerable matron should show greater decorum. Her outrageous behavior was bringing the pope, his family, and the entire

Vatican into disrepute. Cornered, Olimpia blamed the whole thing on her coachman and fired him. Once again, Innocent had lost his temper with her. After thirty-five years of docile submissiveness, it was becoming an unnerving habit.

Perhaps Innocent's rising irritation was caused by the continuing famine. After Cardinal Pallotta's outburst, the pope looked into the bread shortage and was horrified at what he learned. He sent men house to house asking the rich merchants and wealthy nobles for alms for the poor. When this didn't raise much—even the well off had to pay a fortune for food—he decided to requisition grain from Fermo, a town in the area of the Papal States called the Marches. Having been spared the devastating floods that had swept across the environs of Rome, Fermo seemed to have a bit of a surplus.

But when the governor arrived on July 6, 1648, to commandeer the grain, he was torn to pieces by an angry mob, and the revolt spread to other areas in the Marches. On July 14 the people of Viterbo rose up against their tax collector, Olimpia's half-brother, Andrea Maidalchini, who had wanted to take their grain and sell it to Rome at a high price. The crowd chased him through the streets firing guns at him, but he managed to escape. Other towns rose in revolt as enraged citizens chased out the pope's grain collectors.

The prosperous Giacinto Gigli did not eat the *pagnotta* but bought them periodically to try them out and see what the poor had to subsist on. "The bread was very bad in color and in odor," he reported, "and they said that beans and other vegetables had been thrown in, and the people lamented and could not eat it, and I noted with admiration that the dog and cats in my house would not eat it, but if you gave them better bread they would eat it willingly, so that dumb animals know which bread is not good."[5] In July the bread was whiter but oddly crunchy; it contained pieces of plaster.

Gigli noted that many people sold their few sticks of furniture for money to buy bread and when hunger returned found themselves sitting on the floor with nothing left to sell. Others hunted sewer rats and made them into stew. When the Jesuits opened a soup kitchen, such crowds of desperate people thundered in that many were trampled to death and many others suffered broken bones. No matter how many people the Jesuits fed, more would show up the following day. Even the whitest loaf soothed an empty stomach for only a few hours.

Lawlessness set in as starving people stole whatever they could to sell or trade for bread. Gigli wrote, "During this time it seemed as if Rome had become Naples, so that in the evening after the Ave Maria had rung, one could not leave the house with a hat for the danger that it would be stolen, and there were those who were wounded in trying to defend themselves."[6]

On November 27, the pope traveled to various vineyards and gardens in Rome for some fresh air. Gigli reported, "Many people went to him crying at the top of their voice, bread bread! Holy Father we cannot find bread, we want bread. The pope replied, You will have some. . . . Some people retorted that bread would be found in his own house, and that another should govern than a woman."[7]

Innocent was so devastated by the scene that he took to his bed again. He had hoped to be a just pope ruling over a prosperous people. But now his people were starving, and they were shouting terrible things about Olimpia. By the end of November, it looked as though Innocent might die. Numb with terror at the thought, Olimpia exposed the Holy Sacrament in the Church of Saint Mary of the Peace. Masses were held across Rome to implore God to spare the pontiff.

Innocent slowly recovered, and Olimpia held the usual Christmas celebrations in her palazzo, though the mood was somber. At one of these events, a lady politely inquired as to how Her Excellency was doing. Shrugging, Olimpia replied with an old Italian saying: "I am like a beaten horse. The beatings just make my coat glossier."[8]

Many of Olimpia's beatings took place right outside the rear of her palace. Pasquino had always had a lot to say about her, and looking out her corner window each morning, she could see the crowds gaping, elbowing one another, and laughing. Ever since Innocent became pope, most of the pasquinades had been about her. One cartoon showed the main entrance of Olimpia's palazzo. In one frame, her valet was portrayed inviting inside a priest with a full purse, crying, "Come in, blessed father." In the second frame the valet is shown chasing off a priest with

an empty purse, crying, "Go away, accursed one, into eternal ignominy."[9] An unflattering caricature of Olimpia was leaning out of the
window, crying, "Why do you trouble me? I will have nothing to do
with the ungrateful."[10]

In addition to charges of bribe taking, the exact nature of Olimpia's
relationship with the pope was the object of intense speculation. One
particularly popular Latin pasquinade made a pun on her name. *"Olim
pia, nunc impia,"* it said: Once pious, now impious.[11]

The pasquinades became more vicious when bread ran short in
Rome. One poem, which rhymes beautifully in Italian, stated:

Who says "lady" says harm.
Who says "woman" says misfortune.
Who says Olimpia Maidalchini
Says lady, harm, ruin.[12]

On one occasion Pasquino quipped:

"The Roman people are dying of hunger,"
It was said in the Vatican hall
So the pope, to put an end to the loss,
Said Maidalchini would eat for us all.[13]

Pasquino starting referring to Olimpia as the Pimpaccia of the Piazza
Navona. Pimpa was a power-hungry, greedy vixen in a popular play, and
the Italian ending *accia* means something like "incredibly horrible."

It was believed that the princess of Rossano was responsible for some
of the pasquinades, epigrams, and cartoons against her mother-in-law.
After all, she held contests in her palazzo to create such witty masterpieces, and oddly enough, a short time later they appeared on the talking
statues of Rome. Olimpia would have liked nothing more than to tie the
slanderous pasquinades to her daughter-in-law. Giacinto Gigli wrote that
she convinced the pope to station spies near Pasquino "who mixed with
the crowds clothed in silk to look like gentlemen."[14] Many pasquinade
writers were arrested, including three mischievous brothers, but this
didn't put a dent in the heaps of biting verses piled on the statue.

More serious than the pasquinades were the *avvisi* sent to foreign governments. The agent of the duke of Modena was arrested because in his newsletter he wrote that the ministers of the tax department had held a meeting before the *papessa*—the female pope—where it was decided that the *pagnotta* should fall by two ounces. It was a great insult to the Holy See to call a woman the *papessa* and to insinuate that Olimpia was responsible for holding meetings to decide the vital issue of the bread supply. The worst part of it was that this *avvisi* was being sent to a foreign ruler. What messages had been sent out that had not been caught by the censors? What were heads of state thinking about Innocent?

Olimpia knew that the pope cared a great deal for the dignity of his office. All popes had to put up with nasty pasquinades, of course; that came with the office. But most of the pasquinades during Innocent's reign were about Olimpia, not the pope. She was the cause of scandal, the cause of the waning dignity of the papacy. In front of the pope, she shrugged off the popular hatred, hid a great deal of what was going on, and presented a smiling face. But deep down she was worried. If it really came to a contest between Olimpia and the dignity of the papacy, she was not completely certain which one Innocent would choose.

The pope's bouts with kidney stones led him to seek improved health in ways that would avoid encounters with doctors, whom he despised. In truth, seventeenth-century medical care was often more fatal than the disease it attempted to treat. The human body can often cure itself of many life-threatening ailments if given bed rest and hot soup; but the doctors' interventions so weakened the body that it simply gave up and died. Blood was drained out in alarming quantities, and the nutrition needed for healing was forced either to explode upward or downward after the doctors' administration of pukes or purges.

The pope decided that perhaps the only nonviolent way to improve his health was to improve the air he breathed. He moved to the Quirinal Palace on one of the Seven Hills of ancient Rome. The palace was also known as Monte Cavallo, or the Hill of Horses. Two immense sculptural groups of the Dioscuri, or Horse Tamers, had been unearthed from a nearby ancient temple and placed in the piazza in front of the palace.

The palace had its origins as a papal dwelling in 1587 when Pope Sixtus V bought a luxurious villa with extensive gardens as his summer residence. It offered the advantage of a good location still in the heart of Rome but lacked the mosquitoes and miasmas of the sunken Vatican. Sixtus added long wings around a large internal courtyard, and subsequent popes left their own marks on the palace and gardens. It was more comfortable than the ancient, moldy Vatican, and just as beautiful. It even boasted a replica of the Sistine Chapel with the same dimensions.

When the rest of Rome sweltered, the Quirinal was cooled by refreshing breezes. Upon moving in, Innocent liked the palace so much he decided he would stay there year-round and sleep at the Vatican only if he was required to perform ceremonial functions early the next morning. He must have been elated when his doctors cried out that this was a terrible idea, and he must return to the Vatican every winter for the sake of his health. With a gleam in his eye, he told them he wouldn't budge.

~~~~~

Detested at home because of the famine, Innocent found himself humiliated on the international level by the ignominious end of the Thirty Years' War. Having started in 1618 as a religious quarrel between Catholic and Protestant states, over time it had become a multinational free-for-all to grab territory from neighbors.

The Thirty Years' War was the bloodiest, widest-ranging war of the early modern age. Much of Germany was devastated. Hundreds of thousands of civilians had been killed, thousands of villages burned to the ground, millions of acres destroyed, and all in the name of God. The lesson learned by both Catholics and Protestants alike was that war in the name of religion clearly wasn't worth it. The costs of defending religious beliefs were too high. Better to have people worship as they pleased and wage war only for sensible reasons, like taking a neighbor's land or stealing his money.

By 1648 Europe was bled white and ready for a peace that settled both religious and territorial questions. The Treaty of Westphalia stipulated that the Lutheran and Calvinist religions were to be officially tolerated by the Catholic princes of Germany, and ecclesiastical

lands, whether Protestant or Catholic, were to be returned to whom-
ever owned them in a year arbitrarily chosen, which happened to be
1624.

For the first time since Martin Luther questioned papal authority in
1517, European monarchs accepted that the religious divide was irreparable. There would be no forcing the heretics back to the fold of the
Mother Church. Heretics, the treaty acknowledged, were here to stay
and were rich and powerful to boot. It was a humiliating acknowledg-
ment for Pope Innocent X.

When Innocent heard the terms of the peace treaty, he was furious.
He wanted heretics converted, not tolerated, in Germany. And according to the treaty, the church had to hand over to Protestants numerous
territories it had conquered since 1624—three archbishoprics and thirteen bishoprics, a total of sixteen huge territories including thousands of
churches, monasteries, and pious foundations.

The papal envoy to the negotiations, Monsignor Fabio Chigi, stated
that the Austrian ambassador, Count Maximilian von Trauttmansdorff,
would sign over Saint Peter's Basilica itself to the Protestants if they
asked for it. No one at the table seemed to take the church seriously.
Chigi wrote, "To pass the time, these gentlemen play with bishoprics
and monasteries as boys play with nuts and marbles."[15]

For centuries, the Vatican had been the great negotiator, the media-
tor of European wars. Not only was Innocent *not* invited to mediate the
treaty, it was signed over his shrieking protests. Times were changing.
Nation-states were rising even as the secular importance of the papacy
fell. The Treaty of Westphalia was a watershed event for the Vatican,
marking the end of its diplomatic hegemony and signaling the rise of
the modern state. Sadly, everyone knew that Innocent couldn't keep his
own fractious family members from making war on one another, much
less European nations.

Innocent issued a bull dated November 20, 1648, declaring the Treaty
of Westphalia "null, void, invalid, iniquitous, unjust, damnable, repro-
bate, inane, empty of meaning and effect for all time."[16] He was politely
ignored. The Catholic German nations, eager to clean up the debris and
move forward, didn't want the pope making any trouble about the

treaty and prohibited his bull from being distributed. Like a bad would-be author, the pope couldn't even get published.

To his great disappointment, the real victor of the Thirty Years' War was France, which emerged from the conflict triumphant. Spain and Austria climbed out of the ashes exhausted, though Spain was still too proud to sign a treaty with France and would continue the war, sort of, until 1659. Having trounced its ancient enemies, the path would be open for France to rise to glory under Louis XIV. But that was in the future, and when the Treaty of Westphalia was signed, the brilliant Sun King was yet a slender ray, playing with toy soldiers.

Other parts of the world presented difficulties for the pontiff. Victorious Muslim fleets continued to conquer Venetian trading posts in the Aegean, sweeping ever westward. England was ruled by the Puritans, the most virulent heretics ever seen, who cut off the head of the Catholic sympathizer King Charles I in January 1649. They executed priests, stripped English Catholics of all their possessions, and sent troops into Ireland, where they massacred more than 100,000 Catholics.

Looking further afield, the pope's missions to South America were fraught with personality conflicts. A nine-month journey from Rome, missions so far from Vatican control were often reduced to brawling among bishops and priests to see who could wield the most power. In North America, missionaries to Canada were being slaughtered by the Iroquois.

But the pope experienced some successes. In terms of spreading the faith in Africa, his missionaries had received a friendly reception in Senegal in 1645 and had converted the king of Benin in 1648. Italian Capuchin monks had entered the kingdom of the Congo in 1646. In India the Jesuits were extremely active. The king of Ceylon became Catholic in 1644. In the Philippines, Innocent built the Dominican College of Manila to teach theology and bestow academic degrees. The Christians in Japan had been destroyed, but in China there were some 150,000 of them.

Missionary efforts were not all in the far-flung corners of the globe. An ongoing program existed in Rome itself. The Jewish community was a source both of pride and embarrassment to the Holy See—pride because unlike other nations, the Papal States had never slaughtered its Jews; embarrassment because just a short walk from the Vatican lived a stubborn population of nonbelievers.

Jews had lived in Rome since at least the time of Jesus. In 1555, Pope Paul IV had crammed all Jews into an eight-acre walled ghetto in Trastevere on the Tiber. During Innocent's reign, the population had risen to some four thousand. Jews were not permitted to own property or work in the government or the military. They were only allowed to sell used goods, run small shops, and lend money. They were also expected to pay enormous taxes to the Roman government. The purpose of these punitive measures was to induce the Jews to convert, and each convert was given his choice of career—possibly a high office in the Vatican itself—a generous pension, and the right to move out of the ghetto. Unmarried female converts were given ample dowries and strapping Christian husbands.

But converts from the ancient, closely knit community were few. Frustrated by this, in 1584 Pope Gregory XIII decreed that 155 Jews over the age of twelve had to attend a church service every Saturday— the Jewish holy day—in which a Dominican friar preached to them of their theological errors. If fewer than the required number showed up, the community was forced to pay a heavy fine. And so they attended, but some stuffed their ears with cotton and others used the opportunity to catch up on their sleep. The church hired a bailiff to patrol the sermon stick in hand and whack those who were not listening. This, too, had little effect.

On January 7, 1645, John Evelyn attended such a service and left us a priceless description of it. "A Sermon was preach'd to the Jewes at Ponte Sisto," he wrote, "who are constrained to sit till the houre is don; but it is with so much malice in their countenances, spitting, hum'ing, coughing, and motion, that it is almost impossible they should heare a word from the preacher." He added, "A conversion is very rare."[17]

Wherever the poor pope looked, whether in his family, in his city, across Europe, or around the globe, there was scandal, war, famine, slaughter, and humiliation. It was enough to give anybody kidney stones.

16

The Shoulder of
Saint Francesca

*For wheresoever the carcass is, there will the vultures
be gathered together.*

—Matthew 24:28

OLIMPIA'S 1646 CARNIVAL PLAY written with Gian Lorenzo
Bernini, in which they made fun of the pope and Camillo,
had resulted in the sculptor's disgrace. Another play that year,
in which she depicted Francesco Barberini as a staggering drunk and
Cardinal Mazarin dressed half-French and half-Italian, had had international repercussions. Nothing is recorded about her 1647 and 1648
plays, but for the Carnival of 1649, Olimpia planned another controversial comedy, the story of a young fool who disobeys his wise mother and
marries an obnoxious woman who renders his life miserable.

By this time Innocent knew that to prevent scandal he had to examine Olimpia's comedies carefully before they were performed at her
palazzo. The grandest nobles in Rome had eagerly auditioned for the
roles and had already memorized their parts when the pope looked into
it and put the kibosh on the performance. Olimpia could put on a play
if she wanted, Innocent said, but it had to be something less likely to

cause further uproar in the family. Whatever she put on, it probably did not please the pope. In his *avvisi* of February 6, 1649, Teodoro Amayden noted, "Signora Donna Olimpia has begun her comedies, which are licentious enough."[1]

On February 9, the Jews were forced to perform their Carnival race through a torrential downpour, to the delight of spectators. After the skies cleared, the weather became unusually warm, and Olimpia took a carriage ride along the Corso. As she passed the Palazzo Aldobrandini she looked up and saw her son and the princess standing in the front window watching the Carnival revelers below. But when they spotted Olimpia, instead of bowing politely as etiquette demanded, they "removed themselves from the window so she would not see them," Amayden recounted.[2]

Furious at the insult, Olimpia ordered her driver to go around the block. When she returned, she saw Camillo and the princess standing in the window again. And when they saw her, they once more stepped backward into the shadows. Amayden added that the snub "was seen by all."[3]

Olimpia raced to complain to the pope. But having told him of the public insult, she was astonished to find that he was angry at *her*. Certainly Camillo and the princess of Rossano had behaved badly by backing away from the window when they saw her, Innocent agreed, but why did she so pointedly stick her head out of the carriage window and look up? And if that weren't bad enough, why did she order her coachman to go around the block again, stop her carriage and lean out *again*, squinting and grimacing at the princess's window?

Olimpia, the pope continued, should have politely pretended not to notice the snub and kept on rolling. It was *her* behavior that had made everybody look up at the window in the first place. She, too, must bear some responsibility for creating scandal, and he was tired of her blaming everything on her daughter-in-law.

The princess of Rossano was racking up victories in the War of the Olimpias. She had given birth to an undisputed Pamphili heir despite her mother-in-law's purported plans to cast doubt on the child's heritage. She had received permission to remain in Rome despite Olimpia's hostile campaign for exile. She had emerged triumphant in the public skirmishes of the carriages, the insulting epigram contests, and Olimpia's never-performed Carnival comedy. Yet not all was victory; the princess began to see signs of defeat very close to home.

The bloom was off the bud in terms of her marriage. After two years with Camillo, the thrill of the forbidden love affair had gone, and the steamy sexual passions had burned themselves out. Now, looking across the breakfast table, the princess realized that she was married to a dolt. Cardinal Pallavicino put it diplomatically when he described Camillo as "a man very much inferior to the mediocrity of others, while his wife was far above the mediocrity of other women."[4]

Using his wife's money, Camillo designed improvements to her gardens and collected statues. He spent an inordinate amount of time trying to give the Pamphili family an ancient noble lineage, instead of the unimpressive descent from the fifteenth-century Pamphilis of the Umbrian backwater of Gubbio. The legendary king of Rome in the sixth century B.C. was called Numa Pompilio. In writing his history of the family, Camillo fudged the name to Numa Pamphilio and claimed direct descent. He was terribly proud of his genealogical accomplishment and didn't seem to notice that people—including his wife—were laughing.

Olimpia was an avid collector of relics. Catholics believed that the body parts of saints retain the essence of holiness that can perform miracles or at least bring good luck. Saints' bones, blood, hair, skin, teeth, and even clothing and household items were treasured as miracle-working totems, encased in gold and crystal and studded with diamonds.

The royal family of Spain was fortunate to possess entire saintly cadavers, which, if a member of the dynasty became gravely ill, would be put into the sickbed. Sometimes the royal four-poster became a charnel house of moldering corpses, with the bright eyes of a feverish prince or princess peering out from beneath them. Oddly, the miraculous corpses sometimes affected a cure. Or perhaps, if that experience didn't kill the invalid, nothing would.

In the Dark and Middle Ages, merchants in the Byzantine Empire, hearing of the European thirst for relics, were seen in crumbling cemeteries digging up rotten bones—of pagans—calling them the bones of early Christian martyrs, and selling them to pilgrims for high prices. Not only human remains were sold. No one seemed to mind that some saints' bones had a disturbingly canine appearance.

One of the most daring feats of relic stealing occurred in A.D. 828 when two Venetians smuggled the body of Saint Mark the Evangelist out of Muslim-controlled Egypt, where he had been buried. It was thought that Muslims, who had their own cult of saints, would never allow their enemies the Catholics to cart off such a powerful relic, which could even be used against them in battle. They would sooner hide it or destroy it than let it fall into the hands of Christians.

The two Venetians, having secretly dug up the body, took it to their ship, and stashed it into a barrel of pickled pork, a food abhorred by Islam. Then, when Muslim customs officers arrived on board to check the cargo, the smugglers smilingly opened the barrel. "Unclean!" the Muslims cried, running off the ship in terror. And that is why Saint Mark is in Venice to this day, and crowds still throng to see the magnificent church that sprouted around his bones.

One of Martin Luther's beefs with the Catholic Church was the veneration of false relics and the belief that such veneration would confer a get-out-of-purgatory-free card. Until Luther's followers tossed them into the trash, one German church boasted a feather from the wing of the angel Gabriel, and the bishop of Mainz had a magically solidified flame from Moses' burning bush. Even today, the cathedral at Aachen has Jesus' diaper and the loincloth he wore on the cross. Most of all, Luther was disturbed that eighteen disciples were buried on German soil, when Christ had had only twelve.

The multiplication of relics didn't disturb Catholics, however. If a Protestant visitor to Italy politely asked a priest how there could be, for instance, two heads or three feet of a particular saint, he would smile, shrug, and say, "It's a miracle!" One Italian church reportedly possessed the head of John the Baptist as a child.

A sure sign of God's approval was a corpse that remained fresh long after death. In 1599 the body of Saint Cecilia, an early Christian martyr, was found under the high altar of the Roman church named after her.

Her corpse was surprisingly well preserved, with skin and hair intact. Over several days before the sacred body was reburied, thousands streamed into the church to see it.

The phrase "odor of sanctity" has its origins in reports that certain saintly bodies, when dug up, were not only intact but also exuded the delicate fragrance of roses. A rank, rapidly deteriorating corpse, on the other hand, was the mark of God's displeasure. Catholics were delighted to hear that no sooner had Martin Luther died in 1546 than his body turned black and began to stink, a sure sign of a quick trip south to a very hot place.

The body parts of saints were called first-class relics. Some Italian churches boasted magnificent first-class items—drops of the Virgin Mary's breast milk, the foreskin of Jesus' penis, and his umbilical cord. Other churches offered second-class relics, articles that had been intimately connected with the holy person during his or her life. One Roman church exposed Jesus' cradle from the manger, and another the marble pedestal on which Pontius Pilate had had him flogged.

In the Vatican itself was the lance that the Roman centurion Longinus used to pierce the Savior's side on the cross; a portrait of Christ on the handkerchief of Saint Veronica, which she had used to wipe the sweat from his face as he carried the cross; and the papal throne of Saint Peter (though carbon dating recently determined that it was, in fact, from the ninth century).

Across Europe, many churches and lucky individuals had splinters of the true cross on which Jesus had been crucified. The cross had been brought to Rome in about A.D. 327 by Constantine's mother, the devout empress Helena, who had purchased it on a relic-shopping trip to Jerusalem. There the empress had been approached by a group of Jews who claimed to know where the cross had been hidden centuries earlier. Considering the cruelty with which the Roman emperors had walloped Middle Eastern Jews—obliterating more than a million, and knocking down their holy Jerusalem temple—we can only hope that as Helena sailed back to Rome, those who sold her the cross were not laughing, imagining Constantine's mother worshipping a piece of rotten wood they had buried the night before.

Third-class relics were articles that had touched the saint when alive or his bones after death. Even these were thought to have healing powers, having soaked up the magical properties of the saint's body through physical contact. It was, however, generally not accepted that a person with whom a saint had shaken hands could set himself up in a church for public veneration as a third-class relic.

The pope's relatives usually showed their piety by endowing their own churches. But because every church worth its salt had to have a first-class relic, and so few new saints were forthcoming in such a degenerate age, somewhere a saintly corpse had to be dismembered.

In 1638 Anna Colonna wanted a chunk of the body of Saint Filippo Neri to send to her new chapel in Naples. Neri, who died in 1595, had been a friend of Saint Ignatius of Loyola's and had founded a religious order called the Congregation of the Oratory. Because he had died only some forty years earlier, his body had not yet been sliced up and distributed as those of ancient martyrs and medieval saints had been, and this corpsely integrity was a great source of pride to the Oratorians. Each year on his saint's day, the body was brought out from under the altar and exposed to the faithful.

One day a priest who had some business in the Vatican happened to glance at a table bearing decrees awaiting Urban VIII's signature. To his horror, on the top of the stack was a decree ordering Saint Filippo Neri's exhumation and dismemberment. The priest ran to the Oratorians and told them that they were about to be robbed. The monks immediately appointed two of their brothers to hide the body without telling anyone its location, and then to hide themselves.

When the church officials came with their long knives, they had the tomb opened and found that the body was gone. The assembled monks said—quite honestly—that they didn't know where the body was. Furious, the officials had to be satisfied with carting off some silver vases in which had been placed the saint's heart, intestines, a nerve, a tooth, and some hair. Though sad to lose such valuable relics, the Oratorian fathers were happy they still had an intact saintly body—which the two monks dragged out of a closet once the furor had died down. But this intactness was not destined to last much longer. Once Anna Colonna heard they had put the body back, she sent someone by with a pair of clippers to snip off a rib.

And now in 1649 the new first lady of Rome wanted an impressive saintly relic. Olimpia truly needed such heavenly protection now, given the rising public hatred of her and its consequent dangers. And worse, the pope seemed to be distancing himself from her, ever so slightly. Perhaps it was just the stress of the job, but sometimes she didn't like the look in his eyes or the tone in his voice.

Olimpia planned to put her relic in the Church of San Martino, which she had refurbished with Francesco Borromini. Olimpia's new town and restored church urgently needed a holy relic to encourage pilgrims on their way to Rome to stop by and stimulate the local economy. And Olimpia knew exactly whose body she wanted to raid.

In 1638 the corpse of the fifteenth-century saint Francesca was found in the Church of Saint Mary on a hill overlooking the Roman Forum, where it had been buried 198 years earlier. Immediately the bones began to perform miracles. Sister Teodora Celsi, whose body had been withered and twisted for sixteen years, dangled her useless arms among the bones and suddenly felt warmth revive them. She opened her hands, which had been so tightly closed that her nails had grown into her palms. Two days later she returned to the saint to have her paralyzed legs healed. A blind person was restored to sight, two people possessed by demons were liberated, another cripple leaped up with joy, throwing away his crutches, and many were healed of fever.

After several days of performing miracles, the bones were dressed in fine new clothes, covered with silk flowers, and reburied in the original humble tomb. Bernini designed a grand new tomb in the same church, of exquisite marble crowned with bronze figures. On the night of March 9, 1649, the saint's feast day, Saint Francesca's coffin was to be moved to the new tomb. This translation, as it was called, was the perfect opportunity to pocket a relic.

Naturally there would be a stink if Olimpia swiped the whole body. Decorum decreed that she take only a piece. The best portion of a saintly corpse was always the head, which was thought to have the greatest power. And indeed, most saints' bodies had already lost their heads to another church.

No, Olimpia decided, the head was too much to steal. And besides, somebody would certainly notice it had gone missing. She could take a finger or a tooth; probably no one would miss that. But such a small item would not give her church the prestige it needed. Then she hit upon the solution—the shoulder bone. Big enough to impress more than, say, a toe, it was a solid chunk of bone, but not as controversial as the head. She would pilfer the shoulder bone.

Saint Francesca had founded the Tor de' Specchi Convent, where Innocent's sister Agatha resided. The nuns there were looking forward to the translation as the most exciting event of their careers. They would leave the convent at sunset to make a torchlight procession through Rome up the hill to the church. There they would see the coffin opened, venerate the bones of their patroness, and watch the solemn entombment.

But when the nuns arrived after an hourlong procession, they found to their horror that the saint's casket had been sealed with lead and already placed in the new tomb. Why hadn't they been allowed to see the sacred relics? Then someone whispered that the monsignor charged with the translation had yanked the saint's shoulder bone off and stuck it under his priestly tunic for Olimpia.

Giacinto Gigli wrote in his diary, "Anyone can imagine the chagrin that the nuns felt, the cries and lamentations that were heard through the whole Forum, and they said they would have thought that for the love of Sister Agatha, Pope Innocent's sister, who should have been more respected and honored, they would have expected the contrary."

But the monsignor who had done the dirty deed, Gigli continued, and "did not want to hear the cries of the nuns . . . was impolite. The next morning Sister Agatha went to the Vatican to see her brother the pope to complain and quarrel about it. He, at the insistence of Donna Olimpia, sent the shoulder to a place called San Martino near Viterbo."[5]

Though Olimpia caught the most flack, she was not alone in abstracting something from Saint Francesca's coffin. The august cardinals and government officials who witnessed the translation had also fished for plunder. There was no protest from the nuns because they had only taken third-class relics—snippets of clothing and silk flowers that had been put in the coffin back in 1638. But a first-class shoulder was a different matter altogether. A sacrilege, they cried. Pasquino roared against the pope, who permitted his sister-in-law to profane the holy bones.

They could complain all they wanted. Olimpia, for her part, was thrilled to have such an illustrious relic for her church. And surely the power of the bone would protect her from anything the Roman people tried to do to her. Perhaps it would make her brother-in-law return to his formerly docile self, obedient to her commands and grateful for her help. This new, independent Innocent made her oddly uneasy.

While he was looking around for funds to ease the bread situation in Rome, it occurred to the pope that the duke of Parma still owed the apostolic treasury some 1.6 million scudi. In 1644, Urban VIII had gone to war over the debt, but having spent 12 million scudi with inconclusive results, the pope made a humiliating peace. The issue, however, had never been resolved.

On September 11, 1646, the swashbuckling Odoardo Farnese, duke of Parma, Piacenza, and Castro, had died, leaving his sixteen-year-old son, Ranuccio II, heir to his considerable debts. Innocent approached the young man in a friendly manner, suggesting how he could pay off the debt by selling various properties or simply handing them over to the Holy See.

For some two years negotiations continued, and it seemed that young Farnese was prepared to sign over a portion of his territory to satisfy his debt. But just before he did, the bishop of Castro died and a replacement was needed. Ranuccio insisted on naming the new bishop, but the pope declared that he and he alone had the right. When Innocent sent his newly appointed bishop to Castro, the bishop was murdered by Ranuccio's assassins.

Insulted at home and abroad, Innocent couldn't stand any more. Prodded by Olimpia, who hated the duke of Parma for supporting the princess of Rossano, the pope declared war. He hired an army, which he could ill afford, and stormed the fortress of Castro later that month. The garrison surrendered on September 2. Tired of Castro as a thorn in the papal side, and perhaps encouraged again by Olimpia, Innocent gave orders to raze to the ground not just the castle but the entire town. No two stones were left standing. The residents were dispersed, but not before one of them carved a sad stone for the site which read, HERE STOOD CASTRO.[6]

Olimpia carted off the image of the Immaculate Virgin and two sets of church bells. Taking the church bells of a vanquished enemy was a Mediterranean tradition to flout one's victory over an enemy, much the way Germanic warriors had turned the skulls of their enemies into drinking cups. Though Olimpia might have liked to drink from the silver-plated skull of the princess of Rossano, she had to be satisfied with the church bells of the princess's closest ally. One set she placed in her Church of San Martino, and another she kept for the new Church of Saint Agnes she was planning to build next to her Piazza Navona palazzo.

During the Castro war, Olimpia lost her beloved half-brother. On July 29, Andrea Maidalchini died at Viterbo at the age of about sixty-eight. But if Olimpia mourned him, the people of Viterbo did not. Gigli commented, "He was much disliked because he bought all the grain, all the wine and oil, and then resold it at profit. He did not want to increase the bread at Viterbo where he was despised as the author of the famine. After his death the loaves became bigger in Viterbo."[7]

The loaves also became bigger in Rome as a plentiful grain harvest put an end to the lingering famine. Gigli reported that on August 1, bread rose to a normal eight-ounce *pagnotta*. He added, "For this the people stopped murmuring and many were happy enough."[8]

The day of Innocent's election he had named his old friend Monsignor Domenico Cecchini to the most important Vatican office—that of datary, a word that refers not only to the office but also to its director. The datary was the pope's personal bank account. Each penny the church collected from indulgences, benefices, graces, privileges, offices, and taxes went into the datary, which then dispensed the funds to other departments, or to the pope's relatives and friends, according to papal instructions.

The individual who served as datary was in the enviable position of being able to put his hand in the till without anybody knowing about it, at least as long as his theft was acceptably modest. In an era when accounting referred to scribes scratching lists of numbers on pieces of paper, there was ample room for fraud. Moreover, the position guaranteed the datary large bribes from those seeking pensions and honors from the church.

The selling of church and government offices was standard practice and a reliable way for the Vatican to make money. Each office was an investment that brought a guaranteed annual income. The position of protonotary, for instance—whose job it was to write the lives of the saints—was sold for 7,000 scudi and offered 400 scudi revenue a year. The office of lead, which ensured that all papal bulls had lead seals attached, cost an impressive 23,000 scudi up front but brought an annual income of 3,000. The transaction was a gamble for both the buyer and seller of the office. If the buyer lived for decades, the church lost money. If he died immediately after purchasing it, the church could turn around and sell it again.

The problem with office selling was that the most qualified candidate for the position was usually not the candidate with the deepest pockets. Many who bought an office had no intention of doing the work and subcontracted it out for a lower price, pocketing the profit. Sometimes the buyer was too cheap to hire a replacement and pocketed the entire salary without doing any of the work; in this case someone else in the office would have to write about the saints or order the lead.

Rome was not alone in selling offices and titles. In England, kings routinely sold noble titles to raise money for an empty exchequer. James I (reigned 1603–1625) came up with a new title—baronet—which he sold for over a thousand pounds to whoever wanted it. Many butchers and tailors who had run profitable businesses were suddenly able to buy their way into English nobility. His first year as king, James sold 838 knighthoods—including one to a barber and another to a man who had married a laundress.

As usual, France did things on a grander scale than England, selling thousands of duplicate positions to raise money for its aggressive military campaigns. One French courtier wrote, "One of the most wonderful privileges of the kings of France is that when the king creates an office, God, at that very instant, creates a fool to buy it."[9] An extremely prestigious position was the groom of the stool, the man who had the rare honor of wiping the royal rear end. This position was highly prized because it allowed the owner to be very close to the king—closer than most of us would wish.

But unlike royal courts, the Vatican court had a theological problem with the selling of offices. Simony was the name for the buying and selling of spiritual things. In the biblical book of Acts, a magician named Simon saw the miracles worked by Peter and the apostles and offered them money to buy their spiritual power. Peter responded, "Your silver perish with you because you thought you could obtain God's gift with money!" Over the centuries, popes and church councils had harshly forbidden simony and declared offices purchased with it to be held illegally.

Faced with the contradictory requirements of theology and finance, by the fifteenth century the church reached a compromise—only mid-level positions could be sold. Top Vatican positions, such as papal ministers or the datary, were too important to sell and were given to truly qualified men. On the other end of the spectrum, minor positions were to be bestowed free of charge on worthy prelates as a reward for years of hard service. Many clerics, having worked for decades in poor parishes comforting the sick and feeding the hungry, came to Rome to make it known that they would like some modest bequest—the income that came with running a small diocese, perhaps. Church committees were supposed to investigate these requests and grant them to worthy candidates. But for centuries the pope's family members had sold even the most minor positions, pocketing the sales price.

By seventeenth-century standards, Innocent was thought to be financially incorrupt. Though he had given and received bribes on the way up, as everyone did, he was never accused in any capacity whatsoever of stealing money from the church, and his lifestyle had always been abstemious. And so, when Innocent appointed a datary on his very first day as pope, he chose the most honest man he knew. In March 1645, Innocent further rewarded Cecchini by bestowing on him the cardinal's hat.

Born in 1589, Cecchini exercised his functions with great rectitude, accounting for every *bajocco* that came in or went out of the datary. This was a problem for Olimpia, who like most papal relatives expected a cut from datary transactions. Innocent would not live forever, and she would need every penny to keep the family afloat and out of jail during the next pontificate. She was losing huge amounts of money because of Cecchini's stubborn honesty.

Olimpia had another bone to pick with Cecchini. The cardinal lived with a widowed sister-in-law, Clemenzia, a greedy, ambitious woman who was said to have a tremendous influence over him. It was a situation oddly similar to that of Olimpia and the pope, and in this case, too, people whispered that the two were having an affair. Because the honorable Cecchini did not accept outright bribes, the bribers went to Clemenzia and loaded her with jewels and gifts, which she cheerfully accepted. Everyone in Rome knew that Clemenzia influenced the datary and Olimpia did not. Olimpia found that she was losing power and money by Cecchini's honesty and Clemenzia's greed.

Having studied Olimpia's career path, Clemenzia had become a kind of mini-Olimpia and hoped to wheel and deal her brother-in-law onto the papal throne in the next conclave. He was, after all, an important and highly respected cardinal, and in 1647 he was fifty-eight, just two years shy of the *papabile* age of sixty. But Clemenzia was not so clever by half as Olimpia, who had studied human nature for decades and worked subtly.

The brash Clemenzia made fatal mistakes. She did not court the first lady of Rome. She did not offer to share her commissions, gifts, and bribes with her. Instead, she tried to upstage her at every opportunity. If Olimpia trotted around town in an elegant new coach and six, Clemenzia bought a more luxurious one. If Olimpia gave a party, Clemenzia gave a bigger one. If Olimpia appeared in public shining in diamonds, Clemenzia appeared wearing brighter ones.

Clemenzia was no worthy rival, and it was an easy matter for Olimpia to carefully aim a poison blow dart, puff up her cheeks, blow hard, and send it flying. It found its mark. Olimpia pointed out to Innocent that Clemenzia was prancing around Rome in new carriages, ablaze in jewels. She insinuated that his datary was, perhaps, not so incorrupt. Money that came into the datary to send to Jesuit missions abroad or build hospitals for the poor was obviously funding Clemenzia's extravagant lifestyle. Innocent had been certain of Cecchini's honesty, but as time passed, and Olimpia whispered, and Clemenzia pranced, he became unsure.

Cecchini's subdatary, the number two man in the office, was not as incorruptible as his boss. Francesco Canonici, called Mascambruno, had been born a country bumpkin in 1610. As a young man he found a job as a scribe in the Roman law office of Camillo Mascambruno. The wealthy church lawyer became quite fond of his scribe, some said too fond, as a homosexual relationship was suspected. He adopted the younger man, giving him his name, and left him his entire estate.

Francesco Mascambruno first came to the attention of the Pamphili family in 1644 when Olimpia's son-in-law Andrea Giustiniani hired him to transfer properties into his name from his uncle's estate. The ambitious Mascambruno fastened himself to the new papal family like a leech, becoming especially close to Olimpia, rendering every possible service with great efficiency. At Olimpia's instigation, the pope appointed Mascambruno the subdatary.

Mascambruno was an unusual Vatican bureaucrat. In contrast to the bright silks, frothy lace, and gleaming gold embroidery of his colleagues, he wore dark colors and plain fabrics. He seemed to be a frugal soul, a hardworking functionary with an obsequious manner. His winning formula was to slink silently into the background and pounce forward when needed, the indispensable man. He had a flat, broad face and strange eyes, his colleagues later recalled. Frightened eyes, as if always waiting for doom to strike. The French ambassador, Saint-Nicolas, wrote to Cardinal Mazarin that Mascambruno "was a dangerous type who was not thought of as very sincere."[10]

With Cecchini fired, Olimpia and Mascambruno could skim the datary profits. They set to work to convince the pope that Cecchini was not as honorable as he seemed. They were joined in their disparagement by Cardinal Panciroli, who was violently jealous of the pope's affection for Cecchini. Panciroli told Innocent that Cecchini aspired to be the next pope—the sooner the better—and was supported in this aim by the grand duke of Tuscany. "Panzirole never missed an opportunity to vomit at me all his poison," Cecchini wrote in his autobiography.[11]

The poison eventually had an effect. In a public audience on June 22, 1649, "the pope, saturated and stimulated by the slander of Donna Olimpia and Panzirole, was ready to burst . . . and called me a rascal, a rogue, and a simoniac."[12] Innocent summoned the Swiss Guard and told them that Cecchini was never to show his face to the pope again.

After that outburst, everyone thought Cecchini was finished at the Vatican. Olimpia promised him she would convince the pope to send him away honorably to a bishopric far from Vatican intrigues. But it is likely that the pope was not so sure about the accusations after all; he did not take away Cecchini's titles and incomes and allowed him to remain the datary in name. But Innocent no longer called for Cecchini to bring him the daily financial reports; he called for Mascambruno. Each day when Mascambruno returned from his papal audience, Cecchini, vegetating in his offices, asked him if the pope had mentioned him, and each day Mascambruno replied that he had not, but he certainly would soon. The datary waited uneasily, and his sister-in-law Clemenzia stopped prancing.

According to the Venetian ambassador, Giovanni Giustiniani, Olimpia wrote up her own petitions and handed them to Mascambruno, who passed them on to the pope. Seeing they were from his sister-in-law, Innocent didn't bother to read them but signed them and handed them back to Mascambruno.

Though the pope and Olimpia were unaware of it, Mascambruno began writing up his own petitions and presenting them as Olimpia's. The pope immediately signed them and handed them back, and Mascambruno found himself in the enviable position of selling papal indulgences and offices without having to split the money with a member of the pope's family.

~~~~~

Throughout history, art has been a primary tool of propaganda, a means the powerful used to awe their subjects into submissive obedience. When poor wretches stood blinking in wonder at temples, pyramids, statues, and obelisks, they meekly emptied their pockets of their last penny to give to the tax man. It was clearly no use arguing with a power that could produce such marvels.

Art was also a means of grasping at eternity from beyond the grave. Olimpia knew that the pope would not live forever. Even worse, she would not live forever. And the line started by Camillo might dwindle and die out, as so many noble families did. But if she left behind her extraordinary palaces, gardens, and fountains, a part of Olimpia Maidalchini Pamphili would live for all eternity, proclaiming the wealth, power, and position to which the dowerless girl from Viterbo had risen.

As work finished up on her magnificent Piazza Navona palace, Olimpia took a long hard look out her front windows and didn't like what she saw. The vegetable sellers were long gone, by papal decree. But the plain fountains in the piazza—low enough for donkeys and horses to drink from—were unimpressive. She resolved to turn the area into a worthy replacement of Emperor Domitian's grand marble stadium.

There was no room for a garden, of course, in the highly trafficked piazza, but Olimpia could create pleasure grounds nonetheless, complete with a resplendent fountain in the center, unique in all the world. When she discussed her plan with the pope, Innocent liked the idea of a fountain. He was also interested in resurrecting an obelisk that the emperor Caligula had brought to Rome from Egypt in the first century. The obelisk had been knocked down by Totila the Goth in A.D. 547 and now lay in five pieces, poking out of the dirt outside the Saint Sebastian Gate. Innocent decided to incorporate the obelisk into the design of the fountain.

He asked Francesco Borromini for ideas. Borromini suggested representing the four major rivers of the world—the Nile in Africa, the
Danube in Europe, the Ganges in Asia, and the Plate in South America, as the obelisk towered above them. Innocent was intrigued by Borromini's idea and instructed him to divert water from the nearest
aqueduct—the Acqua Vergine—to the Piazza Navona. The pope made
tin and lead available for the pipes.

Moving the fallen obelisk to the Piazza Navona was an arduous engineering task. The heavy slabs were dug up and hoisted out of ditches with
ropes and pulleys. Once on flat ground, each slab was harnessed to four
pairs of buffalo and hauled, inch by painful inch, to its new location.

With the pipes in place and the obelisk ready for resurrection, Innocent held a competition for several artists to make models of the fountain, but he wasn't thrilled by the results, not even by the model created
by Borromini, which was stiffly somber. Gian Lorenzo Bernini, who
had been on the outs with the pope since 1646 when his bell towers had
been dismantled, had not been invited to compete.

But Prince Ludovisi was a good friend of Bernini's who felt that the
artist had been given a raw deal. One day the prince asked Bernini to
call on him, and when the sculptor arrived Ludovisi told him his secret
plan. If Bernini would craft a model for the fountain, he would make
sure that the pope saw it. A short time later, on August 15, 1647, when
Innocent visited Olimpia for lunch, he walked by a table on which the
prince had placed Bernini's model of wood and gesso. The pope was
thunderstruck by its originality and beauty. The rivers were represented
by four enormous river gods; in its breathtaking entirety, the fountain
was a baroque jumble of dramatic surprises.

"This design must be by Bernini!" Innocent cried. Bernini's son Domenico wrote that the pope walked around the model for half an hour,
studying it from all angles. "The pope called for Bernini and apologized for not having him work for him before, and ordered him to
make the fountain according to his design."[13]

When Borromini heard that his ancient rival, whom he thought he
had vanquished once and for all, had been given the enviable commission,
he was foaming-at-the-mouth angry. It had been *his* idea to represent the

four rivers. *He* had done the dirty, thankless grunt work of diverting the aqueduct and laying down the conduits. And now Bernini was to plunk his frothy creation on top and have all the credit and glory. Several times Borromini stormed into the pope's presence screaming and stomping his feet. Many people thought that the episode had so unhinged the emotionally unstable Borromini that he would throw himself into the Tiber as the most dramatic protest possible.

To create his fountain, Bernini first built the travertine base, into which the obelisk was set in August 1649. He hired other sculptors to create four river gods according to his specifications. It is debatable exactly how much of the fountain Bernini carved. But he certainly created the design and supervised construction from beginning to end.

The Four Rivers Fountain is a seventeenth-century wonder, a tourist attraction to this very day. The center looks like a primeval rock from which water gushes and the obelisk rises. At the bottom of the rock are a horse, a lion, and a palm tree, writhing in theatrical contortions. Around the edges of the basin sit the four river gods, twisting themselves to better show their exaggerated muscles to admiring spectators.

The South American figure looks oddly African because Bernini had never seen a native of South America; however, he had probably seen Africans, as the 1650 census recorded thirteen of them living in Rome (out of a population of 126,192), and many noble visitors brought with them fashionable African child servants. Near the South American figure is what is supposed to be an armadillo, but since there were none of those living in Rome either, Bernini's armadillo looks more like a dragon. The Nile river god has his head covered with a drape, as if he were inhaling menthol fumes for a head cold. But the drape indicated that no one had seen the source, or head, of the Nile.

At the base of the fountain is the huge marble coat of arms of Pope Innocent X, with the dove holding the olive sprig in its mouth. Art aside, the propaganda statement was clear—the Pamphili family and the Roman Catholic Church reigned supreme over all four continents. On top of the fifty-four-foot obelisk was placed the Pamphili dove, which represented the pope and the Holy Spirit triumphing over pagan empires. Moreover, the living waters of the fountain symbolized

Christian baptism sanctifying the ancient pagan arena. Olimpia, casting her glance to the left out of her parlor windows as the fountain rose, must have sighed with contentment.

But the people of Rome were not content. Just moving the obelisk cost twelve thousand scudi, and the fountain cost an additional eighty thousand, which the pope squeezed out of the Romans by placing a special tax on them in the middle of a famine. One morning the engineers arrived at the Piazza Navona to find a placard on the obelisk that read, "This obelisk is consecrated in eternity in the Piazza Navona of Innocent at the cost of the innocents."[14] Pasquino cried: "We don't want an obelisk and a fountain head. Give us bread, bread, bread!"[15]

Though Olimpia was not able to create a real garden in the Piazza Navona, she found an opportunity elsewhere to build one of the most beautiful gardens of the seventeenth century. With Camillo back in Rome but instructed not to involve himself with anything important, Olimpia took over the design of his gardens at his pleasure villa, Bel Respiro. Unhappy over the fact that curious passersby on the Via Aurelia could look up the sloping hill and stare at her villa, she wanted more privacy out front and a fashionable sunken garden out back.

To this end she had hundreds of workmen cart thousands of wheelbarrows full of dirt out of her backyard and dump them on the slope in the front of the house. Then she built a massive retaining wall, which was all that the gawkers below would now see. She planted the sunken gardens with rare blooms, fragrant trees, and thick hedges, and decorated with fountains, statues, and grottoes. She even placed a fountain on the lower floor of the villa, which opened onto the terrace. There her guests could relax or dine to the playful sound of falling water and look out over her acres of stunning sunken gardens.

Many of the statues adorning her gardens were recent finds. It seemed that whenever a spade hit dirt in or around Rome, the glories of the ancient past resurfaced. In 1649, excavators digging in the Baths of Trajan found a room with a floor of lapis lazuli and fifty-four intact statues. Cemeteries were unearthed on the Via Latina, each tomb bursting with carved urns, sarcophagi, frescoes, inscriptions, vases, and jewels. In both cases, construction workers immediately sent word to Olimpia, who raced over with wagons and porters. Cartloads of priceless antiquities rumbled back to the Piazza Navona.

In acquiring new artifacts for her collections in this manner, Olimpia was doing nothing different from what Cardinal Nephew Scipione Borghese had done thirty years earlier, and indeed, she had never stolen paintings from church walls the way Borghese had. But a woman was not supposed to greedily snap up antiquities, and when people saw the ancient statues disappear behind the doors of her palazzo, they murmured.

17

The Holy Jubilee Year

We are all Pilgrims, who seek Italy.

—Johann Wolfgang von Goethe

T HOUGH HE WAS HUMILIATED at home and abroad, Innocent's luck was about to change. For he had the good fortune to be pope during the jubilee, a yearlong religious festival that Pope Boniface VIII had started in 1300 to bring God into the hearts of men and money into the coffers of Rome. During the jubilee, held every twenty-five years, the pope was the star of the European stage, and the church reigned triumphant.

Pilgrims flocked to Rome to obtain the indulgence of sins. The Catholic sacrament of penance affirms that in order to have sins forgiven the sinner must have a sincerely contrite heart, confess to a priest, who represents God, and make restitution to those he has harmed. Finally, he must endure either an earthly punishment or suffer in purgatory after death. It was far safer, Catholics believed, for the sinner to choose his own chastisement than to wait until after death and let God concoct the appropriate penalty. Self-imposed punishments included fasting, prayer, almsgiving, and making a long journey to a holy site. A pilgrimage was a popular form of punishment as it allowed the sinner to get in a great deal of sightseeing.

Holy Year pilgrims obtained the indulgence of sins by visiting the four major Roman basilicas the number of times specified by the reigning pontiff. They shaved extra time off purgatory by touring the catacombs where early Christians had buried their dead and worshipped in frescoed underground chapels. More heavenly brownie points accrued by praying at the Colosseum, believed to be the site of the martyrdom of so many Christians, and asking for heavenly intercession at the shrines of the saints.

This influx of sinners was a huge stimulus for the Roman economy, with hundreds of thousands of visitors staying at inns, eating and drinking, and shopping for necessities, souvenirs, and luxury items. Most pilgrims piously gave donations to the churches they visited.

But it wasn't all profit for the Vatican, which invested in preparations years in advance. Hospitals and dormitories were built, trees were planted, and streets were paved. In addition, Rome in the jubilee year was a kind of baroque Catholic Disney World, with easily recognizable biblical characters walking the piazzas in impressive costumes, exquisitely constructed stage sets on every street, and tacky expensive souvenirs for sale on every corner. Holy-Year celebrations awed and inspired with fireworks, feasts, and fountains running with wine.

The Vatican also bore the substantial cost of refurbishing Rome's famous churches to strike wonder into the hearts of pilgrims. Innocent ordered that all churches be cleaned, repaired, and ornamented. But particular attention was paid to the four jubilee churches—Saint Peter's, Saint John Lateran, Saint Mary Major, and Saint Paul's Outside the Walls.

Starting in 1647, Innocent began major renovations at two of these churches. Saint John Lateran was a fourth-century basilica built by Constantine, which over time had been sacked by barbarians, rattled by earthquakes, and blackened by fires. The beautiful Roman columns had become so unstable that earlier popes had surrounded them with ungainly bricks. The floor was wobbly, and some of the walls were leaning out of kilter.

When the first Saint Peter's Basilica had been in a similar condition in the early sixteenth century, Pope Julius II demolished it and built a grand new church. But times had changed. Seventeenth-century Romans had an appreciation of antiquity that their great-grandfathers had lacked. Though delighted with the new magnificent Saint Peter's, they realized that the priceless historical and sacred value of the old one was forever lost. It had been a grievous waste to knock it down and throw it out with the trash to build something bigger and newer.

To overhaul Saint John Lateran, Innocent hired Francesco Borromini to recommend repairs. The architect was hell-bent on completely redesigning the building from top to bottom, making it into the Church of Saint John Borromini. Innocent gently reined him in and instructed him to preserve as much of the ancient church as possible. No walls were torn down, and the ancient proportions were retained. Borromini reinforced the wobbly foundations, stabilized the walls, and adorned the church with magnificent decorations.

Meanwhile, Innocent turned his attention to Saint Peter's. The interior decoration was not yet complete. The pilasters in the nave that held up the giant arches were of plain marble, which, people of the baroque felt, just cried out for adornment. With an eye toward the jubilee, soon after Bernini's rehabilitation Innocent hired him to decorate the pilasters. Bernini and his team carved cherubs holding three-dimensional medallions of the first thirty-eight popes. The Pamphili dove and olive branch were visible on each pilaster, an eternal reminder of Innocent X's generosity. Innocent also commissioned Bernini to design and lay down the sumptuous marble pavement in the nave.

In October 1649 Giacinto Gigli wrote that the churches "in other holy years were never this ornamented or beautiful. Because Saint Peter's looked fabulous with its new floor of colored marble and the chapels of Paul V newly inlaid with marble and all the altars embellished and everything carefully washed and polished."[1]

Given the astronomical expenses, the Holy Year was like a Broadway show with elaborate stage sets and a huge cast that had to be paid for before the first ticket was sold. All wealthy Romans were expected to make significant contributions the year before the jubilee. As first lady of Rome, Olimpia was assigned the Trinity Institute of Pilgrims, a huge guest house open for the Holy Year. The Roman people, aware of her avarice, were curious to see how much she would donate.

Using her well-honed administrative skills, Olimpia organized a group of forty-two influential ladies to collect money for the maintenance of pilgrims. A team of three ladies canvassed each of Rome's fourteen *rioni,* or districts. Olimpia's team of fund-raisers collected 16,582 scudi, enough money to feed and shelter 226,771 men, 81,822 women, and 25,902 convalescents for three days each. It was a magnificent sum. It was noted, however, that Olimpia had not contributed a penny of her own.

Dormitories such as Olimpia's Trinity Institute were never sufficient to shelter all pilgrims. In a day and age when hotel rooms were not reserved in advance—unless you sent someone ahead of you on a horse to do so—many exhausted visitors would arrive in the Eternal City to find there was not a single bed available in inns, pilgrim dormitories, or private homes. They would bed down where they could—in stables with cows and horses, under the loggias of public buildings, or in the vineyards just outside the walls of Rome. In 1649 the pope ordered tens of thousands of comfortable straw pallets for unsheltered pilgrims to buy at cost, as well as blankets, wine, and food.

To protect the pilgrims from racketeering, in 1648 Innocent had already passed a law prohibiting the raising of rents. Severe fines would be imposed on innkeepers and apartment owners who raised their prices to fleece the flock. The cost of food and wine, too, was carefully looked into. Any tavern keeper charging exorbitant prices during the jubilee would be fined and, if he continued, jailed.

On December 10, 1649, the pope issued various edicts regarding the approaching Holy Year. Priests were not allowed to wear long hair, and prostitutes were not allowed to wear crinolines or, as Gigli wrote, "go about in dresses similar to good women."[2]

In a rare fit of frivolity, on December 21 Innocent hired back all the bell ringers Olimpia had made him fire in 1644 to save money. He decreed that to show joy during the jubilee, all churches ring their bells three times daily for the next year, at nine in the morning, at one, and at sunset. Considering that Rome boasted 355 churches, it must have made for a merry cacophony.

The jubilee year was officially inaugurated on Christmas Eve by the ceremonial opening of the holy doors of the four basilicas. These doors, which were bricked up during regular years, were opened by the cardinal who was archpriest of the basilica. In front of cheering crowds, the cardinal tapped on the bricks with a ceremonial hammer. The bricks had already been loosened by masons, who were standing behind them. When the masons heard the tapping, they pulled down the bricks, creating a thunderous drama.

Embedded in each holy door was a chest of gold medals minted to celebrate the previous jubilee and struck with the image of the last Holy Year pope. This box was to be given to the door-opening cardinal. The medals were highly coveted and extremely valuable. As soon as the cardinal had taken his chest of holy medals and the masons had carted off the rubble, the crowds of excited pilgrims would race through the door to be the first to claim the indulgence.

On the afternoon of December 24, 1649, four cavalcades wound their way to the four basilicas. Penitents beat their breasts and whipped themselves as they walked. Some of the pious crept forward on their knees. Most pilgrims walked, some barefoot, while the better-off rode on mules or horses. The majority were Catholic, though each procession included several Protestants and a handful of Muslims and Jews who just wanted to see a good show.

Olimpia was itching to get her hands on the holy medals. Luckily, the archpriest of Saint John Lateran, Cardinal Girolamo Colonna, was a friend of hers. He opened the door with due dignity and took the heavy chest of Urban VIII's 1625 jubilee medals. Without opening it, he gave it to a soldier, who wrapped it in his cloak and took it posthaste to Olimpia.

Cardinal Francesco Barberini, the archpriest of Saint Peter's, would not open his holy door, as that honor was saved for the pope. But as archpriest, Francesco was entitled to the medals. Since Olimpia had recalled his family from exile and returned most of their property to them, he agreed to give her his medals. He instructed the masons to have a wheelbarrow placed behind the holy door so that the moment the masonry collapsed, the box of medals would fall into the wheelbarrow, which would be covered with a canvas and carted off to Olimpia. But it was not carted off quickly enough, as it was noticed by many of the faithful, including Giacinto Gigli, who recorded it in his diary.

While these two ceremonies went off without a hitch, the others did not. Over at Saint Paul's Basilica, when eighty-eight-year-old Cardinal Marcello Lante arrived to open the holy door, he found it already open. The masons waiting behind it, unable to see outside, had thought they heard the cardinal tapping and pulled down the door. Some two hundred pilgrims were inside the church milling around and gawking at the decorations.

Seeing the mess that awaited him, Cardinal Lante had the church cleared out and instructed the masons to pile up the bricks as best they could. He then ceremonially tapped on the dusty heap, declaring the church open for pilgrims. The box of medals was already gone, but it was not in Olimpia's hands. The dean of the basilica, knowing she wanted it, had locked it up in Saint Paul's treasury.

The archpriest of the fourth jubilee church, Saint Mary Major, was none other than Cardinal Antonio Barberini, but he was still huffing and puffing in self-imposed exile in France. Cardinal Alderano Cibo was next in line to perform the ceremony, but Olimpia insisted that her nephew Cardinal Maidalchini do the honors. She specifically instructed him to get the medals as quickly as possible and bring them to her.

Upon hearing that Cardinal Maidalchini had been chosen to replace Antonio Barberini for the job, Cardinal Federico Sforza raced to the pope to explain that this was a poor choice. The clumsy Cardinal Maidalchini could not represent the holy Catholic Church at such a crucial ceremony with thousands of spectators from around the world, some of them heretics. Another cardinal, Sforza begged, must do the honors. But the pope had already promised Olimpia. And when he told her about Sforza's plea, she had the popular cardinal exiled to his bishopric on the east coast of Italy.

Cardinal Sforza's prediction was accurate. The crowds of pilgrims murmured at the sight of the ungainly pimple-faced boy who seemed not to know how to hold the holy hammer. Nervous church officials suggested maybe they should call in another cardinal. But somehow Maidalchini figured out which end was up and managed to tap on the door, and the bricks promptly fell.

The young cardinal reached inside to grab the casket of holy medals, but the church canons, expecting such a move, were waiting behind the door and tried to yank the box out of his hands. The medals, they declared, belonged to them, and not to Cardinal Maidalchini, who was not the archpriest or even a proper substitute. Cardinal Maidalchini, terrified of Aunt Olimpia's fury, got into a brawl with the canons over possession of the box.

The spectators were furious at Cardinal Maidalchini for several reasons. First of all, he was ugly. Second, he had botched the sacred ceremony. Third, he was trying to steal the holy medals. The crowd rushed him, almost crushing him against the wall of the church. The little cardinal somehow wriggled out of their clutches and in the confusion raced out of the church clutching the box of medals. He jumped into his coach and galloped to the Piazza Navona palace with his mission accomplished.

And so, on the evening of December 24, 1649, Olimpia was the proud possessor of three of the four boxes of holy medals. It wasn't a bad take, but still, it could have been better.

On January 8, 1650, Innocent, irritated at tourists smoking pipes in the sacred space of Saint Peter's, became perhaps the first person ever to set up a no-smoking sign. All smokers would be excommunicated immediately and, without the sacraments of the church, would go to hell. Smoking stopped.

On January 9, Olimpia made a pompous cavalcade to the four jubilee churches. She had in her carriage her daughter Maria, Princess Giustiniani, and a retinue of many noble ladies followed in their own carriages. They rode first to Saint John Lateran, where on their knees, they climbed the holy stair, which was believed to have come from the Jerusalem palace of Pontius Pilate, and down which Jesus was said to have walked carrying the cross. Spots of miraculously indelible blood could still be seen on certain stairs. Saying a Hail Mary or an Our Father on each step, they made the painful ascent. It must have been agonizing for Olimpia, whose knees swelled and ached with arthritis.

Olimpia and other wealthy Catholics made the rounds of the four churches in comfortable carriages. For most people, however, the exhausting journey in all kinds of weather was done on foot. The entire circuit was twenty-five miles, since Saint Paul's was a few miles outside Rome. Innocent had decreed that pilgrims coming from afar were required to make the rounds of the four churches fifteen times to obtain the indulgence, while Romans, who hadn't already made a long trip to get to Rome, were required to visit all four churches thirty times.

Traditionally, with the pope's permission sick people could obtain the indulgence with fewer visits than required from the healthy. And historically most popes smiled, gave a benediction, and granted the indulgence to any incommoded person who asked for it. But Innocent, ever the strict jurist, was not quick to grant it to those who hadn't made even one round of the churches, and he inquired carefully into their efforts.

Giacinto Gigli thought the pontiff a bit stingy. "A gentlewoman sick to death begged the pope to give her the indulgence without going to the churches," he recounted. "The pope asked how many times she had gone and she said none, and he said what did she expect if she didn't go? She said she hoped to go in the month of May in warmer weather and the pope replied that in May we will give you the indulgence. Similarly other people who were ready to die sent to ask for the indulgence and it was asked how many times they had visited the churches and if they had never gone it was not conceded to them."[3]

Strict though he was, when the pope visited the churches he showed willingness to listen to all those pilgrims who wanted to talk to him. As a canon lawyer he had always listened to petitioners with compassion and patience, and in this way he was no different as pope.

The pope had forbidden Carnival, as the Holy Year was no time for Jews and prostitutes to race down the Corso. The parade of nude hunchbacks was canceled, as was the procession of farters carrying the King of the Defecators on a toilet chair. Those who wished to produce rowdy comedies had to do so in their private palaces outside the gates of Rome. Plays of a sacred nature were, of course, permitted.

The high point of every Holy Year was Easter, and this Easter the number of pilgrims swelled to sixty thousand. During Holy Week the pope several times washed the feet of poor pilgrims, in imitation of Jesus washing his disciples' feet. But Olimpia, it was noted, was never seen to wash a single poor foot.

As Easter dawned on April 17, the Spanish confraternity of the Holy Resurrection marched into the Piazza Navona holding aloft the Holy Sacrament. The architect Carlo Rainaldi had transformed the piazza into a peristyle of columns, creating 116 arches, surrounded by vines that flickered with the light of 1,600 candles. At each end of the piazza was a magnificent arch and cupola that seemed to be of heavy colored marble but was really made of flimsy painted wood. Inside one was the risen Christ, and inside the other was his Virgin Mother.

Bernini's fountain of the Four Rivers was still being constructed behind scaffolding. For Holy Week the artist surrounded the fountain with a crenellated wooden enclosure resembling a medieval castle, hung with beautiful religious paintings. On each corner he built a castle tower, on top of which musicians played. Lit by colored lights, the obelisk rose above the construction and at times shot off fireworks.

The jubilee year was a time of frequent miracles. Miracles occurred throughout Italy even in non-jubilee years, of course, but the hysteria of the Holy Year seemed to cause swarms of them. Prayers were answered. Crutches were left at altars. The moribund rose from their deathbeds and danced in the streets. Looking at these miracles from a modern perspective, we are unsure whether they were caused by mind over matter, natural healing, trickery, or divine intervention.

Innocent and Olimpia were kept closely informed of any miracles that took place in the Papal States. It was important, from both a church and governmental point of view, to determine the source of the miracles. Some of them were found to be real, caused by God and his saints to boost faith in the true church. Others were no less real but caused by Satan and his demons to fool the devout, and these had to be driven out by exorcists. The clearest sign of demonic possession was a gyrating pelvis. Anyone caught doing a seventeenth-century version of Elvis Presley—no matter how many cripples he healed—would have been drenched with holy water immediately and would, most likely, have responded with hisses and howls. Alas, most miracles were faked, caused by men and women hoping to defraud the pious.

Throughout Innocent's reign, the most fascinating case was that of Joseph of Cupertino. Known as "the Flying Friar," Joseph would go into a trance and then, with a shriek, fly up into the air. His superiors forbade him to meditate in the monastery gardens as his brothers were tired of hauling out the ladder and plucking him out of trees. Joseph was also forbidden to attend Mass in church, as he would go crashing through the air and knock into the high altar, screaming as the candles burned him, or land atop a column, sending the entire service into disorder. Nor was Joseph allowed to eat in the refectory with the other monks; he tended to launch himself airborne while holding a tray of hot soup, spilling it on those below. On some occasions as Joseph started to soar he grabbed hold of a fellow friar and carried the horrified monk into the air with him. Joseph was confined to a low cell, where he could do no flying. At one point he was reportedly brought to the Vatican so Urban VIII could meet him, and he duly soared upward, arms and legs gesticulating wildly, and landed at the pope's feet with a loud thud.

In 1650 the staunchly Lutheran duke of Brunswick, Johann Friedrich, traveled to Rome to experience the jubilee. On his way, he stopped off at Joseph's monastery in Assisi to see the Flying Friar. Whatever he saw amazed him so much that he immediately declared he would convert to Catholicism.

While most who witnessed Joseph's amazing feats were certain they were caused by God, the Inquisition was not so sure. To make sure his levitation was not the work of the devil, Innocent's chief inquisitor of miracles kept a firm eye on Joseph until his death in 1663. In 1767, Pope Clement XIII decided it had been the hand of God that lifted him up, and he canonized him. Church officials of the twentieth century—no strangers to things flying through the air—have since declared Joseph the patron saint of aviation. As for us, we can offer no explanation and must, for the moment, leave the case of Saint Joseph of Cupertino up in the air.

Not all miracles were as inexplicable as the Flying Friar. In May 1650 a group of Florentines brought to Rome a miraculous cross—which was said to fly from church to church of its own accord—and placed it in the Church of Saint John of the Florentines. Praying before the cross on his knees, a poor crippled Florentine suddenly jumped up and threw away his crutches. A woman possessed of a demon was healed, and another woman threw away her crutches. As a large crowd thronged the church to gape at the miracles unfolding before their very eyes, the vice-regent of Rome marched in to maintain order. He took the cross to the Inquisition so that investigations could be conducted on its healing power. Interrogations revealed that the crippled Florentine who threw away his crutches was a charlatan, hoping to draw excited crowds who in their religious fervor wouldn't notice when his associates picked their pockets.

Giacinto Gigli wrote, "Every day things get more confusing because no one knows if the miracles are truly done by God, or are false and lies."[4]

It was the biggest Holy Year ever, with some 700,000 pilgrims coming from all parts of Europe over the course of twelve months. While many travelers shuffled into Rome anonymous, dusty, and tired, others arrived with ostentatious panache. The emperor of China sent a delegation bursting with silken Oriental splendor, years in the planning and two years on the road. The king of the Congo sent warriors draped in leopard skin, laden with thick ivory and gold bangles, and brandishing ceremonial spears.

The most spectacular entourage, however, was clearly that of the Spanish ambassador, the duke of Infantado, representing King Philip IV. He arrived escorted by 300 carriages, 100 of them rounded up by Prince Ludovisi from his friends and neighbors. This was a satisfying number because the French ambassador had only managed to scare up an embarrassing 160 carriages for his procession. The duke of Infantado had in his train hundreds of grooms holding the reins of gaily caparisoned horses, a squadron of tall Africans in plumed turbans, and a team of hunchbacks riding small white mules with jangling silver bells on their saddles.

Of all jubilee visitors, the great Spanish portrait painter Diego Velázquez left us the most lasting souvenir. During the artist's papal audience, he studied Innocent intently. Back in his rooms, he painted the pope without a single sitting. When he presented the portrait to the pope, Innocent took one look at it and cried, "Too true!"[5]

It is, indeed, almost a photograph of Innocent in all his pontifical majesty, sitting in a red velvet papal chair with gilded woodwork and finials. He wears a frothy white knee-length rochet edged with lace, a shining red satin mozzetta over his shoulders, and on his head the red satin *camauro*. His small, suspicious eyes look critically at the viewer. His brow is furrowed into a perturbed scowl. His lips are slightly pursed, as if he is about to say something unpleasant. The background, perhaps meant to represent a drape, appears unfinished, almost impressionistic, angry swatches of red and black.

The month of May saw the arrival of another famous pilgrim. Princess Maria of Savoy, great-aunt of the reigning duke, clattered into Rome with impressive pageantry. The princess was a fifty-six-year-old spinster and Capuchin lay nun—she lived the life of a nun but had never taken a nun's vows. She had, however, founded a convent in Turin where she spent her days in prayer, penance, and good works. She and her ladies wore enormous hoods and billowing coats of many wide folds that made the Romans laugh. She was profoundly deaf and used a silver ear horn to help her hear.

Princess Maria went first to visit the pope, to whom she gave a gorgeous reproduction of the Shroud of Turin encrusted with jewels. Immediately after her papal audience, she should have called on Olimpia as first lady of Rome. But instead of going to the Piazza Navona, the princess's carriage rumbled straight to the Tor de' Specchi Convent, where she would be residing. And there she remained.

It was a huge snub to Olimpia because everyone in Rome knew the princess had not visited her. But the devout Princess Maria had no intention of calling on a woman who had been born a nobody and who, it was thought, ruled Rome only because she was the pope's mistress. At the convent, Princess Maria's bias against Olimpia was exacerbated by Sister Agatha, who yelled into her ear horn the story of poor Camillo's miserable exile, the noble suffering of the pregnant princess of Rossano, and their continued estrangement from the pope, all at Olimpia's wicked instigation. The princess stayed put, and Olimpia's enemies roared with laughter.

As the days passed and still the princess did not call, Olimpia realized she needed to do something or she would be the laughingstock of Rome. She came up with an invitation so tantalizing that the devout princess would not be able to turn it down. Olimpia's private chapel in the Piazza Navona palace was stuffed with the relics of saints and a splinter of the true cross. Surely the princess would like to pray before such holy objects. Practically salivating at the very thought, Princess Maria agreed to make a brief private visit as long as no one else knew about it. She certainly didn't want the Roman public to know she had debased herself by visiting such an awful woman.

When Princess Maria arrived at the Piazza Navona palace, Olimpia smilingly guided her upstairs and opened the doors to her *galleria*. The princess entered, thinking it was the chapel with the holy relics. To her dismay, she found a crowd of hundreds bowing and clapping. Cardinals, bishops, ambassadors, noblemen, and their wives were standing on both sides of the gallery to witness Olimpia's triumph. Giacinto Gigli wrote, "There she found all the prelates of Rome, and a good part of the ladies, and she never saw the chapel, and went home disgusted."[6]

One of the goals of the jubilee was to encourage conversions. It was hoped that heretics—Protestants—or apostates—Muslims and Jews—would be so overcome by the pageantry and glory of the church that they would recant their false beliefs and spring into the arms of Catholicism.

There were never many conversions, but in a church under threat every single one was greeted with great fanfare. In 1650 six Jews converted, as well as a Turk and several heretics, including a Huguenot who threw himself at the feet of the pope while he conducted Mass and begged to be admitted into the Roman Catholic Church. Innocent embraced the reformed heretic and welcomed him back into the fold.

Sometimes pilgrims were so overcome with religious zeal that they forgot themselves. One gentleman, seeing the papal procession coming out of Saint Peter's, became so emotional that he darted into the procession, flung his arms around His Holiness, and kissed him.

Unfortunately, he had kissed the pope's bearded, exquisitely robed butler. Innocent was standing farther back, enjoying a good laugh at the comical scene.

Not all pilgrims were so devout. Numerous groups, lining up to march to church to proclaim their Christian devotion, got into bloody fights with other groups who were butting in front of them in the parade line. Some of these fights spilled over into churches, and the high altars were littered with dead bodies.

In June, Giacinto Gigli described a riot involving some two thousand pilgrims marching in two different religious parades, both of whom tried to push in front of the other. "Many were wounded with cudgels, among them the Marchese Santa Croce who was beaten in the head. . . . The marchese's coachman was taken to the hospital badly wounded in the face by a paving stone. These tumults happen on the street almost every day because these villains come from their own countries to Rome for the jubilee . . . and are so haughty they give room to no one and go processing through the streets and won't let anyone pass by. . . . If they come upon another group, they fight with their fists, because each wants precedence."[7]

The *avvisi* noted that some pilgrims, after begging God to forgive their sins and whipping themselves, ran to an inn and ate meat instead of fish, got wretchedly drunk, and had sex with whores. A French visitor observed, "No one abstained from eating forbidden meat, and despite their libertinage, you could see them praying and crying out for mercy, mercy, and beating their breasts as if they were the greatest saints in the world."[8]

Giacinto Gigli lamented, "Devotion is lost, and the Jubilee will create scandal and damage and make us Christians look like fools to the Jews, the Heretics, and the Gentiles who see and hear of these mishaps."[9]

But there were more serious concerns than unruly pilgrims. Crowd control had not yet been mastered, and well-attended events presented mortal dangers. On May 16 a huge throng surged toward the Quirinal Palace to see the pope bestow his blessing from a balcony. Many pilgrims were crushed, trampled, and suffocated, and Innocent was devastated to hear of the deaths and injuries.

Then there was the drought. For the first eight months of 1650 it barely rained at all, which prompted fears of another famine. Every day the pilgrims trudged to the four churches in a thick cloud of dust. An epidemic of some sort began to cull its victims. Gigli wrote, "Many people grew sick and many of the pilgrims and workers and even noble and rich people died suddenly."[10]

⁓

Pilgrims who came to Rome for the jubilee of 1650 had a long list of things to see—festive celebrations, Roman ruins, medieval churches, the beautiful new Saint Peter's Basilica, and most fascinating of all, the pope's sister-in-law, who, everyone knew, ran the Vatican.

Those who lived outside Rome had a hard time picturing this woman who ruled a pope, a church, and a nation. Some thought she had achieved her influence through her beauty. She must be drop-dead gorgeous, a Helen of Troy whose face mesmerized even the most dried-up old churchmen. Others, knowing she was fifty-nine, an age bordering on decrepitude, thought perhaps she was more like Cleopatra, no classic beauty but redolent of charm and seduction. After all, there were many such women at the courts of Europe who were still desirable despite having left the freshness of youth far behind. Yet others, who heard she was neither beautiful nor fascinating, believed her influence was the result of witchcraft. She was in league with the devil, they said, to ruin God's church. She must be inherently evil, a very monster of iniquity trafficking with Satan himself.

When they saw Olimpia, all three groups of pilgrims must have been grievously disappointed. For what they saw was a short, heavy woman in late middle age whose face once had been handsome but now sported a double chin and sagging jowls, a graying bourgeois matron in plain black widow's weeds. She was neither radiantly beautiful, nor scintillatingly seductive, nor manifestly malevolent.

This mistress of the Vatican was a woman no one would ever look at twice, had they not known who she was. Here was a woman who could pass unnoticed in a crowd of colorful Italian nobles, bold prostitutes, pompous clerics, prosperous merchants, and ragged beggars. Of all the miraculous wonders the pilgrims saw in Rome that jubilee year of 1650, Olimpia Maidalchini was the most amazing.

Those curious pilgrims who were not worthy of being invited to her festivities at the Piazza Navona palace camped outside, much as modern-day fans might do outside a hotel where their favorite movie star is staying. They studied the countless windows across the broad façade, hoping for a glimpse of her. Whenever the high doors of her courtyard swung open and a carriage clattered out, Olimpia fans thronged it. We can hear them crying, "There she is!" as they rushed her carriage. Had it been the fashion, they surely would have thrust autograph books into her carriage windows.

Pilgrims stationed in front of Olimpia's house were often treated to the sight of the pope coming by to have lunch with her. But the pope was, after all, just another old man with a beard and funny hat. Popes were pretty much interchangeable—paper-doll figures who all wore the same paper-doll clothes. Olimpia, by virtue of her unique position, truly fascinated them. In 1650 she was a kind of baroque rock star, ruling over the most important event in the world, in the most important city in the world, as if she were a queen.

As the year went by, the pope became uncomfortably aware of Olimpia's popularity with the pilgrims. As Saint Peter's successor and the Vicar of Christ, *he* should have been the center of attention during the jubilee year, and Olimpia was stealing his thunder. One day Innocent's secretary showed him a letter from a Neapolitan who wrote that most of the pilgrims who left Naples for Rome had done so not for the indulgence of sins or to see the pope but out of curiosity to see his sister-in-law. The Olimpia fans were almost all women, fascinated that another woman had climbed so high against all social restrictions and church regulations.

One day when the pope walked to the loggia of Saint Peter's to bless the crowds gathered below, a cardinal wondered aloud that there were so many women; usually women were left at home on long, dangerous journeys. The pope replied bitterly that since the pilgrims came to see Olimpia, there were naturally more women among them than men, as curiosity was a strictly female trait.

Some devout pilgrims were confused to see tarted-up prostitutes rolling through the streets of Rome with the pope's family coat of arms on the doors. True, the emblem lacked the triple tiara and crossed keys of Saint Peter, which Innocent had taken as his papal coat of arms. But it still had the Pamphili dove with the olive sprig in its mouth. What were prostitutes doing with that crest? When it was explained that the pope's sister-in-law was the official lobbyist of that particular profession, some visitors became angry. What kind of behavior was that? How could the pope allow such a thing? These opinions filtered up to the pope.

As Innocent became more and more uneasy with Olimpia's image in the Holy Year, he was struck by a bitter blow. On April 25 his sister Prudenzia died suddenly in her Convent of Saint Marta. According to Gigli, "The pope in the first years of his reign went sometimes to visit her and his sister Agatha in the Tor di' Specchi. But after these nuns favored and welcomed the princess of Rossano who married Don Camillo against the will of Donna Olimpia, the pope stopped going to see them, and the one parted and the other remained with rancor."[11] Because of Olimpia, Innocent had not spoken to his sister in three years, and now she was dead.

One morning, as the devout flocked to the Church of Saint John Lateran, they saw that the wall inscription INNOCENT X, PONTIFEX MAXIMUS had been partially covered with a banner that some enterprising soul had hung in the night. "Olimpia I, Pontifex Maximus," it said.[12] Others started sprouting overnight in various churches, including, "Olimpia, the first female pope."[13]

Innocent's small, suspicious eyes alighted on her, and he decided some changes were in order. Unbeknownst to Olimpia, on June 20, 1650, he made a new will, in which he revoked the total freedom to dispose of all her possessions that he had given her in his will of 1644. The new will specified that everything she had, and everything she would yet acquire, would be left to Camillo.

18

Crisis of Conscience

We shall find no fiend in hell can match the fury
of a disappointed woman,—scorned, slighted, dismissed
without a parting pang.

—Colley Cibber

I NNOCENT, WHO USUALLY AGONIZED over every little decision, had been putting off a big one. Ever since Francesco Maidalchini became cardinal nephew in the fall of 1647, the pope had known that he was completely unfit for the job. None of the burden of work had been removed from the pontiff's elderly shoulders. Cardinal Maidalchini's tasks were shifted upward to where they had been while Camillo played at the office—to Cardinal Panciroli and to the pope himself.

But now the stalwart workhorse Panciroli was sick, and *all* the work devolved upon the aged pontiff. Innocent could not keep up with it, especially in a jubilee year when daily public ceremonies crammed his schedule. With Panciroli in bed for days at a time, ambassadors, cardinals, and municipal officials sometimes waited fuming in an antechamber for hours until the pope could see them.

An efficient cardinal nephew would solve all the problems. "The responsibilities of a cardinal nephew," Leti explained, ". . . included being obliged, when the pope was indisposed or if he wanted some repose, to give audience to the ambassadors with whom he could negotiate. . . . One handles business with him as if he were the pope. Until then Innocent had not had this relief which was so necessary at his advanced age and which caused much anger to the ambassadors who had affairs to negotiate with him."[1]

Cardinal Maidalchini compounded the problem of his uselessness by diminishing the dignity of the Catholic Church. Though Innocent had politely ignored his ridiculous charade as cardinal nephew, he could not forgive his very public disgrace at the opening of the holy door when he had not been able to figure out what to do with the holy hammer and the angry crowd had mashed him against the wall. The heretics were laughing, and the Catholics were ashamed, and it was all Olimpia's fault for pushing her idiot nephew into the position and then insisting he open the door to grab the medals.

It was clear that Innocent must name a new cardinal nephew. But no matter whom he chose, Olimpia would be outraged. Though the crowds of favor seekers had stopped coming by her house to call on Cardinal Maidalchini, at least the cardinal nephew did not take power *away* from her. Olimpia would never stand for an ambitious young prelate helping the pope run the Vatican, leaving her twiddling her thumbs on the sidelines. Innocent had been studying the young clerics at the papal court for some time. The families that Olimpia's two haughty daughters had married into—the Ludovisi and Giustiniani clans—were aware of the need for a new nephew and were quietly pushing forward several grinning relatives. But the pope wasn't interested.

Cardinal Panciroli, with whom the pope often discussed his dilemma, pointed out to him a promising young man named Camillo Astalli. Cardinal Pallavicino described Astalli, a darkly handsome thirty-year-old, as "a prelate of noble Roman family, who seemed to him a youth of merit and expectations. . . . The pope brooded on this plan and was pulled by his liking for Astalli, so that when he saw him he had a violent commotion of the heart."[2]

The pope, readily attracted to good-looking people, imagined that Astalli would add luster to the papal throne by simply standing next to it. Leti wrote that Innocent began to "have great contentment in the good grace of this young man and discussed the means of relieving His Holiness in the administration of great affairs during which he found no one among his family who was capable of filling the post of nephew other than those he disliked."[3]

Olimpia did not have an inkling of what the pope was planning. But when she, as matchmaker for the rich and famous of the Papal States, was looking for a wife for Camillo Astalli's brother, the pope insisted loudly that she arrange a match with one of her own nieces, a daughter of Andrea Maidalchini. Olimpia must have been surprised. Innocent had never before evinced much interest in the marriages of the nobility, matches that so fascinated her. Mystified, Olimpia complied, and Tiberio Astalli duly married Caterina Maidalchini. It was a clever move. When the pope finally proclaimed Camillo Astalli the new nephew, no one could say he was not related to the pope.

The pope trod carefully in his preparations; he knew that as soon as Olimpia got wind of his plan, she would make a huge squawk about it and quite possibly derail the whole thing. She would find out only when it had already been done, and then she could squawk all she wanted and it would be too late to stop it. In mid-September 1650 the pope confided to the French ambassador that within the next few days he would do something to amaze everyone. The ambassador spread the word, and all of Rome watched with bated breath. It was not long in coming.

On Monday, September 19, 1650, without having said a word to anybody other than Cardinal Panciroli, who wholeheartedly approved of the choice, the pope announced the imminent creation of Camillo Astalli as cardinal. He would be the pope's nephew operating as cardinal *padrone,* a position of authority that neither Camillo Pamphili nor Francesco Maidalchini ever held. Furthermore, the pope bestowed upon Astalli the invaluable honor of using the Pamphili name and coat of arms. It was as if he had been adopted as the pope's son.

This, however, created confusion. Innocent was now on his third cardinal nephew and all three were living, an unprecedented situation in the history of the papacy. And two of them had exactly the same name. Camillo Pamphili, Olimpia's son and now no longer cardinal, was called Camillo Pamphili the real nephew. Camillo Pamphili, formerly Camillo Astalli and a new cardinal, was called Camillo Pamphili the fake nephew. And poor little Cardinal Maidalchini was dubbed the imbecile nephew. For the sake of clarity we will refer to the third nephew as Cardinal Astalli-Pamphili.

The new nephew was given the right to live in and control the Palazzo Pamphili in the Piazza Navona and the villa of Bel Respiro, and to have the use of all the furnishings, statues, silver, and tapestries in both residences. He was assigned the governance of the papal city of Fermo and the legation of Avignon. He received ten thousand scudi as a welcome gift, and an annual income of thirty thousand scudi. In a matter of days, Camillo Astalli-Pamphili had gone from an unimportant prelate to the second-highest-ranking position in the Papal States and Catholic Church.

We can imagine Olimpia's shock. No sooner had she heard the news than this stranger was moving his baggage into her house, taking over the best rooms facing the Piazza Navona. The worst part of it was that Innocent, the man who had always asked her opinion about everything, was suddenly doing things behind her back. She must have been seized with a deep sense of panic. Certainly she was angry.

There is no report of her reaction until Thursday, September 22, three days after the pope's announcement. On that morning Cardinal Astalli-Pamphili received his red hat from the hands of the pope at the Quirinal Palace and after the celebratory feast was planning to make his courtesy call on Olimpia. But according to Gigli, Olimpia knew "that she was losing her dominion and her control. She scorned him greatly, and entered into a great frenzy." Olimpia intercepted the cardinal, sending a message that "she did not want to receive him, saying she had no other nephew than Cardinal Maidalchini, and she did not recognize him as being of the house of Pamphili."[4] She added that she was sick, and her daughters were sick, and all of their servants were sick, and it was better not to visit any of them.

Hearing this strange message, the new cardinal smiled and instructed his entourage to follow him "to the sick people." Upon arriving at the Piazza Navona house, he found that Olimpia really was in bed ill. Her servants explained to him that she had just returned from visiting the pope, "lamenting and making the greatest noise" about Cardinal Astalli-Pamphili, but the pope brusquely told her not to interfere. And she "returned home full of this mania and displeasure" and took to her bed.[5]

Olimpia's confrontation with the pope had, indeed, been an angry one. It was reported that she stomped into the Quirinal in high dudgeon, accusing Innocent of trying to ruin her. She said that if he did not demote and exile Cardinal Astalli-Pamphili immediately, she would create a great scandal by leaving the Piazza Navona house to avoid running into the new nephew. She would live with her son in the Villa Aldobrandini in Frascati outside Rome, a threat that must have terrified both Camillo and the princess of Rossano. Though the pope had exiled Camillo at Olimpia's instigation three years earlier, this time he would not do her bidding and started yelling back at her. It was no wonder she took to her bed.

When Rome and the international community heard about the meteoric rise of Camillo Astalli-Pamphili, they immediately assumed the promotion had been done at Olimpia's instigation. After all, she had had a hand in everything the pope did, and the young man's brother had married her niece. The two of them must have made a pact to jointly share power. But word leaked out that Olimpia had had nothing to do with it and was, in fact, furious about it. She confirmed the rumors by galloping out of Rome to Camillo's villa in Frascati, where she stayed for several days.

Teodoro Amayden's *avvisi* of October 1 reported, "The invention of the new Cardinal Pamfilio is due only to Cardinal Panzirolo, and Signora Donna Olimpia had no part in it, a thing that is difficult to believe. Because she went to Frascati, and they say she will leave the Piazza Navona and live with her son, and they say publicly that Cardinal Panzirolo is the author of this resolution. . . . Speaking of this signora, Cardinal Panzirolo said, 'She is too ill-tempered and wants everything her own way.'"[6]

What had changed Innocent from the docile, obedient man she had always known? Olimpia imagined it had been Cardinal Panciroli, the only other person the pope had ever listened to or confided in. One day Olimpia stormed into the Quirinal Palace and called Panciroli into the audience hall. When he arrived, she vented her fury, accusing him of masterminding Astalli's promotion to ruin her and Cardinal Maidalchini. She threatened him. She cursed him. But Cardinal Panciroli, who must have been delighted that for the first time in the six-year pontificate he would no longer have to share his power with Olimpia, gravely replied that "things did not, as she might think, depend upon his councels, but upon the Popes inclinations, who lov'd to do what he pleased, and nothing else."[7]

Olimpia stirred up her daughters' families, both of whom had been hoping to have one of *their* relatives named the new nephew. Prince Ludovisi, who took all of his family disappointments out on his helpless wife, yelled at Costanza that the pope held the Maidalchini relatives in greater esteem than the Pamphilis. If he had married Olimpia's niece, instead of the pope's niece, his reward would have been far more honorable. Andrea Giustiniani believed the pope was going senile. How else could he choose as nephew his brother's wife's half-brother's daughter's husband's brother, which was a stretch even for Italian concepts of family? Princes Giustiniani and Ludovisi galloped out of Rome in a huff.

Olimpia and her in-laws were not the only ones shocked at the choice of nephew. Though handsome and charming, Cardinal Astalli-Pamphili had very little in the way of diplomatic experience and found himself suddenly standing in for the pope. Cardinal Pallavicino wrote, "This was done to the wonder of the court which saw in Astalli only mediocrity and nothing so distinguished or attractive as to warrant such advantages."[8]

On October 8, Teodoro Amayden wrote, "The court believes that the pope preferred a youth without experience to all of them, among whom are men of great merit."[9]

Leti stated, "This astonished the whole court, seeing a man elevated to such an important position to assist the pope in the most urgent matters of state and in all other political affairs while he was still so inexperienced, not having had the occasion to receive instruction in the management of such affairs."[10] Others found it odd that the new cardinal nephew, assigned the responsibility of conducting foreign affairs, had never been more than a few miles from Rome in his life.

The diplomatic community was confused as to the protocol of visiting the Piazza Navona palace. Having called on the new cardinal nephew, should they also pay a courtesy call on Olimpia, or would this offend the pope? But what if the pope fired this cardinal nephew as well, and put Olimpia back in power? Wouldn't she be keeping a list of all those diplomats who had snubbed her? Everyone in Rome knew that Olimpia's paybacks were hell.

But the new cardinal, feeling uneasy about living in Olimpia's domain, solved the problem by moving into the cardinal nephew's apartments in the Quirinal Palace. And Rome's elite followed him. Olimpia's antechambers became eerily empty, and the Piazza Navona was strangely devoid of luxurious carriages. Now it was Cardinal Astalli-Pamphili who was wined and dined, and loaded with valuable presents, and given the seat of honor at all the jubilee celebrations. Olimpia wasn't invited.

Seeing the futility of pretending that Cardinal Maidalchini had any power at all, Olimpia dropped him like a hot potato. And her nephew began to despise her. She was the one who had forced him to become a cardinal at the age of seventeen in the first place. She had used him as a pawn to make her own political moves. She had insisted he open the holy door, even though he had had no right to, without telling him how to hold the holy hammer. She had pushed him to steal the sacred jubilee medals and get into a fight with the church canons. And now that she had made him the laughingstock of Europe, she dropped him. She had, in fact, placed not a cardinal's cap on his head so much as a dunce cap.

Well, the pope was seventy-six and couldn't live much longer. One day soon there would be a conclave, and even if Francesco Maidalchini was the dumbest member of the Sacred College, his vote to elect a new pope was worth as much as any other cardinal's. He would do his utmost to elect a pope who despised Olimpia as much as he did.

Carried away by her feelings of betrayal, Olimpia made the tactical error of storming into the Quirinal and throwing temper tantrums before the pope and Cardinal Panciroli. Perhaps she felt she could bully

Innocent into bowing to her demands. It was a rare miscalculation for Olimpia, who had ruled the pope for decades with a calm and jovial manner. Not only did her rage irritate Innocent, but it obscured from her a more subtle and effective tactic. Had she pretended to welcome Cardinal Astalli-Pamphili's promotion, she could have stayed at the pope's side and, when the time was right, sabotaged the interloper.

As it was, Olimpia's horrific scenes only made the pope realize there was another issue to be addressed, an issue far more disturbing than the selection of a new cardinal nephew. And this issue had been weighing on him for nearly six years. But Innocent, the eternal procrastinator, had put it off.

The pope's dilemma was this: the woman who had placed him on the pinnacle of power, carrying him step by step on her strong shoulders, guiding him with her agile mind, was now pulling him down. Worse for Innocent, she was pulling the church down, the church he loved and honored. It was the joke of Europe that Olimpia had insisted on taking the prostitutes of Rome under her protection, allowing them to use the Pamphili coat of arms. Then she had exiled Camillo and the princess of Rossano, which caused people to murmur against the pope's unnatural severity toward his closest relatives. The pope had never even seen the little grandnephew named after him. She had polluted the Sacred College with the creation of two idiot cardinals—Francesco Maidalchini and Michel Mazarin, although the latter had considerately died within a year of taking office.

There was, of course, the public spectacle she had made of herself when she insulted Cardinal Pallotta in the street, prompting him to call her a whore. Her grain speculation during the Masaniello revolt had given rise to the rumor that Olimpia had caused the subsequent Roman famine. She had pilfered the sacred shoulder of Saint Francesca and put on licentious comedies poking fun at the pope, Camillo, and major public figures. She had stolen the pope's thunder during the Holy Year. Most painful, because of Olimpia's actions he had not spoken to his sister Prudenzia for three years before she died.

And that was just Rome. There was the additional matter of international humiliation. The duchy of Savoy had been irked by the nasty trick Olimpia had played on the deaf princess. The Portuguese were crying that they had bribed Olimpia with the jeweled portrait frame and not gotten anything in return.

Worse, the pope was still smarting from the Treaty of Westphalia. Despite the Catholics' efforts at reform, the heretics were looking for the least bit of gossip—a powerful cardinal eaten up with venereal disease, for instance, or a highly respected Vatican official caught stealing a sacrament cup—and *laughing*. It would have been less insulting if the heretics had taken up arms and marched south to attack the Papal States. In that case, at least, they would be taking the Mother Church seriously.

But ridicule has a profoundly withering effect. This cackling laughter, slicing through the Alps like bitter gusts of wind, whistled all the way down the Italian peninsula and whipped between the Seven Hills of Rome. And now the heretics were enjoying a gut-wrenching, belly-aching, falling-on-the-floor howl because the Vatican was being run by a woman who was the star of the Holy Year instead of the pope.

Of course, Innocent had known about the criticism for years. The Venetian ambassador Giovanni Giustiniani wrote that in the first years of his reign he had pretended not to know, as he was "not yet resolute enough in himself to find a solution to put a stop to the tongues, not only in Rome, but throughout all Christendom, and in particular in those northern parts where the Protestants, taking this female liberty as a great joke . . . mocked him licentiously."[11]

On August 16, 1647, Fabio Chigi, the pope's diplomat to the peace negotiations of the Thirty Years' War, had written him of the "liberties of the gazetteers of Rome who with bold-faced lies and calumnies injure the holy and innocent current pontificate in such a way that they are more dangerous to the holy Catholic religion than all the sermons of the Calvinists and Lutherans. . . . Is it possible that you cannot remedy this? While the world burns, and religion is in danger of being lost, they speak of nothing other than of . . . giving hats for a price, of female popes and of a thousand infamous sacrileges."[12] But in response to Chigi's plea, Innocent had done nothing.

In the months leading up to Cardinal Astalli-Pamphili's promotion, several events had occurred that greatly concerned the pope. A comedy was reportedly put on at the London court of the Lord Protector of England, the Puritan Oliver Cromwell. Called *The Marriage of the Pope,* it told the story of Innocent's attempts to get his sister-in-law to marry him. Olimpia refused, saying she would never marry such an ugly man, and the desperate pope offered to give her Saint Peter's key to heaven. Olimpia replied, "I want the other one, too, because otherwise, when you are tired of me, you will have the devils carry me away."[13] Having received both of Saint Peter's keys, Olimpia consented to marry him. The joyful announcement was followed by a ballet of friars and nuns, looking forward to their own marriages.

Word got back to the pope that a certain European king, upon sending an ambassador to Rome, bade him farewell with these instructions: "If you cannot make a breach in the mind of the pope through our authority, try to gain it through the authority of Donna Olimpia with our money."[14]

On one occasion a foreign ambassador, frustrated that Innocent had refused his request, said sarcastically, "Maybe what Your Holiness won't do for my king, Donna Olimpia will do, and I will now go to see her."[15]

The pope was infuriated. Having smartly dismissed the ambassador, he banged his hand on a table, crying, "Cursed be women and those who have brought them forward."[16] It is likely he was referring to himself.

On another occasion a papal secretary stationed in Paris traveled to Rome via Geneva. When Innocent heard he had traveled through that infamous bastion of heretics, he asked him what they were saying about the Catholic Church there. At first the secretary demurred, saying no one could expect Calvinists to say anything good about Catholics. When the pope pressed him for details, he finally admitted having attended a Calvinist church service out of curiosity. The minister had chosen as his sermon the letter of Saint Paul to Timothy: "I don't permit women to lead, neither to dominate men." The secretary said, "On the subject he exaggerated a great deal and with great contempt for the Church of Rome that allowed herself to be so scandalously governed by a woman."[17]

With the honest Cardinal Cecchini sidelined in the datary, Olimpia had reaped a fortune selling offices. Word had gotten out and winged its way upward to the pope. The cardinal nephew in skirts, as they called her, was reported to have sold the same office seven times, having poisoned the officeholders to sell it again. A story circulating in Paris confidently asserted that she had poisoned no fewer than 150 people to take their benefices and resell them.

The Venetian ambassador Nicolò Sagredo summed up the general feeling when he wrote his senate, "It is not edifying to Catholicism to see that all spiritual graces, concessions of the datary, and dignities depend on her consensus as if the fisherman's ring was on *her* finger."[18]

It is possible that Cardinal Astalli-Pamphili helped nudge the pope to break completely with Olimpia, who, he knew, hated him as a vile intruder and was plotting some revenge. One day he gave the pope a gold medal that had been mailed to him anonymously in a packet full of slander, he said. On one side was a portrait of Olimpia wearing the papal tiara, with the keys of Saint Peter in her hand. The other side showed the pope with long hair coifed like a woman, holding in one hand a spindle and in the other a distaff. The pope was horrified. He soon learned that numerous such medals had been struck in silver and gold and were collected throughout the courts of Europe, even in Rome.

The worst embarrassment was when Nuncio Melzi, the pope's representative in Vienna, handed the Holy Roman Emperor a letter from Innocent chastising him for making peace with the heretics to the shame of Christendom. The emperor replied bitterly that the real shame was a pope who "has placed his government in the hands of a woman about whom all the heretics are laughing."[19] The emperor then gave the nuncio a book of unflattering cartoons of Innocent and his sister-in-law, along with some medals, cast by heretics, showing Olimpia majestically enthroned and wearing the papal crown, with the pope sitting abjectly at her feet.

When the nuncio returned to Rome and had his private audience with Innocent, he gave him the book and the medals and told him of the emperor's reply. This "opened the eyes of the pope who, reflecting on himself, said, If the Catholic princes such as those of Austria and Germany make me such reproaches, what will those do who do not have the same veneration for the Holy See?" The pope was "noticeably touched by these discourses, to the depths of his soul."[20]

Gregorio Leti summed up the situation. "In fact, no pope had ever been so little esteemed as Innocent was. The Catholic princes could not help but laugh sometimes to see this form of female government because they saw the Protestant princes laughing about it agreeably. And, at the same time, they deplored the miserable condition of the Roman church because they saw it exposed to the jokes of the heretics. And who would not have shed tears to see that one didn't speak anymore of sending ambassadors to the pope but to Donna Olimpia, not to the court of the head of the church, but to the palace of a woman."[21]

But for all the scandal Olimpia brought to the church and to the pope personally, Innocent knew that he owed her everything. It was she who had jump-started his career back in 1612, helping him adjudicate his cases in the Rota. It was she who had thrown the right parties and given the right gifts to encourage Pope Gregory XV to make him papal nuncio to Naples. It was Olimpia who had arranged for him to become the number one Vatican ambassador, the nuncio to Madrid. And it was Olimpia who, in his absence, had connived at getting him made cardinal. And then, in the conclave of 1644, it was her smuggled letter that had convinced the Barberinis to swing their votes to his side and elect him pope.

For nearly forty years Olimpia had unflaggingly supported Gianbattista Pamphili, devoting her extensive fortune and her incisive intelligence to his worldly success. She had single-handedly raised the Pamphili family from living in a narrow tumbledown house to the pinnacle of power, wealth, and fame. True, Gianbattista had always been hardworking, intelligent, and fair-minded. But so were thousands of other Roman clerics who never became nuncio, let alone pope. With his strong sense of justice and gratitude, how could Innocent throw Olimpia to the dogs? How could he?

It was a crisis of conscience the likes of which he had never faced before. We can picture the blindfolded, Grecian-draped figure of Justice holding her scales. On the one side was the love and gratitude Innocent felt for Olimpia. On the other side was his duty as the Vicar of Christ to protect Jesus' church. For so long they had been balanced, one side or the other dipping a bit but bobbing back up. Now a final decision must be made by the most indecisive pope ever. He must have felt that he was torn in two; either way his decision went, it would be the most hurtful, wretched choice anybody ever had to make.

It was Olimpia who actually decided it for him, her angry voice bellowing from the sedan chair before the porters even set it down in the Quirinal audience chamber. Emerging, she threw another hysterical tirade against Cardinal Panciroli in the presence of the pope.

And suddenly Innocent found that thirty-two years of minor irritations, when he had wanted to disagree with her but had held his tongue, and six years of major irritations, when she ran the Vatican for him and he felt compelled to obey her, came rolling out in a torrent. He told her to shut up. Just shut up. If she did not, he would throw her into a convent and lock the doors behind her and she would never be seen again. Urban VIII had done just that with his bossy sister, Lavinia Barberini, who had gone around town slandering *his* cardinal nephew. And Innocent would do it to Olimpia if she didn't stop telling him what to do that very moment.

We can imagine Innocent with thunder on his brow, sitting grimly in his imposing high-backed papal chair, the father of all Christians, yelling at her that she is only a woman, that she has no right to say anything, no right to intervene in business affairs. That this is a man's world, where men rule, and she would obey, not instruct. *That the only place for a woman like her is in the convent.* He rises, towering over her, his angry words melting into a blur as the blood throbs in her ears.

She stands before him, short and plump and old now, and becomes smaller and smaller, shrinking beneath the verbal blows, the insults, the threats. And as she shrinks, something inside her hardens. The pope, the one man who was supposed to love and protect her, is betraying her in the worst way possible. She will never forgive him. She will never forget. And she will find a way to wreak her revenge.

It was a betrayal far worse than Sforza's had been all those years ago.

After all, she had never placed her father at the peak of greatness. But she had labored for decades for Gianbattista, the only man she thought she could trust. All of that work for what? To be cast off as a useless woman, unwanted in the world of men's affairs? To be locked up in the prison she had so deftly evaded for forty-four years? Was this what it had come to? The work of a lifetime had set her right back where she started, a defenseless fifteen-year-old whose father was going to put her away.

Sforza Maidalchini had not been able to force Olimpia into a convent, but her father had not been pope. If the Vicar of Christ and monarch of the Papal States decreed she had to go, then go she must. And here was the greatest irony: the pope that she had created was the only person in the world who was in a position to make her nightmare come true. The anger drained out of her and was replaced by icy fear.

She quietly turned on her heel and mechanically sat in her sedan chair, unnaturally calm. Silent, unmoving as a statue, she was carried down to her carriage and climbed in for the ride to the Piazza Navona. There would be no more temper tantrums. But Innocent, whose festering irritation was finally uncorked after forty years, was not through. He informed his staff that Olimpia was not to interfere any more in Vatican affairs, nor was she to ever visit him again, or even wait outside the door of his apartment.

Olimpia's power vanished instantly. The day after that last horrible altercation, Amayden reported, "The new Governor did not post the arms of the signora above the door of his house as his predecessors had; and all the prelates of the court have taken theirs down."[22] The *avvisi* of October 23, 1650, noted, "When she sent someone to call the subdatary of the Vatican, who had been totally subordinate to her, he did not come."[23] The subdatary was none other than her close friend Francesco Mascambruno, for whom she had obtained the position. Now, seeing her disgrace, he immediately washed his hands of her.

The butler of the Quirinal Palace asked Olimpia to remove one of her carriages from the stables there as Cardinal Astalli-Pamphili needed the space for his own carriage. In response, Olimpia cleared all her carriages out of the stables.

According to an *avvisi* of October 28, the pope sent a messenger to Olimpia asking her to return his undergarments, which she had been laundering. Appearing at the papal palace on her behalf clutching the pope's underwear, Olimpia's doctor, Fonseca, told the pope that she was unwell and that her indisposition was caused by her conflict with the pope. Innocent cut him off, saying, "Do not speak if not about your profession."[24]

Word on the street was that Olimpia would be immured in a convent outside Rome.

With Olimpia disgraced, even more stories filtered up to the pope about her corruption. Innocent asked for a list of Olimpia's servants and fired them. He had her accountant carted off to prison for questioning. He asked her butler for a list of visitors who called most frequently on her over the years to investigate their financial dealings. It was more than Olimpia could bear. On December 5 her carriage left Rome, headed for sanctuary in San Martino.

On the evening of December 24, the pope ceremonially laid the first bricks to wall up the holy door of Saint Peter's. At the three other jubilee churches, three other cardinals performed the same task, and not one of them was Cardinal Maidalchini. In each holy door was a cask of medals stamped with Innocent's likeness. These would be opened in 1675.

Later that night, Giacinto Gigli sat at his desk by the light of a candle and wrote, "So ends the Holy Year of 1650. . . . Many people died of suffering in the burning sun of the summer, and the unbelievable dust that was mostly on the streets leading to Saint Paul's and Saint John Lateran, and then by the rains, which were infrequent but violent, and the ice and wind that afflicted many people on the visits to the four churches. There were many who for the discomforts and difficulties could not go to the churches thirty times and therefore could not hope of having obtained the jubilee. But the pope, who was rigorous with others, did not go there more than fourteen or fifteen times."[25]

With Olimpia and the Holy Year out of the way, the pope was determined to embark on a new course. His first goal was to reconcile with his family. Though he had let himself be guided by his sister-in-law in alienating Camillo, the princess of Rossano, and Sister Agatha, Innocent was a tenderhearted man and had been deeply hurt by the estrangement. He first summoned Agatha from the convent, and she readily forgave him.

When the princess of Rossano received the long-awaited invitation to visit the pope, she was undeterred by the fact that she was nine months pregnant with Camillo's second child. She raced to the Quirinal and waddled into the audience chamber, where she stayed tête-à-tête with His Holiness for three hours. Then she went home laden with gorgeous gifts and gave birth to a healthy daughter. The pope stood as godfather in a Vatican baptism.

On January 8, 1651, Camillo accepted his uncle's invitation to call on him in the Quirinal with his two-year-old son. When Innocent saw little Gianbattista Pamphili for the first time, he burst into tears. Then he gave the child a silver statue of his patron saint, Saint John the Baptist.

Olimpia could not bear for her triumphant enemies to see her in such disgrace. Though the pope had only exiled her from the halls of power, it was Olimpia who, for the most part, had exiled herself from Rome. When she did come to Rome it was incognito, in an unmarked carriage. If she made too much noise, she feared Innocent might put her in a convent.

Olimpia stayed mostly in San Martino, the town she had created from scratch, and Viterbo, the town that still proudly pointed to her as the local girl made good. Here the intrigues of Rome were far away, and here Olimpia would always be queen, honored and fêted.

Ambassador Giustiniani of Venice praised Olimpia for confronting her disgrace "with matronly decorum, refusing to appear in public and showing not the least shadow of authority."[26] Another contemporary wrote, "After Donna Olimpia finally fell into the hole that she had been digging for herself for a long time, she learned, in her great need, to use prudence."[27]

The new queen of Rome was the princess of Rossano, who showed neither matronly decorum nor prudence but gloated openly about the change of fortunes. For the Carnival of 1651, the princess held a magnificent joust outside her palazzo on the Corso and built wooden stands enclosed with glass for her noble spectators. She invited Olimpia's enemies to lavish parties and made a point to insult and neglect those who had been close to her mother-in-law. Every week, the princess spent several hours alone with the pope, advising him on policy. This betrayal of Innocent's must have rankled the most deeply in Olimpia, but she would never have given her daughter-in-law the satisfaction of knowing it.

The most famous image of Olimpia, the bust by Alessandro Algardi, is said to have come from the first months after her downfall. The artist had known Olimpia personally for many years, and those who knew her said he captured her likeness and character exactly. The sculpture shows steely resolve, incomparable determination in the face of disaster, the widow's veil billowing behind her as if she remains erect in a hurricane wind through sheer strength of will. It reminds us of the captain of the *Titanic* grimly gripping his wheel as the ship starts to sink into the icy depths. Or Custer, tight-lipped and clench-jawed, looking his Last Stand in the eye. *Come and get me,* she seems to be saying. *Do your worst. I don't care.*

Sculpted subtly just below the strength are the bruises of the soul. Strength is, after all, only a defense against pain. We who boldly strike out to shape the world according to our tastes usually do so to prevent others from shaping it according to theirs and crushing us in the process.

I am alone, she says. *I have to face this alone.*

Part Three

UNFORGIVENESS

19

Honor and Dishonor

Mine honor is my life, both grow in one.
Take honor from me, and my life is done.

—William Shakespeare, *Richard II*

HERE WERE WORSE THINGS for a woman to do than retire to her palace in the countryside and queen it over her feudal territory. And while Olimpia must have spent many hours grieving privately and hating ardently, she was never one to sink into a paralyzing depression. Other than a few hours of emotional collapse after she realized she had lost her power, misfortune never seemed to have serious long-term effects on her health, as it did the pope's. She had always remained vulgarly robust in the face of pregnancy, childbirth, epidemics, widowhood, and now public disgrace.

Whenever Olimpia was upset, she rolled up her sleeves and got to work, and in San Martino there was still much to do that she had not been able to attend to while living in Rome. She hired architects to build more houses and bring new families to the town, and continued decorating her palazzo and the church.

Olimpia's native land was refreshing, relaxing, and it must have soothed her to be away from the turmoil of Rome. Yet she must have hoped that Innocent would find himself adrift without her, the clever captain who had guided his ship for nearly forty years. Plagued by indecision, mistrustful of the men who now advised him, surely the pope would eventually call for her.

It is almost certain that she had spies in Rome—and in the Vatican itself—sending her frequent reports. Her friends, and she still had many of them, would have kept in close contact. Cardinals and ambassadors would have informed her of the pope's doings, his moods, and any word he dropped about her. But the best spies were servants, those who could peer through keyholes, listen at doors, and fish letters out of the trash. Many servants earned several times their official salary for their spying activities.

Letters sent to her at San Martino would have been written partly in code, or with invisible lemon-juice ink, or in invisible ink *and* in code, and burned immediately after being read. Codes such as these were changed regularly to confuse the spies of enemies.

In a heap of miscellaneous family papers in the Doria Pamphilj Archives, there is a code cipher from Innocent's pontificate that, given the strong, clear handwriting, could have been written by Olimpia:

Pope	100
Panzirole	101
Cherubino	102 [Cardinal Francesco Cherubini]
Maidalchini	103 [Cardinal Francesco Maidalchini]
Brancaici	104 [Cardinal Francesco Maria Brancaccio]
Olimpia	105
Prince Camillo	106
Giustiniani	107
Ludovisio	108
Rome	109
Viterbo	110

a	b	c	d	e	f	g	h	i	l	m	n	o	p	q	r	s
6	7	8	9	10	11	12	13	14	15	16	17	18	19	20	21	22

t	u	y	z
23	24	25	26[1]

In early June 1651, Olimpia's correspondents would have told her that the Four Rivers Fountain in the Piazza Navona was finally completed after four years of design and construction. Spewing sour grapes, Francesco Borromini looked at his enemy's masterpiece and declared it would never shoot out water. Gian Lorenzo Bernini heard his rival's prediction and decided to play a little trick.

On June 8, when the pope visited the fountain in a great cavalcade, he walked around it for half an hour, admiring it from all angles. Innocent then asked Bernini where the water was, and the sculptor hung his head and shamefacedly admitted that it wasn't yet ready to flow. The pope was a bit disappointed and said that without water Bernini's masterpiece was not a fountain, it was a statue. As the pope was leaving the Piazza Navona, Bernini opened the faucets and the sound of rushing water filled the square. The pope raced back and marveled at the water dancing over the sculpted figures.

Proved wrong about the water, Borromini next spread word that the obelisk was in danger of toppling and crushing those beneath it. Bernini had done a terrible engineering job with Saint Peter's bell towers, he bellowed, and now he had done a terrible job with the Four Rivers obelisk. One day in a heavy wind, as passersby eyed the obelisk with concern, Bernini's carriage stopped. The sculptor got out and squinted at the obelisk, scratching his head. A crowd gathered around him, all nervously staring at the obelisk.

Then Bernini suddenly seemed to get an idea. He went into his carriage and pulled out some string. Then he climbed up onto the fountain and wrapped it around the obelisk, attaching the ends to iron torch hooks on the houses on either side of the piazza. With a satisfied nod, he got into his carriage and rode off, as all the spectators had a hearty laugh. It was a brilliant move; Borromini's nasty rumors had been laughed to death.

The new fountain was the talk of Europe. All the kings requested drawings of it, and the fountains of Versailles would be based on it. But Olimpia, whose idea it had been, had not been invited to its inauguration.

Though Olimpia was being pointedly ignored by many former

friends, the wily Jesuits understood that she could jump back into power at any time and corresponded cheerfully with her. In the summer of 1651, the Jesuit Father Albergati invited her to a magnificent celebration honoring Saint Ignatius of Loyola in the Roman College. Her reply was bitter; they should invite the queen—the princess of Rossano—and not the poor exile. The Jesuit replied cheerfully that the queen had also been invited, along with all the nephews and nieces of His Holiness.

Olimpia loved Jesuit services and very much wanted to go. Yet she couldn't imagine herself sitting in the same church with the princess of Rossano exulting in a more honorable chair. She decided to attend after the evening bell when most people hastened home. "And I will go, too," she wrote, "but privately and after the Ave Maria."[2] That way her enemies could not gloat over her defeat.

After Olimpia's fall, Cardinal Panciroli had hoped to be the sole advisor to the pope, with Cardinal Astalli-Pamphili working as his assistant. He envisioned that at a certain point years in the future when he died or retired, he would leave his position to the new cardinal nephew. But very soon after the young man's promotion, Astalli-Pamphili's manner went from ingratiating to haughty. Panciroli realized that his protégé was not a helpmeet but a rival. He had nourished a viper in the breast.

His sudden elevation had gone to Camillo Astalli-Pamphili's head. He was deified by courtiers and lauded by ambassadors; he received magnificent gifts from kings. Why should a prelate as great as he sit still and listen to the boring instructions of a sick old man? Cardinal Panciroli complained bitterly to the pope about the rash, ungrateful Cardinal Astalli-Pamphili, and Cardinal Astalli-Pamphili complained bitterly to the pope about the jealous old Cardinal Panciroli.

The pope, for his part, had grown tired of Cardinal Panciroli and preferred speaking to this young, charming man instead. Innocent began to distance himself from his old friend. But he soon realized that the third cardinal nephew was not all he thought he would be. "Cardinal [Astalli] Pamphili," wrote the French ambassador de Valençais, "was adopted into the pope's family, and it would have been good for him if together with his red hat they had been able to also give him a brain. . . . There were no stellar qualities in him, and certainly he had greater proclivities for pastimes than for work."[3]

The new cardinal nephew was not only inexperienced in international diplomacy, he was vain, shallow, and lazy. He loved the honor and wealth of the job, the sumptuous palaces and gardens, and the gorgeous carriages pulled by splendid horses wearing ostrich-feather hats. He loved having the seat of honor at all the best parties. But he wasn't up to the work. Oddly, the first Cardinal Nephew, Camillo Pamphili and the second Cardinal Nephew, Camillo Pamphili were quite similar— all swashbuckling swagger, swirls of red robes, and little else.

In addition to Cardinal Astalli-Pamphili's increasingly apparent uselessness, Innocent was experiencing family problems. As long as Olimpia had ruled in Rome, she had reined in her children and their families to prevent them from badgering the pope. Now the Giustinianis, Ludovisis, and Pamphilis hammered him incessantly with requests for honors, titles, and incomes, sometimes pointing fingers at one another as being unworthy of the same. Nor did he have the strength to ban them from the papal palace. According to the Venetian ambassador, Innocent "will never know how to free himself of this, by refusing to admit his relatives who visit him so frequently."[4] As always when under stress, Innocent became ill. On July 20, he grew extremely feverish from a bladder infection.

At least Olimpia's family members could agree on one thing: they hated Cardinal Astalli-Pamphili. Camillo in particular loathed him for taking over his pleasure villa, Bel Respiro. Like Olimpia, her son saw Cardinal Panciroli as the architect of Cardinal Astalli-Pamphili's meteoric rise and passionately despised him. Camillo soon wreaked his revenge. When Cardinal Panciroli went to visit the recovering pope on August 4, Camillo barred his path. It would only disturb Innocent to see him, he said. It would not be good to stress His Holiness.

It was a deadly insult to the old cardinal, who had been instrumental in Innocent's election, had harmed his health shouldering the pope's workload, and had lost papal favor to the inept Cardinal Astalli-Pamphili. Gigli reported that Panciroli "returned to his apartments with a bitterness and a pain in his heart so great that reaching the door he could go no further but entered into the room of his servant and threw himself facedown on the bed where he stayed a long while and then he was carried into his room and put in his own bed."[5] He would not rise from it.

At 7 P.M. on September 3, Cardinal Giangiacomo Panciroli died at the age of sixty-four, disillusioned by his change of fortune. In his last days he had repeatedly called for the pope, but Innocent did not come. Cardinal Astalli-Pamphili, perhaps afraid of what Panciroli would say about him, told the pope that the disease was contagious. Innocent was, however, greatly saddened by his death, and "went into deep mourning for several days without being able to console himself."[6]

Olimpia did not mourn. She viewed Cardinal Panciroli as the author of her downfall. It was he who had convinced Innocent to create a new cardinal nephew and cut his ties with her. It was he who was responsible for the ruinous collapse of everything she had built. And it was he, four years earlier, who had engineered Camillo's marriage to the despicable princess of Rossano. Hearing the news that Cardinal Panciroli was no more, she replied with bitter satisfaction, "He is dead, but I am alive."[7]

The timing of Cardinal Panciroli's death was unfortunate. For months the French ambassador had been planning a grand celebration to mark the thirteenth birthday and official coming of age of King Louis XIV on September 5. When the fireworks blasted off, lighting up the night sky in jubilation, many Romans thought the French were celebrating Cardinal Panciroli's demise two days earlier, as he had always been partial to Spain.

Now that Panciroli was dead, there was only Cardinal Astalli-Pamphili to help Innocent with the workload. Those who liked the fake nephew politely remarked that he was still young and inexperienced in the ways of diplomacy. Those who disliked him called him a blithering dunderhead. Cardinal Pallavicino wrote that "the pope, full of years, was leaning on an inexperienced and unknown crutch."[8] Though Cardinal Astalli-Pamphili wanted to have all the powers of a secretary of state, Innocent knew that would be disastrous. He must replace Cardinal Panciroli.

The pope had, by this point, given up on the idea of bringing in a family member to assist him. The only man who had ever helped him run the Vatican had been Cardinal Panciroli, who had not been related in any way, shape, or form. The successful candidate for secretary of state should be an older man with extensive international diplomatic and legal experience.

Cardinal Astalli-Pamphili was frightened as to who might be chosen as his new boss. A truly brilliant man would recognize his defects and point them out to the pope. A mediocre man would be better for him, or at least someone he could call a friend and who would cover for him. He proposed his cousin, Francesco Gaetani, and received a crisp papal refusal. He next suggested the clever young cleric Decio Azzolini, his friend, but he was equally inexperienced.

The subdatary, Francesco Mascambruno, who continued to be in the pope's favor, pushed himself forward for the job. But Innocent knew that despite his legal knowledge Mascambruno had no diplomatic experience. Besides, the pope had a surprise in store for Mascambruno. He would make him a cardinal in the next creation. Unaware of the forthcoming honor, Mascambruno was deeply stung by Innocent's refusal to make him secretary of state. After everything he had done for Innocent and his family, the subdatary felt cheated.

Cardinal Bernardino Spada suggested that Innocent consider Monsignor Fabio Chigi, apostolic nuncio to Münster, Germany. This suggestion received the pope's immediate consent. Though Innocent had never met Chigi, he had received his weekly dispatches since 1644 and had them copied in larger handwriting so that he could read them personally. "This is a man of purpose!" the pope said to Cardinal Panciroli after reading his correspondence, and told everyone that there had never been a better nuncio than Fabio Chigi.[9] Though the Thirty Year's War had ended in 1648, Chigi remained in Germany to hammer out secondary treaties with the still-squabbling parties.

Fabio Chigi was, indeed, the perfect man for the job. He had spent twelve years in the highly charged, vitriolic German peace negotiations putting up with all kinds of egotistical foolishness. The Swedish envoy rose, went to bed, and ate to the sounds of blaring trumpets, disturbing all the other diplomats. The French envoy refused to speak Latin and insisted everyone speak French. The Austrian envoy was ready to give away the entire Catholic Church if only he could go home. The diplomats outdid one another in throwing lavish drunken banquets and racing their horses instead of focusing on the peace treaty. And through it all, Fabio Chigi's wisdom, calmness, and integrity had won the respect of his sniping, petty counterparts.

In addition to his extensive diplomatic and legal experience, Fabio Chigi had the rare reputation for strict Catholic virtues. He lived a chaste life, keeping far from women. He slept on a board instead of in a feather bed, drank from a cup with a skull on it, and kept no fire in his cold damp German rooms, which resulted in the saintly suffering of bad health.

Chigi was an anomaly in the church hierarchy—he had no ambition other than to serve God. He lived simply, gave most of his money to the poor, and as bad as the intrigues of Germany were, he was thrilled to be far removed from that snake pit of intrigue, Rome.

Within days of Panciroli's death, Innocent sent a swift messenger to Germany with instructions for Monsignor Chigi to leave for Rome immediately as Cardinal Astalli-Pamphili wanted to bestow an honor upon him. The pope did not tell him that he would be appointed secretary of state; if Chigi knew in advance, he might very well politely decline and stay in Germany. As it was, even the mysterious message was disturbing. Cardinal Pallavicino stated, "Chigi received this news with a doubtful heart. As much as he wanted to return to the Italian sky, he was terrified to enter the troubles of the court."[10]

Chigi left Germany on October 1, 1651, and arrived on November 30 in Rome, where he was told to call on the pope immediately. The moment Innocent saw Chigi he was smitten with his serious demeanor. He had a long, narrow face, a long, bony nose, and a dark mustache and goatee. His heavily hooded dark eyes were large and expressive. After a bit of conversation, the pope dropped the bomb: Chigi would be his new secretary of state, working with Cardinal Astalli-Pamphili. Chigi reluctantly accepted the position.

Noticing Chigi's frugality, Innocent told Cardinal Astalli-Pamphili,

"We must think about this man because he does not think about him-self."[11] The pope presented Chigi with several bags of gold—the enormous sum of three thousand scudi—for his expenses in establishing an honorable household in Rome. Chigi was shocked to receive such a gift but accepted it to please the pope.

Imitating the pope, when Cardinal Astalli-Pamphili discovered that Chigi's Roman palace was mostly bereft of furniture, he declared that he would give him one thousand gold pieces to furnish it. Chigi was horrified at the announcement but finally had to accept the gift to avoid offending the cardinal nephew.

The rigorous Fabio Chigi squirmed in discomfort at the gift-giving culture of Rome, which often blurred into bribery and influence buying. "He disliked giving and receiving," wrote Cardinal Pallavicino, "this trafficking in gifts of the ambitious and the self-interested, and the ostentation of the wasteful. He preferred to give alms to the poor rather than fatten the powerful with gifts."[12]

Within days of his arrival in Rome, Chigi learned that etiquette demanded he give presents to Cardinal Astalli-Pamphili and Camillo as an expression of gratitude for his good fortune. Not to do so would be the cause of great offense, and he would acquire the reputation of being either ignorant or cheap. Chigi bowed to the reigning custom, but his gifts were thoughtful rather than sumptuous—hard-to-find spices from the Orient, rare books, exquisite perfumes, and delicious pastries. "But having allowed himself to overcome his repugnance to giving, he remained inflexibly opposed to receiving."[13]

Chigi's incorruptibility was the talk of Rome. He refused bribes and gifts from the French and Spaniards alike, and from family factions in Rome; stranger yet, the pope had to force him to accept incomes and benefices becoming his office. Unlike other courtiers, Chigi was as friendly to those known to be in disgrace at court as he was to the favorites, treating all with equal kindness and respect. No one in the Vatican had ever seen anything like it.

Before Chigi had been called to Rome, Innocent had given in to Cardinal Astalli-Pamphili's pleas to keep him a monsignor. Making the older, wiser man a cardinal would give him more power than that of the young and foolish cardinal nephew. But even so, the insightful, efficient Chigi soon took over the office, becoming the cardinal nephew's boss in fact, if not in title. Suddenly the honorable Fabio Chigi was the pope's favorite, and the charming Cardinal Astalli-Pamphili was on the outs.

Well informed in her exile, Olimpia knew who held the reins of power that had been so violently wrenched from her hands. She traded courteous letters with Monsignor Chigi, who replied with equal courtesy. Though they had never met, they sent each other gifts of wine, cheese, and game. She had nothing against Chigi, who had never done her any harm and could, perhaps, be won over as an ally to help her return.

But the princess of Rossano was not about to let the powerful secretary of state become an ally of her despised mother-in-law. She set about winning his allegiance and had a great advantage over Olimpia by being in Rome. She could wine him, dine him, and meet with him, which Olimpia could not. But if the princess thought that batting her long black lashes or appearing in a particularly low-cut gown could dazzle the somber Chigi as it had Innocent, she was dead wrong.

Cardinal Pallavicino explained, "Now, with every studied industry, showing herself eager for his success, she tried to win Chigi as an ally for the house of Pamphili. But this effort, which would have vanquished the sternest puritan at court, didn't work with this man, and he replied that he wanted to be of service to all, but against no one, and that being secretary of state it was his office to negotiate the politics of the nation and not the economics of one particular family."[14] And here she was stuck.

There was no love lost between Cardinal Astalli-Pamphili and the subdatary, Francesco Mascambruno, who both competed for power and the pope's affection. The datary, Cardinal Cecchini, had been in disgrace for two years now and still waited pathetically day after day in his office for the pope to call him. Mascambruno ran the lucrative department, and when the marquess Tiberio Astalli asked him for pensions and incomes, as was his due as the cardinal nephew's brother, Mascambruno angrily rebuffed him. The subdatary sold these positions and was certainly not about to give them away.

To get Tiberio Astalli off his back, Mascambruno complained to the pope that the marquess was importuning him almost daily and should perhaps be banished to his estates in the country. Innocent angrily called in Cardinal Astalli-Pamphili and told him to make sure his brother did not bother Mascambruno anymore, or the whole family would be exiled. The cardinal nephew, knowing Mascambruno's hands were very unclean, conducted a little investigation of his own, found something heinous, and spread the word.

Monsignor Chigi had been in his position as secretary of state for less than three weeks when an angry Jesuit stormed into his office. Father Luigi Brandano, the assistant to the Holy See from Portugal, had heard that the pope had signed a scandalous indulgence for the Portuguese count of Villafranca. The count had been married in a church ceremony by a village priest, which would have been no sin in itself except that the count was already married to a richly dowered lady, and his second bride was a teenaged boy, dressed up like a woman, with whom he fully consummated the marriage that night. When word got out, the Spanish Inquisition threw the groom, the "bride," and the priest into a dungeon.

The penalty for sodomy was usually burning at the stake. But the desperate count had paid forty thousand gold pieces for a papal order to get him out of this hot water. Even now, Father Brandano insisted, a bull signed by the pope was winging its way to Portugal ordering the transfer of the trial from the jurisdiction of the unforgiving Inquisition to that of the local bishop, a friend and relative of the sodomite count who would, no doubt, immediately release the guilty trio and impose a small fine as penance.

The virtuous Monsignor Chigi was so appalled at the Jesuit's story that he immediately arranged a papal audience for Father Brandano. As the Jesuit was retelling the tale, the Portuguese monsignor Mendoza came flapping into the audience chamber and angrily spewed out the same story. The furious pope denied ever having signed a bull that, in effect, permitted two homosexuals to marry and commit sodomy with only a slap on the wrist as penalty.

Innocent refused to believe the story and vehemently defended his employees in the datary. However, given the fact that his reputation and the reputation of the entire church were at stake, the pope agreed to launch an investigation. He sent word for Cardinal Cecchini to come immediately to the papal audience chamber. Eaten up by gout, Cecchini hobbled breathlessly to the pope, hoping that he had been restored to favor. Instead, he heard devastating rumors of forgery in the datary.

The datary offices were searched for the Portuguese bull, but it was not found. A copy was found in the chancery, the department responsible for establishing new dioceses and benefices. The copy of the forged bull had been made by a certain Giuseppe Brignardelli, who had already sent off the original to Portugal. Brignardelli, it was discovered, had fled. But when Cardinal Cecchini's investigators questioned his wife, she said that three days before her husband's disappearance her nephew had shown up with thirteen thousand scudi from Francesco Mascambruno to help him escape. When Mascambruno's lodgings were searched, the investigators found fourteen thousand gold pieces, countless vases and plates of pure gold and silver, and bank records showing enormous deposits. They also found seventy forged papal bulls, which Mascambruno was evidently holding until payment arrived.

Several of the bulls were in the process of being forged, which revealed how he had done it. Official letters of the seventeenth century were works of art, with magnificent calligraphy and pleasing spaces between the paragraphs. Mascambruno had written a summary of the bull at the top of a long sheet of parchment, an innocuous dispensation for third cousins to marry, for instance. The pope, casting barely a glance at the summary, signed at the bottom of a large white space.

Back in his office, Mascambruno cut off the top of the document and wrote a new text, permitting homosexual acts, for example. Then he attached the lead bulla dangling from red ribbons at the bottom and sent it off, not through the datary but through the chancery, where his accomplices worked. Investigators discovered a network of coconspirators across Europe, corrupt officials in different nunciatures forwarding the forged bulls to those who had paid for them. It was a brilliant scheme because the only part of a papal bull that was closely examined for forgery was the signature, and that was always genuine.

On January 22, 1652, Francesco Mascambruno was taken to the infamous Tor di Nona prison. During long interrogations he gave up no information, saying only, "Ask Donna Olimpia," or "The Ludovisis and Giustinianis know all about that."[15] He wanted his captors to know that if he was going down, he would implicate the entire Pamphili family and drag them down with him.

Despite Mascambruno's dark insinuations, the scandal vindicated Olimpia. While she had queened it over Rome, she had been the scapegoat for all famine, flood, war, and vice. But not even her worst enemies could blame Mascambruno's conduct on her. The investigation proved that hundreds of Mascambruno's forged bulls had been written during Olimpia's disgrace and exile, when the subdatary had publicly dumped her and become the ally of her enemy, the princess of Rossano. The princess had become so close to the subdatary that she even permitted his low-born female relatives the signal honor of riding in her carriage.

It also appeared likely that Olimpia's earlier supervision of the datary had kept Mascambruno's corruption within the bounds of polite acceptability. It was only since her exile that Mascambruno had gotten truly out of line, particularly after Innocent's refusal to name him secretary of state. Mascambruno's sullying of the pope's name was a strong brew of greed and revenge.

Reeling from Mascambruno's betrayal, the pope felt increasingly grateful to Monsignor Chigi for his sober efficiency. Though Innocent had promised Cardinal Astalli-Pamphili that the new secretary of state would not be made a cardinal, he soon changed his mind. In Fabio Chigi, Innocent had finally found a man in some ways similar to himself—hardworking, abstemious, and just. Such a man should be rewarded. The pope instructed Cardinal Astalli-Pamphili to give Monsignor Chigi the wonderful news, which he must have done reluctantly.

But when Chigi was told of his imminent assumption into the Sacred College, he "showed no happiness, or change of expression but, as if he were discussing foreign affairs, replied that great thought should be given to that, and that he would perhaps better be able to serve His Holiness in his present position. Then he continued discussing other affairs with the same tranquility as before."[16] It was an unheard-of reply, rather like a lottery player, hearing that he held the winning $100 million ticket, suddenly turning to discuss the weather.

When Chigi held his regular audience with the pope that evening, he didn't fling himself on his knees expressing heartfelt gratitude for the immense honor in store for him. In fact, he didn't even mention the cardinal's cap. After he departed, Innocent called for Cardinal Astalli-Pamphili and angrily accused him of not imparting the news. The young cardinal protested that he had indeed told him. Dumbfounded, the pope exclaimed, "We have not ever seen such a man; nothing moves him."[17]

On February 18, the night before the announcement of his elevation, Chigi told a friend that he accepted the dignity reluctantly because with increased honors came increased responsibilities. "I assure you that if the list were in my possession, I would cross out my name," he said with a sigh.[18]

Innocent assigned Cardinal Chigi three important congregations in addition to his time-consuming duties as secretary of state. He joined the Holy Office of the Inquisition, the Congregation of the Propagation of the Faith, and the congregation that examined potential bishops. Working day and night, Chigi proved himself the most efficient member of the Sacred College.

One evening the pope gave the order that Cardinal Chigi, not Cardinal Astalli-Pamphili, should have the honor of carrying the candles into his office at sunset and staying for a consultation. The two had a long chat behind closed doors while the younger cardinal cooled his heels in the antechamber, fuming that he, as nephew, should have had precedence over the secretary of state and access to the pontiff at all times. And from then on it was Chigi, not the nephew, who carried in the candles.

In the same consistory that saw the creation of Cardinal Chigi, the princess of Rossano saw the elevation of two of her candidates—her cousin Baccio Aldobrandini and the French cleric Jean-François Gondi, who became known as Cardinal de Retz. Until then Olimpia had helped Innocent choose the new cardinals, and now she had clearly been replaced by her daughter-in-law. The *avvisi* commented, "The Rossano is becoming the open competitor of her mother-in-law."[19]

Though Innocent was wracked with grief over the betrayal of Francesco Mascambruno, a man he had implicitly trusted, he hired two of Rome's best lawyers to defend him. After a trial lasting two months, with some eleven thousand pages of witness testimony, Francesco Mascambruno was sentenced to be hanged. Then his head would be cut off and stuck on a skewer, which would be placed on the Castel Sant'Angelo Bridge, along with his body, hanging by his left foot. After being exposed in such a disgraceful manner for several hours, both head and body would be burned, and the ashes tossed into the Tiber.

Accompanied by Mascambruno's lawyers, the princess of Rossano swished into the Quirinal arrayed in her most fetching attire, imploring the pope to pardon the forger, who had promised to devote the remainder of his life to prayer and penance in a distant monastery if spared. Sighing, Innocent said, "Pray God to grant the pardon that we cannot concede for justice sake."[20]

Ironically, it was the usually ineffectual Camillo who obtained the pope's mitigation of the sentence. Mascambruno would be beheaded, his body exposed and then buried decently in a church. But when the forger was informed that the sentence had been mitigated, Mascambruno was not at all grateful. In fact, he did not believe the execution would be carried out. He spoke of other cases where the condemned was brought to the place of execution, forced to lay his neck on the block, and at the last minute pardoned. Surely the pope would not execute him and was plotting an elaborate drama to scare him for his misdeeds.

As an ordained servant of the Holy Mother Church, a priest could not be executed. He must first be defrocked. On April 14, Mascambruno was taken in a heavily guarded carriage from his prison to the

Church of Saint Salvatore in Lauro, where before a crowd of cardinals, nobles, and ambassadors, his priestly vestments were wrested from him. Finally, his fate began to sink in. "Pray Lord God and the Holy Virgin that they forgive every one of them for this great persecution!" he shrieked. "God pardon them, pardon them. Great persecution! Great persecution! Pardon to all, pardon from the heart. Be my witnesses that I pardon them all!"[21] His howling was so unseemly in a church that his guards shoved a gag into his mouth.

When he returned to his cell, Mascambruno found the Brothers of Compassion there, members of the confraternity that comforted those awaiting execution. When he bewailed his unjust fate, they consoled him with the fact that he would not die unconfessed and unrepentant. If death had struck him down still stained with his foul sins, he would have gone to hell. Now, given holy absolution after confession, he would spend only a little time in purgatory and still might make it into heaven. Mascambruno took them at their word. His final confession lasted seven hours, during which time he admitted countless acts of theft and forgery that he had not even been charged with, including pilfering 35,000 scudi that had been set aside for Olimpia's granddaughter, Olimpiuccia Giustiniani, in 1650. Stealing from an innocent child of nine was considered as low as a person could possibly sink.

The following day at dawn, the brothers conducted him to the prison courtyard. Given Mascambruno's frightful theatrics the day before, it was decided to do the job with merciful speed. After the forger said only one short prayer, the executioner pushed him down and struck off his head. For its journey to the Castel Sant'Angelo Bridge, the head was, oddly enough, "sewn onto the body from which blood trickled and the dogs licked it," a spectator observed.[22] The body remained there from eleven in the morning until four in the afternoon, thronged by the curious, the jeering, and the compassionate. Finally it was interred in a nearby church.

The day of Mascambruno's execution, the pope was seen sitting in his Quirinal apartments, crying. The scandal was far-ranging. Dozens of other offenders were in prison and would be tortured, executed, exiled, fined, imprisoned, or sentenced to the galleys. By exiling Olimpia,

Innocent had hoped to clean up the reputation of the Holy See. But now it was much worse than when she had been at the helm, and no one could blame *her* for this. The Catholics hung their heads in shame, and the heretics laughed at him.

Over time, the princess of Rossano's star dimmed a bit, and she found it increasingly difficult to compete with Olimpia's forty years of interaction with the pope. For if Olimpia had been like an old comfortable pair of loafers, the princess was a new pair of stylish high-heeled shoes that pinched. Innocent had always been able to relax with the older Olimpia. This young Olimpia, though easier to look at, was always prickling him with requests for favors, honors, and money for herself, her family, and her friends. Her shrill, incessant demands were more irritating than his sister-in-law's measured advice and behind-the-scenes maneuvering.

The princess's Vatican politicking took the place of a happy marriage. Studying her foolish husband through narrowed eyes, she found much to criticize and often ripped into him for the many things he was always doing wrong. She particularly hated it when Camillo still trembled upon hearing his mother's name, even though Olimpia was clearly powerless.

It was a cruel irony that Camillo, who had married the princess to get away from the domination of his bossy mother, now found himself dominated by a bossy wife. In fact, appearances aside, the two Olimpias were remarkably similar; both were ambitious, strong, and far smarter than he, and neither would ever let him forget it.

Scorned by his wife, poor Camillo found solace in the arms of pretty singers and dancers, women who looked up to him and told him what a great and clever man he was. He further punished the princess by carefully controlling her purse strings, which he, as her husband, was legally permitted to do. Whenever the princess wanted to go shopping or throw a party, he cracked open his change purse and reluctantly doled out a few coins from her immense dowry, which infuriated her. He called her a reckless spendthrift, and she called him a womanizing idiot.

Camillo was stung daily by the fact that no one called his wife by the title he had bestowed on her by marriage—the princess Pamphili. Everyone in Rome knew Olimpia Maidalchini as the princess Pamphili, and the matter was further confused because both women had the same first name. And so the princess of Rossano stayed the princess of Rossano, and poor Camillo became the prince of Rossano. The humiliation became too much for him, and he asked the pope to send him to Avignon as legate just to get away.

But Innocent did not send him away. Though he knew his nephew was stupid and useless, the pope was a sentimental fellow who loved his own blood dearly. One day a cardinal asked him about assigning an income to either Camillo or Prince Ludovisi. The pope replied that the shirt was closer to the heart than the coat, and Camillo, who was evidently the shirt, was given the income. Another day the same cardinal asked him which of his three nephews he loved best. Innocent said, "I love Prince Giustiniani out of respect for his wife. I love Prince Ludovisio because he is a good prince. But I love Prince Pamfili because he is my blood."[23]

Sitting motionless in San Martino like a black widow spider eyeing her prey, Olimpia was wreaking her revenge without lifting a finger. Her enemy Cardinal Panciroli was dead. Her enemy Cardinal Astalli-Pamphili had proved ineffectual and had lost his power to Cardinal Chigi. Her enemy the princess of Rossano was losing her initial influence over Innocent with her constant demands, and her fairy-tale-romance marriage was falling apart. Her enemy Pope Innocent X was plagued by constant family squabbles because Olimpia was not there to control her fractious brood.

To top it all off, the pope was embroiled in the most shocking Vatican scandal in nearly a century, a scandal that would never have occurred had Olimpia still been running the show. She knew that, and fretting on his papal throne, so did he.

20

Olimpia's Triumphant
Return

*Where there is hatred, let me sow love. Where
there is injury, pardon.*

—Saint Francis of Assisi

THE POPE WAS SEVERELY DEPRESSED by the Mascambruno
scandal and its withering effect on the international reputation
of the Catholic Church. For the first time since he was elected,
the seventy-eight-year-old pontiff seemed old, fragile. He suffered
from insomnia and an odd trembling in his right hand that made it
difficult for him to celebrate Mass.

Within days of Mascambruno's execution, the pope razed the Tor di
Nona prison, where his subdatary had been held and executed. Innocent had been thinking about building a modern prison for years, but
now he felt compelled to begin the project to erase the revolting memo-
ries of the papal forger.

Many prisoners incarcerated temporarily for lesser offenses—debts
or drunken brawling, for instance—found that instead of a few months
in jail, they had, in effect, received a death sentence due to unhealthy
prison conditions. After heavy rains, the Tiber could rise at a moment's

notice and drown the first-floor prisoners. Mice, lice, fleas, and human waste turned the cells into sewers raging with infection. One Roman confraternity had the sole purpose of visiting nonviolent prisoners weekly to determine which ones were becoming ill. The confraternity members would then petition the courts for early release, reminding the judges that the penalty imposed had been a few months' incarceration, and not death. Most of these requests were granted.

As a just monarch, Innocent saw great injustice in the prison system. It was not fair for someone convicted of a misdemeanor to die for the crime. Neither was it fair for a criminal to be let off the hook early without paying fully for his misdeeds. It was clear to Innocent that a new prison must be built that was more conducive to inmate health.

Innocent commissioned his friend Monsignor Virgilio Spada to design the Carceri Nuovi, the New Prison. Spada held the vaunted position of papal almoner, distributing Innocent's alms to worthy recipients. In addition, he was a trained architect who advised Innocent on all architectural matters. Prison design had not changed since the Middle Ages, and Spada's plans were trailblazing. Cells had balconies where prisoners, though behind bars, could enjoy fresh air and sunshine. Large courtyards permitted the inmates—who previously had not seen much daylight for the length of their sentences—to exercise regularly. The spacious cells were all well above ground—no more drownings—and would be cleaned regularly to avoid contagion. Convicts could complete their sentences in health, and justice would be served.

Though Mascambruno's prison had swiftly disappeared, his legacy of crime and punishment continued. On July 27, 1652, two associates of Mascambruno's were hanged, their bodies burned and the ashes thrown in the Tiber. Two others fled to Geneva, where they were heartily welcomed by the heretics. Another one, hearing the tromping of the guards on his stairs coming to get him, flung himself out of an upper window, committing suicide.

The depressed pope began to think about building his tomb. When he first became pope, he and Olimpia had discussed plans to turn the tiny Chapel of Saint Agnes into a grand church facing the Piazza Navona, a baroque confection worthy of the bones of the Pamphili family and the pope himself. The chapel had originally been built in one of the arches of the Domitian stadium, the site of the supposed saint's supposed martyrdom.

By the time houses were built in the piazza in the fourteenth century, the Chapel of Saint Agnes was submerged some fifteen feet below ground. A large town house was constructed on top of it, facing the piazza, while a little church and entry to the chapel were built on the Via dell'Anima, behind the piazza. Innocent planned to buy the house, now owned by the Mellini family, tear it down along with the old church behind it, and create his grand new church. Connected to the enlarged Palazzo Pamphili, the church would be an extension of the palace complex and a political statement of the power and grandeur of the Pamphili family. In the belfry he would place the church bells taken from his victory over Castro.

Innocent commissioned the father-and-son architects Girolamo and Carlo Rainaldi to design the edifice. Camillo, who preened himself over his vast architectural expertise, was given the honor of overseeing the project. In a grand ceremony, attended by numerous cardinals, the pope laid the foundation stone on August 15.

Despite his excitement over the new building projects, the pope's temper became unusually short. In September he finally fired his old friend Cardinal Cecchini from the post of datary, the exact reason for which has never clearly been determined. Giacinto Gigli wrote, "No one knew if it was because he had been complicit in the errors of Mascambruno or for some other reason. . . . Those waiting in the antechamber for an audience with the pope heard a big argument in which the pope was very angry and the cardinal said that he had always been an honest gentleman and the pope said, If that is so we will see soon. And he told him not to appear in consistory or in church or anywhere else."[1]

Querulous and suspicious, on October 2 the pope fired both the majordomo and the head butler of Cardinal Astalli-Pamphili. In November the grouchy pontiff fired his own majordomo and his wardrobe master. He took an inveterate dislike to his friend and architectural advisor Virgilio Spada and to Monsignor Farnese, the governor of Rome.

The Holy Father was becoming a holy terror, lashing out in uncontrollable anger at his family members, his staff, his old friends, and even the cardinals. He granted very few favors. Those who sought favors knew the only person the pope listened to was Cardinal Chigi, who refused to intercede on behalf of greedy favor seekers. The unofficial business of the court—the bestowing of pensions, titles, honors, and incomes—came to a grinding halt. Many courtiers began to believe that only if Olimpia came back could things return to normal. Only she could truly calm the fretful pontiff. Olimpia alone could make him laugh and shrug off for a few moments the crushing weight of his office. Only she could convince him to listen to the requests of courtiers—for a commission, of course, the accepted price of doing business.

Cardinal Pallavicino huffed, "The most highly regarded prelates and cardinals of the court, who knew of this abomination of the monstrous power of a woman in the Vatican, and knew of her pomp and greed and how she abused it, being intolerant of Innocent's hardness, desired the sister-in-law back to help them with favors, as an angel of intercession."[2]

For the same reason, the Pamphili family, too—with the exception of the princess of Rossano—wanted Olimpia back. Without her mediation, they had received very few favors from the pope, who lately had been chasing them out of his audience chamber with angry words whenever they requested anything. Only Olimpia could convince the pope to fulfill his duties to his family. Eyeing Cardinal Astalli-Pamphili warily, the family knew that only Olimpia could deal effectively with this arrogant intruder siphoning off the Pamphili patrimony.

And so Camillo, Prince Ludovisi, Prince Giustiniani, and several cardinals, when listening to the pope's venting about unruly servants or difficult politics, nodded with compassionate understanding. Things had never been the same for the poor pope since Olimpia left, they said. Only Olimpia could muzzle her clamorous family members. Only Olimpia could run his large household with strict efficiency so that he did not have to upset himself over bad help. Only Olimpia could supervise the datary and the other departments, keeping an unblinking eye on all financial transactions, and making sure that corruption did not go beyond the bounds of good taste. Perhaps the pope should consider bringing Olimpia back? Why should he torment himself, at his age, with such irritating details, when his brilliant sister-in-law could do all that for him?

The pope had to agree. He desperately wanted Olimpia back. He had valiantly taken a stand against her to maintain the honor of the Catholic Church, but without her the honor of the church had fallen to new lows. He missed his old comfortable pair of loafers. He missed chuckling and gossiping with her, unveiling his deepest fears, something he couldn't do with anyone else. Nothing had been right since she left.

But Innocent found himself in a quandary. Back in 1650 when he banished Olimpia from his presence, he had launched into angry mono-logues against her in front of ambassadors and cardinals. He had criti-cized her thieving from the papal treasury, her bossiness in running the Vatican, and her selfish cruelty against her son, daughter-in-law, and grandson. The pope had sworn that for six years he had known nothing about her corruption, and now that he knew, he was exiling her from the Vatican. Those who listened to his tirades had applauded his firm-ness. If he brought her back despite her crimes, they would laugh at his weakness.

The pope knew that he would look ridiculous if he suddenly issued a pardon to Olimpia. He would need to canvas the Sacred College, as advisors to the church, to see whether they would support her return. That way he wouldn't be making the decision alone. He began timidly asking his cardinals individually what they thought of allowing Olim-pia back. Even those who did not particularly like Olimpia believed that she would provide a soothing influence on the pope, rendering him much easier to work with.

Some cardinals thought that the pope's open contempt for his sister-in-law had been unseemly; he should bring her back to a position of modified favor, giving her the role of friend and first lady of Rome but not of running the government. These cardinals told the pope that Olimpia had learned her lesson; she would henceforth restrain her greed and ambition and restrict herself to a more womanly role—the pope's hostess and companion.

Cardinal Pallavicino scoffed at this opinion. "And this is wondrous in sage men, all assuming that she could return to a state in between, in which she would have helped with the petitions of others but would not have regained her former power or sold the palace positions as best she could."[3]

While most cardinals told the pope that pardoning Olimpia was an excellent idea, the one assent he truly wanted was that of Cardinal Chigi, the man he respected most. If the incorruptible Chigi supported Olimpia's return for the good of the pope and the church, few would question it. Cardinal Pallavicino reported, "One day, finding himself alone with Cardinal Chigi, he asked his opinion if it were opportune to rehabilitate her for the peace and quiet of the family, and to relieve him of these tedious matters."[4]

Cardinal Chigi found himself in a bind. "He knew that the pope having Olimpia by his side the second time around would be much more dishonorable than the first, when one could presume he was ignorant of the indecent occurrences."[5] But Chigi also knew that even if he were adamantly opposed to Olimpia's pardon, the pope would call her back anyway. Restored to power, Olimpia, realizing Chigi was an enemy, would sideline or fire him, and he would not be in a position to mitigate the scandal she would cause for the church. And yet the honest cardinal could not lie to the pope.

Sighing, Chigi said he feared that Olimpia's return would result in an immediate public brawl with the princess of Rossano, who would not be likely to graciously yield her position as first lady of Rome to her mother-in-law. He would not wish to see His Holiness brought low by further family squabbles.

The pope, who had wanted an enthusiastic affirmation of his proposal, was dissatisfied with this cool response. He hesitated. And his family remained on tenterhooks. Realizing that Cardinal Chigi was responsible for the pope's hesitation, Prince Ludovisi called on him one day to convince him that Olimpia's return was for the good of the Catholic Church and the Papal States.

"Cardinal Chigi," his biographer wrote, "knew well that the evil of her return was inevitable, but did not want to be seen as a participant in it." When Prince Ludovisi pressed Chigi for his opinion, he replied "that this business had nothing to do with him, that he had never been opposed to her return with a single word, and that the pope and his sister-in-law should try with all sincerity to live tranquilly."[6] And that was all they were going to get out of Cardinal Chigi.

It was enough for the pope to move forward. Seventeenth-century protocol required that Olimpia be rehabilitated in a ceremonial way, having made peace with her former enemies before she was pardoned by the pope. Her first step was to win over Sister Agatha, who had never forgiven her for stealing Saint Francesca's shoulder bone. Olimpia explained her pilfering of the holy relic as an excess of religious zeal. She, too, loved and venerated the saint and wanted the relic to restore the luster to a neglected church in San Martino. What she had done might have been wrong, indeed, but her motives had been pure—it was all for the glory of God.

This was an explanation likely to win the nun's approval. Olimpia asked her forgiveness for the theft, which the pious, peacemaking nun readily granted. Olimpia confessed the pain and humiliation of her exile—we can imagine Sister Agatha in tears at this point—and her wish to be reinstated in the bosom of her family. And the kindhearted nun promised to help.

On March 11, 1653, Romans were flabbergasted by the sight of Olimpia making a courtesy call on the princess of Rossano at her palace on the Corso. Camillo was absent from Rome, but there, in front of the palazzo, the heavily pregnant princess, eighty-three-year-old Sister Agatha, and four-year-old Gianbattista Pamphili were lined up to welcome Olimpia as if she were a queen. It must have been difficult for Olimpia to extend her hand to her daughter-in-law, and even more difficult for the princess to take that hand.

Cardinal Astalli-Pamphili then visited Olimpia at the Piazza Navona palace for a public, if superficial, reconciliation. But the most important ceremony occurred when Sister Agatha led Olimpia by the arm into the Quirinal Palace for a private meeting with the pope. She remained there until after midnight, the *avvisi* stated, which indicates that the journalists had stationed themselves outside the palace to see what time she reentered her carriage.

One of Olimpia's first acts delighted her family. She convinced the pope to give Prince Ludovisi 100,000 scudi from the papal treasury, the dowry he should have received back in 1644 for marrying Costanza Pamphili. For decades the going rate for a papal niece had been 100,000 scudi, and he had only received 20,000. Now the fat prince could no longer berate his wife for her lack of dowry or tromp around Rome complaining of his bad bargain, which must have gladdened Costanza more than the cash itself. He used this money to buy a palace and began to incorporate the houses next door into it.

Once more, Olimpia's carriage rumbled up to the Quirinal, where she emerged carrying a stack of petitions for the pope to sign. Once again the Piazza Navona was crammed with the carriages of cardinals and ambassadors whom she received like an empress, surrounded by a bevy of noblewomen waiting on her. The ambassador of the Venetian republic traveled to the Piazza Navona in great pomp to beg Olimpia's assistance in convincing the pope to help Venice fight the Turks.

She received everyone graciously except Monsignor Melzi, the nuncio to Vienna who had helped topple her in 1650 by telling Innocent of the emperor's comment, that the shame of Christendom was a pope who "has placed his government in the hands of a woman about whom all the heretics are laughing."[7] As a peace offering, Nuncio Melzi sent Olimpia two beautiful scent bottles filled with rare perfume. To no avail. He was her enemy and would never be forgiven. But she kept the perfume.

In addition to the old enemies, there was a new one. Cardinal Chigi, though always polite to Olimpia, was furious about her regained power. Upon her return, Olimpia had immediately tried to win him over, but he remained adamantly impartial, polite but reserved, and never discussed state or church business with her. He returned the expensive gifts she sent him with an apologetic note, and sent her strange presents of soap and capons, not the usual gold, silver, and diamonds she was used to.

Despite his careful courtesy toward Olimpia, Chigi couldn't bear to see how even the greatest cardinals bowed and scraped before her at public events, and one day he lost his temper with them. "You should know that among these people there are many Germans and French and maybe some heretics," he roared. "Have therefore greater regard for your own dignity, that you do not show contempt for it."[8] This comment winged its way back to Olimpia within the hour.

One evening Prince Ludovisi, who had been so supportive of Olimpia's return, marched up to Cardinal Chigi in the Quirinal and began complaining bitterly about her. He "deposited in his ears an infinity of complaints about his mother-in-law, which stupefied the cardinal, and were such as he could not believe, so the other [Prince Ludovisi] became even more heated in telling details and circumstances and in confirming them with lively assertions."[9]

Listening to the ridiculous tirade, Chigi burst out laughing so hard that he was unable to speak. The prince added that the cardinal would be right to reprove him for helping his mother-in-law back into power, when he should have trampled her underfoot. And so the two parted.

Perhaps for reasons of delicacy, Cardinal Pallavicino does not relate the exact nature of Olimpia's atrocities. It is likely that her wheeling and dealing in offices would not have shocked the cardinal, as he had fully expected this behavior. It is possible that the accusations were of a sexual nature, which truly would have astonished the fifty-four-year-old virgin Chigi.

Those seeking the pope's favor were still officially supposed to call on the cardinal nephew, Cardinal Astalli-Pamphili. But everyone knew that he had absolutely no influence on Innocent; they stopped calling on him and instead visited Olimpia, who delivered immediate results. The cardinal nephew, who had wholly lost the pope's favor to Cardinal Chigi, now lost even the pretense of power, and stewed bitterly about it. Innocent was grouchy and impatient with him, criticizing him roundly for his ineptitude.

But the pope reveled in Olimpia's presence. On one occasion soon after her return it seemed as if she had truly brought him magic. The spring of 1653 saw an invasion of crickets and locusts, who munched their way through the fields outside Rome, prompting fears of yet another devastating famine. The skies turned black when swarms of biblical proportions buzzed overhead. Local farmers, desperate for help, came to Rome and begged Innocent to excommunicate the critters, to curse them and send them to hell.

The pope graciously complied. In an elaborate ceremony he commanded all the bugs to fall into the Tiber River and drown. It is likely that no one was more surprised than the pope when the insects actually obeyed him. "It was a thing marvelous to see," Giacinto Gigli wrote, "that these animals ran all at once into the Tiber, and they filled it up so that you couldn't see the water anymore, which was black as ink . . . and remained so for several days."[10]

The same month, filled with renewed pontifical vigor, Innocent issued a papal decree against Jansenism, a religious movement in France named after its founder, Cornelius Jansen, bishop of Ypres (1585–1638). Jansenism claimed to return to the pure virtues of the fifth-century church father Saint Augustine and turn away from the decadent church that had developed in the following centuries. Though Jansenists maintained that they were strict Catholics, their beliefs smacked oddly of that most right-wing of all heresies, Calvinism. Jesus did not die for all men, the Jansenists declared, as some of them were clearly beyond saving and were predestined to hell. They decried church art and the veneration of saints and relics. They tossed out confession as they believed that only God could forgive sins, not a priest as God's representative. The church should become stricter, they said, as the path to heaven was narrow. The church, and the Jesuits, who hated the Jansenists believed that the path to God was rather wide, given his compassionate forgiveness of human sin.

The Jansenist movement swiftly became popular in France. The French monarchy, which supported the Jesuits, perceived Jansenism as a political threat and begged the pope to do something about it. In 1651, Innocent assembled a special congregation in Rome comprising five cardinals and fifteen theologians. Based on their findings, on May 31, 1653, after two years of investigation and debate, Innocent issued a bull declaring Jansenism heretical.

With Olimpia back in town, she was once more the scapegoat for the complaints of all and sundry. The Jansenists accused her of accepting a huge bribe from her friends the Jesuits to persuade the pope to condemn the movement. But the commission, which had labored and debated for two years before her return to power, had made up its mind without her, and the pope had merely accepted its recommendation.

If Olimpia had influenced the congregation, she would have pushed for condemnation of Jansenism even if no money had traded hands. Certainly the image of a comfortably wide path to heaven, wide enough for her both physically and spiritually, was more appealing than the Jansenist concept of the narrow path, where her broad rear end and her wide range of sins were destined to become irretrievably stuck. She hated the idea of an angry, unforgiving God pitching sinners helter-skelter into hell; one of them might very well be *her.*

After two and a half years of bitter exile, Olimpia enjoyed her position as mistress of the Vatican more than ever before. But this time around, her work was not about enjoyment. It was about revenge and safety.

She would revenge herself on all who had hurt her. The princess of Rossano was, except for family events and social occasions, barred from the pope's presence. She would no longer be advising him on politics or nominating her friends as cardinals. Officially, the two women had made peace with each other, and the princess had stopped sponsoring poetry contests to see who could pen the nastiest epigram about her mother-in-law. But their frigid courtesy to each other chilled even the warmest reception room. The War of the Olimpias had become a cold war.

Then there was Cardinal Astalli-Pamphili to deal with. In sweeping into the Vatican, he had swept Olimpia out and taken a good chunk of her possessions for himself. In an effort to get rid of her for good, he had shown the pope the gold medal featuring her wearing the papal tiara and Innocent wearing curls. Though the cardinal had been sidelined from power and was disliked by the pope, this was not enough for Olimpia. She would cook something up to make sure his ruin was entire and very public.

And then, last but not least, there was the pope. Though he had spurned her in anger, now he welcomed her back with joy and forgiveness, letting bygones be bygones. But there was no forgiveness in Olimpia's heart, and she didn't know the meaning of the word *bygones*. Once an enemy, always an enemy. And the pope, more than the princess of Rossano, more than Cardinals Astalli-Pamphili and Chigi, more than Nuncio Melzi, was her enemy. The extent of her revenge would be equal to the depth of her former love, her betrayed trust, and her agonizing pain.

She had loved Gianbattista Pamphili for thirty-eight years, devoted her life to him, made him rich, and made him pope. As a reward, he had thrown her to the dogs, stripped her of prestige and power, humiliated her internationally, and caressed her enemies. But no one else was smart enough to run the Vatican in her absence, and she had laughed when everything fell to pieces. Now he called her back. Well, she returned, chirping apologies, dripping syrupy smiles, and Innocent was naïve enough to think she was sincere. She was not sincere. She would make him pay for what he had done every single day until he died, and even then she would not be through with him. Sitting in San Martino, she had had a great deal of time to plot her revenge, a great deal of time indeed.

Olimpia's second urgent need was safety. She knew that she had numerous enemies in the Sacred College. If one of them were elected the next pope, she would find herself exiled, as she had exiled the Barberinis.

Even worse, she might be imprisoned, with all her property confiscated to repay the papal treasury for her depradations. Everything she had worked for hinged on which cardinal would be elected the next pope. And, casting a sidelong glance at Innocent, his right hand shaking violently, she knew the next conclave would not be too far in the future. She must work fast.

One cardinal often mentioned as the future pontiff was none other than Antonio Barberini, still fuming in self-imposed exile in Paris. Olimpia had to get Cardinal Antonio firmly on her side. Even if he were not elected pope, he would control a large block of votes, which he could swing against Olimpia as his revenge for what she had done to him. Or he could swing his votes for Olimpia, electing a cardinal known to be a friend of hers.

The idea of a marriage between the Pamphili and Barberini families, protecting each family from the other, had always appealed to them both. Camillo had, of course, botched everything by first becoming a cardinal and then marrying the princess of Rossano. But now there was a new generation of Pamphilis and Barberinis of marriageable age. Another alliance could be formed. And Olimpia decided it would be her beloved granddaughter, Olimpiuccia Giustiniani, who would finally join the two great papal houses.

Olimpiuccia had turned twelve, the minimum age required by the church for a girl to marry. Olimpia decided her granddaughter would marry the second son of Anna Colonna and the deceased Taddeo Barberini. Twenty-year-old Prince Maffeo was better-looking and less scholarly than his twenty-two-year-old brother, Carlo, who would be ordered by his cardinal uncles to give up his birthright and become a cardinal himself. Innocent should have named a Barberini cardinal in his first creation after becoming pope, as a sign of gratitude to the family that had made him a cardinal and led him on the road to the papal throne. But better late than never.

Olimpia had cooked up the marriage while still in exile and made it known to her family in Rome that their future was bleak indeed if the match did not go through. The Pamphilis, Giustinianis, and Ludovisis could lose everything if the next pope was unfriendly, she pointed out, and her relatives agreed. The historian Ludovico Muratori wrote in his annals of 1652, "Now Donna Olimpia, sister-in-law of the pope, and others of the Pamphili family, seeing the decline of the decrepit pope, decided to end the enmity of the Barberinis and cement friendship with a house so powerful for its riches and protection."[11]

Gregorio Leti explained, "So in order to prevent the peril which threatened her with entire ruin, she resolved, despite everything, to strike a blow so strange that many people had difficulty believing it after it was done. She negotiated a close alliance with the Barberinis to oblige them with the union of blood, not only to pardon her all the past, but also to defend her when the time came against all her enemies."[12]

No sooner was Olimpia back in Rome than she met with Francesco Barberini about the proposed marriage and sent an offer to Cardinal

Antonio in Paris. But now, given Innocent's slide into decrepitude, the Barberinis were in the driver's seat. They demanded the standard enormous dowry of a papal niece, which Olimpia readily agreed to provide. They wanted the remainder of their confiscated property returned. Olimpia consented.

With great excitement, Olimpia informed her granddaughter of the glorious marriage she had arranged for her. Olimpiuccia would be a princess in her own right, with a conspicuous dowry, living in her own palace, allied to the most important family in Rome. But upon hearing the news, she informed her grandmother that she had no intention of marrying Maffeo Barberini. She wanted to become a nun.

Olimpia waved away this response as childish nonsense. Who in their right mind would want to become a nun? She took Olimpiuccia for a few days to meet the groom at the Barberini estate of Palestrina outside Rome. But the little girl did not like the groom. And the groom did not like the bride, who at twelve had a chest as flat as a board and a figure as curvaceous as a pencil. He wearily assented to the marriage for the good of his family. And there was always the hope that she would, in time, fill out. But the bride was not as resigned to her fate. When she and Olimpia returned to the Piazza Navona, Olimpiuccia ran away to her parents' house, the Villa Giustiniani.

At first Olimpiuccia's father, Prince Andrea, refused to return her to Olimpia. His mother-in-law's interference with his daughter had always irritated him. But finally he realized that the future of the Pamphili family depended on the marriage. If the Pamphilis had any hope of obtaining a friendly pope in the next conclave, Olimpiuccia must be sacrificed. And so he reluctantly drove her back to the Piazza Navona but told everyone who would listen that his daughter's unhappy fate was caused by his nasty, meddling mother-in-law, who had originally planned to marry her to that imbecile Francesco Maidalchini, who had, thank God, gone into the church.

In May 1653 the haughty Cardinal Antonio Barberini set out from Paris with a great entourage to return to Rome, where he would be welcomed with triumphal arches and numerous festivities. And on May 30, the dowry documents, written in the florid style of the time, were signed.

The Most Excellent Signora Donna Olimpia Maidalchini
Pamphili, Princess of San Martino, promises the Most Excellent
Signor Don Maffeo Barberini, son of the Most Excellent Signor
Don Taddeo Barberini of Most Happy Memory, and of the Most
Excellent Donna Anna Colonna, to give him as his legitimate
wife the Most Excellent Signorina Donna Olimpia Giustiniani
her granddaughter and daughter of the Most Excellent Signor
Andrea Giustiniani, and of the Most Excellent Signora Maria
Pamphili, niece of His Holiness, which granddaughter the
Signora Princess of San Martino has educated since the first
months after her birth, and loved as if she were her own
daughter . . ."[13]

The dowry was 100,000 scudi given by the bride's father, but the
avvisi noted that Olimpia had provided 70,000 of it herself.

On June 15, the sobbing child bride and the morose groom were married by the pope himself in an elaborate ceremony in the Sistine Chapel,
attended by the entire Sacred College. Immediately after the ceremony, the
marriage feast was held at the Pamphili Palace. The bride's grandmother
was absolutely delighted, the groom's mother less so. Anna Colonna, who
had avoided for nearly a decade marrying a blue-blooded child of hers to a
parvenu Pamphili, looked on the marriage as a degradation and a necessary evil. Having Olimpia in her family would be a daily martyrdom for
the haughty princess. We can imagine her sour-faced and purse-lipped,
picking at her food with a silver fork—not tin anymore—while a beaming Olimpia dug into her meal with hearty gusto.

After the feast, the groom was supposed to take his bride to her new
home, the exquisite Palace of the Four Fountains. But Olimpiuccia
raced up to her old bedroom and locked the door. The wedding guests
could hear her loud sobs echoing through the walls. Then she threw
open the window and cried at the top of her lungs that she wanted to
become a nun, that she wanted to die a virgin and poor, and that she
had never agreed to marry for money. She shrieked that she knew what
her husband expected of her that night because a waiting woman had
told her, and she wanted no part of it.

The people milling around the Piazza Navona admiring the carriages of the wedding guests stopped talking and listened intently. The bride then swore that she would not unlock her door until Maffeo Barberini went home without her. Olimpia had never imagined that her moment of greatest triumph—the union of the Pamphilis and Barberinis that she had planned for nine years—would be spoiled by the stubbornness of a twelve-year-old.

The humiliated groom hung around disconsolately, not knowing what to do. Finally, Olimpia persuaded him to go home. She had raised Olimpiuccia from birth and knew her better than anyone; she would talk to her and bring her to his palace the following day. But now Olimpiuccia proved herself to be Olimpia's granddaughter and vowed to use church law against the fate concocted for her. Since in the eyes of the church a marriage was no marriage until consummation, she knew that she was, technically, not married. If she held out long enough, embarrassed the Barberinis long enough, perhaps they would annul the contract and she could get out of the whole thing.

To a great extent Olimpiuccia's behavior was the fault of her grandmother, who had raised her to be brash and strong in a world that endeavored to crush weak females. Teodoro Amayden informed his readers that Olimpia had told the child again and again, "Olimpiuccia, never let anyone underestimate you! You must be the boss of everything."[14] Little had Olimpia considered that this lesson would be used against herself.

Days turned into weeks, then months. Messengers galloped back and forth between the Piazza Navona and the Barberini Palace. Maffeo visited periodically, hoping that his bride would get used to him. Olimpia convinced her granddaughter to permit Maffeo to hold her hand and give her a little kiss, but that was all she could get out of her.

Surely it helped Maffeo's marital humiliation to be treated as a reigning prince; ambassadors called on the new "nephew," bowing and offering him rich gifts. Whenever he visited a noble palazzo, the bells pealed in celebration. Yet his hold on the title of papal lay nephew was tenuous because the marriage had not yet been consummated.

Olimpia tried to cajole Olimpiuccia to join her husband and, mistakenly thinking she was speaking to a younger version of herself, raved about the social prestige she would enjoy, and the lavish entertainments she would give in salons far larger and more beautiful than those in the Palazzo Pamphili. For Olimpiuccia would live in the magnificent Palazzo Barberini, the palace Olimpia had always had her eye on, with its triumphal staircase, forty-foot ceilings, and splendid fragrant gardens. But here Olimpiuccia differed from her grandmother. She did not care for such things, she said, and preferred the deprivations of the convent to the luxuries of the Palazzo Barberini. She wanted to die a virgin, and poor.

Olimpia called in her daughter Maria, Olimpiuccia's mother, who had never been very involved in the girl's upbringing, to do what she could. Maria begged her daughter to obey for the sake of the family. Many young girls, she pointed out cheerfully, were forced to marry ugly, sick old men. Maffeo Barberini was only twenty and not bad-looking. But Olimpiuccia—old enough to understand sex but young enough to despise the idea of it—repeated that she wanted to remain a virgin for life.

All Rome gossiped about this unconsummated marriage, and the pope grew troubled. Easily angered, he fired his *maestro di camera,* Monsignor Centofiorini, and other household employees for poor performance. He ordered his doctor, Gabriele Fonseca, not to come into his presence unless summoned. Giacinto Gigli noted, "And he has become so grouchy that all his servants fear being fired."[15]

On June 29, after celebrating the feast of Saints Peter and Paul, the cranky pope stopped by the Piazza Navona to see how work was coming along on the Church of Saint Agnes. He noticed that ungainly stairs had just been built, which jutted out into the piazza, ruining its oval symmetry. They were so ugly, in fact, that people had begun saying the Four Rivers Fountain figure of the Nile had draped its head so it wouldn't have to look at them.

Seeing the pope, the masons ran up to him and complained that Camillo had not paid them. Innocent was furious. He ordered that the stairs be demolished. He fired Camillo as overseer of the project and the Rainaldis as architects. To finish the job he brought in Francesco Borromini, who had the challenge of making major modifications to a building already half constructed. It would be a long process, and the pope despaired of ever seeing the church finished. Where would his bones rest when he died? He became depressed, and as usual, his health suffered.

Worried about the pope's health, Olimpia decided he needed an invigorating visit to Viterbo and San Martino. The pope, who usually disliked travel, was actually looking forward to the diversion. When Dr. Fonseca forced his way into the pope's room to warn him of the dangers of the journey, the pope fired him. Cardinal Chigi, too, advised him not to go. He was concerned not only with the pope's health but with the glorification of Olimpia, which seemed to him the sole purpose of the journey she had arranged. The pope, of course, didn't listen. On Sunday, October 12, at 8 A.M., the entourage left Rome.

Innocent was so eager to see San Martino that he bypassed Viterbo entirely, leaving the welcoming committee twiddling their thumbs. He was carried up the double-snail staircase of Olimpia's palace and settled into the bedroom she had built specially for him, with an interior door connecting to hers. When the dignitaries of Viterbo, hearing of the pontiff's sudden change in plans, raced to see him, he received them on the papal throne of the audience chamber Olimpia had designed for him. Above him was the gilded ceiling that could be raised or lowered; on three sides were long windows looking out over the green hills. For several hours Innocent graciously granted audiences to local churchmen, officials, and nobles.

Cardinal Chigi, who had been dragged along unwillingly, was shocked to see an inscription on the gate outside Olimpia's palace that stated that Pope Innocent X had given her the principality. He pointed out to the pope that Rome-bound travelers rumbling by on the main road—Catholic and heretic alike—would see the inscription and, knowing all the scurrilous stories about the pope and his sister-in-law, would laugh at it. Innocent reluctantly agreed that it had to be removed and told Olimpia, who now held another grudge against Chigi.

The following day, the entourage rode the three miles to Viterbo, where the pope was received in the cathedral by none other than Cardinal Francesco Maidalchini. The little cardinal had been assigned the benefice with the sole purpose of getting him out of Rome so that the pope wouldn't have to look at him anymore. Compared to the intrigues of Rome, the peace and quiet of Viterbo had suited Cardinal Maidalchini, who was still only twenty-three. Perhaps he was nervous as the pope was carried in his litter up to the altar—Innocent had been known to yell at him in front of the most important visitors. But when Innocent emerged, he was in high spirits and showed unusual kindness to Olimpia's nephew.

The pope next visited Olimpia's younger sisters in the Convent of Saint Dominic. Having left the convent, the papal carriages rolled to Olimpia's Nini palace for a reception. Here was where her worldly success had begun. Here she had known wealth of her own for the first time. Here she had discovered sex. Here she had borne two children; and here she had lost two children. Here she had become a widow when twenty-three-year-old Nino breathed his last. Here she had plotted her further advance in the world and had gone looking for Pamphilio Pamphili, nobleman of Rome. It must have meant a great deal for Olimpia, bringing the pope into her past, in full sight of the citizens of Viterbo. If there were any still alive who had treated her badly when she was young, she must have doubly relished her victory.

On the road back to San Martino, the cavalcade stopped for refreshments at the hunting lodge called Il Barco, built by Olimpia's half-brother, Andrea, who had died four years earlier. It was a frescoed jewel of a house, with a floor-length wall fountain in the entry-level hall and bedrooms leading out onto charming balconies with outside staircases. A little church stood behind it, and orchards all around it.

The self-important Andrea had always hated it when people pointed to his younger half-sister as the source of his power and wealth. She alone, they said, had given him the wherewithal to build his hunting lodge. But they were wrong. As tax collector of Viterbo, Andrea had stolen the money all by himself. Still, the insults rankled. He had inserted a marble slab into the outside wall where carriages drove up, stating that he had built the residence in 1625, "before his sister Olimpia went as wife to the brother of Pope Innocent X." Yet his sister Olimpia had gone as wife to the brother of Pope Innocent X in 1612.

At Il Barco, Olimpia played a joke on the pope. In and around Viterbo, October was the time of the famous chestnut harvest. Olimpia had secretly arranged for roasted chestnuts to be tied on the trees. She then instructed the Swiss Guard to gather them for the pope, and he laughed heartily when he tasted them, proclaiming it a miracle. When Monsignor Acquapendente, the governor of Viterbo, paid his respects, Innocent was so jolly that he promised to make him a cardinal in the next creation, a promise that he kept.

The entire visit was a great success. Innocent enjoyed it immensely, and away from the cares of Rome he felt younger and healthier than he had in years. He didn't even let the usual family disturbances unduly worry him. On the road home, a group of laborers blocked the papal carriage and informed the pontiff that Prince Giustiniani had hired them to fill potholes for the pope's visit but now that the work was done wouldn't pay them. As punishment, the pope refused to honor the prince's castle with the expected visit. Camillo had come along on the trip, leaving the princess of Rossano in Rome, and told the pope that his marriage was unbearable. The princess never stopped nagging him, and he wished he could be cardinal nephew again.

Glowing with good health and high spirits, when the pope arrived in Rome he went first to Saint Peter's, then to the Palazzo Pamphili, and then to the Quirinal, insisting at each stop that he get out of his chair and go up the stairs on foot. People marveled at his firm step, bright eyes, and easy smile.

While all were agreed on the pope's miraculous regeneration, not everyone believed this was a good thing. One *avvisi* writer told of the general disappointment that the voyage had probably given the pontiff another ten years of life.

21

The Sudden Disgrace
of Cardinal Astalli

He who blinded by ambition, raises himself to
a position whence he cannot mount higher, must thereafter
fall with the greatest loss.

—Niccolò Machiavelli

I‌T WAS NOT LONG BEFORE the old stresses and strains of Rome took their toll on Innocent. There was, for instance, the perplexing dilemma of what to do about the recalcitrant Olimpiuccia, who still refused to move in with her husband. The Barberinis began to wonder if this wasn't another one of Olimpia's tricks—she had, after all, promised them Camillo back in 1644, and everyone knew how disastrous that had been.

Aware of their suspicions, Olimpia began to panic. This marriage had been crafted to win them as her friends, not to make them fiercer enemies than ever before. She simply had to figure out how to get Olimpiuccia into Maffeo Barberini's bed.

Given the girl's professed piety, Olimpia called in a priest to convince her to do her duty to her family, an ironic parallel to Sforza Maidalchini's action back in 1606. Perhaps Olimpia truly could not see that what she was doing to a twelve-year-old was what Sforza had done to a fifteen-year-old; her father had tried to drag her into a convent, while she kicked and screamed that she wanted to marry, and now Olimpia was dragging her granddaughter into a marriage, while she kicked and screamed that she wanted to become a nun. Olimpia, as cruel as Agamemnon himself, was sacrificing her own little Iphigenia on the altar of family loyalty. The priest duly arrived and spoke solemnly with Olimpiuccia about the grave sin she was committing by not obeying her family. The little girl shrugged.

Finally, Olimpia had enough. One evening, after five months of putting up with her granddaughter's stubborn refusal to consummate her illustrious marriage, she dragged her into a carriage and took her to Palazzo Barberini herself. There she shoved her into the arms of Maffeo. An *avvisi* sent to Paris on November 24, 1653, stated, "Olimpiuccia was carried to the palace of the Four Fountains to the great relief of the pope."[1] The ambassador of Mantua wrote, "The grandmother took her there almost violently one evening."[2]

Shortly thereafter, the marriage was consummated. Olimpia heaved a loud sigh of relief. On January 6, 1654, Innocent X ordered the Vatican treasury to wipe out all remaining Barberini debts. The Barberini cardinals were no longer required to restore the money they had stolen, and now they were in an excellent position to start stealing afresh. Poor Lucrezia Barberini, dangling like rancid meat on the marriage market for a decade, was married to the widowed duke of Modena and became a duchess.

After ten years shuttered in darkness, the three-thousand-seat Barberini theater was opened for a musical comedy. Costly gifts flowed in from all over the world as recognition of the family's return to power. And now that their interests were the same, the Barberini cardinals worked hand in hand with Olimpia in running the Vatican. "Having not yet forgotten their former custom of amassing money," Gregorio Leti wrote, "they tried everything possible to obtain it for themselves and for Donna Olimpia, to whom they taught new methods of squeezing money from all sides."[3]

On January 4 Olimpia changed her will, albeit reluctantly. Leti explained, "The pope was heard to say several times to Donna Olimpia, in promising to return her to all her former authority, which he absolutely wanted, that she should give all or at least the greater part of the wealth she had amassed to Don Camillo. . . . He had been well informed that she doted more on her daughters than on her son and he found it strange that she was thinking of leaving her wealth not to those in the direct line of Pamfili, of whom his nephew was the only one left. . . . Donna Olimpia had great repugnance to consenting to do this."[4]

Since her birth in 1641, Olimpiuccia had been Olimpia's primary heir, but now she was eminently provided for as a Barberini princess. Obeying the pope, Olimpia made Camillo her heir, though it must have irked her to leave her money, in effect, to the princess of Rossano. But it would eventually descend to Olimpia's grandchildren, and the fruitful princess had by now considerably provided four of them, two boys and two girls.

Olimpia further stated in her will that she wanted two thousand Masses to be said for her soul in San Martino, and another two thousand in Viterbo, and two thousand more in Rome. Surely these Masses, winging their way to heaven, would help clear that wide path necessary for her ascent. In addition, she gave dowries to seven poor girls in San Martino who otherwise would not be able to marry. In a touching tribute to her immured sister, Olimpia stipulated that for twenty years after her death, seven poor women would receive a nice dress on the Feast of Saint Orsola, Ortensia's patron saint.

Olimpia left Olimpiuccia a diamond watch and the right to choose whatever other objects she wanted from the Pamphili legacy. Prince Ludovisi and Costanza also had a daughter named Olimpia, who would be given a valuable tiara to wear on her wedding day. Olimpia's daughters, Maria and Costanza, who had already received their dowries, would each inherit one thousand scudi in cash and the same amount in silver plate.

In 1650 Olimpia had purchased a garden in Ripagrande, on the banks of the Tiber in Trastevere, where she sometimes liked to take the air. Now she was building a house there. This property she bequeathed to her little grandson Gianbattista Pamphili. She left Francesco Maidal-chini five hundred scudi, a rather slender sum, and her servants received legacies. As for her state bonds, they were to be sold and the money given to charity. The rest of her estate was to be given to her primary heir, Camillo.

The pope could count himself fortunate that several irritating issues had been resolved to his satisfaction. Olimpia was back, soothing his doubts and worries and taking care of Vatican business. Olimpiuccia had finally consummated her marriage, and Olimpia had agreed to leave her estate to Camillo. But as age and illness tightened their grip, the pope grew cross and angry again.

In December Giacinto Gigli reported that "the pope fired his major-domo, his *maestro di casa*, the deacon of the grooms, and many other ministers, and made them all give an exact account of the money that they had spent and became suspicious and said that everyone was steal-ing from him."[5] On January 20 the pope went to the Church of Saint Sebastian and hastily knelt to pray. He fell, and when the prior tried to help him up, the pope fired him.

Olimpia was on a mission—to earn as much money as possible before the pope died. Though she was already an extremely wealthy woman, deep inside her lived the powerless little girl of Viterbo who was terri-fied of not having enough. But how much was enough? As soon as In-nocent breathed his last, her income from office selling and influence peddling would dry up immediately. The relatives of the new pope would have their hands out for these transactions. Moreover, she might need large sums to bribe her enemies into leaving her alone.

Olimpia convinced the pope to involve himself less in political mat-ters. He should conserve his health, she said. At his age, too much hard work could kill him, and only she truly looked after his best interests. Olimpia took over many of the pope's duties.

"She did not content herself solely with giving orders for the politi-cal administration of the state, of the church, and of the court," Leti wrote. "She wanted to govern the spiritual realm as well, as she had done before, so that she often convoked the congregations at her palace before their regular meetings."[6] He added, "It was a marvel to see a woman some sixty years old work so hard day and night, treating and negotiating with all and sundry, coming and going, climbing and descending continually, without ever showing any signs of fatigue."[7]

Despite the return of the Barberini cardinals and Olimpia to help the pope run the church, Innocent still relied heavily on Cardinal Chigi, his secretary of state. Innocent wanted Chigi and Olimpia to become friends and work closely together. Otherwise, he would have to listen to Olimpia's constant complaints that Chigi did not respect her.

As a matter of fact, Chigi did *not* respect her, though he could not show it outright. He was appalled at a woman setting foot in papal offices, much less running them. And he was painfully aware of Olimpia's reputation as the pope's mistress, a reputation that tarnished the entire church. When the pope encouraged Chigi to be nicer to Olimpia, the cardinal would duly "visit her on rare occasions which the law of common etiquette required," Cardinal Pallavicino reported, "and then talk to her with serious words, and leave after a short time without having discussed any state business with her, and without giving a single instance of adulation to that idol of the court.

"She could not tolerate it that this man alone in all the palace treated her like this. And the more people talked of Chigi's probity and sense, the more it seemed to her that he diminished her reputation." Olimpia assumed he was on the side of the princess of Rossano. "But truly the cardinal stayed far away from both. He did as little with one as with the other."[8]

When Innocent suggested that Chigi give Olimpia a nice present, he immediately sent her a box of pastries—which we can assume didn't go over too well. In December 1653, someone asked Cardinal Chigi what Christmas present he intended to give Olimpia. The irritated cardinal replied "that he had no gold to give her, nor did he want to offer her incense, and she was not grateful for myrrh, so he really couldn't give her anything."[9] This witticism became the talk of the court and winged its way quickly back to Olimpia, who repeated it to the pope using more scathing terms.

"The pope, therefore, ulcerated by these complaints of hers against the cardinal, and not without a bit of contempt for so stubborn a contrariness of his against the pope's desire and inclination, began to diminish his friendship and trust."[10]

Olimpia found a way to route important correspondence to the pope directly, bypassing Chigi. The papal secretary of briefs and ciphers, Monsignor Decio Azzolini, was a cunning, charming young man of aristocratic family whose great-uncle had been a cardinal. A Machiavellian courtier, he had an uncanny ability to decipher coded letters and to create new codes for the pope's correspondence. All important letters came through his office, and after decoding them, he was supposed to hand them to Cardinal Chigi. But at Olimpia's request, Azzolini began giving them directly to the pope.

Innocent did not object to bypassing Chigi on certain matters. In particular, he did not want him to see documents "pertaining to private advantages for the house of Pamphili, and not for the public service of the Apostolic See."[11] Chigi, however, knew very well what was going on and, far from being angered, was pleased that no one would be able to accuse him of raiding the church treasury for the Pamphili family.

One day Cardinal Chigi learned that his sister had come to Rome and wanted to see him. When he asked the pope's permission to leave his office and visit her, Innocent graciously suggested that he invite her to the papal palace to meet with Chigi in his apartments. Waving his hands in horror, Chigi replied, "Oh no, Holy Father. This palace is not the place to have women come."[12]

Though Olimpia was bit by bit, day by day, wreaking her revenge on the pope in terms of the money she was stealing from him, there was another individual who had yet to pay for what he had done to her—Cardinal Astalli-Pamphili. "The bitter memory of the pain she had suffered for so long did not move her so much to repentance as to the growing hatred against him who was the cause of the whole thing," Cardinal Pallavicino explained.[13]

Cardinal Astalli-Pamphili was, at this point, a rather pathetic enemy.

He had become a figurehead with very few duties. The ambassadors avoided him. The Pamphilis loathed him. The Barberinis disliked him. Cardinal Chigi, who ran a tight ship, kept the dunderheaded fake nephew at a distance. But Olimpia was not satisfied with sidelining him. She planted spies in his office to keep an eagle eye on his doings.

The cardinal nephew was expected to sell a certain number of benefices, or take the money from vacant benefices, to pay for those business expenses that were not reimbursed by the Vatican. Yet the first time Cardinal Astalli-Pamphili did this, Olimpia complained to the pope. The angry pontiff accused his fake nephew of graft and demanded he hand the money over—to Olimpia.

Olimpia frequently told the pope of Astalli-Pamphili's uselessness in his office, giving detailed evidence provided by her spies. Innocent "began to mortify the cardinal with injurious words and deeds, and thought about firing him, saying that Cardinal Chigi could do the work without him idly taking up space."[14]

The pope spoke to Chigi about getting rid of Cardinal Astalli-Pamphili, who had proved to be the third embarrassing cardinal nephew in a row. The Barberini cardinals, who had run the Vatican on behalf of their uncle for twenty-two years, were proving remarkably efficient; Olimpia was back and more involved than ever, and there seemed no reason to have this phony nephew bumbling around pretending to work.

But Chigi "wanted to do good for all. He was zealous that the palace should not become a theater of new disturbances, and the subject of satirical gazettes, and he did not want to appear a happy spectator at the ruin of others or to be seen as stepping on their bodies to climb up. Therefore, he tried to change the pope's mind," Cardinal Pallavicino wrote. Cardinal Chigi told the pope that "firing the cardinal without grave cause would expose the pope to the poor judgment of the world for having, with so many signs of favor, raised an unworthy man, and with such signs of disfavor lowered an innocent one."[15]

In the late fall of 1653, Cardinal Astalli-Pamphili noticed something mysterious going on among the pope, Olimpia, and the Barberini cardinals. Late-night meetings were held, from which he was firmly excluded. As cardinal nephew, he should have signed, or at least seen, most of the pope's letters, yet now coded letters were being sent out covertly. Astalli-Pamphili smelled a plot. Rifling through papal correspondence in the wee hours by candlelight, finding the ciphers to decode letters, he soon discovered what was afoot. It was a bombshell.

During their French exile, the Barberini cardinals had kicked themselves for not having accumulated principalities during their uncle's long reign, as many other papal nephews had; while money was useful, they realized, it could easily be dissipated or confiscated. A principality, on the other hand, provided a family with power and marriage alliances to other royal families; it added glory to the family name long after the papal uncle was dead and forgotten.

They had missed many opportunities. Various dukes had died with no heirs, and Urban had incorporated their territories into the Papal States when he could have given them to his relatives. Pressured by his nephews to acquire some principality for the Barberinis before it was too late, in his last year the ailing pope had tried unsuccessfully to conquer Castro.

But the city of Castro had been demolished by Innocent's forces and now held little appeal to the ambitious Barberinis. Casting around Italy for a weakly defended territory ripe for the picking, their eyes alighted on Naples, a large, fertile, and well-populated kingdom. Naples held the added advantage that it was, technically, owned by the pope, who leased it to Spain for the annual payment of the white horse. What was to prevent the pope from claiming his ancient feudal territory?

Moreover, Spanish hold over Naples remained tenuous. The viceroys were despised; taxes were outrageous, and the people simmered with resentment. Innocent had lost a great opportunity to seize the kingdom in 1647 during the Masaniello revolt. Now, with France on his side, it was not too late to invade Naples. Surely when the people saw papal troops coming to liberate them, they would rise up once more against the Spanish tyrants.

The Barberini cardinals wanted to acquire the duchy of Salerno for themselves. The rest of the kingdom would be given to Maffeo Barberini as king, and his wife, Olimpiuccia, as queen. Olimpia was delighted at this suggestion. She would be the grandmother of a *queen*. The Barberinis promised to field at their own cost an army of twelve thousand men, and started recruiting. The pope would raise his own army to march south in short order and would outfit the papal galleys to bombard Spanish coastal fortresses.

"The pope, almost beside himself due to his old age, easily gave into all their plans," Gregorio Leti wrote.[16] And indeed, the pope's approval of this harebrained scheme seems proof that he was losing his faculties. Spain would never let Naples go without a fight, and Spanish forces were infinitely more powerful than papal ones. France was too far away to offer timely support if, indeed, she ever sent it. For centuries, ardent French promises of dispatching men and ships to defend the pope or conquer the infidel were followed not by the expected tromp of boots and snap of sails but by a bewildering silence.

As Olimpia and the Barberinis secretly prepared for the invasion, word came from the viceroy of Naples that the king of Spain had been informed of their treachery. Neapolitan fortresses were on full alert; additional soldiers were recruited. City walls and gates were manned by crack soldiers ready to open fire on any suspicious visitors. The Spanish fleet was bobbing along the coast ready to sink any papal or French vessels.

The conspirators were flabbergasted. Now all their plans were undone. How on earth could Spain have found out? They had been so careful with their coded letters and disguised messengers. But Olimpia had a clue as to who had betrayed them. She believed it was Cardinal Astalli-Pamphili, a loyal advocate of Spain, but she needed irrevocable proof to present to the pope. Then she could send the cardinal nephew packing.

Olimpia met secretly with Decio Azzolini and asked him to nose around Cardinal Astalli-Pamphili's office, using his ability to decode ciphers, and bring her evidence that the cardinal nephew was the traitor. She promised to make him a cardinal in the upcoming creation if his efforts were successful. Azzolini, who had always shown the greatest friendship to Astalli-Pamphili, poked, prodded, bribed, coaxed, and decoded. He found the irrevocable proof Olimpia wanted in the form of a dispatch to Spain. She handed it to the pope.

On Saturday, January 31, 1654, Giacinto Gigli wrote in his diary that Cardinal Astalli-Pamphili was fast sliding into disgrace. "The pope severely reprimanded him for the many errors he had committed, calling him ungrateful, saying that he was in a plot with the Spaniards against the will of the pope. Cardinal Astalli, seeing the danger all around him, tried to put things right, but could not."[17]

But how to punish him? Olimpia pushed for the harshest penalty possible—removal from all offices, honors, titles, and benefices. She would have liked to see him lose the dignity of cardinal, as well, but this would have created uproarious protest in the Sacred College. In the rough-and-tumble centuries of the Dark and Middle Ages, popes had from time to time defrocked enemy cardinals, thrown them into prison, and even murdered them. But once the Protestants had started laughing at them, Catholic prelates tried to muster as much dignity as possible. The dishonor of one cardinal would dishonor them all. By the seventeenth century, even if a cardinal was an imbecile, a libertine, or a traitor, he might lose all his money and power, but he would never be defrocked—unless, of course, he had turned heretic.

Listening to Olimpia's stern recommendations for justice, the pope was, as usual, hesitant. If he penalized Astalli-Pamphili with the full rigor of his power, would the world laugh at him—again? Yet the traitor deserved nothing less. The pope had raised him from nothing to the highest honors; first he had proved lazy and useless, and now he had betrayed the very man who had so honored him.

As the pope tried to make up his mind, Olimpia came down with an excruciating case of podagra, the gouty inflammation of the big toe. It was a malady common enough in baroque courts heavy on meats, pastries, sauces, and wine. The affected toe was swollen, red, and throbbing, propped up on a pillow as she lay in bed. Usually the least movement could cause the the podagra sufferer paroxysms of bone-shattering pain, and some would have been hard put to stir if the house caught fire. But when, on February 3, Olimpia received a note from Innocent that he had finally decided how to punish Cardinal Astalli-Pamphili, she leaped out of her sickbed and had herself carried—gouty toe and all—to the Quirinal to hear the verdict. The pope had decided to remove Cardinal Astalli-Pamphili from all honors, incomes, benefices, and titles except that of cardinal, to take away his permission to use the Pamphili name and coat of arms, to take away his use of Bel Respiro and the Pamphili Palace, and to exile him immediately.

Gigli explained that Olimpia, "with her usual dexterity, placidly told him that His Holiness, having exalted a stranger to such extraordinary greatness, and told him the most intimate secrets of his heart, was faced with treachery . . . and he would do his best in the following conclave to ruin the exalted house of Pamphili."[18]

At 11 A.M. the pope sent instructions to Cardinal Astalli-Pamphili to clear out of the papal palace and go into exile at his family castle of Sambuci, thirty miles outside Rome. He would not be permitted to take any furniture with him. When Cardinal Chigi heard the news, he was horrified by the scandal it would bring to the church. Twice he went to implore the pope to reconsider, but Innocent impatiently shooed him away.

At 9 P.M. the former cardinal nephew stepped into his carriage and departed Rome. His servants—except his secretary, who had wisely burned his letters and fled—were imprisoned and questioned under torture. All those in Rome who had proudly posted the cardinal's arms above their doors had to take them down that very night.

On February 18, Olimpia's niece Caterina Maidalchini, married to Cardinal Astalli's brother, tried desperately to see her aunt. Having been sent away once by the butler, Caterina tried again and this time forced her way in, shrieking that Olimpia must help her. Hearing the ruckus, Olimpia rustled to the top of the triumphal staircase leading to the courtyard and looked down at the young woman coldly. "And now finally this cardinal *padrone* is finished!" she cried.[19] It would be best for the Astallis, she continued, if they left Rome. If they lived in the same bitter exile to which Cardinal Astalli had condemned her. Caterina staggered out crying, and Olimpia swept back to her rooms. Revenge was sweet.

Cardinal Astalli's bonds in the amount of forty thousand scudi were confiscated by order of the pope. To humiliate him even further, Innocent had all the furniture of his palaces dragged out and auctioned off on the streets for whatever price it could bring. All of his carriages went, along with twenty-three horses and four mules, and the prices fetched were rather low. A friend of Astalli's felt so bad for him that he bought some of the horses, carriages, and furniture and secretly kept them for the cardinal until he could return after the pope's death.

Innocent had to write a papal brief depriving Astalli of his offices and give his reasons for doing so. Yet the pope could hardly tell the truth—that he had been plotting to invade Naples to make Olimpia's granddaughter a queen and that Astalli had informed Spain. The pope stated simply that the cardinal was well aware of the reasons for his disgrace.

Vatican jackals circled the fresh meat, friends of Olimpia and Decio Azzolini jockeying for the titles, honors, benefices, and incomes that had belonged to Cardinal Astalli. Innocent wanted to give something to Cardinal Chigi, who, as usual, asked for nothing, and told him he would receive the lucrative post of protector of the Franciscan monasteries. But Chigi politely declined with various excuses, as he "did not want to enjoy the shipwrecks of others. . . . But the pope understood the real reason behind his refusal, and it pleased him to see Chigi's reverence for those who were in disgrace."[20]

The pope ordered a trial, in which Astalli's colleagues and servants were questioned about his dealings. Giacinto Gigli recorded that the only results from the rigorous inquest were "youthful indiscretions." The good cardinal had built a secret ladder in the Quirinal Palace that led from the room of his majordomo to the stables. Called to testify, the carpenter who had constructed the ladder declared candidly, "Yes, it is true that I worked on that ladder, and all the household said that the cardinal intended to use it to receive or go out to visit with the greatest secrecy the pretty ladies."[21]

Innocent was furious over the secret ladder. For one thing, a cardinal should not be sneaking out of the papal palace to visit pretty ladies at night or, heaven forbid, bringing them into the papal palace. For another, it was a dangerous breach of security, as spies and assassins could have climbed *up* the ladder. And third, the cardinal could have used the ladder to sneak out and visit the Spanish ambassador and other enemies of the pope.

Cardinal Astalli maintained great dignity in the face of his very public disgrace. He did not send the pope letters imploring his mercy. He did not beg the other cardinals to intercede for him. He knew he was facing financial ruin, sitting in his drafty medieval castle with no means of maintaining it. His cash was gone, his bonds had been seized, and his furniture had been sold at auction. He had almost nothing to live on. But he knew the pope could not last much longer, and then he, a cardinal still, would do his utmost to elect as his successor an enemy of the house of Pamphili. In this ambition, Cardinal Astalli had a soul mate.

By the time of Astalli's downfall, Cardinal Maidalchini was no longer a clueless boy. He had had seven years of education and training by some of the brightest men in the church. His association with French diplomats had given his manners a bit of Gallic polish. And though his intelligence would always glimmer feebly in the galaxy of brilliant minds adorning the papal court, he was certainly smart enough to know that Aunt Olimpia had used him vilely to serve her own purposes. The pope, too, had treated him poorly.

To thumb his nose at his aunt and the pope, Cardinal Maidalchini transferred some of his lucrative church pensions to the disgraced Cardinal Astalli so that he could live comfortably in exile. Anyone who was an enemy of Aunt Olimpia was Francesco Maidalchini's best friend.

It must have been with great relief that Romans celebrated the Carnival of 1654. For ten days they could forget papal intrigues, disgrace, and the pope's advancing age and be swept up in parades, feasts, and comedies. Camillo enjoyed this Carnival season greatly. His rival, Cardinal Astalli, was gone, his money and property were restored to the Pamphili family, and in the Palazzo Aldobrandini on the Corso, Camillo performed comedies with his servants almost every evening.

Camillo "takes the lead of the young lover," Giacinto Gigli wrote with disdain.[22] This was seen as ridiculous in a thirty-one-year-old. It is likely that Camillo's wife and mother finally agreed on one thing—that Camillo was adept at making a fool of himself.

On the first day of Lent, the pope went in regal cavalcade to the Church of Saint Sabina, then headed to the Tor de' Specchi Convent to visit Sister Agatha. But according to Gigli, when he realized he was going to pass by Cardinal Astalli's palace, he ordered his litter-bearers to go another way, "and he did this to avoid passing by the Astalli house."[23]

As the pope's strength continued to decline, Olimpia carefully examined the Sacred College to determine which members were her friends and which her enemies. She would need a strong faction within the conclave to ensure the election of a pontiff who would not harm her once he climbed upon the throne. Her most frightening opponent was Cardinal Pallotta, whom she had insulted in the street back in 1648, prompting him to call her a whore.

Cardinal Federico Sforza—whom she had exiled for suggesting that Cardinal Maidalchini should not open the holy door—was no friend of hers, either, and was always "saying very nasty things against her reputation."[24] The former datary, Cardinal Cecchini, knew that Olimpia was behind his disgrace. He would ally himself with the elderly Cardinal Vincenzo Maculano, a dear friend of the princess of Rossano's who hated Olimpia's meddling in Vatican affairs with particular venom. For reasons that were personal rather than political, Cardinals Astalli and Maidalchini would do their utmost to elect a voracious enemy of Olimpia's. Others who detested her as an interfering woman were Cardinals Fabrizio Savelli, Giovanni Lomellini, Lorenzo Imperiale, and Giberto Borromeo. That made ten died-in-the-wool enemies.

But if Olimpia had enemies in the Sacred College, she had powerful friends as well. There were three Barberini cardinals, who would do nothing to damage the house of Pamphili, to which they were now inextricably allied. The Barberinis could pull together a faction of cardinals created by Urban VIII and more recent creations who were on their side.

Also among her friends was Cardinal Francesco Cherubini, who had worked closely with Innocent for more than forty years, first as an auditor of the Rota, then in Naples, Spain, and Rome. Another supporter was Cardinal Benedetto Odescalchi, who, though a worthy churchman, had in 1645 reportedly obtained his cardinal's hat at the age of thirty-four when his rich brother, ambitious for family honor, bribed Olimpia with a silver dinner service. If that was indeed the case, it would prove an excellent bargain—in return for saucers and soup bowls Odescalchi would become Pope Innocent XI in 1676.

On her list of friends and enemies, Olimpia was uncertain where to place Cardinal Chigi. Clearly he disliked her involvement in Vatican affairs. But he had always been courteous to her, unlike many of the other cardinals. Given his horror of any taint of scandal to the church, would he be inclined to rake her over the coals if he became pope? Would a man of great rectitude drag down the family of the pope to whom he owed everything? She was not sure.

No matter where Chigi stood, it was clear that Olimpia needed more supporters to balance her enemies. Though the Sacred College had a limit of seventy members, at the moment it consisted of only sixty-three cardinals. Olimpia handed the pope a list of seven prelates for the next creation of cardinals.

The handsome Decio Azzolini would be amply rewarded for his invaluable espionage in the Astalli case. Well aware of which side his bread was buttered on, he vowed to work closely with Olimpia in conclave. Though the reason for his creation was, perhaps, not the most ethical, he brought multifaceted talents to the Sacred College. At thirty he was highly intelligent, hardworking, and cunning. He had received his doctorates in philosophy, theology, and law. He could maneuver behind the scenes, where most Vatican politics were crafted. But he was not without flaws. "His defects that over-rule him . . . ," Gregorio Leti scoffed, are "amours to all kinds of Ladies, both Virgins and Wives, he passing most of his time in caressing them, not regarding whether the Republique receives any advantage, or no."[25]

Olimpia promoted a relative on her mother's side, forty-year-old Carlo Gualterio of Orvieto, a consistorial lawyer. Leti had a poor opinion of Gualterio's abilities, as did the pope. "Innocent was really in his own mind averse from introducing persons of so small virtue as this and

Maldachino into the Sacred College, amongst so many Eminent persons, and so many great Princes," he explained. "If the qualities of a Maldachino and Gualterio were compar'd, Gualterio's though they are good for little or nothing, are yet less ridiculous than the former."[26] Leti noted that the pope did not keep Gualterio in the papal offices but immediately gave him a bishopric "only to send him packing from Rome, it going against the hair to see in the Consistories and publique meetings such a creature sitting amongst so many Cardinals of renoun."[27]

Ottavio Acquaviva, the governor of Viterbo during Innocent's magical visit the previous October, was given a hat as the pope had promised. For years Acquaviva had been an able governor of several papal territories, and he was a close friend of Olimpia's. Other members of this creation were not known to be blind supporters of Olimpia's, but considering Olimpia chose them, we can assume they were friendly enough and certainly were no enemies.

The oddest thing about the creation was the fact that the pope kept it secret from his secretary of state. Innocent knew that Chigi would adamantly oppose the creation of Olimpia's two favorites—Azzolini and Gualterio—though he thought highly of the others. It was a huge insult to Chigi that he was not informed until the list was officially released. He knew that Olimpia was behind the insult.

Another insult was in store. Olimpia begged the pope to replace Cardinal Chigi as secretary of state with that bright, handsome, young Cardinal Azzolini. But here she was stymied. Cardinal Pallavicino noted, "Those who were intimately informed were aware that the pope did not want to lose Cardinal Chigi; with his sterling reputation he could not be removed without great vituperation, and without great justification."[28]

To appease Olimpia, the pope agreed to speak to Cardinal Chigi only in the presence of Cardinal Azzolini, who would report back to her every word. Cardinal Azzolini began to act as if he were co–secretary of state, walking into the pope's offices throughout the day without inviting Cardinal Chigi as protocol required. Chigi sat alertly in his office, watching the comings and goings, and knew these daily slights were all due to Olimpia.

Cardinals who were also bishops were scheduled to spend a certain amount of time in their seats, administering the bishopric. Important cardinals—and certainly the secretary of state—were expected to ask for a postponement of their bishops' visits, which was automatically granted. Seeing his scheduled visit coming up, Chigi did not ask for a postponement. Perhaps he looked forward to leaving Vatican intrigues and Olimpia's malice for the relative calm of Nardo, a backwater in southern Italy. He sent a note to Innocent listing the men he had appointed to take care of his business during his absence. To Chigi's disappointment, the pope sent back a note postponing his bishop's visit.

It certainly was to Olimpia's disappointment that Chigi was not sent packing to Nardo to deal with priests' squabbles, villagers' complaints, and a leaking church roof. But by mid-1654, looking at the Sacred College, Olimpia could be pleased that she had diluted the power of her enemies and stacked it with as many supporters as she dared. When Innocent died, she would be ready.

22

Death of the Dove

*The last of all the Romans, fare thee well. It is impossible
that ever Rome should breed thy fellow.*

—William Shakespeare, *Julius Caesar*

THOUGH SHE WAS ONCE AGAIN amassing huge amounts of cash,
this did not give Olimpia the feeling of safety. An unfriendly
pope could seize her bank accounts and bonds, as Innocent
had done to the Barberinis and to Cardinal Astalli. And while one
could hide gold in walls and under the floors, this, too, could be discovered. It would be more difficult for the next pope to confiscate property,
especially if it was located outside Rome. The nobles bristled with anger
whenever the government tried to take an estate from a nobleman, realizing theirs could be next.

On April 26, 1654, Olimpia purchased at auction vast tracts of land,
including several castles in Umbria, for 265,000 scudi. It was a relatively
safe investment; if events forced her to remove herself even farther from
Rome than San Martino, she could retire as a feudal princess to her
lovely turreted castle of Alviano.

Soon after Olimpia bought her castles, a messenger galloped into the
papal palace bearing glorious news for the pope. Twenty-seven-year-old
Queen Christina of Sweden, who had been talking secretly to Jesuit

priests since 1651, was prepared to convert from Lutheranism to Catholicism. She would abdicate on June 6 in favor of her cousin, Charles X Gustav, and retire quietly until such time as her pensions and annuities were firmly fixed by the Swedish government. If she became a Catholic before receiving her financial settlement, it was feared that the horrified Lutheran government would make sure she never got a dime.

Her conversion was top secret, known only to the pope, Cardinal Chigi as secretary of state, and a handful of top Jesuits. Innocent must have waited with bated breath to see if the queen would, in fact, abdicate; she had discussed doing so before and had put it off. By July he would have received word that the abdication had taken place. The restless queen left her native land and traveled first to Hamburg, then to Brussels and Antwerp to await her financial settlement. Once the documents were signed, Christina would publicly convert and move to Rome.

In the seventeenth century, Sweden was a major European power. The conversion of its Lutheran monarch would be an absolute triumph for the Catholic Church and almost make up for the humiliating Treaty of Westphalia. Moreover, Christina's father, Gustav II Adolphus, had been one of the most dangerous heretics since Martin Luther; the warrior king had soundly trounced Catholic forces again and again during the Thirty Years' War, paying with his life in the 1632 Battle of Lützen. When Innocent could finally release the news, it would be the crowning glory of his papacy and make up for all the awful scandals.

Though Innocent was greatly cheered by Christina's abdication, his family problems continued. His three nephews—Camillo, Prince Ludovisi, and Prince Giustiniani—were at the moment devout supporters of Spain and were aghast that Innocent was finally planning to receive a Portuguese ambassador. They made a terrible ruckus, storming into the pope's offices at all hours in high dudgeon. Furious, the pope took away Camillo's remunerative position as supreme general of the Papal States and fired Prince Ludovisi from his position as general of the papal galleys. Then he exiled the bunch of them.

The papal brief decreeing these actions declared that the pope had been forced to take these measures because of his nephews' base ingratitude. A few weeks later, the indefatigable Sister Agatha trundled into the Quirinal holding hands with Camillo on one side and Prince Giustiniani on the other, and reconciled them with the pope for the sake of Christian charity. But Prince Ludovisi's Spanish dignity had been severely wounded. He refused to be reconciled and remained on his estates outside Rome in a huff.

The remainder of 1654 was fraught with strange occurrences. Locusts ruined much of the harvest. In May the Colosseum began to rumble and three and a half arches suddenly collapsed. In June fire raced through the neighborhood near the Barberini Palace, miraculously stopped in its tracks by an image of the Virgin on a suitcase maker's house. In August the heavens themselves seemed to proclaim the imminent death of the pope. Strange lights were seen in the Roman night sky, perhaps a rare southerly display of the Northern Lights. "They say that at night they see fires and splendors in the heavens and a procession of many lit torches and it seems there is an empty coffin," Giacinto Gigli wrote the first week of August.[1]

The flames of fear were further fanned by a solar eclipse on August 12 and a lunar one on August 27. Astronomers predicted that the eclipse of the sun would be the darkest in history, except for the one that occurred when Christ had died on the cross. Many Romans, fully expecting to die, went to church and gave confession that day, and stayed there for the length of the eclipse. If they died on sanctified earth, freshly confessed, perhaps God would forgive them their sins more readily.

Giacinto Gigli laughed at such superstitions. On August 12 he stayed home and dined with his family, candles and flints at the ready when darkness came. But it was "not the complete darkness that had been predicted. It was not too dark to read or write or do anything else." He did not have to light his candles. When the sun emerged fully after three hours of twilight, thousands poured out of the churches rejoicing.

But there was one person in Rome who did not rejoice. For millennia, an eclipse was thought to predict the death of a monarch or the end of an age. "There will be signs in sun, moon, and stars," Jesus said.[2] And indeed, the day after the eclipse the pope was wracked with diarrhea that nothing seemed to stanch. He could not perform any official functions or even leave the palace due to his constant need for a chamber pot.

When the pope felt well enough to inquire about the progress on the Church of Saint Agnes, he was furious to learn that during his illness work had stopped completely because the laborers had not been paid. Innocent angrily gave instructions to pay them every Saturday evening. He also called in the police to make sure they worked even on feast days; those who did not work would be rounded up and beaten. The church must be finished to receive the pope's bones, and he felt that death was coming on faster than the construction.

It was six-year-old Gianbattista Pamphili who spoke the words that the pope himself was afraid to utter. One day when the little boy was spending an hour alone with his great-uncle in the Quirinal, the pope asked him if he had seen the church being built. With the wide-eyed frankness of a child repeating what his parents had said, the boy replied, "I've seen it, but if you don't hurry up, you will never see it finished."[3]

Innocent was furious. "And who told you that?" he thundered. Knowing he had said something terribly wrong, Gianbattista clammed up. Seeing that his anger would get him nowhere, the pope led the boy into another room and gave him some candy. Then he repeated the question. But the child, realizing he was already in big trouble, refused to say another word. The pope slapped him hard on the face and told him to get out. He did not permit his grandnephew to visit him again.

On September 1 the pope was once more felled by severe diarrhea. He went to bed and stayed there for forty-five days straight. A new doctor, Matteo Parision, concocted a potion of coral dust specially designed to stop the diarrhea, which it did. The medicine, in fact, turned the pope's intestines into something akin to concrete. Violent enemas were required to unstop him, which gave him diarrhea again and caused him to sputter that he had been right all those years to mistrust doctors.

On October 15 Innocent sent word to Olimpia that he was feeling much better and would call on her at the Piazza Navona. Sprucing herself up for the visit, she went to her jewel box and found that many of her most valuable pieces were missing—a gold cross with a piece of the true cross that had been sent to her by the Holy Roman Emperor, a ring given to her by the grand duke of Tuscany, a crown of pearls, and a gold watch.

Olimpia was beside herself. Before he left the Quirinal, Innocent received an urgent note from her telling him of the theft. He arrived at the Pamphili Palace to find her in hysterics. For once the unflappable Olimpia was reduced to wretched sobs. The pope had brought with him thirty thousand pieces of gold as consolation for her loss, which comforted her somewhat.

As soon as the pope had himself carried back to the Quirinal, a rumor got out that he had died. A jeering crowd gathered in front of Olimpia's palace and hurled itself against her courtyard doors. Olimpia went onto the balcony above the mob and flung down several hundred of the gold pieces the pope had just given her. Satisfied, the crowd melted away.

But there was the jewel thief to deal with, and Olimpia was determined to find the culprit and punish him. She threw one of her pages in prison as well as a goldsmith who had recently appraised her jewels. The page was tortured for fourteen hours without confessing.

Then Olimpia received an audacious letter from the real thief. He informed her exactly when he had stolen the jewels and how he had opened her locked desk. Olimpia should be grateful to him, he added, because he had not taken everything from her, which he could have done had he been so inclined. He signed himself Felice Felicetti, a mocking and obvious alias, as it meant something like "the happy little happy one." Happy he might be, as he was one of the few people on earth ever to pull a fast one on Olimpia.

Ever since Innocent's debilitating bout with diarrhea in August, Olimpia had been in charge of his official audiences. Foreign ambassadors and high church officials who needed to speak with the pope were admitted only for brief discussions. Olimpia didn't want visitors to realize that Innocent's mind was wandering. Seated next to the pope's throne as he nodded off, made odd remarks, or began to dribble, she cut short the discussions with her usual obliging manner. The pope, she apologized, had slept poorly the night before. They must let him get some rest.

If the pope was too weak to get out of bed, visitors with urgent business were admitted into his chamber for a few minutes only. Olimpia, sitting in a chair next to the pope's bed and—if Gregorio Leti can be believed—holding his hand, would answer for him. When Innocent was too weak to give audiences at all, Camillo received the ambassadors in the cardinal nephew's apartments, as if he had resumed his old job.

Those last few months, as the pope slipped into decrepitude, Olimpia was more powerful than ever before. "At the palace one spoke only of Donna Olimpia," Leti declared. "One heard only her name ringing out, Donna Olimpia this and Donna Olimpia that. All letters were delivered to Donna Olimpia and Donna Olimpia read them. No one gave petitions to the pope anymore but only to Donna Olimpia who reported to him the contents. And she always received the same response from him, which was to do what she wanted."[4]

During the first part of December, rain soaked Rome in such quantities that many wondered if God was preparing another biblical deluge as punishment for their sins. The Tiber rose and flooded the Jewish ghetto, the area around the Pantheon, and the Piazza Navona. When the rain stopped and the skies cleared, the pope felt the need for fresh air. On the afternoon of December 14 he had himself carried in a litter to Olimpia's Ripagrande garden on the Tiber, where he sat on a bench with her. We don't know what they discussed as the sun started to set—perhaps politics, or family problems, or the good old times all those years and years ago.

As the shadows lengthened, the pope shivered. Night was coming. It was getting cold. He climbed into his litter. When it disappeared into the courtyard of the Quirinal, he would never again be seen alive by the Roman people. Back in the palace, Innocent began to rave.

Popular discontent, which trickled out harmlessly in the form of pasquinades when a pope was healthy, began to unleash itself in a torrent of rage when it became clear that he was dying. Grievances over bad bread, high taxes, and greedy papal relatives swelled into a tidal wave that flooded the city with riots, murders, and arson until the new pope was elected. Only when the cardinal camerlengo stood on the balcony of the Vatican and announced *"Habemus papam!"* did the mob lay aside cudgels, swords, and pistols and go back to work joyously.

Now, as the riots broke out, they focused on Olimpia. As a woman she was an easy target. With a straight face, Gregorio Leti stated that the rapacity of the Barberini nephews was acceptable, given the fact that they were men. "The Barberinis had certainly also been insatiable in heaping up gold and silver under the pontificate of their uncle," he wrote, but "we should consider that the Barberinis governed a church where they were supposed to remain due to the position of cardinal, which they had, but Donna Olimpia governed a church from which she had to be forced to leave and that far from peacefully, because she was a woman."[5]

Angry Romans stationed themselves outside Olimpia's palazzo during the day, throwing refuse at it and shouting insults. If they could have looked forward 140 years to revolutionary France, they might very well have borrowed the idea of cutting off Olimpia's head and affixing it to a pike. As it was, whenever the huge double doors to her courtyard opened and her carriage rolled out, they attacked it, crying, "Bread! Bread!" She had to fling them coins to prevent her carriage from being toppled.

Olimpia began to leave for the papal palace before sunrise and return at midnight, hiring public sedan-chair carriers rather than risk being seen in a coach bearing the Pamphili coat of arms. But popular outrage did not die down. Children ran through the streets singing songs about the pope's whore. Crowds continued to gather in front of her barricaded palazzo, yelling insults and making threats. Olimpia was extremely nervous that a mob would force its way into her house, sack it, and tear her limb from limb. She had the pope send out priests to the poor sections of town, distributing thousands of scudi in alms.

It would have been safer for Olimpia to retire to one of her country estates during the pope's final illness. No one would have bothered her in a feudal fortress in faraway Umbria. She could have breathed easily in Viterbo, where the citizens still puffed themselves up with pride in the town's greatest daughter. The inhabitants of San Martino, bursting with gratitude for all she had done for them, would have defended her palace with their lives. It was only in Rome where her life was in danger.

But Olimpia had three financial goals to fulfill before the pope died, and she had to be in the papal palace until his last moment to do so. The first goal was to sell as many offices as possible. Ambitious office-seekers knew that now was the time to get a cut-rate deal on prestigious positions. Leti noted that Olimpia was selling them for 50 percent of the usual rate.

Such last-minute negotiations were mutually beneficial to buyer and seller. The buyer knew he might never be able to purchase the position during the next pontificate; if the new pope turned out to be less corrupt, it would be impossible, and if he were more corrupt, it would be unaffordable. The transaction was also beneficial to Olimpia, who pretty soon would not be in a position to sell a Vatican office ever again. Bribes reportedly accompanied the cash payments. "On the Vatican stairs one saw only presents being carried up and never any carried down," Leti asserted.[6] Word got out that Olimpia earned a half million scudi the last ten days of the pope's life.

Olimpia's second goal was to remove everything of value in the papal apartments. Since the ninth century, it had been customary for a pope's servants to plunder his rooms as soon as he died, as a kind of final bonus from their boss. Over time, servants began to strip not only the papal palace bare but the papal corpse, as well. When Innocent III died in 1216, a visitor found the pope's corpse in a bare room, nearly naked and in an advanced state of decomposition. His servants had stripped off the precious vestments in which he had been dressed for burial.

When Sixtus IV died in 1484, his master of ceremonies, Johann Burchard, had a terrible time trying to provide the corpse with a shred of dignity. The pope's sacristan had stolen the bed and left the pope naked on the floor. "And indeed, despite my hunting from the sixth to the tenth hours," Burchard wrote, "I was unable to find either oil or handkerchief, or any sort of receptacle, in which to put the wine and water scented with herbs to wash the corpse; and not even socks or a clean shirt to dress it."[7] The tradition had continued down to Urban VIII's death in 1644 when his master of ceremonies couldn't even find a candle to place beside the body.

Olimpia was not about to let plunderers take any of Innocent's possessions. She ordered covered wagons to roll up to the courtyard of the Quirinal in the wee hours and had her servants carry down the fine tapestries, inlaid mahogany furniture, bed hangings, silverware, candlesticks—every single item of any value except the bed.

Olimpia's third goal was to steal the papal treasury. Usually the gold reserve of the Papal States was kept in the heavily fortified Castel Sant'Angelo. But in the event of the pope's illness or death, the guards would never allow her to simply walk off with the entire Vatican treasury. Somehow she had convinced the pope to take the gold out of Castel Sant'Angelo and hide it under his bed. This was a secret known only to Innocent—who had probably forgotten by this time—and Olimpia.

During the pope's last illness, every day Olimpia was quietly sneaking the gold out of his room. The public sedan-chair carriers took her into the pope's apartments shortly after dawn, left her chair there, and came back for her at midnight. Throughout the day, when the pope was asleep or raving, she would crawl under the bed, drag out one of the chests, and put as much gold as possible into sacks. These she would put inside the sedan chair. The porters began telling stories in taverns of how much heavier Donna Olimpia was to carry at night than she had been in the morning.

Olimpia would have liked to stay in the pope's bedchamber around the clock to keep her eye on the gold. Etiquette, however, demanded that she return home every night if only for a few hours; spies and journalists stood outside the Quirinal Palace and noted what time she left. She was deeply concerned that during her absence a servant or perhaps the doctor would peer under the bed and find the treasure chests. To prevent such an occurrence, when she left the Quirinal at midnight, she locked the pope in his bedroom alone. No matter how sick he was, no matter how urgently he needed water, a piece of bread, or a chamber pot, he would have to wait for assistance until she returned at sunrise the next morning.

Though the pope didn't know it, in Brussels on Christmas Eve, Queen Christina of Sweden was privately received into the Catholic Church, abjuring her Lutheran religion. She would convert publicly in the coming months. It was another tragedy of Innocent's reign that although the queen had converted under his pontificate, his successor would reap all the credit.

⁓

When Olimpia left the pope's bedroom periodically to allow his cardinal advisors in for an audience, she usually found Decio Azzolini waiting in the antechamber, and often Francesco Cherubini, the pope's auditor. These men greeted Olimpia with great courtesy. Oddly, the secretary of state, who should also have been waiting, was nowhere to be found, not even in his office. After a while, it occurred to Olimpia that Cardinal Chigi was *avoiding* her.

Indeed, her suspicion proved correct. Chigi's distaste for Olimpia had become so overpowering that he stationed a groom as a lookout; seeing Olimpia coming out of the bedchamber, the groom would race to Chigi's office crying that Olimpia was on her way. Chigi would quietly slip away to hide from her.

One day Olimpia instructed a butler to ask Cardinal Chigi what she had ever done to him to make him run away from her. She did not expect cardinals to bow on bended knee before her, she added, but why could Chigi not greet her once in the antechamber, as the other cardinals did?

Cardinal Chigi politely sent word that he could be of no service to her in the papal palace, where he had urgent work to do, and a sick pontiff to attend to, and was often on his knees imploring God's mercy for Innocent. But if she ever needed anything from him, she should let him know and he would gladly call on her at the Palazzo Pamphili—a polite way of saying women had no business walking in and out of the papal palace. To which Olimpia bellowed, "Thank God I don't need anything from him!"[8]

That would change. Soon.

⁓

There was an etiquette to seventeenth-century dying. The individual approaching earthly dissolution must summon relatives, friends, and even enemies to gather at his bedside for a rousing final speech. Even a life poorly lived could, to a certain extent, be redeemed by an edifying deathbed monologue decrying vice, groaning in repentance, and imploring forgiveness.

A pope, of course, had additional deathbed duties. According to the 1650 *Relatione della Corte di Roma*, the dying pontiff must call his cardinals to gather around him. He must ask their forgiveness for any wrongs he had done them during his reign, and must endeavor to right those wrongs if possible. He must then give his recommendations for his successor, names they were to ponder deeply in the coming conclave. Finally, he must ask them to pray for his soul.

Innocent's mind had been wandering his last several weeks. But now, just as his body was completely failing, he regained his mental clarity and knew what he had to do. Innocent told his majordomo, Monsignor Scotti, to summon Camillo to him, as well as the Ludovisis and Giustinianis. The monsignor first sent urgent word to Camillo and the princess of Rossano, who came immediately.

Giacinto Gigli wrote, "The pope asked pardon of the princess of Rossano for not having given her the satisfaction she desired, because he could have done better, and he prayed to God to console her with a new pope who would be more to her satisfaction. The princess did not reply." She was, evidently, still seething with anger at him for bringing Olimpia back and giving her all the power.

The princess of Rossano left the death chamber in silence. As she swept down the marble halls, she must have been surprised to see Olimpia at her side asking to have a word with her. Olimpia had decided that now was the time to drop her grudge against her daughter-in-law. Now the Pamphili family must close ranks to present a united front against all enemies.

Olimpia said that she was sorry about the misunderstandings of the past, but that among relatives "there is always some little thing." The princess replied angrily, "Between us there was never some little thing, but some very big things, and it was all the fault of Your Excellency, and how I will revenge myself for it!"[9] And with a swish of her train, she was gone.

Having cast her pearls before swine, Olimpia was livid. She stormed into the pope's bedroom and told him what the princess had just said to her. Dying though he was, he called Camillo back and angrily "ordered the Prince Pamphilio his nephew to render obedience to his mother Donna Olimpia, charging him to profess to her his gratitude with all respect and obsequiousness."[10]

Olimpia next chastised Monsignor Scotti for inviting the princess of Rossano to the deathbed when the pope had only called for Camillo. The majordomo replied that it had seemed the right thing to do and he did not have to obey *her*.

Olimpia's daughters arrived with their husbands and children. Having spoken to his family, Innocent called for his cardinals. He first sent messengers to two he had banished from his presence—Cardinal Cecchini, the former datary, and Cardinal Sforza, whom he had punished for speaking against Olimpia. Gigli recorded that Cardinals Cecchini and Sforza "came right away and the pope reconciled with them and took them by the hand and said many kind things."[11] The one banished cardinal he did not send for was Cardinal Astalli; still stewing about his betrayal, Innocent said that he had plenty of reasons to keep him in exile.

In the meantime, the pope told Camillo to summon all the other cardinals in Rome. Gigli gives a moving description of the pope's final meeting with the Sacred College. "In the dinner hour, they all came running with great haste," he wrote, "and the carriages went to Monte Cavallo and returned to pick up others with such speed that it seemed they were flying, and there was such a crowd of carriages that the piazza in front of the palazzo was full, and the courtyard and street of the four fountains up to the church of Saint Catherine of Siena . . . and all the cardinals were gathering in front of the pope's bed."

Gigli continued, "And he asked pardon of them if during his pontificate he had not given them the satisfaction that was required, saying that sometimes anger had made him do things he should not have done, and then he exhorted them to elect a pastor for the Holy Church who was good and better than he had ever been, and not to guard the interests of the crowns but to think only of the Holy Church."[12]

The pope then expressed his desire to make little Gianbattista Pamphili a cardinal. Though the pope had every right to do so, the cardinals knew that by making a six-year-old a prince of the church the pope would shame the Catholics and make all the heretics laugh. They talked him out of it.

"He said many kind things to all the cardinals and to each one of them he recommended with great sentiment Cardinals Cecchino and Sforza and their families. Almost all the cardinals left, and it was observed that Sforza left crying and Spada had a face as red as fire."[13]

On the morning of December 27, Dr. Matteo Parision suggested that Innocent fulfill the other requirement of papal death etiquette—the distribution of vacant benefices and pensions to cardinals of moderate means, as well as to deserving court prelates and his own household servants. Innocent called for his datary and gave him instructions.

That evening, seeing the worried looks on the doctors' faces, Cardinal Chigi asked them if the time might be right for the pope to receive the last rites, and they sadly nodded. Chigi called for the pope's private confessor, the Jesuit Father Giovanni Paolo Oliva. When told it was time, Innocent received the news calmly, according to Cardinal Pallavicino, and "with admirable readiness and tranquility disposed himself for the sacraments of penitence and the viaticum."[14]

The pope first confessed, whisking away the last cobwebs of sin clinging to the corners of his soul. Then he took the viaticum, his final Eucharist and last spiritual meal for the road. Father Oliva dipped his thumb in consecrated olive oil and anointed the pope's eyes, saying, "By this holy unction, and through his great mercy, may God indulge thee whatever sins thou hast committed by sight."[15] He then moved on to the pope's ears, lips, nostrils, hands, feet, and groin, asking God to forgive the sins committed through those body parts.

Olimpia had discreetly slipped away before the last rites, and Cardinal Chigi hoped that she had gone for good. At such a solemn moment he believed the dying pope should set his sights on God, not on his reputed mistress. Looking in the nooks and crannies of the papal apartments, Chigi could find no trace of Olimpia. Satisfied, he went downstairs to the papal kitchens.

The exhausted cardinal sat down to his meal. But before he could plunge a fork into his food, a servant came running up with the unwelcome news that Olimpia had tried to enter the pope's bedroom as Father Oliva was anointing him with holy oil. Chigi was furious. Another messenger raced up to him—this one from Cardinal Francesco Barberini—with the urgent request that he return to the pope's side immediately.

But Chigi refused to enter the pope's chamber as long as Olimpia was there. Only when he heard she had gone did he go back upstairs to visit the pope. When Chigi learned that Olimpia and her daughters had not left the palace but were stubbornly sitting in an antechamber, "he could not hold back his exclamations against this annoying occurrence."[16]

His anger was exacerbated when Signor Febei, the pope's master of ceremonies, told him that a delegation of honored persons had appeared at the foot of the Quirinal with a message of reproach for Chigi, whom they knew to be in charge of the deathbed. "The luster that the pope had acquired in the last preparations for death was stained when women came to recommend his soul," they said.[17]

Hearing that he was being blamed for Olimpia's presence, Cardinal Chigi burst into a tirade against her in front of Cardinal Antonio Barberini and several other cardinals, who exchanged meaningful looks. Now the Barberinis would never allow him to be elected the next pope. "But Chigi," wrote his biographer, "had no ambition, and therefore had no fear."[18]

When Olimpia finally left the Quirinal that night, she was in quite a quandary. She could hardly throw out all the priests and cardinals standing around the pope's bed and lock the doors behind them. She was forced to go home and leave them all there with the remaining two beautiful chests of gold under the bed. As she left the Quirinal, she was overheard to sigh, "So soon, so soon."[19] Believing that the pope would die that very night and her house might be sacked and burned, she did not return to the Piazza Navona but stayed with Olimpiuccia at the Palace of the Four Fountains.

The cardinals were horrified that Olimpia had locked the pope up alone at night, but since he hadn't complained, they hadn't been sure how to proceed. But once the pope had been given last rites, the cardinals circled their wagons around him. The following morning at dawn, as Olimpia cheerfully marched into the pope's chambers hoping to find the gold still under his bed, what she found instead was Father Oliva blocking the door.

This authoritative figure, holding a crucifix as if Olimpia were a vampire, prevented her from entering the pope's bedroom. When she started to argue, he actually put his hands on her shoulders and turned her around, saying she had no further business there. Fluttering, chirping about her concern for the pope, she hovered in the antechamber, ready to swoop in at a moment's notice and get her gold.

During the pope's last days, countless courtiers hoped to take advantage of his weakened state and request favors—pardons, indulgences, judicial judgments, and offices. But Cardinal Chigi stationed himself by the bedroom door like a dragon, telling favor seekers the pope's thoughts must wend their way heavenward and not be tied to earth by earthly matters. Petitioners must save their requests for the next pope.

But Chigi could not prevent a scene on December 29 when Dr. Parision, who two days earlier had persuaded the pope to distribute various vacancies, discovered that the pope had granted *him* no money. The datary had told him that now there was nothing left. Thinking the doctor was checking on the pope's health, Chigi allowed him into the death chamber, where Parision threw a temper tantrum, yelling that the pope owed him money.

"Hearing this, the pope began to whimper and called the datary, and asked him if there was nothing to dispense. He replied that there was a pension for 50 scudi and a benefice in Calabria for 160, and the pope ordered that these be given to the doctor."[20] And now the Vatican bank was empty.

On December 30 the pope lost the power of speech and couldn't eat for two days. His legs had swollen horribly, and one of them burst, "and out of it issued much water, and his delirium left and he came back to himself."[21]

During Innocent's final illness, "Chigi stood by with assistance and orations, paying scarcely enough time to the needs of nature. The sadness, the stench, the application of his mind, and the long unease of kneeling in prayer gave him great bodily suffering, but he showed no fatigue of spirit."[22]

The first week of January 1655, Gigli gave a gripping account of the pope's final days. "The pope, against the opinions of the doctors and everyone else, was still alive," he wrote, "and was in such bad shape that many had compassion for him. . . . The palace was so empty that there wasn't even a bowl or a spoon to give the pope a bit of soup, and it was necessary to send someone to buy a bowl and spoon. And in bed the pope was under a vile blanket like the kind used by a poor person in a hospital. He had only the shirt on his back, all the other ones were gone. And there was only one candlestick of brass, which soon disappeared, and was replaced by one of wood."[23]

Before Innocent expired, he made two requests. He asked the cardinals to choose a worthy successor—he highly recommended Cardinal Chigi—and he begged his family to stop fighting. Between seven and eight on the morning of Thursday, January 7, 1655, Pope Innocent X died. Cardinal Chigi closed his eyes.

Cardinal Pallavicino wrote, "Innocent X finally died on January 7, 1655 with the assistance of Cardinal Chigi, having reigned ten years, three months and 23 days, pretty much feared, not at all loved, not without some glory and happiness in foreign affairs, but ingloriously and miserably for the continuation of tragedies or comedies in his domestic life."[24]

Gregorio Leti summed up Innocent as follows: "This was truly a pope worthy of the best memory if his sister-in-law had not lost him his reputation. . . . Instead, one was constrained to bury him in eternal oblivion so as not to mention his sister-in-law."[25] He wrote, "His suffering Donna Olimpia to rule all, his exaltation and abasing of his adopted nephew Astalli, his banishing and recalling Don Camillo his nephew, his persecuting and reingratiating with the Barberinis, in a word, his changing will and judgment every moment, and his inconstancy in everything, would have embroiled any government whatsoever, and much more the papal government, which is naturally full of confusion."[26]

Giacinto Gigli was disturbed by a pamphlet published shortly after the pope's death that denied a bit too vigorously that Innocent had died "with his eyes open and his face frightened and in great poverty, having been robbed of everything." He added, "Unfortunately, it was all true, and it would have been better if this pamphlet had not furnished such information to the heretics."[27]

It had been more than forty-two years since Gianbattista Pamphili, a thirty-eight-year-old monsignor living in a dilapidated row house, had met Olimpia Maidalchini, the twenty-one-year-old bride of his brother. Ambitious and energetic, with flashing dark eyes and an obliging smile, she had swept into his house and completely changed the trajectory of his life. And now that relationship, which had shocked first Rome and then the world, was over.

The pope's master of ceremonies and his assistants removed his body from the bed and carried it to another room to be washed with cold water and herbs. His barber shaved his head and beard. His body was washed again with white wine warmed with fragrant herbs, then oiled with balsam.

The moment the body was gone and the room was empty, Olimpia ran in. She fell to her knees, scrambled under the bed, and dragged out both chests of gold. She had brought with her several burly servants to carry them quickly out of the palace and load them into her carriage. As the chests were being removed from the pope's bedroom, papal servants raced inside to despoil what was left of the bed.

Olimpia galloped home, hoping no one would attack her carriage once the bells started tolling their news of the pope's death. Once her carriage raced into the courtyard of the Piazza Navona palace, she barred the doors behind her.

Olimpia was now locked inside a prison from which she dared not emerge. Her greatest fear all those years of what men would do to her had come true, but they had not done it to her. Tragically, she had done it to herself.

23

Unforgiveness

Heaven has no rage like love to hatred turned,
Nor hell a fury like a woman scorned.

—William Congreve

WHEN INNOCENT'S SERVANTS RETURNED his body to the bed, they found that the sheets had been stolen. They were forced to wrap him in a coarse wool blanket on the bare mattress while they went to find decent clothes to bury him in.

The bell ringers of Saint Peter's Basilica began pulling on the ropes; the huge bells started to sway and, after several strenuous tugs, to ring. Churches across the city had been waiting for this signal for two weeks, and their bell ringers ran into their belfries and began tugging on the ropes. Soon all the church bells of Rome rang out, not the joyous pealing of a papal election or a jubilee but the slow thudding tones that signified the death of a pope.

As soon as the bells tolled, Pasquino, his friend Marforio, and the other talking statues of Rome were covered head to toe with nasty poems. A shocked Gigli noted, "There were published many verses and pasquinades that cursed the dead pope and Donna Olimpia, composed by ingenious but unwise people. Some were too biting, and some were impious, modeled on the Lord's Prayer . . . and other prayers. Innocent was cursed as having satisfied the greed of a very greedy and infamous woman, and many other unworthy things."[1]

The heretic cousin of King Charles X Gustav of Sweden happened to be in Rome and started collecting pasquinades to take back home. He ripped them off the talking statues and let the poets of Rome know he would pay gold for the most outrageous ones. Perhaps hearing of Queen Christina's secret conversion, he intended to show Lutherans how Catholics revered their recently deceased pontiff. But as usual the worst ones were reserved for Olimpia.

Pasquino roared:

Finished is the lust
Of this old bag
Of the Piazza Navona
Let's call the hangman!
Finished is the lust
The pastor is dead
The cow remains with us
Let's have a feast of her
Let's take out her heart!
The pastor is dead.[2]

Because of the vicious verses, "many were imprisoned who had written such compositions, and four copyists were sent to the galleys, and others led to the prisons of the Inquisition of the Holy Office."[3]

At eight o'clock on the evening of January 7, a sad torchlight procession wound its way from the Quirinal Palace down to Saint Peter's Basilica. The pope's body lay on a mattress covered in red silk, on a cart pulled by black horses. Innocent's master of ceremonies had rifled through the palace and found some decent clothing that had not been stolen. The corpse was dressed in red vestments and a red cap, white leather gloves, red velvet shoes embroidered with gold crosses, and a pallium, or white stole, that had rested overnight on the tomb of Saint Peter. A silk funeral cloth was placed over the body for the journey, leaving only the feet visible, and around these were wound a thin piece of gauze.

The funeral procession was led by cavalry officers in full armor, followed by two cannon, each pulled by three horses. The pope's grooms and other servants followed carrying torches. Directly in front of the hearse marched Camillo, Prince Ludovisi, and Prince Giustiniani. Next came the open hearse surrounded by a choir chanting psalms. The Swiss Guard, fully armed, marched just behind the hearse, followed by light infantry and three more pieces of artillery.

As the torchlight procession wound its mournful way toward the basilica, thunder rang out and it began to spit rain. Several minutes later, lightning ripped across the sky and a deluge drenched the mourners. They bolted for cover, every man for himself, leaving the dead pope in the middle of the street. When the rain subsided, the procession clumsily re-formed and brought the soaking-wet body to Saint Peter's, where it was placed on the high altar, under Gian Lorenzo Bernini's great baldachino, and over the tomb of the saint.

The morning of January 8 the pope's body was exposed for the traditional three-day viewing. On January 10 the funeral was held. Olimpia is not mentioned in any reports of the funeral, and it seems that she stayed home, locked up with her gold, fearful of being torn to bits by the mob. Gregorio Leti assured his readers that she remained inside during the entire vacant See. "One certainly feared that during the vacant See the furor of the people would be carried to pillage her palace," he explained, "and to insult her person so that she did not appear in public."[4]

At the funeral the cardinals appeared in their traditional fuchsia-colored mourning garb, with no lace rochets over their gowns. But Cardinal Astalli, who had jumped onto his horse the moment he heard of the pope's death, appeared wearing bright red robes loaded with lace. He had not forgiven Innocent for having disgraced and exiled him. During the funeral Mass, he refused to kneel, cross himself, or pray.

As shocking as Cardinal Astalli's behavior was, there was a much greater problem at hand. The cardinals did not know what to do with the body after the funeral. It was customary for a pope's family—who always milked the Vatican treasury dry—to at least pay for his funeral.

Usually the family brought to Saint Peter's the two traditional caskets of mahogany and bronze, into which the body was reverently placed. The family then had the corpse carried to its final resting place.

It was known that Innocent had wanted to be buried in the Church of Saint Agnes. Though it was still a far cry from finished, he could have been interred in a temporary tomb until the church was completed and a suitable monument sculpted. But the cardinals had not received any word from the Pamphilis as to where the pope was to be taken. Worse, when the funeral broke up, the pope was still lying under the baldachino on a slab, and no coffins had arrived. The cardinals and other officials stood around the body awkwardly, not knowing what to do with it. Had the pope's family, in their grief, forgotten the coffins?

Naturally, church officials thought first of Olimpia. The pope had made her a princess, given her several towns, castles, palaces, and art collections, and she had raked in countless millions of gold scudi in pensions and bribes. A delegation was dispatched to the Piazza Navona to call on her. They respectfully asked her when the coffins would arrive at Saint Peter's and where she wanted to entomb the body.

But now it was payback time. Looking at the expectant faces of the burial committee, Olimpia politely replied that she could not afford to pay for the coffins, being, as she said, only "a poor widow."[5] They should ask her son, Prince Camillo, who was the male head of the Pamphili family and the pope's heir. She was, after all, just a woman.

Perplexed by this response, the burial committee called on Camillo in his immense palace on the Corso. Having heard their request, Camillo stated that his mother had always received much more money from the pope than he ever had, and even if he was the heir, *she* should pay for the burial. They should go back to his mother and ask her again.

Back they went to Olimpia. Seated in her palatial rooms crammed with valuable furniture, she twittered apologies that she could not afford to bury the pope, and they must once again ask Camillo. Back they went to Camillo, who replied that if his mother was too niggardly to bury the pope, the expenses should be borne by the Vatican treasury, certainly not by *him*.

Realizing they were getting nowhere, the burial committee next called on Princes Ludovisi and Giustiniani, who had both profited handsomely as papal nephews. These worthy gentlemen declared that if Olimpia and Camillo were too grasping to pay for the coffins, they didn't see why *they,* being more distant relatives, should have to bear the expense.

The body was, by now, beginning to stink. It couldn't be left to decompose in the middle of Saint Peter's Basilica in full view of the faithful. Something had to be done with it.

It was suggested that the body could be stored in a room of Saint Peter's sacristy, an area adjoining the church where the holy vestments, chalices, prayer books, and other sacred objects were kept. But the sacristans objected to having a dead body, even a papal one, in their place of work. The chief sacristan said the body should be taken to Donna Olimpia, who was, after all, responsible for it. Yet the burial committee was reluctant to cart the blackened corpse on a plank through the streets of Rome and knock on Olimpia's door. Surely her servants would not allow it to be brought inside, and they couldn't very well leave it at her doorstep, where people would steal the clothes and leave the pope lying naked in the Piazza Navona.

An anonymous contemporary manuscript reported the dilemma. "They did not give a sepulcher to the majestic cadaver because no one had prepared the coffin to put him in, and finding that no one wanted to pay for it, Monsignor Sacristan, in the presence of all those princes, attested to having many times insisted and warned Donna Olimpia. . . . So it is no marvel that the following day there multiplied the imprecations of avarice against this family, which abhorred the cost of 100 scudi for custody of the bones of that pope who had eviscerated the treasury of the church to enrich each one of them, leaving it with a debt of 8 million."[6]

The Basilica of Saint Peter's required constant maintenance, and the custodians had a workroom in the basement where carpenters kept their saws, hammers, and other tools. It was decided to carry the pope on a plank of wood into this janitor's closet. There they would leave him until someone in the family called for him.

On January 13, the sixth day after the pope's death, Marchese Riccardi, ambassador of the grand duke of Tuscany, wrote, "The Pope has not yet been buried, because no one can be found who will pay for it. Don Camillo says that he never received anything from His Beatitude and suggests we contact Donna Olimpia, who she says she is not the heir. And so His Beatitude remains there in a corner."[7]

Cardinal Pallavicino wrote that the pope's body was placed "in a vile room subjected to the injuries of humidity and filthy animals because no one wanted to pay for burial. This is a great lesson for popes as to what affection they can expect from their relatives for whom they risk conscience and honor."[8]

And indeed, there was a problem with filthy animals. Rats scuttled out of the woodwork to nibble on the pope. The carpenters who used the room were horrified that the papal corpse was becoming a feast for vermin. One of them kept a candle lit at the head of the corpse, while another stood guard with a two-by-four, ready to whack any adventurous rodents.

And this was Olimpia's ultimate revenge. Innocent had thrown her to the dogs. Now she was throwing him to the rats.

Finally Monsignor Scotti, the pope's majordomo, couldn't stand it anymore and bought a cheap wooden coffin with his own money. Monsignor Segni, a former majordomo whom Innocent had unjustly fired, came forward with his savings of five scudi to pay for grave diggers to inter him in an unmarked grave in the basement of the basilica.

On his coronation day, October 4, 1644, Innocent's master of ceremonies had held out burning flax in front of him to remind him of his mortality, saying, "*Pater sancte, sic transit gloria mundi.*" Holy Father, thus passes the glory of the world.

For years Cardinal Maidalchini had been chomping at the bit to show openly his disrespect of his aunt, and now the time had come. As camerlengo during the vacant See, Antonio Barberini temporarily held papal power. Maidalchini convinced Antonio to return to Cardinal Astalli all the benefices the pope had unjustly taken away from him, benefices that Olimpia in the meantime had bestowed on her friends.

Olimpia was furious to hear what her nephew had done and decided to get back at him. He had returned to Rome during the pope's final illness and was living in a palace owned by Olimpia near the Trevi Fountain, which he had filled with his furniture. Olimpia ordered him to leave the palace and take every stick of his furniture with him. The cardinal informed Olimpia that it was a vacant See, and there was no reason, when another pope was created, that she should tell anyone what to do. But vacant See or not, the palace he had been living in was her property. Cardinal Maidalchini had to move. He stored his tables and chairs at the palace of Prince Ludovisi.

Huffing and puffing on his way out, Cardinal Maidalchini "was so mad at his aunt that he said publicly that when there was a new pope the first favor he would ask was this, that she be punished severely."[9]

It was a sign of things to come.

24

Pope Alexander VII

Malice sucks up the greater part
of her own venom, and poisons herself.

—Michel de Montaigne

EVERY FAMILY OF A FRESHLY deceased pope teetered on the brink of ruin at the conclave, and the Pamphilis were no exception. Everything Olimpia had worked for over the previous forty years could be snatched from her in an instant if the wrong cardinal were elected pope.

On January 18, 1655, sixty-six cardinals solemnly entered the Sistine Chapel. In his last creation of 1654, Innocent had filled the college up to its limit of seventy. In the meantime one had died, two elderly cardinals living in Spain didn't want to budge, and Cardinal Mazarin remained in Paris running the country for the king and sleeping with the queen mother.

In the Sistine Chapel, Cardinal Francesco Barberini, as vice deacon of the Sacred College, started off the proceedings by singing the Mass of the Holy Spirit. The conclave remained open for foreign ambassadors throughout that day and all the next. For several months, the Spanish and French ambassadors had been sitting on instructions from their kings as to which cardinals to exclude in conclave and which to support.

Now that the conclave was about to begin, their meetings with the cardinals were so urgent, and lasted so long, that the conclave was not officially sealed until after 2 A.M. on January 20, when the Spanish ambassador almost had to be physically ejected.

This conclave was unusual because there was no cardinal nephew of the freshly deceased pope to rally the allies of his uncle into an impressive faction. Cardinal Francesco Barberini, cardinal nephew of the pope-before-last, gathered many of his uncle's creations around him. Cardinal Carlo de' Medici was in charge of the Spanish clique, and Rinaldo d'Este, supported by Cardinal Antonio Barberini, was in charge of the French partisans.

But there was a fourth group, consisting of ten "young" cardinals— most in their forties—many of whom had been promoted in Innocent's last creation the year before. Led by Olimpia's supporter Decio Azzolini, they formed a faction independent of France or Spain. They called themselves "the Flying Squadron," or *squadrone volante,* a term for an auxiliary military unit that was deployed with great speed to that spot on the battlefield where its assistance was most urgently needed. The Flying Squadron vowed to elect the best pontiff possible, regardless of French or Spanish interests. Most of its members were close friends of Olimpia's.

Before the conclave began, Olimpia and Cardinal Azzolini had decided their first choice would be Cardinal Giulio Sacchetti, a mild-mannered and scholarly prelate of exactly the right age—sixty-eight— who would do no harm to the Pamphilis. Sacchetti, who would have won in 1644 had Spain not excluded him, was also the favorite of Cardinal Mazarin and therefore had many of the French votes.

On January 21 the first scrutiny was held. Cardinal Sacchetti received thirty-nine votes, only five fewer than was required to become pope. Several other candidates, including Cardinal Chigi, were proposed but received far less support.

On January 22, the seventy-three-year-old Cardinal Pierluigi Carafa received forty-one votes. Later that day he began to feel ill, along with Cardinals Pallotta, Caffarelli, Rapaccioli, and Ceva. Only two days after the doors were sealed, an epidemic had broken out, which was unusual for a winter conclave.

Tensions already ran high. That evening, Giacinto Gigli noted, Cardinals Astalli and Azzolini fell into a violent shouting match and ended up slapping each other. Given the fact that Astalli was Olimpia's vicious enemy, and Azzolini her staunchest supporter, it is likely that the subject of the argument was Olimpia.

On January 24, the rumor raced across Rome that Cardinal Francesco Barberini would become pope. Olimpia, Maffeo, and Olimpiuccia received the news with glad hearts, and the bookies changed their odds to favor him. But it proved untrue. Other *papabili* were proposed and ditched for various reasons. Cardinal Spada was highly regarded but not well liked. Spain supported the election of Cardinal Francesco Rapaccioli, but at forty-six, he would likely have such a long reign that none of the older cardinals would get a chance to be pope.

Cardinal Ulderico Carpegna was pushed by France if Sacchetti fell out of the running. At fifty-nine he was almost of suitable age. But his greatest disadvantage was his young, vivacious sister-in-law, who was best friends with the princess of Rossano and despised Olimpia. The sister-in-law had not only numerous poor relatives but insatiable ambition. The cardinals shuddered to think of another Olimpia storming into the Vatican and telling them all what to do.

Cardinal Cecchini, the former datary, was well respected but suffered from family disadvantages, which also reminded the cardinals of Innocent. "He lets himself be dominated by his sister-in-law more than is usual," the Venetian ambassador wrote. "His only nephew has very little in the way of a brain, and of the countless other relatives, none is very smart."[1]

On January 27 the conclave was opened briefly to allow the just-arrived ambassador of the Holy Roman Emperor to meet with cardinals. In the meantime word leaked out that Cardinal Maidalchini was denouncing his aunt Olimpia in dramatic speeches.

On January 30, the Florentine envoy Riccardi reported, "Signora Donna Olimpia said that she is more mortified by the way Maidalchini is acting, having allied himself with her enemies, than of the death of the pope and of the many pasquinades and writings against her. . . . I hear that in conclave he continues to speak ill of his aunt, as he used to do outside."[2] Gregorio Leti asserted that Cardinal Maidalchini "declaimed with more noise than all the others against his aunt, although everyone laughed at all his discourses because no one esteemed him much in the conclave."[3]

It was generally believed that the Holy Spirit was listening intently to every word the cardinals said in conclave. But Olimpia had no fear that God was paying any attention at all to her wayward nephew. "The braying of an ass," she said, shaking her head, "is not heard as far as heaven."[4]

As the conclave slowly ground forward in the chilly chambers, the bored cardinals began to wheel and deal—often literally, playing cards for small sums when the boredom became unbearable. At night they met secretly in one another's cells to encourage votes for a favorite candidate, and they sent and received messages to the outside world concealed in their food platters.

To relieve the unending tedium, the young cardinals played "carnivalesque pranks" on the older ones, according to Cardinal Spada, who spotted them sneaking around at night holding candles.[5] The young cardinals discovered that Cardinal Carafa had built a secret door in his cell, which opened up on a passage behind the cell of Cardinal de' Medici, leader of the Spanish faction. This enabled Carafa's *conclavistas* to eavesdrop on the plotting and planning of the Spaniards. Cardinal Maidalchini, who was by now twenty-five, wrapped himself in a sheet and tiptoed through the passage. He planned to enter Cardinal Carafa's cell through the hidden door and shriek like a ghost. But Carafa was a light sleeper and had become aware of strange sounds in the passageway. Though he lay still in bed, he was, in fact, wide awake. When the white form moved past him, he whacked it hard with the cane he kept in his bed. Sobbing in pain, Cardinal Maidalchini staggered out the way he had come.

On February 9, Cardinal Giangiacomo Trivulzio left the conclave feverish with a rash on his face. Three days later Cardinal Vincenzo Maculano became ill but refused to leave the conclave because he wanted to become pope. On February 15, Cardinal Carafa, who had also refused to leave despite a fever, died in his cell.

Olimpia was hell-bent on preventing her enemies from becoming pope. There were three in particular who for years had poured forth vitriolic monologues about her greed, lust for power, and sexual immorality: Giovan Battista Pallotta, Federico Sforza, and Vincenzo Maculano. She was also terrified of the former datary, Domenico Cecchini; though he seemed to hold no grudge against her for alienating him from the pope, payback time could come the moment he plopped the triple tiara on his head. Whenever these four cardinals were nominated, Cardinal Francesco Barberini shot them down on Olimpia's behalf.

But it was much easier to prevent the election of an enemy than to secure the election of a friend. Scrutinies were held every day for Cardinal Sacchetti, who, though he was popular with the other cardinals, had been vetoed again by Spain, who still thought him too friendly with Mazarin. Those cardinals with pensions from the king of Spain, and from his ally the duke of Tuscany, were reluctant to vote for him.

Olimpia was receiving conclave news every day from a spy, Francesco Ravizza, the *conclavista* of her cousin Cardinal Gualterio. But on March 3, Ravizza was taken to jail in the Castel Sant'Angelo. Gigli wrote, "It was discovered that in a certain place he sent letters which were carried to Donna Olimpia and which told her all the negotiations of the conclave about the creation of a new pope."[6]

One of the letters found was from Olimpia with instructions to prevent the election of her old enemy, Cardinal Maculano, at all costs. The discovery of Olimpia's spy sparked heated debate. Some cardinals declared it was bad enough that a woman had elected one pope; they would do everything in their power to prevent her from electing a second.

On March 4 news leaked out of the conclave that Cardinal Bernardino Spada had become delirious with fever and believed that he had been elected pope. He began making loud plans for his coronation and issuing proclamations. Cardinal Spada was forcibly removed from the conclave and taken to his palace to recuperate. But many believed that he had feigned his illness so that he could meet with the French ambassador and Olimpia for urgent negotiations.

Cardinal Spada knew that France had given instructions to Cardinal d'Este to exclude Fabio Chigi if voting seemed to be going in his favor. During Chigi's tenure as papal nuncio to Germany, he had often remarked that the French in general, and Cardinal Mazarin in particular, were strangely opposed to making peace. Mazarin, with his long memory and delicate ego, refused to see this man as pope.

Yet more and more cardinals were talking about Chigi. True, he was too young at fifty-six and had been a cardinal for only three years, but his incorruptible standards, his international legal and diplomatic experience, and his irreproachable way of life might make up for those defects. The members of the Flying Squadron, in fact, supposing that Sacchetti might very well fail because of Spanish opposition, were holding Chigi in reserve as their backup candidate.

Given the increasing support for Chigi, it was urgent that Spada meet with the French ambassador and Olimpia to see if Chigi would be acceptable to them. For in this election there were not the usual two great powers with veto privileges—France and Spain. There were now three: France, Spain, and Olimpia. Before Spada returned to the conclave, he was seen entering the Palazzo Pamphili.

Gregorio Leti harrumphed, "Because, to tell the truth, putting aside the interests of Spain and France, everything centered on either the protection or the ruin of Donna Olimpia. To see her ruined, the cardinals who were her enemies would have given their vote not only to an unworthy candidate, but to the devil himself as long as he was her enemy. And, on the other side, those who were looking out for her interests would have had no difficulty in rejecting a saint if he had shown the least aversion to this woman."[7]

Certainly Chigi would not have been Olimpia's preference. Yet if Chigi were elected, would he go out of his way to punish the family of the pope who had plucked him from obscurity and made him a cardinal? Would he hold a grudge against her for all those prickling insults? Olimpia was not sure. But the Flying Squadron and the Barberini cardinals, all loyal supporters of Olimpia, believed that the selfless Chigi would not be one to exact his pound of flesh.

Ironically, even Olimpia's worst enemies—Cardinals Sforza, Pallotta, and Maculano—were supportive of Chigi. With his strict sense of justice, they believed he could not ignore her depradations of the papal treasury and would prosecute her to the fullest extent of the law.

Evidently Olimpia grudgingly gave her approval to vote for Chigi if Sacchetti could not be elected. Now there was only Mazarin to deal with. Cardinal Antonio Barberini wrote a letter urging Mazarin to withdraw his secret exclusion of Chigi. He was the best candidate for the job, Antonio explained, and harbored no resentment toward France. Besides, the conclave had been going on for two months. Rome was in chaos, and Milan had gone to war with Modena. A new pontiff was urgently needed to establish law and order at home and negotiate peace abroad.

Cardinal Sacchetti also sent a letter, generously stepping aside as the French candidate, imploring Mazarin to allow the election of the worthy Chigi for the good of Christendom. If the Most Christian King did not withdraw the exclusion, the cardinals, more of whom were falling sick, might elect Chigi anyway, and for the second time in a row the new pope would bear no love for France, which had tried to prevent his election.

The cardinals' letters were posted with special messengers who rode like the wind. Finally, the verdict was delivered. Mazarin and the sixteen-year-old Louis XIV would be absolutely delighted if the virtuous Cardinal Chigi became pope.

With France, Spain, and Olimpia accepting the choice, on the evening of April 6 the cardinals went to Chigi's cell to give him the glorious news that on the following morning he would become pope. When the cardinals knocked on his cell door they found that he was taking a nap. Chigi listened to their news with no change of expression and then asked them to reconsider their choice. He had many obvious imperfections, he said, and quite a few they didn't even know about. But this self-deprecating statement only increased the cardinals' eagerness to elect him.

The following day, Cardinal Chigi received a unanimous vote, except for his own, which he gave to Sacchetti. When the last vote was taken out of the chalice and read, Chigi fell to his knees and prayed. With tears streaming down his face, he stood and announced that he would be called Alexander VII to honor the twelfth-century Alexander III, who had come from Chigi's hometown of Siena.

Four days after the election, on the night of April 11, a great storm hammered Rome. Amidst the rain, hail, thunder, and lightning, a carriage and four headless horses of fire were seen racing through the city. When they arrived at Olimpia's garden on the Tiber, they sprang into an abyss and disappeared. Word got out that in this carriage was the soul of Olimpia Maidalchini Pamphili.

While Rome's nobility were calling on the new pontiff to congratulate him, Olimpia was afraid to do so. Would he physically eject her from the papal palace? He had always said he didn't want women running around the Vatican. She sent Camillo to render homage in the name of the Pamphilis and sound out the pope's response. Alexander accepted Camillo's wishes with dignity but not great warmth. This worried Olimpia.

Next she sent her majordomo to present her congratulations. Alexander merely told him to thank his mistress for her good wishes. And that was it. Not satisfied, Olimpia sent Cardinal Azzolini to let the pope know how delighted she was at his exaltation. Once more, the pope replied with alarming coolness. Shortly thereafter, he granted the vegetable vendors' request to reopen the Piazza Navona for their Wednesday market. Then he ordered Olimpia to clear out the construction material for the Church of Saint Agnes, which was littering the piazza.

Olimpia was, for once, uncertain what to do. How would she win over this new pope, who held her very life in his hands? Projecting her own tastes onto Alexander, she completely misjudged him. She sent her majordomo to the papal palace with two enormous gold vases and the wish that she could come and kiss his feet. But the Holy Father sent her majordomo back with the vases and a message that she was to keep herself far removed from the Vatican as it was not a place for women.

Pope Alexander immediately embarked on numerous acts of goodwill and charity. He sold his silverware for six thousand scudi and gave the money to the poor. He ordered his butler to replenish the papal cupboards with plates and bowls of earthenware on which was painted the skull and crossbones. He personally paid the debts of up to thirty scudi of every debtor in prison, thereby permitting many of them to go home. He sent cartloads of white bread to the prisoners who remained.

The new pope ordered a lead coffin in which he planned to be buried and placed it in his bedroom. Alexander hoped that by having the image of his death before him, he would always remain a humble servant of God no matter how rich and powerful he was. But there was perhaps a second reason for this macabre décor—to make sure his body would never end up on a plank of wood in a janitor's closet.

On April 18, 1655, Pope Alexander VII was crowned in Saint Peter's to the great joy of the Roman people. Though the Pamphilis had emptied the papal treasury completely, in the three months since Innocent's death taxes and contributions from all over the Catholic world had been rolling in. Alexander, however, tried to cut expenses where he could. For his May 9 *possesso* he wanted no pompous cavalcade with trumpeters, drummers, and gaily caparisoned horses. He wanted to go on foot, and humbly.

But, Giacinto Gigli noted, "he was persuaded to consider that the cavalcade gave joy to the people and that the money of the Apostolic Camera went to the Romans to make clothes for the officials and pages, and other pious works, because this money went to poor gentlemen and paid poor artists and so the pope let his decision be changed and allowed the cavalcade at a moderate cost."[8]

Olimpia was not in town for the coronation. She had left some time earlier for a visit to San Martino. Perhaps she vacated Rome because she was afraid of attracting any attention to herself. Or maybe she simply couldn't bear to watch the crowning of a new pope, clear proof that her power was gone forever. It must have been soothing for her to escape the insults, noise, filth, and fear of Rome for her country palace. There the air was sweet and fresh, and in April the hills were alive with the color of emeralds.

One day shortly before the coronation, as she sat in her sitting room overlooking her little town and the medieval church, Olimpia was handed a letter bearing, for a change, extremely good news. On April 12 her beloved granddaughter, Olimpiuccia, had given birth to her first child, a month before her fourteenth birthday. The labor was fairly easy, and both mother and daughter were healthy. She called her baby Costanza, after her aunt and the little girl Olimpia had lost as a young woman in Viterbo.

Upon hearing the news of Cardinal Chigi's election, Romans tried to learn more about his family, whom they expected to come racing to Rome. Did he have nephews of the appropriate age to become cardinals and help him run the church? What secular relatives would be made princes and princesses? How greedy were they? Were there any women in the family who might try to take over?

The new pope had a brother in Siena, sixty-year-old Mario Chigi, a man whose means were far more modest than his ambitions. When a messenger raced to Siena with the glorious news of the election, Mario was beside himself with joy. He had just won the billion-dollar papal lottery. Leti observed, "Without so much as putting on new clothes, as his Wife would have had him, he caused a Horse to be saddled, and with two servants took his journey towards Rome, having first receiv'd from one and the other a number of submissive complements, not without the title of Excellence."[9]

But Pope Alexander VII refused to embark on the slippery slope of nepotism and sent a messenger to Siena. Before Mario had ridden many miles from town, he was met by "a gentleman from the Pope with Letters to him, in which his Holiness did most strictly command that neither he, nor any of his Relations should stir from Siena to go towards Rome, under pain of incurring their brothers indignation for ever."[10]

Reading the letter, "poor Don Mario was as if he had been thunderstruck. . . . All his blood retired to his heart, and left him pale, like a Ghost, though otherwise corpulent enough. . . . He resolv'd to return by night to Siena, being asham'd to enter the City by day."[11]

Mario returned home dejected, but his spirits rose when the duke of Tuscany sent him expensive gifts, and when cardinals and princes lavished him with congratulations and silverware. He was elated when the Venetian senate sent him a solemn embassy with letters patent declaring him a nobleman of the most serene republic. But when the French ambassador was ready to set out from Rome to congratulate Mario personally, word came from the pope to stay put.

Undeterred, Mario wrote to Monsignor Scotti, the pope's majordomo, expressing his heartfelt desire to come to Rome and kiss the pope's feet. If, however, he was not allowed to do so, he would like Monsignor Scotti to kiss the pope's feet for him. When Monsignor Scotti read the letter to Alexander, the pontiff proffered his foot and said, "Kiss it."[12]

Several cardinals asked the pope when he would bring his family to Rome and which positions they would fill. Alexander replied that Fabio Chigi had had relatives, but Alexander VII had no family other than the church. If anyone cared to look in the baptismal register of Siena, he would find no person by the name of Alexander VII. The cardinals were shocked at this reply and warned him that if he didn't show affection for his family, he would look pusillanimous, selfish, and cheap. How could a pope be expected to take care of tens of millions of Christians if he wasn't willing to take care of his own family?

The ambassadors were also greatly displeased at the new pontiff's stubborn opposition to nepotism. The Venetian ambassador stated that the republic would not send the traditional *obbedienza* parade if it would be dishonored by a lack of papal nephews. Besides, he said, the more a pope spent on his family, the less money he would have to make war on other Italian kingdoms and stir up trouble.

The Spanish ambassador explained to the pope that papal relatives were required to take part in the ostentatious cavalcade for the presentation of the *chinea* each June 28. If no papal relatives marched in the parade, Spain would be dishonored and would not give the white horse at all. Spain insisted on having a cardinal nephew with whom the ambassador could negotiate, as the pope was often too busy. Moreover, Spain was ready to hand over rich possessions in the kingdom of Naples to the pope's secular nephews, along with fat pensions and noble Spanish brides with generous dowries. How could they influence the new pope if they were not permitted to bestow their munificence on his nephews?

France and Tuscany found themselves in a similar perplexity. Knowing that the new pontiff was incorruptible, Cardinal Mazarin and the Medici duke had amassed large amounts of gold to bribe the pope's family members to influence him. Now they had sacks of gold sitting around their embassies collecting dust, and they didn't know what to do with them.

The relatives of past popes—the Ludovisis, Borgheses, Barberinis, and Pamphilis—were aghast that this new incorrupt system made them all look like crooks. If Alexander refused to enrich his relatives at the expense of the poor, what did that say about *them*? Plus, if the new pope didn't bring his relatives to Rome, there would be no marriages to bind them all together so he couldn't throw them in jail.

Many prelates looking to rise in the church were disturbed at having to do so on merit alone; bribes and personal connections were so much easier. Minor courtiers hoping to serve in the households of papal relatives as secretaries, masters of ceremonies, and gentlemen-in-waiting were furious at the lack of new job openings.

Rome's service industries were also unhappy at the shocking news that the pope was keeping his family firmly in Siena. Papal relatives bought carriages, furniture, jewels, and clothing; they hired servants, architects, painters, sculptors, and gardeners. They threw elaborate parties to the delight of bakers, butchers, and grocers. They held opera performances to the benefit of actors, singers, and stage-set designers. Nepotism provided an important boost to the Roman economy.

But Cardinal Girolamo Grimaldi, for one, was delighted that the new pope was opposed to nepotism. He had done some calculations and found that there were only enough church properties left for two more papal families to steal.

25

The Two Queens of Rome

Alas! I am a woman, friendless, hopeless!

—Queen Katharine of Aragon, Shakespeare, *Henry VIII*

T HE MOMENT THE NEW PONTIFF climbed onto the throne of Saint Peter there was much for him to do. There was the bread supply to deal with—lately the *pagnotta* had become darker and smaller and people were beginning to complain. There was the new conflict between Milan and Modena, and the war between France and Spain, which had been limping along for decades. There was heresy to suppress and missionary work to support across the globe. But in his first weeks in office, Alexander found that much of his time was spent on requests from citizens and church officials to punish Olimpia.

In fact, within weeks of his election Alexander received hundreds of petitions and letters denouncing her. Many of the claims were, no doubt, true; others were probably false, as everyone jumped on the bandwagon attacking the *woman* who had dared run the Vatican. Had she been a corrupt papal brother-in-law, popular resentment would have been tempered by admiration.

As it was, letters poured in to the pope every day accusing Olimpia of having sold offices to unworthy candidates, let violent criminals out of jail for a price, and hoarded grain while the Roman poor starved. Some even claimed that she had used butter knives to pry gems out of altar-pieces in Saint Peter's and other churches, and that she had stuffed the Holy Communion chalices into her pockets.

"The pope did not have a very good opinion of this woman," Gregorio Leti observed. "Yet he did not yet wish her to feel his violent anger, nor to suspect any resentment. The pope wanted to do everything with great prudence and good conduct."[1]

As former secretary of state, Alexander was well versed in diplomacy and international law, but he had had very little to do with the datary. In his first weeks in office, he threw himself into learning how the datary was run and looking over financial reports. With each audit brought to him from Innocent's reign, Alexander became more and more disturbed at how much money had gone missing and how much of it seemed to have landed in Olimpia's lap.

Leti affirmed, "The pope found every day, whether in church affairs or political affairs, so many crimes and embezzlements that he had not only reason to mistreat her, but to put her in prison for life. He found only deceipt and corruption in the datary. He discovered only simony practiced by this woman, all the posts having been sold, the finances exhausted, and a thousand other things. . . . The pope had too much zeal for the good of the state to see so many crimes without at the same time building up resentment."[2]

It is likely that Alexander would have preferred to let the matter drop. Innocent had made him cardinal and secretary of state, putting him on the road to the papacy. He did not want to terrorize Innocent's family or bring scandal to the church. Yet the scope of the embezzlement was such that Alexander, a stickler for justice, felt he could not turn a blind eye. If Olimpia was indeed guilty, she must be forced to disgorge her ill-gotten gains and return them to the Vatican treasury, where they could be used for the poor.

The pope called all his cardinals to consistory, where he announced that he would launch an investigation into Olimpia's financial transactions under Innocent. He said the proceedings should be undertaken with prudence and caution, as he did not want to provoke new scandals but to clean up old ones. He appointed Cardinal Gualterio, a friend and relative of Olimpia's, to devise a list of all property that she had owned before Gianbattista became pope, and all property that he had accumulated as pope and had legally given to his family. This property would not be subject to investigation and possible confiscation.

The pope appointed a group of cardinals to look into the charges against Olimpia and collect irrefutable proof of wrongdoing if such was available. Within a few weeks, they had amassed damning evidence, thousands of pages of incriminating documents, as well as dozens of witnesses willing to testify against her. Word on the street was that Olimpia would lose her head, just like Mascambruno and Beatrice Cenci, and have it impaled on a spear on the Castel Sant'Angelo Bridge.

Olimpia's Vatican friends kept her well informed of the investigation against her. Having returned to Rome, she must have been absolutely terrified. While her Piazza Navona palace had turned into a prison from which she had rarely, if ever, emerged since Innocent's death, she certainly didn't want to trade its comforts for a real cell with bars on the windows. That would have been much like a convent, but even worse.

Olimpia instructed Camillo to visit the pope again and ask him not to believe the slander being spread about by her enemies. She had entire confidence, Camillo said, in the goodness and justice of such a pope. But Alexander merely replied that Camillo should tell his mother that the pope would see justice done. Olimpia could not have found this reply very soothing.

Olimpia next conferred with Cardinal Francesco Barberini, who was highly respected by the pope, and begged him to speak to Alexander personally. After the cardinal finished his speech imploring the pope's mercy, Alexander coolly replied, "We will be more merciful towards Donna Olimpia than she was to your family."

"We pardoned her," the cardinal reminded him.

"That was to your profit," the pope retorted. "For us, such a pardon would only damage our conscience."[3]

The commissioners, questioning the keepers of the Castel Sant'Angelo treasury, learned that on Innocent's orders several chests of gold had been taken from the treasury to the Quirinal Palace. The gold had mysteriously disappeared. But sedan-chair carriers who had taken Olimpia to and from the Quirinal during Innocent's last days told how much heavier Olimpia's chair was at night than it had been in the morning.

The papal tax collector, Marchese Carlo Maria Lanci, who had held his position since 1639, testified that every year since Innocent became pope he had turned over 32 million scudi to the treasury and had dropped off another 5 million at the Palazzo Pamphili. From 1647 to 1650, he had also given 3 million a year to Cardinal Maidalchini at Olimpia's insistence. Much of this money had come from the tax on salt and bread that particularly inconvenienced the poor.

When the investigators had lined up the main charges against Olimpia, Alexander sent her a list of accusations and demanded that she respond. She must give an accounting of the money she had taken from the church treasury, which she had used as her personal bank account. She must come forward with the names of all individuals who had bought their church offices from her, and the amounts they had paid.

Furthermore, Olimpia must make restitution for all bribes she had received from criminals to let them out of jail. She must give an accounting of the grain that she had sent out of the country. She must account for all the taxes on foodstuffs that had gone into her hands instead of church coffers. And she must return immediately all jewels that she had pried out of church altarpieces and swiped from the papal palace.

Olimpia's written response was short and clear. As monarch of the Papal States, Innocent had been legally entitled to do whatever he wanted with church property. He had given her access to church funds, had permitted her to keep a portion of the tax on food, and had allowed her to sell some offices. She added that this was nothing extraordinary, as for centuries almost all popes had done the same thing with their relatives.

Olimpia's defense was, to a great extent, true. If Innocent had known and approved of all of her dealings, they would have been legal. But obtaining money secretly and without the pope's blessing would have been illegal. Alexander's investigators had the difficult job of determining which transactions the dead pope had approved of and which he had not known about.

It remains unclear how much Innocent knew about Olimpia's shady dealings. Though blatant nepotism had become part of church tradition, Innocent himself had been honest and thrifty. He had loved the church and had compassion for the poor. Just how much money would he have allowed her to keep? Her replacement of the honest Cecchini in the datary with the corrupt Mascambruno was proof that Innocent would not have approved of all her graft, and she was forced to hide at least some of it from him.

But there was another tricky legal question. Innocent had exiled Olimpia from the Vatican, discovered the extent of her corruption, and then invited her back and pardoned her. Was that, in effect, papal permission to keep all the money she had taken?

After a fair trial in which Olimpia would be given lawyers and every means of defending herself, the pope wanted her to make a full restitution of money determined to be illegally obtained. The investigative committee of cardinals held debates about how much of the Pamphili family wealth and property should be sequestered until a verdict was rendered.

Now the entire family felt threatened. Prince Ludovisi took the opportunity to visit Spain. The rest of the family met periodically at the Piazza Navona palace to devise a strategy. The princess of Rossano felt that Olimpia would be better off leaving Rome under the old adage "Out of sight, out of mind." She could pretend her health required her to take the country air at one of her estates, or she could go on a religious pilgrimage somewhere.

But Camillo thought a hasty exit would make Olimpia look guilty. He reportedly advised his mother, "Madam, only a crazy person would flee his house before it burned. Stay in Rome and seek no other retreat. Take care of yourself, and we will take care of the rest."[4] But Olimpia must have been worried about leaving her fate in the hands of her bungling son.

The decision whether to stay or leave was made for her. One day she received word from the pope telling her to leave Rome within three days. Camillo raced to the Vatican for an audience with the pope, hoping to change his mind. But Alexander sent word that he would not see

Camillo until Olimpia had left Rome. On July 22, 1655, she rattled out of the city gate incognito and traveled to her palace at San Martino. The same day, the pope gave orders for witnesses against her to begin giving testimony in a court of law.

The next day, Camillo raced back to the Vatican and asked for another audience now that his mother had left town. When he saw Alexander, Camillo told him that punishing Olimpia would scandalize the heretics, who would laugh at proof that the former pope had given his relatives money and power. Alexander replied that heretics would be more scandalized to see wickedness left unpunished rather than justice served, "and that it would be good if the relatives rendered an accounting to the pope while waiting for him to render an accounting to God."[5]

On October 21 the pope learned that the despite his earlier instructions to Olimpia to clear the construction material out of the Piazza Navona, it was still littered with heaps of marble stones, planks of wood, and barrels of lime. He sent her notice of a large fine along with the threat of more fines if she did not comply.

But Olimpia had no place to put the building materials, as construction was not moving forward; Borromini felt the foundations built by the Rainaldis would not bear the weight he wanted to add. Stewing in exile, Olimpia was hardly in a position to badger the builders to get back to work. She gave the job to Camillo, along with the expense, as he was now the male head of the Pamphili family. She was, after all, only a woman.

Five months after the former queen of Rome trundled out in disgrace, a new queen of Rome was arriving in triumph. The most successful conversion of a heretic had taken place; on November 3, Queen Christina of Sweden had publicly abjured her Lutheran faith and converted to Catholicism in a ceremony held in Innsbruck. On the afternoon of December 23, she entered Rome through the Porta del Popolo in a carriage designed by Gian Lorenzo Bernini. The pope had restored the gate in honor of the occasion with an inscription that read TO COMMEMORATE A HAPPY AND BLESSED ARRIVAL 1655.

All of Rome took a holiday to see the queen. Tapestries hung from windows and balconies. The procession was led by Rome's nobility—gentlemen on horseback and ladies in carriages. Camillo Pamphili continued to wear mourning for the uncle he had refused to bury, perhaps to remind the world that he had been the papal nephew. His black velvet suit was studded with precious diamonds valued at 100,000 scudi. Sewn onto his black hat were several enormous diamonds shining in the winter sun. Riding behind him was the princess of Rossano, also in black, shimmering in gemstones said to be worth seven times as much as her husband's. The couple was accompanied by numerous pages in expensive black livery.

Behind them came the pope's guards, and then the queen herself, riding sidesaddle as women were supposed to, and not astride, as many spectators had hoped. She wore a simple gray dress embroidered with a bit of gold, a black shawl, a plain black hat, and no jewels. Many Romans were disappointed that she looked so normal. They had heard strange things about her.

Giacinto Gigli took a good look at her. "Many say that the queen is certainly a hermaphrodite," he noted, "but professes to be a woman. She is rather short, with a big forehead, big and lively eyes, an aquiline nose, a small mouth, the voice of a man, the movement and gestures of a man. . . . They say she rides like a man . . . and doesn't ride so much as fly."[6]

When Christina was born in 1626, the Swedish people knew that a twenty-one-gun salute would be sounded for the birth of a princess and a one-hundred-gun salute for the birth of a prince. At the twenty-second salute, the populace went wild with joy. But oddly, the guns stopped firing after thirty salutes. In 1965 archeologists, poking around in her coffin in Saint Peter's Basilica, hoped to find evidence of the queen's gender(s) but remained confused.

Christina's hermaphroditic tendencies were one reason for her abdication. She was romantically attracted to women, and the thought of marriage and childbearing appalled her. Whenever her ladies-in-waiting got pregnant, she called them "cows" and refused to see them until after they had been delivered. Yet as queen, Christina was expected to marry and have children. Her aversion to marriage, however, does not explain her conversion to Catholicism. After all, she could have abdicated, remained Lutheran, and lived at the Swedish court as a member of the royal family honored for her years of service and her renowned scholarship.

Christina's free spirit felt stifled by the colorless Lutheran religion and was drawn to the incense, drama, and music of the Roman Church. She spoke eleven languages, ancient and modern, discoursed on the philosophy of Plato and Aristotle, eagerly followed scientific advances and encouraged the arts. The flamboyant queen had read much about former popes—the Borgia orgies; the Medici feasts with dwarves, clowns, and jugglers; and the intellectual, artistic, and scientific fecundity of Rome. Ruling socially over this rollicking world, she imagined, would be much more fun than ruling as monarch over the stiff prudes of Sweden.

Unfortunately, Christina was mistaken in her image of Roman life. The freewheeling early-sixteenth-century papal court was a far cry from the priggish Vatican after the Council of Trent. Seventeenth-century Rome was almost as strict—at least on the surface—as uptight Stockholm. Fascinated as she was by science, Christina was disappointed to find that ever since the Galileo trial of 1633, many top scientists had left Italy and scientific academies had closed their doors for fear of being hauled up before the Inquisition as heretics.

One of the greatest art patrons of her time, the queen was horrified upon moving into the Palazzo Farnese to see magnificent classical nude statues in her palace and gardens defaced by metal bras and underpants and ridiculous fig leaves. She insisted they be removed. The pope, for his part, did not want the fig leaves and metal underpants removed. They had been put there for a purpose. Nudity, even in great art, was no longer appropriate. He insisted the queen put them back on her statues. She refused.

Those who had enjoyed Olimpia's rowdy Carnival performances found a speedy replacement in Christina's "lascivious and sinful comedies" held in her palazzo, which numerous cardinals attended.[7] Invariably the audience included Camillo and the princess of Rossano, who became one of Christina's best friends. The pope was not amused.

Alexander was further dismayed that the queen tromped around the Vatican wearing thick men's boots and men's clothes. The Bible, he pointed out, instructed Christians to wear only those clothes appropriate for their own gender. Christina must stop dressing like a man. The queen, in this instance at least, complied with the pope's request. She started appearing at Vatican receptions wearing gowns so low-cut her nipples popped out.

Initially, church officials thought that the most proper thing for Christina to do in Rome, considering that she was an unmarried female, was to enter a convent, either as a nun or simply to retire from the world. But though Christina visited convents often—mainly to ogle the nuns—she said that she would rather *marry* than become a nun. Then she surprised all Rome by having a passionate love affair with a man. The pope felt her choice was most unfortunate; it was Olimpia's protégé Cardinal Decio Azzolini.

Olimpia had been exiled from Rome some five months before Christina's arrival. The old queen of Rome, who had clawed her way to the top, never met the new queen of Rome, who had been born at the pinnacle and gracefully slid down of her own free will. The one hoped that in her exile from Rome the scandal of her life would be forgotten, while the other hoped to foment as much scandal as possible for the sheer fun of it. Yet it is fascinating to speculate on a meeting between the two women. We can picture the queen marching into Olimpia's palazzo one day in her thick boots and men's breeches, flopping down on a chair with legs spread wide, and gulping wine. We can picture Olimpia, in her virtuous black silk, letting slip a hearty guffaw.

When Christina was snubbed by a haughty Roman noblewoman who refused to accompany her down the stairs after a visit, the feisty former queen grabbed her hostess by the hands and dragged her down kicking and screaming. Olimpia, who had been snubbed herself in her early years in Rome, would have approved.

Though they had few, if any, similar interests, and completely different backgrounds, these two remarkable women had one striking characteristic in common—despite the oppressive misogyny of their world, they had both completely taken charge of their lives and not allowed men to dictate to them. They lived exactly as they wished to—no matter how loudly the men squawked. It is possible that Christina and Olimpia would have truly liked each other.

On January 17, 1656, Sister Agatha Pamphili died at the age of eighty-six. Camillo wrote Olimpia, "Yesterday morning the signora Sister Agatha rendered her spirit to God with such exemplary resignation that we cannot doubt that she is enjoying eternal glory."[8] Indeed, if any member of the Pamphili family ever passed Go in purgatory and flew directly to heaven, it must have been Agatha. For decades she had done all she could to instill the Catholic virtue of forgiveness in her wayward relatives. Now she could finally rest, leaving them to their fractious selves.

There was no rest for Olimpiuccia, a bride at twelve and mother at thirteen. With her grandmother exiled from Rome, the girl felt terribly alone. Her husband and in-laws used her as a brood mare, and neither could she find comfort with girlfriends. According to the French ambassador, "The noblewomen of Rome concluded that the princess wasn't very smart, basing this judgment on the aversion she had to sleeping with her husband."[9]

Her letters make it clear that Olimpiuccia lacked her grandmother's intelligence. Whereas Olimpia expressed herself well with a clear and lovely handwriting, Olimpiuccia would scrawl ungrammatical missives for the rest of her life. Despite all the tutors Olimpia had brought in for her granddaughter, Olimpiuccia remained barely literate.

January 31, 1656. Signora Grandmother, my most illustrious heart, don't forget me. Most illustrious, consider that I am alone also I don't have anyone that does anything for me my mother has other daughters to think about if Your Excellency doesn't think about me I don't have anyone to think about me. My Signora Grandmother, I have been pregnant since July.

This pregnancy, evidently, resulted in a miscarriage or stillbirth. Nothing more was ever heard of it.

"Don't forget me," Olimpiuccia repeated, "and I humbly kiss you."[10]

26

The Scourge of God

Like as the waves make towards the pebbled shore,
so do our minutes hasten to their end.

—William Shakespeare

WHILE QUEEN CHRISTINA DELIGHTED ROME with her scandal, and the trial against Olimpia ground forward, Olimpia flitted among her many castles and palaces. She spent much of her time in her Nini town house in Viterbo. Perhaps she enjoyed reliving those few happy years with the cheerful young man she had married at seventeen. Then life had been a banquet of mouthwatering possibilities. Now, after all those possibilities had become reality, the taste had become oddly bitter.

In Rome, Alexander VII was having his own change of heart. After a year of fighting against nepotistic traditions, the pope's resolve began to crack under the pressure. In April 1656, Alexander asked his cardinals whether he should invite his relatives to Rome and give them church and governmental positions or if, given the cost, he should break the tradition. The cardinals almost unanimously agreed that it was unseemly for him to keep his family in poverty in Siena. The Jesuit Father Oliva, one of the most respected churchmen of his time and the pope's private confessor, solemnly stated, "The Pope would have committed a sin if he had not called to him his nephews."[1]

The pope sent word to his brother Mario and two nephews to join him. Mario, who had worked in an administrative post in Tuscany, was made governor of Rome, governor of Castel Sant'Angelo, and general of the holy Church. Gregorio Leti scoffed, "Was it not a fine sight to see Don Mario, who had never worn a sword in his life, declared Generalissimo of the Holy Church?"[2]

In the same vein, Alexander's nephew Flavio, a hard-drinking womanizer, took holy orders in preparation to become the cardinal nephew. The pope decided that his other nephew, Agostino, would be the secular member of the family and was appointed general of the guards. Alexander took the precaution of moving the whole clan into the Vatican Palace so he could keep an eye on them.

Olimpia must have been relieved to hear that the incorruptible pope had caved in to the clamorous requests to bring his family to Rome. Perhaps he was not so incorruptible after all, and if that were the case, he would not be in such a hurry to point the finger at *her.*

In May, word would have reached Olimpia that the first cases of bubonic plague had been confirmed in Naples. Plague had raged across Europe every generation or so since it first struck in the Black Death of 1348, when a merchant ship from the Orient docked in Venice and unloaded its cargo of destruction.

The first European exposure to the bacterium was so deadly that some people were reported to fall down dead in the street in the middle of a conversation before they felt any symptoms. An estimated 40 percent of Europe's population died in the pandemic, and epidemics flared up every thirty years or so in different parts of the continent. While smallpox and measles offered lifelong immunity to survivors, those who outlived the plague were not so fortunate. Immunity lasted at least a year or two—the length of most epidemics—but decreased over time. When the next epidemic washed over a community decades later, those who had survived the plague could catch it again. No one was safe, and for this reason plague was more feared than war, famine, flood, or fire. Whenever the word *plague* was mentioned, people would cross themselves and say, "God deliver us from it."

Fortunately, Italy had by far the most modern health facilities in Europe. The traveling Englishman John Evelyn was greatly impressed when he toured Rome's Christ Hospital in 1645; London had nothing like it. "The Infirmitory where the sick lay was paved with various colour'd marbles, and the walls hung with noble pieces," he gushed. "The beds are very faire. . . . The organs are very fine, and frequently play'd on to recreate the people in paine. . . . Under the portico the sick may walk out and take the ayre. . . . At the end of the long corridore is an apothecary's shop, fair and very well stor'd. . . . Indeed 'tis one of the most pious and worthy foundations I ever saw."[3]

Though Italy boasted the most educated doctors and cleanest hospitals, it was difficult for physicians to cure illnesses when they had no idea what caused them. Plague was thought to be induced by "miasmas," or poisonous air. The atoms of miasma were believed to be stickier than normal atoms and would cling to clothing, furnishings, skin, and hair. When a person or animal inhaled the miasmas or absorbed them through the pores of the skin, the venomous atoms would poison the body, causing illness and, in at least half the cases, death. Doctors noted that the epidemic festered in dirty places, and assumed that filth exuded the corrupt, plague-inducing miasmas.

To combat plague, city officials cleaned up the sources of corrupt air—plugged sewers, overflowing outhouses, and dirty straw in homes and stables. Filthy areas were aired out, swept, washed with soap and water, doused with vinegar, smoked with sulfur, and covered with lime. Dirty walls were whitewashed. Grungy mattresses were burned, and when the poor objected to losing their mattresses and started to hide them from inspectors, the government bought them new ones. Such measures promoting basic cleanliness often helped keep down incidents of plague, thereby confirming the doctors' theory of miasmas.

In the 1630 plague epidemic of northern Italy, French physicians invented an anti-miasma suit for doctors to treat victims without fear of infection. A certain Dr. Pona of Verona agreed to try out the suit, which he described as "a long robe of thin, waxed cloth. The robe had to be hooded and the doctors had to visit the patients with the head covered and wearing spectacles."[4] The beaklike nose of the sinister costume was filled with perfumes, herbs, and vinegar to filter the miasmas out of the air the doctor breathed. Gloves protected the hands. Oddly, the costumes worked. Doctors who wore it rarely caught the plague even though they worked amongst the most virulent contagion, once again confirming the miasma theory.

But the plague doctor's costume was unbearably hot most of the year and made it awkward to examine patients. Some physicians refused to wear it. When the Neapolitan plague hit Genoa in 1656, Father Antero Maria da San Bonaventure complained, "The waxed robe in a pesthouse is good only to protect one from the fleas which cannot nest in it."[5]

And that, of course, was the real cause of the plague, though no one knew it. The fleas. A part of everyday life in the seventeenth century, fleas carried the plague bacillus we call *Yersinia pestis*. The bacillus, lodged in the flea's stomach, prevented feeding, and the infected flea threw up its lunch—including the *Yersinia pestis*—into the wound it had made on its human host. Once in the wound, the bacillus raced to the nearest lymph nodes and spread like wildfire. A single flea bite could bring death.

Fleas nested in dirty mattresses, piles of refuse, filthy barns, and unwashed bodies. By cleaning up the filth, people were also getting rid of plague-infected fleas. One scientist, the German Jesuit priest Athanasius Kircher (1602–1680), almost hit upon the real cause of plague but never managed to connect the dots. When examining the blood of plague victims under an early microscope, Kircher was shocked to find "little worms" wriggling around in it.[6] And he left it at that. Fleas were never even considered, and it wasn't until 1894 that they were found to be the cause.

In the spring of 1656, plague spread quickly in Naples, which unlike the rest of Italy had no measures in place to tackle an epidemic. Given the squalid conditions of some 300,000 people living cheek by jowl, infection raced through the city. Soon 2,000 people a day were dying.

Hearing of the epidemic in Naples, on May 20 the Roman government closed its ports to all traffic from the stricken city. Only five of Rome's twelve gates remained open, and here soldiers and doctors carefully examined visitors and animals entering the city. Those who were dripping with feverish sweat, staggering in pain, and covered with black boils were not allowed to enter. But in June a Neapolitan fisherman made it into Rome, where, feeling ill, he went to the Hospital of Saint John. Within hours black boils appeared, and within days he died. No one knew how many Romans the sick fisherman had infected with his miasmas. Plague had hit Rome.

The Roman authorities immediately sequestered large buildings located away from the bulk of the population in which to immure plague victims, keeping them separated from those who remained healthy. Called lazarettos after Lazarus, whom Jesus had raised from the dead, each hospital had hundreds of beds and a staff of doctors and nurses to attend to them. One lazaretto was for the ill and dying; another for those thought to be recovering; and a third for travelers waiting outside the gates of Rome for a health certificate before they were permitted to enter. Although the incubation period of bubonic plague is only three to six days, seventeenth-century doctors insisted on a quarantine of twenty-two days, just to be sure.

Two lazarettos were outside the city of Rome and another was on an island in the Tiber, a convent requisitioned from nuns. In the lazarettos, doctors fortified the sick with meat and eggs, along with special concoctions of hot chickpea juice. The most important step to save the sick was to pop the buboes—black abscesses the size of lemons or oranges that formed in the armpits and groins of the victims and contained foul-smelling seedlike structures. If the buboes could be popped and their poisonous contents extracted from the body, the victim stood a good chance of recuperating. If they did not reach a head, and the poison remained, the victim usually died.

Doctors believed that causing the patient to sweat would make the buboes form a head; patients were covered with hot blankets and seated next to raging fires. If the buboes remained unpoppable, doctors placed over them hot glass suction cups usually used for bleeding, or daubed them with roasted white onion. And if that didn't work, a skilled physician could try to cut them out, though the bone-shattering pain of such an operation without anesthesia and the resulting infection often carried off an already weakened patient.

Doctors, their assistants, and courageous volunteers were each given a certain number of houses to visit once a week to check on the health of their inhabitants. At the slightest sign of illness an individual would be taken on a cart to the lazaretto. Many people, believing they were merely getting a cold, refused to enter the contagious miasmas of the plague hospital where, if they didn't have plague already, they would surely catch it. Their relatives tried to hide them in the basement behind wine barrels or in the thatched roof over the attic, but the doctors, aware of these tricks, usually plucked them out and carted them off. It was especially unfortunate when entire families were dragged away; sometimes upon their return they found their houses cleaned out by robbers.

Those houses from which a resident had been taken to a lazaretto were boarded up on the ground floor to prevent the other inhabitants—who were not yet showing symptoms but might also be infected—from wandering about town. Volunteers trolled the streets in donkey carts, dispensing food to baskets lowered from upstairs windows. Those who could pay for the food did so, while those who could not received it for free.

Every morning in the papal palace, doctors gave reports on the ill and the dead to the pope, the congregation of cardinals, and other ministers. Having worked on the plague commission of Siena in 1630, Mario Chigi was appointed chairman of the antiplague task force and superintendent of the food supply. Going out into the most infected sections of the city to help the sick and poor, the pope, Cardinal Antonio Barberini, and the pope's brother and nephews were greatly admired for their fearlessness in their fight against the plague. Some cardinals suggested that to avoid the miasmas Alexander should travel in a glass case, a kind of early pope-mobile. But the pope insisted on breathing the same air, and taking the same risks, as his people.

The first activities banned by the authorities were those not considered necessary to sustain life: dances, concerts, games, and parties. Holy water was no longer used in churches, as the dipping of plague-stricken fingers was thought to cause contagion. A sheepskin was hung in the confessional between the priest and sinner, quite effectively preventing infected fleas from jumping from one person to the other.

As more Romans came down with the plague, on June 26 law courts and schools were closed, as well as markets and shops. The economy ground to a standstill. Those whose businesses were closed couldn't earn any money, nor could their employees, who were told to stay home. Yet all but the very poor were expected to give alms to the authorities to pay for the plague hospitals.

Camillo evidently wanted to join the exodus of families from Rome to the healthier areas in the countryside. He felt that Viterbo would be safe and prepared to join his mother there. But his wife balked. She would not go with him, even though she was legally obligated to obey her husband by joining him if he insisted. With a rare surge of testosterone, Camillo insisted.

But it seemed that the princess of Rossano would rather die in Rome than live in Viterbo with Olimpia. Giacinto Gigli noted in his diary entry of June 27 that the princess "with permission of the pope entered into the convent of Tor di' Specchi to not be constrained by her husband Don Camillo to go to Viterbo where her mother-in-law Donna Olimpia was staying."[7]

On June 28, Alexander canceled the annual procession of the *chinea*. The white horse was given privately to the pope at the Quirinal Palace. He did not, however, close the churches, as it was believed that fervent prayer might make an avenging God more merciful.

During the worst weeks in the summer of 1656, all Romans were ordered to stay inside for forty days or face the death penalty. The pope had gallows built in several main squares of the city as a clear warning of the punishment for breaking quarantine. One thirteen-year-old girl, chasing an errant chicken onto the street, was caught by the patrol and hanged as an example to others.

Despite the best efforts of the health commissioners to take the sick to the lazarettos, many still died at home. Cart drivers processed solemnly through the empty streets crying, "Bring out your dead!" Bodies were taken to a graveyard outside the city near Saint Paul's Basilica.

There they were buried very deeply to prevent the corpses' miasmas from seeping up through the ground and contaminating the air.

Jews were always viewed with suspicion whenever an epidemic struck; in late June they were all walled up in their Trastevere ghetto to prevent them from intentionally spreading the plague among good Christians by throwing dead bodies down their wells. But after three weeks the situation in the ghetto was becoming desperate due to lack of food. On July 18 the Roman government deputized fourteen Jews of respectable character to leave the ghetto to bring back food and medicine. In the cramped conditions, plague was rampant; some eight hundred of the ghetto's four thousand residents would die.

As the number of plague victims grew, the Carceri Nuovi, Innocent's model prison, which had recently been completed by Pope Alexander, was sequestered as another lazaretto. Though in the heart of the city, it offered spacious cells with balconies and fresh air facing an inner courtyard, from which, it was assumed, the miasmas would not spread to neighboring houses. Cardinal Decio Azzolini was named superintendent of the new lazaretto.

In September 1656 Giacinto Gigli and his family obtained permission to go to a vineyard outside the city gates for fifteen days. "I heard news that 100 or more were dying of the plague every day," he wrote. "When I returned to Rome with all my family safe and sound, by the grace of God, it was a terrible thing to see. The cadavers were being carried in carts covered with waxed cloth with a cross on top, pulled by horses, and big bells were rung so that the people on the streets knew to stand aside as the carts passed by on the way to Saint Paul's meadow to bury them. . . . I could relate many other things but I will not because they are disgusting things."[8]

As the plague raged into the fall, Camillo found that in addition to worrying about infection, he was suffering serious financial problems. Pope Alexander had forced him personally to pay the costs of building Saint Agnes, and given the structural problems, the amount continued to skyrocket. In October 1656 Camillo wrote his mother that he had sold many properties to pay for the construction, though "the jewels they cannot touch because my wife has taken them away. The contagion is getting worse and worse, and more than eighty a day are dying. See now that I merit the sympathy of your Excellency. Here in the house, God be praised, all are well, especially my children, who ask your blessing."[9]

On October 7, Costanza Pamphili wrote her mother, "I cannot with my pen describe this evil contagion, but I ask you to make all necessary precautions in San Martino, more precisely, a good doctor and a barber [a medical assistant], to have one come from Rome if necessary, because if your Excellency has not arranged this from Viterbo there is now no time to have anyone come." Referring to her brother's troubled marriage, she added, "I can give you news of Don Camillo; by the grace of God things go better with his wife and we hope this will continue."[10]

On November 11, Camillo wrote Olimpia that he had resorted to selling furniture to pay for Saint Agnes. But a week later, there was something worse to worry about. In his letter of November 20 he informed his mother, "With flourishing contagion Girolamo the wardrobe master was taken to the lazaretto where, we later learned, he died."[11] Others in the house nervously checked their groins and armpits for buboes and felt their foreheads for fever.

With the advent of the first frost, the epidemic slowed. In the bitter cold, fleas died or hibernated. Was the sickness over? Or would it sprout again in the spring with the return of the fleas? Most plague epidemics lasted two warm seasons.

On December 20, 1656, Olimpiuccia wrote her grandmother, "With the Christmas season I did not want to neglect giving Your Excellency my best wishes. . . . To tell you how I am there is no longer any doubt because I am five months pregnant with a creature that I feel very much. My mother says that I am certainly pregnant."[12] Olimpiuccia would safely deliver another daughter, Camilla, on April 28.

The princess of Rossano, meanwhile, agitated for more money for her monthly maintenance from Camillo. Her dowry documents had stated that she would receive 500 scudi a month, but ever since their 1647 marriage she had only received 250 a month. She wanted not only the higher amount starting immediately but also the money in arrears.

Given his burdensome financial commitments, Camillo refused, the princess shrieked, and the pope intervened.

In his 1656 Christmas letter, Camillo informed Olimpia, "His Holiness ordered me by a decree of Monsignor the vice regent to give to the princess my wife 6,000 scudi and 300 a month, and that I give her three carriages each with two horses. I know how little sympathy Your Excellency will have," he added bitterly. He was right. He had gotten himself into the pickle by marrying the one woman Olimpia had expressly forbidden him to marry, and now she had very little sympathy for him indeed.

"I hope that it is worthwhile to reflect on my state," he continued, "and I ask your blessing, as do my children."[13]

Since June 1656, Roman officials had given every available hour to fighting the plague. All law courts had closed. All criminal investigations had come to a grinding halt. The sick needed to be quarantined; the healthy needed to be fed; the dead needed to be buried. Plague-stricken doctors and grave diggers—usually those who refused to wear their anti-miasma suits—had to be replaced at exorbitant rates. With commerce stagnating, the regular taxes were not available to pay for the costly measures, and the pope had to find the money somewhere, even if it meant taking out high-interest loans.

Given Rome's rising death toll and empty treasury, the pope and his commission temporarily dropped the investigation against Olimpia. Her embezzlement, as shocking as it had been, had suddenly become a minor matter when Death stalked all the streets of Rome, mercilessly wielding his sickle.

Death was aided and abetted by the Romans themselves, many of whom did not follow the rules. Boredom caused many to break their quarantine. At night, some of the more adventurous climbed down the ropes dangling from the second floor, used to haul up food. They visited bored-to-tears friends for rousing wine-soaked card parties where fleas silently jumped from one player to the next.

Grave diggers presented their own problems. They were a surly, muscle-bound lot at the very bottom of the social ladder. Some of them grew tired of hauling the nonstop cartloads of dead bodies far out of town and burying them eight feet under; it was easier to bury them closer to town. Sometimes as a joke they would dump the bodies into shallow graves next to the homes of people they didn't like. Additionally, grave diggers were supposed to burn the contagious clothing and bedding of the deceased, but they often sold them, along with the bubonic fleas they harbored.

The valuable lazaretto doctors were supposed to limit their contact with plague victims, standing in plague suits several feet away to oversee their less esteemed assistants—the barbers—administer medicine and provide the patients with cleanliness, nourishment, and comfort. But some doctors, bored stiff, removed their sweaty plague suits and engaged the patients in card games, sitting by their bedsides for hours at a time. Others brought prostitutes in for sex and sent them back out to carry on their trade and, quite possibly, spread the disease. Some physicians, displeased with the wine delivered to the lazarettos, made runs out to liquor stores.

And so plague spread throughout much of Italy returning with virulence in the spring. Naples lost 50 percent of its population, some 150,000 out of 300,000. Genoa lost 60 percent, or 120,000 out of 200,000. Rome lost comparatively few, an estimated 15,000 to 20,000 dead out of a population of 120,000, a death rate of only 12 to 16 percent. And then, as mysteriously as the plague started, it began to abate.

On August 15, 1657, Costanza wrote her mother with two pieces of good news. "Finally, by the grace of God, the princess of Rossano has returned to the house of her husband and I hope that all the gossiping will be over. I did not want to neglect to inform Your Excellency of this, knowing how it will please you to hear it. . . . It was she who went to find him and they talked so that these arguments will not occur again." Even more important than the tempestuous marriage of Camillo and the princess was the news that the plague was ending in Rome. "Soon they will open the lazarettos here and put the holy water back in the churches."[14]

But the plague, releasing its grasp on Rome, marched on to Viterbo. In her letter of September 2, Olimpiuccia begged her grandmother to leave the city. San Martino, she added, was too close. She should visit a healthier place farther away. But Olimpia did not listen. She rattled the three miles to her lovely palace and there ensconced herself to wait out the epidemic.

On September 3, 1657, Olimpia's nine-year-old grandson, Gianbattista Pamphili, sent her a remarkably well-expressed letter written in loopy schoolboy cursive.

> The contagion in Viterbo is worrying everyone in the house, and me particularly for the great love I have for Your Excellency because I would want to see you far removed from such a grave danger. Or I would willingly want to serve you, in person, and I think I could do so profitably being now very practical regarding matters of contagion, from which we have known how to resolutely guard ourselves here. But since this is not permitted me, believe me that prayers are not lacking, being made continually by my sisters, for your health. May it please God to grant them, and Your Excellency to bless us all.[15]

On September 15, Camillo wrote, "Seeing that the contagion of Viterbo is losing steam and virulence, this news fills my soul with joy in every respect, but particularly on behalf of Your Excellency, and of my aunts the nuns, to whom I ask Your Excellency to commend me. Here, God be praised, we are completely free from any illness. In our house we all enjoy perfect health."[16]

At some point between September 17 and 20, perhaps in the magnificent frescoed rooms designed for her by Bernini, a flea jumped onto Olimpia. Perhaps it sprang onto her black wool stocking and worked its way up, past the leather garter buckled just above the knee, onto the flesh of the thigh.

Three or four days after the flea bite, Olimpia shivered in the September warmth. Shrugging it off, perhaps she reached for a shawl. But then her body temperature rose rapidly to between 103 and 106 degrees. Buboes appeared. Examining the sore black boils in her groin and armpits, Olimpia could no longer deny that she had caught the plague.

She was tormented by unquenchable thirst, vomiting, diarrhea, headache, and hallucinations. She probably knew that death normally occurred within three to six days after the first symptoms. If she could hold out till the seventh or eighth day, she would have a good chance of recovery.

Gripped by utter exhaustion, Olimpia took quickly to her bed. After Innocent's death, she had removed his papal throne from the audience chamber she had built for him and placed her bed there, where the throne had stood on its dais. It was the largest, most beautiful room in the palace, with its ornate movable ceiling, windows on three sides, and a gorgeous view of the medieval church, the town crouched at its stone feet, and the blue hills in the distance.

Though doctors must have been hard to come by, evidently Olimpia found one, according to a letter written by her relative Cardinal Gualterio. The most important step to save her life was to drain the buboes. But Olimpia's buboes did not come to a head. "They could not pop the nodes without great inconvenience, if they did not cut them out," Gualterio wrote.[17]

None of Olimpia's family or friends was with her during her illness. It was reported that her servants, fearful of contagion, deserted her. Gregorio Leti stated that there was no priest at hand to take her last confession and ease her way to the next world with the comforting sacred rites. This could very well have been true, considering that the San Martino priests might have died or fled town.

For decades Olimpia had accumulated, acquired, and embezzled to stanch her fear and keep herself safe. But now not all the money in the world could help her, not all the gorgeous palaces could stop the infection, not all the power she had ever wielded could prevent destruction caused by a microbe lodged inside the stomach of a flea.

On September 26, 1657, the indomitable Olimpia Maidalchini Pamphili, princess of San Martino and former mistress of the Vatican, died, and quite possibly she died alone.

We can imagine her soul rising through the gold-embroidered velvet hangings of her four-poster bed, up to the painted movable ceiling and through the huge white dove on the papal crest of Innocent X. She rose through the empty space above the ceiling, with its pulleys and levers, and out through the roof. Above the palace, she could see the 250 houses she had built for dowerless girls.

In the distance soared the spires of Viterbo, the town of her birth, which had threatened to devour her but which she had long ago conquered. And farther south in Rome rose the magnificent dome of Saint Peter's, which she had also subjugated, even though she had had the misfortune to be born a woman.

Now that her pain had stopped, and her heart had stopped, she was suddenly truly free for the first time in sixty-six years. Free in a way she had never imagined. In this freedom she needed neither wealth, position, nor power, for no prison threatened her now. Now, finally, she was free of greed, free of flesh.

Free, even, of fear. Olimpia was finally safe.

27

After Olimpia

All our yesterdays have lighted fools
the way to dusty death. Out, out, brief candle!
Life's but a walking shadow, a poor player
that struts and frets his hour upon the stage
And then is heard no more.

—William Shakespeare, *Macbeth*

CAMILLO WAS SUMMONED from Rome. According to some reports, he found his mother naked on a stripped bed because her servants, having come back to check on her, had robbed the corpse and bed hangings.

Given the threat of contagion, the body had to be buried immediately. Luckily, her tomb was already prepared in the Church of San Martino, right next door to her palace. But there was the little matter of a coffin. With so many recent deaths, all the coffins in San Martino, and in Viterbo for that matter, were already six feet under—actually, eight feet under in the case of plague victims. Camillo rooted around the palace and in the basement found some packing crates that had been used to bring furniture from Olimpia's Piazza Navona palace out to San Martino. These were hammered into a makeshift coffin. Washed and dressed, Olimpia was interred in the shabby box, which many saw as divine retribution for her having caused the same treatment of Innocent.

There is an unconfirmed story that when they lifted Olimpia's body into the coffin, the head turned to one side, the mouth dropped open, and Camillo saw three huge diamonds hidden inside her cheek. Given her attention to worldly goods, it is possible that Olimpia, knowing she could very well fall into a coma and be robbed by her servants, might have secreted such valuable gems in a place where she would wake to find them. No one would stick their hands into the miasma-spewing mouth of a comatose plague victim.

We have a detailed description of how Olimpia was dressed for burial, given by a certain Antonio Bernardini, who opened her tomb in 1762. Camillo's grandson Prince Girolamo Pamphili had died, having uttered the express wish to be buried next to the illustrious ancestress responsible for all subsequent greatness of the Pamphili family. Ashamed of the story that she had been buried in a furniture crate, the family prepared an elaborate coffin into which they would transfer her remains.

On Monday, March 30, on the occasion of digging in the Church of San Martino to inter the body of His Majesty, Signor Prince Don Girolamo, they had to remove the tombstone of Donna Olimpia, and under the headstone they found the cadaver of Donna Olimpia in a wooden box placed in a space surrounded by masonry which had been made under the tombstone. The cadaver consisted only of bones that were a bit consumed by time.

The dress was recognized as a ribbed silk, the color of crimson. A brass crucifix with an ebony cross, about as long as a palm, was placed on the chest, a crown of coconut palm threaded with red ribbon, two small medallions of silver and one of brass and a little Agnus Dei [a small wax lamb blessed by the pope]. Under the body was a cushion, but no one could tell what material it was made of.

All the hair was still on the skull, and part of it was a wiglet and part was woven into a part of the wiglet and another part braids, and wound by means of cardboard. You could recognize the well-done braids by their gold color and they are as pretty as can be. A new casket was made and was the same size as the planks of the old one that were underneath. She was placed in the new casket the same way she had been in the old one, along with all that was there without removing anything.[1]

It is fascinating that Olimpia was buried not in her traditional black widow's weeds and peaked cap but in a gown of ribbed crimson silk, with golden false braids woven into her hair. It is possible that her servants had stolen all her gowns and Camillo hurriedly obtained clothing from someone else to place on Olimpia. It might have been Camillo's last, bungling attempt to please his mother, tarting her up in a red dress and blond wig for her trip to meet God.

When news of Olimpia's death reached the city, it aroused various reactions. Her relative and friend Cardinal Gualterio was devastated by the death of the woman who had single-handedly made him a cardinal. On October 9 he poured out his grief to a friend, Niccolò Caferri.

> Donna Olimpia has died with no friends around her. I feel such great despair that I don't know where I am. To vent this grief I have written two very long letters to my dear Signor Don Camillo. And he alone will be the object of my most obliging and heartfelt gratitude. If he cares for me as does Your Holiness, I ask you to please extend to him the kindest affection I have for that most Illustrious woman of, unfortunately, happy memory.
>
> Oh my dear, dear signora, whom I can no longer serve. Now she has been lifted up and where is she? Oh the pain. God have compassion for that soul and give me the light of understanding from this lesson, as He has done in similar circumstances.

Gualterio then added the surprising news that Olimpia had made up her differences with the princess of Rossano.

> I am consoled that her death occurred after having made peace with the Princess. . . . The goodness of God postponed the death of the mother until she made peace with the wife.

I assure you that . . . the lady of the P.M. *[Pontifex Maximus?]* served well and diligently, and she never received any of the recognition she should have.[2]

Many rejoiced at Olimpia's demise. Gregorio Leti saw her death as God's vengeance for her sins. He moralized, "But if men had abandoned chastisement of this woman, or if, better said, the pope had been forced to postpone it until a more convenient time, God, who watches constantly while men sleep, threw the powerful thunderbolt against the woman who was guilty of so many crimes."[3]

But if God had truly wanted to punish Olimpia, it would have been years earlier, certainly not after allowing her to run the Vatican for the better part of a decade, and certainly not at the ripe old age of sixty-six, which in the 1650s was more like eighty in our own times. At that age, a quick death after a few days of fever was not so much a punishment as a blessing.

Olimpia's death sealed the triumph of her family. The pope was not inclined to punish innocent relatives, even though they had clearly profited from her corruption. The embezzler was dead, and it was far more dignified to let the matter rest. Moreover, having found the time to look carefully into the financial records of Urban VIII, the pope found that the Barberini family had stolen many times what the Pamphilis had pocketed. Some estimates indicate that Taddeo Barberini had pilfered 42 million scudi, while Cardinal Francesco reportedly stole 29 million, and Cardinal Antonio another 20 million. Whatever Olimpia had purloined, it was a drop in the bucket by comparison.

Therefore, if Alexander were to prosecute the Pamphilis, he would also have to prosecute the Barberinis, who now boasted three cardinals in top church positions. If he did that, he would have to look into the ill-gotten gains of other papal families—the Ludovisis, Borgheses, Aldobrandinis, Perettis, and Buoncompagnis, just to mention a few. He could hardly prosecute *all* papal families for corruption and confiscate their wealth. If he did so, given the intricate marriage alliances, not a single noble line in Rome would be left unscathed. Moreover, he would have to prosecute himself, given the rampant nepotism he had begun to practice. Clearly it was in the best interests of the Holy Roman Church to drop the case against Olimpia's heirs.

"As they say in Rome, dead dog, dead rabies," Gregorio Leti wrote. "So that no one thought any more of her."[4]

~~~

Camillo and the princess of Rossano enjoyed Olimpia's wealth. They now owned two enormous palaces in Rome—the Palazzo Pamphili and the Palazzo Aldobrandini, which came in handy when the couple had a knock-down, drag-out fight and temporarily separated. Camillo lived principally in the Piazza Navona. His inheritance included not only Olimpia's properties, furniture, and art collections but also the astonishing sum of two million gold pieces.

Camillo died in 1666 at the age of forty-four. It is not known exactly what killed him, though those who knew of the deplorable state of his marriage suspected that he had, in fact, been nagged to death. His wife, the princess of Rossano, died in 1681 at the age of fifty-eight, having connived to get their second son, Benedetto, made a cardinal.

The Church of Saint Agnes did eventually become the resting place for Innocent's bones, but not until 1677, when Camillo's son Gianbattista had them dug up from the shoddy grave in Saint Peter's basement and transferred there. His funerary monument was not completed until 1729. It was placed above the main door, so that visitors rarely, if ever, notice it.

Those exiting the church have to crane their necks upward. Among the shafts of light stabbing the soft gloom they will see a powerful old man wearing a bulbous papal tiara so high it scrapes the ceiling; indeed, the entire monument seems to have been squeezed in as an afterthought. But Innocent had always been a man of modest needs; he would not have demanded a huge tomb next to the altar. His statue seems pleased that he finally has a tomb at all. He extends his right hand in benediction and, perhaps, forgiveness.

Though Olimpia's nephew Cardinal Francesco Maidalchini had started off as the laughingstock of the Sacred College, he would, over time, mature into a man esteemed for his pure morals, steadfast loyalty, and dedication to his duties, dying in 1700 at the age of seventy. If he wasn't given any important responsibilities, at least he never shamed the church. It is likely that the only lifelong passion of this mild-mannered soul was his detestation of his crafty aunt.

After the election of Alexander VII, Cardinal Camillo Astalli became an honored member of the Sacred College. Perhaps in gratitude for the timely news of Innocent's plans to invade Naples, Philip IV of Spain bestowed on Astalli many honors. He appointed him the Spanish protector of the kingdom of Naples and of Sicily. Cardinal Astalli died in 1662 at the age of forty-two.

The year after Olimpia's death, Alexander VII married his nephew Agostino to Maria Virginia Borghese, the daughter of the princess of Rossano by her first husband. The pope spent a reported 100,000 scudi on the wedding festivities and bought for 275,000 scudi the principalities of Farnese and Ariccia, making his nephew a prince and duke. Dipping into Olimpia's pots of gold, the princess of Rossano gave her daughter a dowry of 200,000 scudi. Gregorio Leti saw Machiavellian manipulation behind the exorbitant sum; the princess did this "to get the Popes favor, and have some part in the Vatican, which she hath always been ambitious of."[5]

Leti recounted that the pope's brother, Don Mario, raked up so much Vatican money that the people of Rome "cry out more against him than ever they did against Don Taddeo, nay, more than they did against Donna Olimpia herself. He hath invented so many new subtleties to get money out of those Offices which are ordinarily bestowed upon the Popes nearest Relations, that the Barberinis, who thought themselves masters in that Craft, do remain astonished to see themselves outdone by a new beginner."[6]

Leti observed that while the pope had nothing against his male relatives raping the treasury, he was terrified of bringing his sister-in-law to Rome, "the very name of a sister-in-law being a most odious thing to the Romans, for Donna Olimpia's sake." But when Mario's wife was allowed to come to Rome, the pope was relieved to see that unlike Olimpia, she knew her place. "Indeed, Donna Berenice is another sort of Woman, and one who shews modesty and reservedness in all her carriage, being unwilling to meddle with anything to which she is not call'd."[7]

Pope Innocent XII finally outlawed nepotism in 1692, declaring the poor to be his real nephews. His relatives were not permitted to set foot in the Vatican. When the cardinals suggested he add to the Sacred College the archbishop of Taranto, a respected prelate worthy of the honor, the pope replied, "That is true, but he is my nephew."[8] His name was removed from the list of candidates. Though Innocent XII's laws reduced the excesses, nepotism limped along for two more centuries. The last pope to practice it was Leo XIII (reigned 1878–1903), who in 1879 made his brother Giuseppe a cardinal.

The Papal States were folded into the new nation of Italy in 1861 when King Victor Emmanuel II united the squabbling, disparate principalities into one kingdom. After Rome was declared the capital of Italy in 1870, popes refused to accept the loss of their temporal kingdom, calling it completely illegal and an insult to religion. Anyone who voted in an Italian election could consider themselves excommunicated. For sixty years the Vicars of Christ hid in the Vatican rather than spot an Italian flag flying over Rome. But in 1929, in return for a huge lump sum, the church accepted the 109-acre Vatican City as its temporal territory, making it the smallest nation in the world.

Ironically, the loss of his kingdom was a great boon to the pope, who could now concentrate on religion. As Jesus himself said, it is impossible to serve two masters.

Most of Olimpia's exquisite properties are still in use today. Her birthplace in Viterbo, a large town house, has been divided into spacious apartments. The walls are adorned with magnificent frescoes from Olimpia's time, and the wooden ceiling beams are decorated with the eight-pointed gold Maidalchini star. In the garden, residents digging holes for plants find Etruscan vases, medieval pottery, and marble papal shields—layer upon layer of history. In 1944, serious bomb damage destroyed Viterbo's Convent of Saint Dominic, where Olimpia's sisters had lived into their seventies, and its records. Today Viterbo is a bustling modern city operating in beautifully preserved thirteenth-century buildings.

Olimpia's masterpiece, the Piazza Navona palace, has been the home of the Brazilian Embassy since 1920. The façade has recently undergone a thorough cleaning and restoration to bring it back to the pale-gray shade she had painted it in the 1640s. The embassy staff is well aware of Olimpia's fascinating history and is proud to have offices in her former home. The ballroom where she threw magnificent parties still echoes with the clink of champagne glasses whenever the ambassador holds a reception. Her music room, where she held her lascivious comedies, Jesuit orations, and operas, is still used for embassy concerts.

The town of San Martino sits almost unchanged from Olimpia's time. Many of the current 2,500 residents are direct descendants of the dowerless girls Olimpia brought in. Her palace houses the local tourism board and cultural exhibits and is used as a conference center.

The Pamphili villa of Bel Respiro, with its strange glued-together statues and fabulous sunken gardens, was sold in 1985 to the government of Italy. Currently being restored, it will be used as a venue for the prime minister's social functions.

The Il Barco villa outside Viterbo, built by Olimpia's brother, Andrea, is sliding into a state of poetic decrepitude. Many of the plaster ceilings have fallen, and many of the frescoes are flaking and bubbling with water damage. Recently the Italian government decided to restore the villa to its former glory and fixed the roof before it ran out of funds. The little church behind the villa has lost its roof entirely. The chestnut trees on which Olimpia hung roasted chestnuts for the pope's delight are long gone, replaced by gnarled olive trees and tangled waist-high grass.

Innocent's model prison, the Carceri Nuovi, is currently the anti-Mafia headquarters of the Italian government, guarded by handsome burly men wielding machine guns. The Quirinal Palace, where Innocent died, was taken from the pope by the Italian government in 1870 and used as the royal residence of the king of Italy. It currently houses the offices of Italy's president and is used for presidential ceremonies.

The two geniuses that Olimpia commissioned for her architectural projects continued their competition after her death, meeting with very different ends. In 1657 Camillo fired Francesco Borromini as architect of the Church of Saint Agnes. He was fired from other important projects, or never considered for the commissions, or when he was awarded the jobs he would soon after storm off in a rage. As Borromini's star continued to fall, the star of his deadly rival, Gian Lorenzo Bernini, continued to rise.

In 1656, Pope Alexander gave Bernini the commission for the embracing columned portico surrounding Saint Peter's Square. It was an immense, challenging, and prestigious job, completed to great acclaim in 1666. Bernini undertook it with characteristic zeal, but his success pushed his ancient competitor over the edge. Deeply depressed, in 1667 Borromini ran himself through with his sword. The forty-year clash of Rome's artistic titans was over.

Bernini died in 1680 at the age of eighty-one. He sculpted right up until the end, standing on a platform with a young man on either side holding him so he would not fall. One day he had a stroke, which paralyzed his right hand. "It is right," the dying man said to his son, "that before death this hand, which has done so much work in life, should get a little rest."[9]

Queen Christina continued to shock Rome. She discovered that a life of art and philosophy was not all she had imagined it to be. She missed power. Up to her elbows in political intrigue, she decided to become queen of a Catholic nation and chose, as Olimpia had a few years earlier, Naples. But when her private secretary betrayed her plans to Spain, she had him murdered in cold blood, begging for his life on his knees. The pope was disgusted, but he could hardly imprison for murder the personification of Catholicism's triumph over the heretics.

Christina continued to love Cardinal Decio Azzolini until her death, though his initial interest in her soon cooled and became platonic. At the end of her life she declared that she, too, had become an ancient Roman monument and one of the sights of Rome. Her last wish was to be buried in the Pantheon, that ancient pagan temple to all the gods. But when she died in 1689 at the age of sixty-two, she was interred in that most Catholic of tombs, the papal grottoes below Saint Peter's Basilica, as if to force her finally to become a good Catholic.

While Olimpia is somewhat known in Rome, Viterbo, and other places associated with her, the stories about her are bleared with time and spiced with sex. In Viterbo it is said that Olimpia was a beautiful woman who stuck her head out of the window, tantalizing men with her lovely hair and inviting them to come up to her room. In her castle of Alviano in Umbria, there is a well in the courtyard. Down the well, it is said, the black widow Olimpia threw the bodies of the men she had slept with and murdered.

Wherever Olimpia lived, rumors abound that millions of pieces of gold are stashed there, somewhere. Olimpia's castle of Attigliano, included in her auction purchase of 1654, is now razed except for a few picturesque walls. There, it is said, in the covered-over dungeons, sits Olimpia's gold. And in her Nini town house in Viterbo the gold is thought to be hidden in the apartment walls. One young resident, Annalisa Marinetti, remembers as a child in the 1990s tapping on the walls with her brother to find the hollow space where Olimpia's treasure was stored. It's in there somewhere, her father, now deceased, told the children.

Anyone who visits the glorious Doria Pamphilj Galleries in Rome will see where the treasure actually went. It was not hidden in walls or dungeons but bequeathed to Camillo and the princess of Rossano. There, in their palace on the Corso, the couple started an immense art collection, which was added to by later generations. There Olimpia's gold—including what she had taken from under the pope's bed—hangs on the wall in the form of Raphaels, Tintorettos, Brueghels, and Titians.

In 1671 Camillo's eighteen-year-old daughter, Anna, married Giovanni Andrea Doria, scion of a powerful Genoese family. In 1763, when the male Pamphili line died out, Anna's descendants took the combined name of Doria Pamphilj so that the illustrious papal name would continue. A more famous descendant is the actress Brooke Shields, who goes back twelve generations to Olimpia through Olimpiuccia. One of Brooke's half sisters is named Olympia.

But Olimpia Maidalchini Pamphili has a far more important legacy than illustrious descendants or a fabulous art collection. Her legacy is that of a woman who refused to conform to the misogynistic traditions of her time. She would not become a nun. She refused to remain poor and powerless. She grasped power with outstretched hands and ended up running the most antifemale institution in history, the Vatican, with the pope himself and many of his cardinals her puppets.

Though she was the most notorious woman of her time, the memory of Olimpia has almost completely vanished. The Catholic Church must be glad. After all, within a two-thousand-year history encompassing thousands of leading actors, there are bound to be regrettable stories mixed in with those of holy saints and martyrs. The Church still has to contend with the image of the incestuous Lucrezia Borgia, her golden ankle-length hair shining in the candlelight as she smilingly slips arsenic from a poison ring into her guest's wine—a story that is blatantly untrue. Then there's that pesky tale of Pope Joan, giving birth while processing through the streets—another falsehood. And they will always have to contend with nasty rumors about that unfortunate testicle-groping coronation chair—a lie if ever there was one.

But Olimpia's story, completely true, has been completely forgotten. New church scandals fill the newspapers. New saints inspire the faithful. And in an age when other Christian churches have permitted female priests, the Catholic Church adamantly refuses to consider doing so, citing tradition. The church does not concede that a woman has already run the Vatican itself, and her name was Olimpia Maidalchini.

Notes

Introduction

1. Coville, p. 31.
2. Pallavicino, p. 192.
3. Ibid., p. 190.
4. Leti, *Nipotismo,* Part 1, Book 3, p. 126.
5. Leti, *Olimpia,* p. 42.
6. Ibid., p. 103.
7. Ciampi, p. 330.
8. Pallavicino, pp. 189–90.
9. Vassalli, p. 124.

1: The Convent

1. Bell, p. 66.
2. Torjesen, p. 159.
3. Leti, *Olimpia,* p. 7.
4. Vassalli, p. 17.
5. Cavoli, p. 19.
6. Sella, p. 119.
7. Vassalli, p. 16.
8. Pietrini, p. 83.
9. Ciaffei, p. 99.

2: The Wealthy Landowner's Wife

1. Laven, p. 24.
2. Somerset, p. 90.

3: *The Roman Noblewoman*

1. Erlanger, p. 216.
2. Colonna, p. 35.
3. Archivio Doria Pamphilj, 93.57.
4. Leti, *Olimpia,* p. 7.

4: *The Brother-in-Law*

1. Leti, *Olimpia,* p. 10.
2. Ibid., p. 14.
3. Liberati, p. 45.
4. Ibid., p. 33.
5. Hammond, p. 124.
6. Archivio Doria Pamphilj, archiovolo, doc. 193.
7. Ibid.
8. Strozzi, *Relatione della Corte . . . Contarino,* vol. 146, folio 116b.
9. Leti, *Olimpia,* p. 10.
10. Ibid., p. 9.
11. Ibid., pp. 9–11.
12. Ibid., p. 15.

5: *The Papal Nuncio*

1. Archivio Doria Pamphilj, archiovolo doc. 151.
2. Strozzi, *Relatione della Corte . . . Contarino,* vol. 146, folio 122b.
3. Pallavicino, pp. 189–90.
4. Colonna, p. 36.
5. Archivio Doria Pamphilj, archiovolo doc. 151.
6. Lees-Milne, p. 247.
7. Gigli, vol. 1, p. 121.
8. Ibid., p. 125.
9. Pirie, p. 158.
10. Ibid., p. 159.
11. Strozzi, *Relatione della Corte . . . Contarino,* vol. 146, folio 117b.
12. Duffy, p. 231.
13. Archivio Doria Pamphilj, doc. 93.57.
14. Leti, *Olimpia,* pp. 12–14.

6: *Cardinals*

1. Archivio Doria Pamphilj, doc. 93.60.134.
2. Carocci, pp. 149–50.
3. Leti, *Cardinalismo,* p. 123.
4. Vassalli, p. 40.
5. Leti, *Cardinalismo,* p. 146.
6. Vassalli, p. 61.
7. Leti, *Nipotismo,* Part 2, Book 3, p. 137.

8. Gigli, vol. 1, p. 195.
9. Leti, *Cardinalismo,* p. 96.
10. Ibid.
11. Coville, p. 29.
12. Bainton, p. 71.
13. Pastor, vol. 29, pp. 167–68.
14. Chambers, p. 294.
15. Ibid.
16. Leti, *Cardinalismo,* p. 82.
17. Strozzi, *Relatione delle Corte . . . Contarino,* vol. 146, folio 133b.
18. Leti, *Olimpia,* p. 22.

7: *The Black Widow*

1. Maland, p. 60.
2. Sella, p. 229.
3. Ibid., p. 232.
4. Hammond, p. 248.
5. Ibid.
6. Archivio Doria Pamphilj, doc. 93.69.2.
7. Vassalli, p. 53.
8. Leti, *Olimpia,* p. 18.
9. Strozzi, *Istruttione,* vol. 171, folio 159b.
10. Leti, *Olimpia,* p. 17.
11. Strozzi, *Istruttione,* vol. 171, folio 158b.
12. Vassalli, p. 53.
13. Leti, *Olimpia,* p. 15.
14. Ibid., p. 22.
15. Ibid., pp. 22–23.
16. Barberini, p. 190.
17. Bastiaanse, p. 117.
18. Vassalli, p. 57.
19. Gigli, vol. 1, p. 427.

8: *Conclave*

1. Gigli, vol. 2, pp. 429–30.
2. Paravicini-Bagliani, p. 181.
3. Colonna, p. 55.
4. Leti, *Olimpia,* p. 26.
5. Ibid., p. 28.
6. Gigli, vol. 2, p. 427.
7. Coville, p. 5.
8. Ibid., p. 12.
9. Leti, *Olimpia,* pp. 27–28.
10. Strozzi, *Relatione della Corte . . . Contarino,* vol. 146, folio 117b.
11. Colonna, p. 60.

12. Leti, *Olimpia,* p. 29.
13. Colonna, p. 60.
14. Vassalli, p. 62.
15. Ibid., p. 66.
16. Majanlahti, p. 175.
17. Coville, p. 17.
18. Bastiaanse, p. 364.
19. Strozzi, *Conclave dopo la morte di Urbano VIII,* vol. 148, folio 93a.
20. Ibid., *Vita del Cardinale Cecchini,* vol. 175, folio 216a.
21. Leti, *Olimpia,* p. 32.
22. Strozzi, *Conclave dopo la morte di Urbano VIII,* vol. 148, folio 141b.
23. Coville, p. 23.
24. Strozzi, *D'Innocenzo Decimo,* vol. 21, folio 59a.
25. Coville, p. 31.

9: *The Vicar of Christ*

1. Lunadoro, p. 199.
2. Gigli, vol. 2, p. 431.
3. Ibid., p. 432.
4. Leti, *Olimpia,* p. 33.
5. Ciaffei, p. 53.
6. Leti, *Olimpia,* p. 33.
7. Ibid., p. 34.
8. Ibid., p. 35.
9. Ibid., p. 34.
10. Leti, *Olimpia,* pp. 38–39.
11. Partner, p. 16.

10: *Celebrations*

1. Paravicini-Bagliani, p. 38.
2. Lunadoro, p. 214.
3. Vassalli, p. 77.
4. Cavoli, p. 71.
5. Lunadoro, p. 216.
6. Vassalli, p. 75.
7. Strozzi, *Relatione della Corte . . . Contarino,* vol. 146, folio 121a.
8. Ciampi, p. 121 n.
9. Vassalli, p. 77.
10. Colonna, p. 175.
11. Evelyn, p. 109.
12. Gigli, vol. 2, p. 436.
13. Cawthorne, p. 58.
14. Martinelli, p. 155.
15. Evelyn, p. 109.

11: Women in the Vatican

1. Vassalli, p. 17.
2. Cavoli, p. 125.
3. Vassalli, pp. 124–25.
4. Ibid., p. 123.
5. Pastor, vol. 30, p. 34.
6. Pallavicino, p. 190.
7. Leti, *Nipotismo,* Part 1, Book 3, pp. 112–13.
8. Pallavicino, p. 190.
9. Strozzi, *Prosperita infelice,* vol. 175, folio 238a.
10. Ciampi, pp. 330–31.
11. Strozzi, *Relatione della Corte . . . Sagredo,* vol. 59, folio 263b.
12. Leti, *Olimpia,* p. 67.
13. Vassalli, p. 124.
14. Leti, *Olimpia,* p. 55.
15. Gigli, vol. 2, p. 437.
16. Vassalli, p. 125.
17. Strozzi, *Relatione della Corte . . . Contarino,* vol. 146, folio 121a.
18. Vassalli, pp. 86–87.
19. Maland, p. 464.
20. Cavoli, p. 101.
21. Stanford, p. 52.
22. Boase, p. 361.
23. Chamberlin, p. 133.
24. La Bella, p. 39.

12: Vengeance on the Barberinis

1. Vassalli, p. 87.
2. Ibid., pp. 87–88.
3. Colonna, p. 74.
4. Coville, p. 108.
5. Vassalli, p. 101.
6. Ibid., p. 103.
7. Ibid., p. 106.
8. Leti, *Nipotismo,* Part 2, Book 3, p. 135.
9. Leti, *Olimpia,* p. 43.
10. Leti, *Nipotismo,* Part 1, Book 3, p. 116.
11. Strozzi, *Istruttione,* vol. 171, folio 159b.
12. Leti, *Olimpia,* p. 65.
13. Ibid., *Nipotismo,* Part 1, Book 3, p. 116.
14. Bernini, p. 24.
15. Morrissey, p. 92.
16. Ibid., p. 155.
17. Ibid., p. 158.
18. Ibid.
19. Ibid., p. 166.

20. Ibid.
21. Ibid., p. 163.

13: *The Despised Daughter-in-law*

1. Pallavicino, p. 154.
2. Ibid., p. 169.
3. Coville, p. 143.
4. Leti, *Olimpia,* p. 51.
5. Strozzi, *Relatione, della Corte . . . Contarino,* vol. 146, folio 127b.
6. Coville, p. 144.
7. Leti, *Olimpia,* p. 49.
8. Ciaffei, p. 92.
9. Colonna, p. 180.
10. Gigli, vol. 2, p. 495.
11. Ibid.
12. Colonna, p. 181.
13. Ciampi, p. 131.
14. Cavoli, p. 111.

14: *The Imbecile Cardinals*

1. Coville, p. 149.
2. Vassalli, p. 114.
3. Ibid., p. 115.
4. Leti, *Olimpia,* pp. 76–77.
5. Leti, *Cardinalismo,* p. 158.
6. Ibid., pp. 72–73.
7. Vassalli, p. 118.
8. Leti, *Olimpia,* p. 77.
9. Ibid.
10. Ibid., p. 78.
11. Colonna, p. 184.
12. Leti, *Cardinalismo,* p. 158.
13. Coville, p. 182.
14. Vassalli, p. 127.
15. Ibid., p. 96.
16. Gigli, vol. 2, pp. 508–10.
17. Ciampi, p. 142 n.
18. Gigli, vol. 2, p. 508.
19. Ibid., p. 510.
20. Vassalli, p. 135.

15: *Birth, Famine, and Bitter Peace*

1. Ciampi, p. 135 n.
2. Ibid., p. 139.

3. Ciampi, p. 138.
4. Gigli, vol. 2, p. 527.
5. Ibid., p. 524.
6. Ibid., p. 551.
7. Ibid., p. 507.
8. Ciaffei, p. 99
9. Colonna, p. 196.
10. Ibid.
11. Leti, *Olimpia,* p. 16.
12. Majanlahti, p. 282.
13. Colonna, p. 143.
14. Ibid.
15. Pastor, vol. 30, p. 123.
16. Maland, p. 161.
17. Evelyn, p. 113.

16: The Shoulder of Saint Francesca

1. Colonna, p. 170.
2. Cavoli, p. 114.
3. Ibid.
4. Pallavicino, p. 169.
5. Gigli, vol. 2, p. 554.
6. Pastor, vol. 30, p. 371.
7. Gigli, vol. 2, p. 560.
8. Ibid., p. 561.
9. Maland, p. 299.
10. Vassalli, p. 138.
11. Strozzi, *Vita di Cardinal Cecchini,* vol. 175, folio 231b.
12. Ibid., folio 225a.
13. Colonna, p. 131.
14. Vassalli, p. 148.
15. Gigli, vol. 2, p. 534.

17: The Holy Jubilee Year

1. Gigli, vol. 2, p. 562.
2. Ibid., p. 563.
3. Ibid., p. 578.
4. Ibid., p. 592.
5. Colonna, p. 42.
6. Vassalli, p. 157.
7. Gigli, vol. 2, p. 594.
8. Vassalli, p. 155.
9. Gigli, vol. 2, pp. 594–95.
10. Ibid., p. 591.

11. Ibid., p. 587.
12. Ciampi, p. 142.
13. Vassalli, p. 159.

18: Crisis of Conscience

1. Leti, *Olimpia,* pp. 79–80.
2. Pallavicino, p. 155.
3. Leti, *Olimpia,* p. 85.
4. Gigli, vol. 2, p. 603.
5. Ibid.
6. Bastiaanse, p. 312.
7. Leti, *Nipotismo*, Part I, Book 3, p. 122.
8. Pallavicino, p. 155.
9. Bastiaanse, p. 313.
10. Leti, *Olimpia,* pp. 82–83.
11. Colonna, p. 198.
12. Ciampi, p. 145 n.
13. Colonna, p. 197.
14. Leti, *Olimpia,* p. 103.
15. Ibid., p. 102.
16. Ibid.
17. Ibid., p. 106.
18. Strozzi, *Relatione, della Corte . . . Sagredo*, vol. 59.
19. Gigli, vol. 2, p. 604.
20. Leti, *Olimpia,* p. 99.
21. Ibid., pp. 102–3.
22. Vassalli, p. 168.
23. Bastiaanse, p. 314.
24. Ibid., p. 314.
25. Gigli, vol. 2, p. 612.
26. Vassalli, pp. 168–69.
27. Strozzi, *Prosperita Infelice,* vol. 175, folio 237b.

19: Honor and Dishonor

1. Archivio Doria Pamphilj, doc. 93.60.
2. Colonna, p. 221.
3. Cavoli, p. 158.
4. Strozzi, *Relatione della Corte . . . Contarino,* vol. 146, folio 140a.
5. Gigli, vol. 2, p. 633.
6. Leti, *Olimpia,* p. 115.
7. Ibid., p. 114.
8. Pallavicino, p. 156.
9. Ibid., p. 127.
10. Ibid., p. 159.

11. Ibid., p. 175.
12. Ibid., p. 168.
13. Ibid., p. 169.
14. Ibid., pp. 169–70.
15. Vassalli, p. 181.
16. Ibid.
17. Ibid., p. 172.
18. Ibid.
19. Vassalli, p. 172.
20. Ibid., p. 183.
21. Strozzi, *Prosperita Infelice*, vol. 175, folio 272a.
22. Vassalli, p. 185.
23. Leti, *Olimpia,* p. 118.

20: Olimpia's Triumphant Return

1. Gigli, vol. 2, pp. 663–64.
2. Pallavicino, p. 192.
3. Ibid.
4. Ibid., p. 191.
5. Ibid., p. 193.
6. Ibid., p. 194.
7. Gigli, vol. 2, p. 604.
8. Colonna, pp. 223–24.
9. Pallavicino, p. 194.
10. Gigli, vol. 2, p. 680.
11. Vassalli, p. 197.
12. Leti, *Olimpia,* pp. 139–40.
13. Archivio Doria Pamphilj, doc. 93.57.
14. Vassalli, p. 199.
15. Gigli, vol. 2, p. 685.

21: The Sudden Disgrace of Cardinal Astalli

1. Vassalli, p. 203.
2. Ibid., p. 203.
3. Leti, *Olimpia,* p. 146.
4. Ibid., pp. 118–19.
5. Gigli, vol. 2, p. 690.
6. Leti, *Olimpia,* pp. 122–23.
7. Ibid., p. 128.
8. Pallavicino, pp. 204–5.
9. Ibid., p. 205.
10. Ibid., p. 206.
11. Ibid.
12. Gigli, vol. 2, p. 739.

13. Pallavicino, p. 199.
14. Ibid.
15. Ibid., pp. 200–1.
16. Leti, *Olimpia,* p. 155.
17. Gigli, vol. 2, pp. 695–96.
18. Vassalli, p. 223.
19. Ibid., p. 225.
20. Pallavicino, p. 203.
21. Colonna, p. 227.
22. Ibid., p. 174.
23. Gigli, vol. 2, p. 698.
24. Leti, *Olimpia,* p. 165.
25. Leti, *Cardinalismo,* p. 167.
26. Ibid., p. 166.
27. Ibid., p. 167.
28. Pallavicino, p. 207.

22: *Death of the Dove*

1. Gigli, vol. 2, p. 711.
2. Luke 21:25.
3. Colonna, p. 230.
4. Leti, *Olimpia,* p. 160.
5. Ibid., pp. 169–70.
6. Leti, *Olimpia,* p. 160.
7. Paravicini-Bagliani, p. 128.
8. Pallavicino, p. 218.
9. Gigli, vol. 2, p. 717.
10. Vassalli, p. 230.
11. Gigli, vol. 2, p. 717.
12. Ibid., p. 718.
13. Ibid.
14. Pallavicino, p. 210.
15. *Catechism,* p. 207.
16. Pallavicino, p. 212.
17. Ibid.
18. Ibid., p. 205.
19. Gigli, vol. 2, p. 719.
20. Ibid.
21. Ibid., p. 720.
22. Pallavicino, p. 211.
23. Gigli, vol. 2, p. 729.
24. Pallavicino, p. 213.
25. Leti, *Olimpia,* pp. 172–73.
26. Ibid., *Nipotismo,* Part 2, Book 3, pp. 116–17.
27. Colonna, p. 240 n.

23: *Unforgiveness*

1. Gigli, vol. 2, p. 733.
2. Cavoli, p. 195.
3. Gigli, vol. 2, p. 734.
4. Leti, *Olimpia,* p. 175.
5. Gigli, vol. 2, p. 731.
6. Colonna, pp. 243–44.
7. Cavoli, p. 199.
8. Pallavicino, p. 213.
9. Gigli, vol. 2, p. 733.

24: *Pope Alexander VII*

1. Strozzi, *Relatione della Corte . . . Contarino* vol. 146, folio 144a.
2. Pastor, vol. 30, p. 46 n.
3. Leti, *Olimpia,* p. 179.
4. Ibid.
5. Strozzi, *Conclave in quale fu creato pontefice Cardinal Fabio Chigi*, vol. 21, folio 213b.
6. Gigli, vol. 2, p. 737.
7. Leti, *Olimpia,* p. 178.
8. Gigli, vol. 2, p. 742.
9. Leti, *Nipotismo,* Part I, Book 3, p. 128.
10. Ibid.
11. Leti, *Nipotismo,* Part I, Book 3, p. 128.
12. Gigli, vol. 2, p. 728.

25: *The Two Queens of Rome*

1. Leti, *Olimpia,* pp. 192–93.
2. Ibid., pp. 193–94.
3. Colonna, p. 253.
4. Leti, *Olimpia,* p. 200.
5. Ibid., p. 205.
6. Gigli, vol. 2, p. 751.
7. Stolpe, p. 284.
8. Archivio Doria Pamphilj, archiovolo doc. 349.
9. Strozzi, *Relatione di Signor di Valenzay*, vol. 171.
10. Archivio Doria Pamphilj, doc. 349.

26: *The Scourge of God*

1. Cavoli, p. 160.
2. Leti, *Nipotismo*, Part II, book 3, p. 134.
3. Evelyn, pp. 119–20.
4. Cipolla, *Fighting the Plague,* p. 11 n.

5. Ibid., p. 12.
6. Lindemann, p. 82.
7. Gigli, vol. 2, p. 765.
8. Ibid., p. 769.
9. Archivio Doria Pamphilj, archiovolo doc. 349.
10. Ibid.
11. Ibid.
12. Ibid.
13. Ibid.
14. Ibid.
15. Ibid.
16. Ibid.
17. Ibid., 93.69.

27: *After Olimpia*

1. Archivio Doria Pamphilj, scaff. 59, n. 64, int. 9.
2. Ibid., doc. 93.69.
3. Leti, *Olimpia,* p. 210.
4. Ibid., p. 175.
5. Ibid., *Nipotismo,* Part 1, Book 3, p. 147.
6. Ibid., Part 1, Book 3, p. 137.
7. Ibid., Part 1, Book 3, p. 153.
8. Rendina, p. 519.
9. Bernini, p. 174.

Bibliography

Adamson, John. *The Princely Courts of Europe: Ritual, Politics and Culture Under the Ancien Regime, 1500–1750.* London: Weidenfeld & Nicolson, 1999.

Alberti-Poja, Antonio. *The House of Peter: The History of the Vatican.* Gerrards Cross, U.K.: Van Duren, 1987.

Amayden, Teodoro. *Storia delle Famiglie Romane.* Rome: Edizioni Romane Colosseum, 1910.

Archivio di Stato di Roma, Rome.

Bainton, Roland, H. *Here I Stand: A Life of Martin Luther.* New York: New American Library, 1950.

Barberini, Francesca, and Micaela Dickman. *I pontefici e gli Anni Santi nella Roma del XVII Secolo: Vita, arte e costume.* Rome: Ugo Bozzi, 2000.

Barcia, Franco. *Gregorio Leti: Informatore politico di principi italiani.* Turin: University of Turin Press, 1987.

Bastiaanse, A. *Teodoro Ameyden (1586–1656): Un Neerlandese alla Corte di Roma.* 'S-Gravenage, Neth.: Staatsdrukkerij, 1967.

Bastianelli, Colombo. *San Martino al Cimino.* San Martino, Italy: Confraternita del SS. Sacramento e S. Rosario di San Martino al Cimino, 1994.

Baumgartner, Frederic J. *Behind Locked Doors: A History of the Papal Elections.* New York: Palgrave Macmillan, 2003.

Beet, William Ernest. *The Rise of the Papacy A.D. 385–461.* London: Charles H. Kelly, 1910.

Bell, Rudolph M. *How to Do It: Guides to Good Living for Renaissance Italians.* Chicago: University of Chicago Press, 1991.

Bernini, Domenico. *Vita del Cavalier Gio.Lorenzo Bernini.* Rome: Rocco Bernabò, 1713.

Boase, T. S. R. *Boniface VIII.* London: Constable, 1933.

Bradford, Sarah. *Lucrezia Borgia.* New York: Viking, 2004.

Brecht, Martin. *Martin Luther: His Road to Reformation, 1483–1521.* Minneapolis: Fortress Press, 1985.

Brentano, Robert. *Rome Before Avignon: A Social History of Thirteenth Century Rome.* Berkeley: University of California Press, 1990.

Burchard, Johann. *At the Court of the Borgia: Being an Account of the Reign of Pope Alexander VI Written by His Master of Ceremonies.* London: Folio Society, 1963.

Carocci, Sandro. *Il nepotismo nel medioevo: Papi, cardinali e famiglie nobili.* Rome: Viella, 1999.

Catalli, Fiorenzo, and Mauro Petrecca. *Villa Pamphili.* Rome: Presidenza del Consiglio dei Ministri.

Catechism of the Catholic Church. Rome: Libreria Editrice Vaticana, 2000.

Catechism of the Council of Trent. New York: Catholic Publication Society, 1829.

Cavoli, Alfio. *La Papessa Olimpia.* Rome: Scipione, 1992.

Cawthorne, Nigel. *Sex Lives of the Popes.* London: Prion, 1997.

Chamberlin, E. R. *The Bad Popes.* New York: Barnes & Noble, 1969.

———. *The Fall of the House of Borgia.* New York: Dorset Press, 1974.

Chambers, D. S. *Renaissance Cardinals and Their Worldly Problems.* Aldershot, U.K.: Variorium, 1997.

Ciaffei, Giuseppe. *La pimpaccia di Piazza Navona: La storia di Olimpia Pamphili, secondo le cronache del tempo, 1594–1657.* Rome: Nuova Editrice Spada, 1978.

Ciampi, Ignazio. *Innocenzo X e la Sua Corte: Storia di Roma dal 1644 al 1655.* Rome: n.p., 1878.

Cipolla, Carlo M. *Cristofano and the Plague: A Study in the History of Public Health in the Age of Galileo.* London: Collins, 1973.

———. *Faith, Reason, and the Plague in Seventeenth-Century Tuscany.* New York: W. W. Norton, 1979.

———. *Fighting the Plague in Seventeenth-Century Italy.* Madison: University of Wisconsin Press, 1981.

———. *Money, Prices and Civilization in the Mediterranean World, Fifth to Seventeenth Century.* Princeton, N.J.: Princeton University Press, 1956.

Cohen, M. J., and John Major. *History in Quotations.* London: Cassell, 2004.

Collinson, Patrick. *The Reformation: A History.* New York: Modern Library, 2004.

Collison-Morley, Lacy. *Italy After the Renaissance: Decadence and Display in the Seventeenth Century.* New York, Henry Holt, n.d.

Colonna, Gustavo Brigante. *Olimpia Pamphili, "Cardinal Padrone," 1594–1657.* Verona: Casa Editrice A. Mondadori, 1941.

Coville, Henry. *Étude sur Mazarin et ses Démêlés avec le Pape Innocent X (1644–1648).* Paris: Librairie Ancienne Honoré Champion, 1914.

Cropper, Elizabeth, Giovanna Perini, and Francesco Solinas, eds. *Documentary Culture: Florence and Rome from Grand-Duke Ferdinand I to Pope Alexander VII.* Bologna: Nuova Alfa Editoriale, 1992.

Dandalet, Thomas James. *Spanish Rome 1500–1700.* New Haven, Conn.: Yale University Press, 2001.

De Gregori, Luigi. *Piazza Navona prima d'Innocenzo X.* Rome: Palombi Editori, ca. 1925.

De Rosa, Peter. *Vicars of Christ: The Dark Side of the Papacy.* London: Corgi Books, 1988.

Dean, Trevor, and K. J. P. Lowe. *Marriage in Italy 1300–1650.* Cambridge, U.K.: Cambridge University Press, 1998.

Della Casa, Giovanni. *Il Galatheo: De Costumi e Modi che si debbono tenere o schifare nella commune conversatione.* Florence: 1560.

Di Capua, Giovanni. *Marozia: La pornacrazia pontificia intorno all'anno Mille.* Valentano, It.: Scipione, 1999.

D'Onofrio, Cesare. *Castel S. Angelo in the History of Rome and the Papacy.* Rome: Romana Societa Editrice, 1986.

Duffy, Eamon. *Saints & Sinners: A History of the Popes.* New Haven, Conn.: Yale University Press, 1997.

Elliott, J. H. *Imperial Spain 1469–1716.* New York: Penguin Books, 1972.

Erlanger, Philippe. *The Age of Courts and Kings: Manners and Morals, 1558–1715.* New York: Harper & Row, 1967.

Evelyn, John. *The Diary of John Evelyn, from 1641 to 1705–6, with Memoir.* London: Frederick Warne, ca. 1900.

Feist, Aubrey. *The Lion of St. Mark. Venice: The Story of a City from Attila to Napoleon.* Indianapolis: Bobbs-Merrill, 1971.

Galilei, Galileo. *Dialogue Concerning the Two Chief World Systems, Ptolemaic & Copernican.* Berkeley: University of California Press, 1967.

Gastineau, Benjamin. *Les courtisanes de l'église.* Paris: Librairie Georges Barba, 1870.

Gigli, Giacinto. *Diario di Roma, 1608–1670.* 2 vols. Rome: Editore Colombo, 1994.

Gregorovius, Ferdinand. *History of the City of Rome in the Middle Ages.* 13 vols. London: George Bell & Sons, 1894.

Guicciardini, Luigi. *The Sack of Rome.* New York: Italica Press, 1993.

Hammond, Frederick. *Music and Spectacle in Baroque Rome: Barberini Patronage under Urban VIII.* New Haven, Conn.: Yale University Press, 1994.

Hibbert, Christopher. *Rome: The Biography of a City.* London: Penguin Books, 1985.

Hofmann, Paul. *The Vatican's Women: Female Influence at the Holy See.* New York: St. Martin's Press, 2002.

Hollingsworth, Mary. *The Cardinal's Hat: Money, Ambition and Everyday Life in the Court of a Borgia Prince.* New York: Overlook Press, 2004.

Infessura, Stefano. *Römisches Tagebuch.* Düsseldorf: Eugen Diederichs Verlag, 1979.

Jurgens, William A. *The Faith of the Early Fathers.* vol. 1. Collegeville, Minn.: Liturgical Press, 1970.

Kirwin, W. Chandler. *Powers Matchless: The Pontificate of Urban VIII, the Baldachin, and Gian Lorenzo Bernini.* New York: Peter Lang, 1997.

Krivatsky, Nati. *Bibliography of the Works of Gregorio Leti.* New Castle, Del.: Oak Knoll, 1982.

La Bella, Angelo. *La venere papale.* Valentano, It.: Scipione, 1995.

Laven, Mary. *Virgins of Venice: Broken Vows and Cloistered Lives in the Renaissance Convent.* New York: Viking, 2002.

Lea, Henry C. *History of Sacerdotal Celibacy in the Christian Church.* London: Watts, 1932.

Lees-Milne, James. *Saint Peter's: The Story of Saint Peter's Basilica in Rome.* Boston: Little, Brown, 1967.

Leone, Stephanie. "Cardinal Pamphilj Builds a Palace: Self-Representation and Familial Ambition in Seventeenth-Century Rome." *Journal of the Society of Architectural Historians* 63, no. 4 (December 2004): 440–71.

Leti, Gregorio. *Histoire de Donna Olimpia Maldachini.* Leyden, Neth: 1666.

———. *Il cardinalismo di Santa Chiesa, or The History of the Cardinals of the Roman Church.* London: 1670.

————. *Il nipotismo di Roma, or The History of the Popes' Nephews from the Time of Sixtus IV, Anno 1471, to the Death of the Late Pope Alexander VII, Anno 1667.* London: John Starkey, 1673.

Liberati, Francesco. *Il perfetto maestro di casa.* Rome: Bernabò, 1668.

Lindemann, Mary. *Medicine and Society in Early Modern Europe.* Cambridge, U.K.: Cambridge University Press, 1999.

Long, Robert J. *The Popes of Rome and the Bishops of the First Five Centuries.* Aurora, Miss.: Menace Publishing, 1914.

Lunadoro, Girolamo. *Relatione della Corte di Rome, e de Riti di osservarsi in essa, e de suoi magistrati, & officij, con la loro distinta giurisdittione.* Venice: Benetto Miloco, 1677.

Magnuson, Torgil. *Rome in the Age of Bernini.* 2 vols. Stockholm: Almquist & Wiksell, 1982.

Majanlahti, Anthony. *The Families Who Made Rome: A History and Guide.* London: Chatto and Windus, 2005.

Maland, David. *Europe in the Seventeenth Century.* London: Macmillan Education, 1983.

Martinelli, Fioravante. *Roma ricercata nel suo sito.* Venice: Benetto Miloco, 1677.

Martos, Joseph. *Doors to the Sacred: A Historical Introduction to Sacraments in the Catholic Church.* Ligouri, Mo.: Triumph Books, 1981.

McBrien, Richard, P. *Lives of the Popes: The Pontiffs from St. Peter to John Paul II.* San Francisco: HarperSanFrancisco, 2000.

Morabito, Maurizio. *Giustizia barocche: Storie di crimini e di pene.* Viterbo, It.: Nuovi Equilibri, 2006.

Morrissey, Jake. *The Genius in the Design: Bernini, Borromini, and the Rivalry That Transformed Rome.* New York: William Morris, 2005.

Neuhaus, Richard John. *Catholic Matters: Confusion, Controversy, and the Splendor of Truth.* New York: Basic Books, 2006.

Noel, Gerard. *The Anatomy of the Catholic Church.* London: Hodder & Stoughton, 1980.

Olin, John C. *The Catholic Reformation: Savonarola to Ignatius Loyola.* New York: Fordham University Press, 1969.

Pallavicino, P. Sforza. *Della vita di Alessandro VII.* Prato, It.: 1839.

Paravicini-Bagliani, Agostino. *The Pope's Body.* Chicago: University of Chicago Press, 1994.

Partner, Peter. *Renaissance Rome, 1500–1559.* Berkeley: University of California Press, 1976.

Pastor, Dr. Ludwig. *The History of the Popes from the Close of the Middle Ages, Drawn from the Secret Archives of the Vatican and Other Original Sources.* 40 vols. London: Routledge & Kegan Paul, 1949.

Pietrini, Francesco. *I vescovi e i diocesi di Viterbo.* Viterbo, It.: Commerciale, 1949.

Pirie, Valérie. *The Triple Crown: An Account of the Papal Conclaves from the Fifteenth Century to Modern Times.* London: Spring Books, 1935.

Ranke, Leopold. *The History of the Popes, Their Church and State, and Especially of Their Conflicts with Protestantism, in the Sixteenth and Seventeenth Centuries.* 3 vols. London: George Bell and Sons, 1881.

Rappoport, Dr. Angelo S. *The Love Affairs of the Vatican, or The Favourites of the Popes.* London: Stanley Paul, 1912.

Reese, Thomas J. *Inside the Vatican: The Politics and Organization of the Catholic Church.* Cambridge, Mass.: Harvard University Press, 1996.

Rendina, Claudio. *The Popes: Histories and Secrets.* Santa Ana, Calif.: Seven Locks Press, 2002.

Renouard, Yves. *The Avignon Papacy: The Popes in Exile 1305–1403.* New York: Barnes & Noble, 1994.

Rodén, Marie-Louise. *Church Politics in Seventeenth-Century Rome: Cardinal Decio Azzolino, Queen Christina of Sweden, and the Squadrone Volante.* Stockholm: Almquist & Wiksell International, 2000.

Rodocanachi, Emmanuel. *Le Saint-Siège et les juifs: Le ghetto à Rome.* Bologna: Forni Editore, 1891.

Rufus, Anneli. *Magnificent Corpses: Searching Through Europe for St. Peter's Head, St. Chiara's Heart, St. Stephen's Hand, and Other Saints' Relics.* New York: Marlowe, 1999.

Sarpi, Paolo. *History of the Benefices and Selections from the History of the Council of Trent.* New York: Washington Square Press, 1967.

Schaff, Philip. *History of the Christian Church.* Vols. 1–3. N.p., n.d.

Sella, Domenico. *Italy in the Seventeenth Century.* New York: Longman, 1997.

Sestini, Francesco da Bibbiena. *Il maestro di Camera.* Rome: Bernabò, 1668.

Somerset, Anne. *Elizabeth I.* New York: Alfred A. Knopf, 1991.

Stanford, Peter. *The She-Pope: A Quest for the Truth Behind the Mystery of Pope Joan.* London: Arrow, 1999.

Starr, Tama. *The Natural Inferiority of Women: Outrageous Pronouncements by Misguided Males.* New York: Poseidon Press, 1991.

Stolpe, Sven. *Christina of Sweden.* New York: Macmillan, 1966.

Strozzi Collection, Vatican Manuscripts, Folger Shakespeare Library, Washington, D.C.:

- *Prosperita infelice di Francesco Canonici detto Mascambruni Sottodatario et Auditore di Papa Innocentio Decimo Composte dall'abbate Gio:Battista Rinalducci da Pesaro. 1652.*

- Strozzi, *Conclave dopo la morte di Urbano VIII. 1644.*

- Strozzi, *Conclave in quale fu creato pontefice Cardinal Fabio Chigi. 1655.*

- *Vita del Cardinale Cecchini scritta da lui medisimo. 1652.*

- *Relatione dell ecc.mo Giovanni da Pesaro, cavaliere e procuratore di San Marco nel ritorno dell'ambasciaria straordinaria alla santita di N.S. P.P. Alessandro VII, serenissimo principe. 1656.*

- *Relatione della Corte di Roma, fatta dal Clarissimo Contarino Ambasciatore Veneto appresso la Santita di Nostro Signore Innocenzo X. 1648.*

- *Istruttione del Ambasciatore Christianissimo Signor Bali di Valenzay al Suo Successore. 1654.*

- *D'Innocenzo Decimo che vogliono sia del cardinal Bernardino Spada. 1644.*

- *Dell'istesso che si crede composte dal segratario del cardinal Egidio Albernozzi. 1644.*

- *D'Alessandro Settimo parimente supposto del Cardinal Spada. 1655.*

- *Del medemo d'incerto. 1655.*

- *Dell'istesso d'incerto. 1655.*

- *Relatione della Corte di Roma fatta da Nicolo Sagredo nel ritorno della sua ambasciaria per la repubblica di Venezia appresso Papa Innocenzo X. 1651.*

Thurston, Herbert. *The Holy Year of the Jubilee: An Account of the History and Ceremonial of the Roman Jubilee.* Westminster, Md.: Newman Press, 1949.

Torjesen, Karen Jo. *When Women Were Priests: Women's Leadership in the Early Church & the Scandal of Their Subordination in the Rise of Christianity.* San Francisco: HarperSanFrancisco, 1993.

Vassalli, Donata Chiomenti. *Donna Olimpia, o del nepotismo nel Seicento.* Milan: Mursia, 1979.

Walsh, John Evangelist. *The Bones of St. Peter: The Fascinating Account of the Search for the Apostle's Body.* London: Victor Gollancz, 1983.

Wills, Garry. *Papal Sin: Structures of Deceit.* New York: Doubleday, 2000.

Woodward, Kenneth L. *Making Saints: How the Catholic Church Determines Who Becomes a Saint, Who Doesn't, and Why.* New York: Simon & Schuster, 1996.

Wright, F. A. *The Works of Luitprand of Cremona.* London: George Routledge & Sons, 1930.

Wright, Jonathan. *God's Soldiers: Adventure, Politics, Intrigue and Power: A History of the Jesuits.* New York: Doubleday, 2004.

Zuccari, Alessandro, and Stefania Macioce, eds. *Innocenzo X Pamphilj: Arte e potere a Roma nell'Età Barocca.* Rome: Logart Press, n.d.

Index